BACKBONE OF THE NATION

BACKBONE OF THE NATION

MINING COMMUNITIES AND THE GREAT STRIKE OF 1984–85

ROBERT GILDEA

YALE UNIVERSITY PRESS
NEW HAVEN AND LONDON

For information about this and other Yale University Press publications, please contact:
U.S. Office: sales.press@yale.edu   yalebooks.com
Europe Office: sales@yaleup.co.uk   yalebooks.co.uk

Set in Adobe Garamond Pro by IDSUK (DataConnection) Ltd
Printed in Great Britain by TJ Books Limited, Padstow, Cornwall

Library of Congress Control Number: 2023937597

ISBN 978-0-300-26658-0

A catalogue record for this book is available from the British Library.

10 9 8 7 6 5 4 3 2 1

CONTENTS

CONTENTS

ILLUSTRATIONS

PLATES

1. General view of Ballingry from north-west, August 1995. OnFife Archives Ballingry 7130. OnFife Archives (Dunfermline Local Studies) on behalf of Fife Council.
2. Mining village of Askern. By permission of Ken Wilkinson. © Ken Wilkinson.
3. Rally in Rotherham, spring 1984. By permission of Ken Wilkinson. © Ken Wilkinson.
4. Chester-le-Street support group, August 1984. Photograph by David Connolly. By permission of Kath Connolly. © Kath Connolly.
5. Elicia Billingham. Photograph by Raissa Page. © Adrianne Jones – courtesy of The Richard Burton Archives, Swansea University.
6. LGSM in Onllwyn, 2 March 1985. By permission of Mike Jackson. © LGSM / Mike Jackson.
7. Battle of Orgreave, 18 June 1984. © John Harris / reportdigital.co.uk.
8. Striking miners and riot police, Hatfield, 21 August 1984. © Ray Rising / reportdigital.co.uk.
9. Mass picket, Bilston Glen, July 1984. © John Sturrock / reportdigital. co.uk.
10. Strike-breakers boarding a bus, winter 1984–85. By permission of Martin Herron. © Martin Herron.

11. 'Village Without Work', a view of Glyncorrwg by Dr Julian Tudor Hart, 15 November 1984. By permission of Mary Hart. © Julian Tudor Hart.

12. Children's Christmas party, Frickley colliery, December 1984. © John Sturrock / reportdigital.co.uk.

13. Striking miners salvaging coal, Yorkshire, 4 January 1985. © John Harris / reportdigital.co.uk.

14. Miners from the Maerdy colliery, South Wales, return to work, 5 March 1985. © Marx Memorial Library / Mary Evans.

15. Durham Miners' Gala, July 2019. By permission of Friends of Durham Miners' Gala. © Friends of Durham Miners' Gala.

16. A woman and her child in Grimethorpe, South Yorkshire. By permission of Anna Wolmuth. © Philip Wolmuth.

MAPS

ACKNOWLEDGEMENTS

Above all, I would like to thank those from mining families and their supporters – from the Swansea Valley to Fife – who shared their powerful, moving and often painful stories with me. These stories provide the material from which this book has been fashioned. Among them I received particular advice and hospitality from Siân James and Carwyn Donovan in South Wales; Jean Crane, Dianne Hogg and Betty Cook in Yorkshire; David and Kath Connolly, Mary and Paul Stratford, David and Dorothy Wray and Lynn Gibson in County Durham; and 'Watty' and Maureen Watson in Fife. Kipp Dawson, activist and former woman miner in Pittsburgh, who knew so many of the striking miners and their families in Britain, has been a source of inspiration.

Among fellow historians, I am indebted above all to Hywel Francis, who greeted me in the South Wales Miners' Library (which he founded), provided many contacts and accorded the project's first interview, but who very sadly died on 14 February 2021. Rebecca Clifford offered me hospitality and encouragement in both Swansea and County Durham. Jim Phillips was my adviser in Fife, opened all the doors, conducted a number of interviews with me and read the manuscript in draft. In Leicestershire, David Bell introduced me to the Dirty Thirty, of whom he is the historian. For further advice and encouragement, I am indebted to Selina Todd, Senia Paseta, Oliver Zimmer, Tom Buchanan and Paul Smith. Eleri Hedley-

Carter, while writing her own undergraduate dissertation on the strike in the Bridgend area, provided me with contacts and helped with transcription. Natalie Braber put me in touch with miners in Nottinghamshire – notably with David Amos, who also made introductions for me. Florence Sutcliffe-Braithwaite and Natalie Thomlinson blazed the trail with their project on women during the strike and provided stimulating discussion. Ruth Harris read and commented on the text, with critical and insightful appreciation.

For funding, I am grateful to the Leverhulme Trust, which granted me an Emeritus Fellowship to undertake this project; and in Oxford to the John Fell Fund and to Merton College. For transcription, I am very grateful to Liz and Jim Coxon and Eirini Tzouma. Once again, I would like to thank Alex Paulin-Booth for constructing the bibliography with such style. I am indebted to Martin Brown for the maps and to Clive Liddiard for the copy-editing.

Catherine Clarke, my agent, as always offered magnificent advice and encouragement. Julian Loose at Yale believed in the book and allowed me to write it as I wanted to. At Yale I would also like to thank the first-class team of Lucy Buchan, Rachael Lonsdale, Frazer Martin, Heather Nathan and James Williams.

CAST OF CHARACTERS

SCOTLAND

In Lochore, Crosshill and Ballingry, Fife

Ronnie Campbell, 'Red Ronnie', furnaceman at Cowdenbeath Workshops

Anna Campbell and Margaret Todd, his daughters

Mark Campbell and Marissa Carr, his grandchildren

Willie Clarke, NUM official, councillor

Willie Clarke, his son, miner at Comrie

Mary Coll, miner's wife, factory worker

Sean Lee, miner at Seafield

Peter McCutcheon, miner at Seafield

Doddy McShane, miner at Comrie

James McShane, his son

Janet Carson, his daughter

David Mitchell, fitter at Seafield

Margaret Mitchell, his wife, factory worker

Kevin Payne, miner's son, builder

Terry Ratcliffe, miner at Solsgirth

Thomas Watson, miner and safety officer, Bogside

Andrew (Watty) Watson, his son, miner at Comrie

CAST OF CHARACTERS

In Cowdenbeath
Iain Chalmers, miner at Seafield
Robert (Rosco) Ross, fitter and turner, Cowdenbeath Workshops
Carol Ross, his wife, sister of Sean Lee

In Glenrothes
Pat Egan, miner at Seafield

In Lochgelly and Cardenden
Linda Erskine, teacher, councillor
George Erskine, her husband, engineer at Comrie
John McClelland, miner at Seafield
Lea McClelland, his daughter, SNP councillor

In West Wemyss
Tom Adams, miner at Frances

ENGLAND

COUNTY DURHAM

In Chester-le-Street
Kath Connolly (formerly Mattheys), teacher
David Connolly, cooperative movement
Jim Coxon, shift charge engineer, Herrington
Bill Frostwick, shift charge engineer, Herrington
Elspeth Frostwick, his wife, shop assistant
Kenny McKitten, pit electrician at Murton
Allyson McKitten, his wife, housing officer
Kath Savory, chemist's assistant, daughter and wife of miner
Paul Stratford, pit mechanic at Easington
Mary Stratford, his wife, civil servant
Peter Stratford, their son, factory worker
Helen Stratford, their daughter, a GP

CAST OF CHARACTERS

In Easington

Heather Wood, miner's daughter, councillor, Save Easington Area Mines

In Leadgate and Blackhill

Peter Byrne, pit electrician at Wearmouth

David Wray, pit electrician at Sacriston

Dorothy Wray, his wife, Post Office employee

Sam Oldfield, their daughter, nurse

Caitlin Oldfield, her daughter, student

In Sacriston

Anna Lawson, activist

In Spennymore

Ernie Foster, miner at Seaham

Lynn Gibson, miner's daughter, research officer

YORKSHIRE

In Askern

Jean Crane, miner's wife, newsagent's manager

Dianne Hogg, miner's wife, newsagent's employee

Frank Holmes, miner at Askern, later an evangelical minister

Ros Jones, miner's daughter, later mayor of Doncaster

Pete Richardson, miner at Askern

Sue Richardson, his wife, factory worker

Lee Richardson, their son, builder

Peter Robson, miner at Askern

In and around Barnsley

Elicia Billingham, miner's wife, seamstress

Betty Cook, miner's wife, USDAW shop steward

Jean McCrindle, lecturer

CAST OF CHARACTERS

Joe Rollin, chair of Orgreave Truth and Justice Campaign

Anne Scargill, factory worker, wife of Arthur Scargill

Steve Walker, miner at Woolley

Paul Winter, miner at Dodworth

Adam Winter, his son, student

In Bentley

Charlie Hogarth, miner at Bentley, local councillor

At Hatfield

David (Dave) Douglass, miner at Hatfield, activist

Maureen Douglass, his wife, art student, actor

In Sheffield

Kate Flannery, secretary of Orgreave Truth and Justice Campaign

Barbara Jackson, NCB employee, secretary of Orgreave Truth and Justice Campaign

NOTTINGHAMSHIRE

Around Annesley

David Amos, pit electrician at Annesley

Mick Marriott, miner at Annesley

Terry Stringfellow, miner at Annesley

Trevor Taylor, miner at Newstead and Annesley

Susan Trevor, his wife, office worker

Steve Williamson, miner pit fitter at Annesley

In Manton and Worksop

Kevin Greaves, miner, businessman

David Hopkins, miner at Manton

Ray Maslin, miner at Manton

Billy Potts, miner at Manton

Josie Potts, his wife, laundry and factory worker

David Potts, his cousin, miner at Manton

Gary Fisher, cousin of Billy and David Potts, miner at Manton

Anne Fisher, his wife, cleaner

Andy Varley, miner at Manton

In Worsop and Warsop Vale

Ken Bonsall, miner at Welbeck, musician

Karen Bonsall, his wife

Anne Hubbell (formerly Heaton), miner's wife, cleaner at Welbeck

Katherine Parker, her daughter

Elsie Potts, wife of miner (Bill) at Warsop Main

Lisa Potts, her daughter, prison officer

LEICESTERSHIRE

In Barlestone and Desford

Cliff Jeffery, miner from Bagworth

Nigel Jeffery, his son, miner from Bagworth

Wendy Jeffery, his wife

Kay Riley (formerly Smith), miner's wife

In Coalville and Ibstock

Bobby Girvan, miner at Bagworth

Sam Girvan, his brother, miner at Bagworth

Mick (Richo) Richmond, miner at Bagworth

Marisa Cortes Richmond, his third wife

Linda Burton, his second wife, factory worker

In Loughborough

Mel Elcock, pit mechanic at Bagworth

CAST OF CHARACTERS

In Leicester

Simone Dawes, tax official, later community worker

In Stoney Stanton and Stapleton

Darren Moore, miner at Bagworth

Malcolm (Benny) Pinnegar, miner at Bagworth

Margaret Pinnegar, his wife, hosiery worker

Claire Pinnegar, their daughter, pub manager

WALES

In the Afan and Llynfi Valleys

Idwal Isaac, miner at Duffryn

Ian Isaac, his son, miner at Maesteg

Gary Jones, miner, fitter

Donna Jones, his wife, clerical officer

Jude Bevan, their daughter, teacher

Julian Tudor Hart, GP and medical researcher

Mary Hart, his wife, medical researcher

Rachel Tudor Hart, their daughter, nurse and artist

Phil White, miner at Maesteg

In Cardiff

John Morgans, United Reformed Church minister

In the Cynon Valley

Dai John Jones, miner at Tower

Ann Jones, his wife, activist

In the Dulais Valley (Onllwyn, Seven Sisters, Crynant)

Phil Bowen, pit electrician at Blaenant

Kay Bowen, his wife, factory employee

Hywel Francis, miner's son, lecturer, later an MP
Mair Francis, his wife, teacher
Dafydd Francis, their son, teacher
Lyn Harper, fitter at Blaenant
Hefina Headon, miner's wife, village postmistress
Jayne Francis Headon, her granddaughter
Philip James, miner at Treforgan
Marilyn James, his wife, shop assistant
Christine Powell, miner's wife, teacher
Ali Thomas, miner at Blaenant
David Williams, miner at Blaenant

In the Swansea Valley (Ystradgynlais, Ystalyfera)
Martin James, miner at Abernant, sheep farmer
Siân James, his wife, later an MP
Kay Jones, miner's wife, school administrator

LONDON

Jonathan Blake, actor, tailor
Jane Bruton, nurse
Paul Mason, her husband, broadcaster
Helen Colley, bus driver, academic
Mike Jackson, gardener
Paul King, print worker
Bernard Regan, teacher

UNITED STATES

Kipp Dawson, activist, woman miner, teacher
Libby Lindsay, woman miner

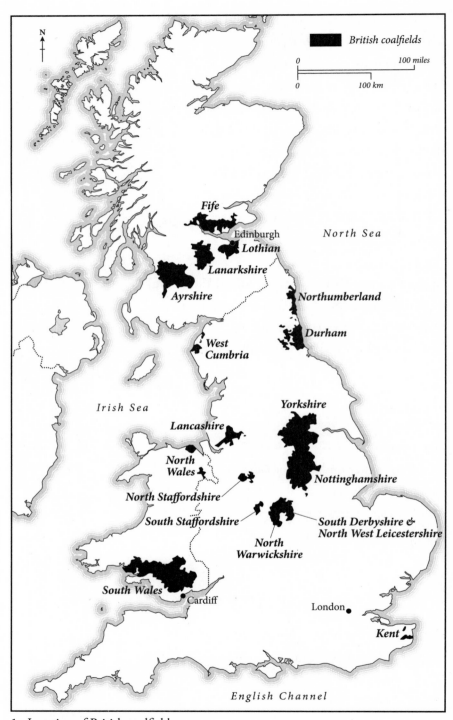

N

British coalfields

0   100 miles

0   100 km

Fife

Edinburgh

North Sea

Lothian

Lanarkshire

Ayrshire

Northumberland

Durham

West Cumbria

Irish Sea

Yorkshire

Lancashire

North Wales

Nottinghamshire

North Staffordshire

South Staffordshire

South Derbyshire & North West Leicestershire

North Warwickshire

South Wales

Cardiff

London

Kent

English Channel

1. Location of British coalfields

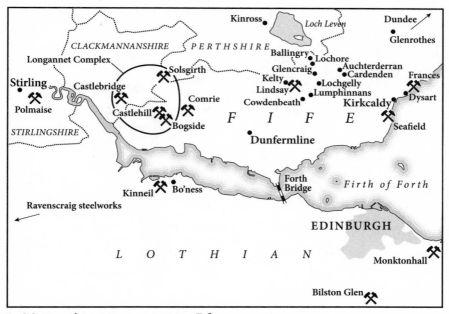

2. Mines and mining communities: Fife

3. Mines and mining communities: County Durham

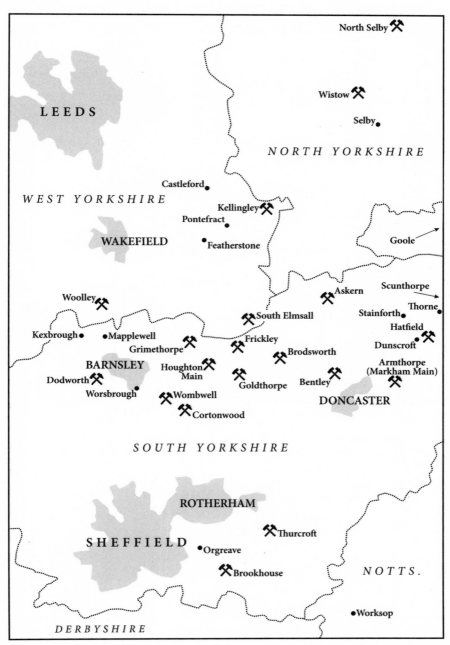

4. Mines and mining communities: Yorkshire

5. Mines and mining communities: Nottinghamshire and Leicestershire

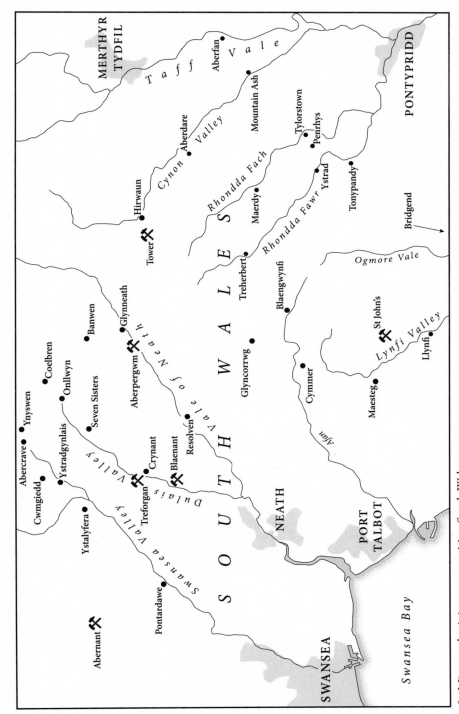

6. Mines and mining communities: South Wales

INTRODUCTION

When I interviewed eighty-seven-year-old former miner Thomas Watson in 2021 at his home in Ballingry, Fife, he recalled the wisdom of his father Andrew, a miner who had fought at the Battle of Mons in 1914:

> My father used to say, the miners are the backbone of the nation. Without them the country just could not go. Without coal you could not run trains. If there were no trains nobody could get to their work. Most of England worked in factories. Factories needed electricity and coal to generate electricity and if there was no coal the factories started to shut down.[1]

The idea that the British working class, epitomised by the miners, were 'the backbone of the nation' was fairly common currency in the mid-twentieth century. Ferdynand Zweig, a year younger than Andrew Watson, a Polish-Jewish law professor from Kraków, who fled to Britain in 1940 and became a social scientist, argued in 1952 that their centrality to the production of wealth, culture and progress compensated in honour for the reality of their 'inferior economic and social position':

> It is pleasant to feel that one belongs to the vanguard of justice and progress, to the giving side, to the backbone of the country, to the

most hard-working and useful layer of the community. Without the worker there is neither leisure nor comfort, and therefore also no culture.[2]

Miners in Britain were all men, the last woman having left surface work at the pit in 1866 and the minimum age having been raised to fourteen in 1911; but there was also a sense that miners' wives were likewise part of that backbone, standing by their husbands, brothers and sons in good times and bad. Heather Wood, born in 1951, the daughter of an Easington miner and herself a Labour activist, known for bringing miners' wives into the Save Easington Area Mines (SEAM) organisation set up in 1983, was clear that historically, in mining families and communities,

mining women have always been the backbone. They've always been the ones who actually went out and did. The men were going to work, most of the women were at home, so they organised and got out on the streets. The 1926 strike, the women were there, as well as some men, helping to provide food.[3]

For two hundred years, the mining industry was the backbone of the country both economically and geographically. Economically, Britain's role as the 'Workshop of the World' and the 'First Industrial Nation' was based on a single fuel: coal.[4] Coal from Newcastle proverbially provided heating for homes in London and other cities. Coal provided coke for the iron and steel industries, power for textile mills and other manufacturing industry, and steam for railways and coastal and international shipping when steam overtook sail in the 1880s. Coal production reached an all-time peak of 287 million tons in 1913, of which over a quarter was exported, mined by over a million miners; one in every ten of the country's male workers was a miner. The height of the coal industry coincided with the height of empire, symbolised by the coronation durbar of King George V and Queen Mary in Delhi in 1911.

Geographically, in 1913 the mining industry stretched from South Wales, where there were 232,000 miners, to the East Midlands, where there were 111,000, to Yorkshire, where there were 159,000. There were 107,000 in Lancashire and Cheshire, 241,000 in Northumberland and Durham and 138,000 in Scotland.[5] Miners were recruited from the rural hinterlands of Britain and Ireland, from Belgium, Germany and, in the case of South Wales, from Spain.[6] Focusing more locally, the population of the village of Onllwyn, at the crossroads of rural, Welsh-speaking, West Wales and the urban, English-speaking Wales of the Rhondda, increased tenfold, from 479 in 1871 to 4,569 in 1911.[7] Askern in South Yorkshire was an elegant spa town, rivalling Harrogate, until coal was discovered there in 1911, after which the plan was to employ 4,000 men.[8] In Fife, the population of Lochore also increased tenfold – from 1,065 in 1881 to 10,349 in 1921 – after the sinking of the Glencraig colliery in 1896 and the Mary colliery in 1906.[9]

The miner was the quintessential *homo faber*, man as maker, whose Promethean work pitted him against the elements of earth, air, fire and water. The combination of those elements exposed teams of men burrowing with rudimentary technology and inadequate safety procedures to catastrophic mining disasters. From 1850 to 1901, there was an average of 981 coalmining fatalities every year.[10] A series of explosions at Oakes colliery, Barnsley, on 12–13 December 1866 killed 361 people, including twenty-seven rescue workers.[11] At the Senghenydd colliery near Caerphilly there was an explosion on 24 May 1901, killing eighty-one men; and then – because improvements under the Coal Mines Act 1911 had not been carried out in good time – another explosion on 14 October 1913 killed 440 men, the worst mining disaster in British history. The manager was fined £24, barely more than a shilling per death, and the company £5 and 5 shillings.[12]

As they fought for safer conditions and better pay, miners became among the best organised of the working class. Organisation enabled them to further their cause by electing union officials to negotiate with employers and to coordinate strike action. The Miners' Federation of Great Britain (MFGB) was formed in 1889 from a large number of county unions, but regional powerbases were more significant.[13] In County Durham, where strikes in 1831 and 1844 by miners portrayed as 'terrible and savage pitmen' were brutally put down, the Durham Miners' Association (DMA) was founded in 1869.[14] Since 1871, the solidarity of the organisation has been on display every July, when miners and their families from 180 collieries parade into the city centre for a mass meeting with their banners flying.[15] The DMA's president and general secretary, William Crawford, defeated a scion of the Londonderry family to become Liberal-Labour MP for Mid-Durham in 1885.[16] The association's magnificent neo-Renaissance headquarters at Redhills, in Durham city, was opened in 1915 to emphasise the miners' equal standing with the employers. More brutally, the Yorkshire Miners' Association, founded in 1881, found itself fighting a 25 per cent wage cut by employers in 1893. Attacks by miners on blacklegs led to infantry and cavalry regiments being brought in, the reading of the 1714 Riot Act and the shooting dead of two miners at Featherstone, near Pontefract, on 7 September 1893.[17] Meanwhile the South Wales Miners' Federation, founded in 1898, was tested in November 1910, when Home Secretary Winston Churchill sent in the army to put down miners rioting against strike-breakers in the Rhondda village of Tonypandy – a deed that has never been forgotten by Welsh miners.[18] *The Miners' Next Step*, a pamphlet drafted in South Wales at the time of a national strike in 1912, advocated 'a policy of open hostility to employers'. A Triple Alliance was forged with railway and transport workers in 1914, and even the war brought no industrial peace: a strike of 200,000 miners in South Wales in 1915 forced the government to take over that coalfield, then all coalfields, under the Defence of the Realm Act.[19]

After the First World War, which was supposed to produce 'homes fit for heroes', there was an upsurge in industrial strife, inspired by the Bolshevik Revolution in Russia. In 1921, the government restored the coalfields to private employers, who immediately imposed a 50 per cent reduction in wages, locked out a million miners for refusing to accept the cut and benefited from the support of the army.[20] A further lockout of miners in April 1926 provoked a General Strike in support; but that lasted a mere nine days, whereas the miners' resistance continued for seven months. Huge amounts of money were collected in support of the strike, over 60 per cent coming from the trade unions of the Soviet Union.[21] Such was the enthusiasm for the USSR that militant mining villages as far apart as Maerdy in the Rhondda Valley, Chopwell in County Durham and Lumphinnans in Fife became known as 'Little Moscows'. Between 1935 and 1950, Willie Gallacher, the Irish–Scottish organiser of the Red Clydeside strike of 1919, was repeatedly returned as Communist MP for West Fife. In South Wales, Arthur Horner, who had been imprisoned during the First World War for refusing to fight and who was a founder member of the Communist Party of Great Britain, served as general secretary of the South Wales Miners' Federation between 1936 and 1946.[22] The MFGB, however, was not united and employers managed to impose settlements district by district. The general secretary of the Nottinghamshire Miners' Association and MP for Broxtowe, George Spencer, called for cooperation between miners and coal owners, agreed a district deal in November 1926 and then formed a breakaway Nottinghamshire and District Miners' Industrial Union. Nicknamed the Spencer Union, it crystallised a separatist tendency that boded ill for the future.[23]

The demands of the Second World War and the victory of a Labour government in 1945 paved the way for the nationalisation of the coal industry on 1 January 1947. The output of coal had fallen from 287 million tons in 1913 to 181 million in 1946, and the number of miners from over a million to 698,000.[24] Private employers had failed to invest adequately or to manage a restive workforce. Nationalisation set up the National Coal Board (NCB), and it worked with the National Union of Mineworkers (NUM) (which replaced the MFGB in 1945) in a battle for coal to supply power stations, gasworks, railways and homes in what was still a 'single-fuel economy'.[25] This was the heroic era of the coalminer: lauded for his strength and skill, his record-breaking feats of productivity received widespread publicity. Interviewed in 1980 by American TV host Dick Cavett, the actor Richard Burton, himself the son of a Welsh miner, contributed – perhaps a little fantastically – to this narrative. Having described the Great Atlantic Fault coal seam that runs from the Basque Country to Pennsylvania via South Wales, he went on:

> My father was a very short man, an ideal height for a miner. He was about 5'3" or 5'4". Very, very powerful, of course. He would look at the seam of coal and almost surgically he would make a mark on it. He would ask his boy – every miner has a boy who works for him – he would say, 'Give me a No. 2 mandrill.' That's a half-headed pick. And then, having stared at this gorgeous display, the black ribbon of shining coal, he would hit it with one enormous blow. And if he hit it right, something like twenty tons of coal would fall out from the coal face . . . Miners believed themselves to be the aristocrats of the working class. They felt superior to all other kinds of manual labourers. They were skilled workers. That coalface was a magical creature.[26]

In addition to their skill, miners celebrated their camaraderie. They looked out for each other at the coal face, where dangers threatened, and socialised both below and above ground, often drinking heavily to slake their thirst. This comradeship was at the root of their solidarity as a class, subsequently developed in the miners' union, which had a lodge or branch at each pit. Durham miner Peter Byrne, born in 1949, recalled his early years at the Eden pit, near Consett:

> My father-in-law worked at Eden, my brother worked at the Eden and I was a face electrician. You were available if there were any break-downs. And having bait [packed lunch], you would be sitting listening to the guys talking. And they sort of educated you about the union, and about your rights, and about standing up for what was right, and

not being afraid to challenge management. And you know, they are not better than you, they just have a different job. And that was something that they instilled in you.[27]

There was, however, a dark side to pit work. Miners were ravaged by the occupational lung disease of pneumoconiosis, caused by inhaling coal dust and actually made worse by the postwar mechanisation of coalmining. About 12 per cent of miners suffered from the disease in 1959–63, but this rose to 25 per cent in South Wales. Between 1955 and 1968, it caused over 1,200 deaths a year.[28] Economically, meanwhile, the golden age of the pits finished around 1959. In the 1960s, oil carried in tankers from the Middle East replaced coal as the major source of fuel for industry, transportation and domestic heating. The Labour government of 1964 decided to close less-efficient mines in Scotland, Northumberland and Durham, and moved 15,000 miners and their families to more efficient pits in Yorkshire and the Midlands.[29]

Overall, the number of pits fell from 698 in 1960 to 292 in 1970, and the coal workforce declined from 602,000 to 287,000.[30] In South Wales, the Dulais Valley lost a thousand souls or 15 per cent of its population between 1961 and 1971.[31] Miners at the head of the valley now took the bus down to the pits at Crynant or Treforgan, travelled east to Aberpergwm in the Neath Valley or west to Abernant in the Swansea Valley. Others migrated to mines in the Midlands, notably Staffordshire. In Scotland, pits closed in Ayrshire, Lanarkshire and Stirlingshire, leaving viable pits only in Midlothian and Fife, nicknamed the Mining Kingdom. Even in Fife, the Glencraig and Mary pits were closed in 1966 and miners were transferred to Frances or Seafield collieries on the coast of the Firth of Forth, or to new pits developed around the Longannet power station: Bogside, Castlebridge, Castlehill and Solsgirth.[32] Tom Watson of Ballingry emigrated to Australia in 1964 to work as an ambulance driver for the port of Melbourne emergency service; then he worked inland at the Yallourn power station. In County Durham, pits in the interior around Chester-le-Street such as

Harraton, Lumley, Pelton Fell and South Pelaw closed between 1964 and 1966, and miners commuted east to more modern, deeper pits on the North Sea coast: Horden, Easington, Dawdon, Seaham and Westhoe. Dave Douglass, born to an Irish Tyneside family in Jarrow in 1948, moved to Hatfield colliery in South Yorkshire in 1966, partly because the pit at Usworth was contracting, but mainly because his young wife Maureen wanted to study at Hull Art College.[33] The migration of miners was experienced differently by David Amos, born in 1957 and brought up in the Nottinghamshire mining village of Annesley. In 1970, after his parents divorced, he moved with his mother to a new estate in Kirkby-in-Ashfield, which was increasingly populated by what he called 'Jocks and Geordies'. 'All the other side of the street was Durham and Northumberland,' he recalled, while 'the Scottish miners that had come down to work in the Nottinghamshire coalfield were given these new council houses.'[34]

Unhappiness among miners built up steadily to the national strikes of 1972 and 1974. Their pay was consistently falling behind that of workers in manufacturing industries, from 22 per cent above that of the average manufacturing worker in 1957 to 2 per cent below in 1969.[35] The world was exploding in 1968, and Dave and Maureen Douglass campaigned against the Vietnam War. In 1970, Dave went to Ruskin College, Oxford, an adult residential college with links to the trade union movement, and joined Sinn Féin in protest at the introduction of internment in Northern Ireland. Academically, he threw himself into Raphael Samuel's History Workshop project, researching and writing pamphlets on labour practices and mining dialect in County Durham.[36] The NUM Annual Conference voted in July 1971 for a wage increase of between 35 and 47 per cent, which was refused by the NCB. The NUM imposed an overtime ban in November and held a national ballot, which voted by 59 per cent for a national strike beginning on 9 January. Flying pickets from Yorkshire were sent to close power stations in East Anglia, and on 3 February a Hatfield picket, Fred Matthews, was run down and killed by a strike-breaking lorry at Keadby power station near Scunthorpe; over five thousand people attended his funeral. Dave Douglass, still at Oxford, picketed nearby Didcot power station. Then news came through that hundreds of lorries were fetching coke from a depot at Saltley Gate, Birmingham. Arthur Scargill, a thirty-four-year-old delegate for Woolley colliery near Barnsley, took 400 Yorkshire miners down there to try to stop the lorries. They were joined by miners from South Wales and Nottinghamshire, and three thousand pickets battled with three thousand police for three days. Scargill then spoke to representatives of the Transport and General Workers' Union (TGWU) and the National Union of Vehicle Builders, urging them to join the picket line. He remembered this as 'the greatest day of my life':

> Over this hill came a banner and I've never seen in my life as many people following a banner. As far as the eye could see it was just a mass of people marching towards Saltley . . . Saltley, the area of Saltley, was now just a mass of human beings, arriving from all over, with banners. The only time this crowd opened was when a delegation of girls from a women's factory came along all dressed in bright white dresses . . . We were in the centre of it and everyone was chanting something different. Some were chanting 'Heath Out', 'Tories Out', 'Support the Miners', 'General Strike'. I got hold of a microphone and started to shout through it, 'Close the Gates! Close the Gates!' and it was taken up, just like a football crowd. [After the gates were closed] I gave a political speech to that mass of people and told them that this was the greatest victory of the working class, certainly in my lifetime.[37]

The Heath government announced a court of inquiry into miners' pay. It recommended substantial increases, resulting in a return to work on 28 February 1972.[38] Unfortunately, the gains made were limited by the statutory pay freeze imposed by the government later that year, while the oil crisis of 1973 strengthened the miners' hand by increasing the demand for coal and coke. In July 1973, the NUM Annual Conference again voted for a wage increase, this time of 31 per cent, but the government would not give ground. Another overtime ban was enforced in November 1973, and a national ballot on 31 January/1 February 1974 resulted in an 81 per cent vote in favour of a national strike, set to begin on 9 February. Edward Heath decided to make this an issue of confidence in his government, and on 7 February called a general election on the question: 'Who Governs Britain?' – the government or the miners? The electorate decided on 28 February 1974 that it was not Edward Heath, who lost his majority, and the incoming Labour government settled with the miners on 5 March.[39]

The miners became more capable of acting together because the National Power Loading Agreement of 1966, which ended wage differentials between collieries and coalfields, gave miners a common cause to defend. This, however, was undone by the introduction of incentive bonus schemes in the 1970s, which rewarded individual pits for beating output targets. Miners in South Wales, Yorkshire, County Durham and Scotland – which were difficult geologically to mine – found themselves being paid less than miners in Leicestershire or Nottinghamshire, who worked in more efficient pits and were handsomely rewarded. It gave them less of an incentive to go on strike in 1984.

Arthur Scargill saw the strikes of 1972 and 1974 as a class war, but in 1984 there was above all a mobilisation of mining communities. These, as we have seen, had grown rapidly at the end of the nineteenth and the beginning of the twentieth centuries. They had a very specific profile, springing up outside major towns and cities; developed a particular solidarity around the Miners' Welfare and other social activities; and, rather than being policed by outside forces, tended to police themselves.

Mining villages grew up around pits sunk by mining companies that had acquired the rights to do so from whichever large landowner owned the site, thus combining industrial and aristocratic feudalism. In Fife, the Lochore estate, which belonged to Lady Scott of Abbotsford, daughter-in-law of Sir Walter Scott, was sold in 1867 to the Lochore and Capledrae Cannel Company, which in due course sold it to the Fife Coal Company that opened the Glencraig and Mary collieries. In County Durham, mines were sunk on the estates of such large landowners as Charles Vane, marquess of Londonderry, who also developed Seaham harbour for exporting coal, and John Lambton, earl of Durham.[40] North Nottinghamshire was known as 'the Dukeries' because the dukes of Portland at Welbeck Abbey, the dukes of Newcastle at Clumber House, the earls Manvers at Thoresby Hall and the barons Savile at Rufford Abbey leased land to mining companies that sank Welbeck colliery in 1912 and Ollerton, Thoresby, Blidworth and Bilsthorpe in the 1920s. Colliery villages were built for labour that was sucked in from nearby Staffordshire, Derbyshire and Yorkshire, County Durham and even Scotland. A little further south-west, at Eastwood, miner's son D.H. Lawrence wrote in *Sons and Lovers* in 1913 that 'Six mines like black studs on the countryside, linked by a loop of fine chain, the railway' were sunk; and 'to accommodate the regiments of miners, Carston, Waite and Co. built the squares, great quadrangles of dwellings on the hillside of Bestwood'.[41]

In the early days, landowners and coal owners sometimes encouraged attendance at church or chapel, or set up cricket, football or rugby clubs in order to reduce class tensions in the mining villages. To achieve the same, the Mining Act 1920 levied a penny per ton of coal on coal companies in order to build miners' halls, where they could indulge in refreshment and recreation after work.[42] At Manton colliery near Worksop in Nottinghamshire, to which many miners had been ferried in wagons by the Wigan Iron and Coal Company, a Miners' Club that opened in 1926 had its own football and athletics club, bowling green and tennis court, reading room, billiard room, card room, bar, and concert and dance hall.[43] At Askern in South Yorkshire, where a pungent Coalite plant that opened in 1929 drove away the spa visitors, a Miners' Welfare was opened in the now redundant Spa Hotel, and a Welfare Park was inaugurated in 1930 with a bowling green, tennis courts, football and cricket pitches, together with a playground for children attending the schools on the Sutton and Selby roads.[44] In Lochore, community life blossomed with a handsome Miners' Institute completed in 1934, pipe bands, football teams and a summer children's gala.[45] In South Wales, community solidarity developed in another way during the 1926 Miners' Strike: soup kitchens were set up in the mining villages; the authorities in the Rhondda fed 18,000 children a week; and borrowings from Miners' Institute libraries increased by 150 per cent.[46]

The sociability of mining communities was sustained by the men, but also by the miners' wives, with their children then being drawn in. In County Durham, Kath Savory, the daughter and granddaughter of miners at Pelton Fell, remembered the peculiar warmth and smell of the local Miners' Welfare in the 1950s, where her uncle Tom was caretaker:

When I was little I would be running up and down the stairs, I would run through the halls where the miners were and they would be sitting reading newspapers, or they would be playing darts, or having general conversations and I loved it, and that memory's with me. I just have to smell a bottle of Jeyes Fluid and that takes me right back to my child-hood, because it stunk of Jeyes Fluid. They used to have weddings and meetings, and that was where all the banners were kept for the whole county; the banners were kept there. So walking into a massive, huge hall and just looking at all the banners going right round, it was fasci-nating; I loved it.[47]

Josie Potts, a miner's wife and mother of four girls at Manton, recalled that the club provided entertainment for the whole family, not least her daughters, and also linked one mining community with another:

They were a close-knit community, very close. And Manton Club, what we had down on Retford Road, that were the place you went at weekends, you know, and all gathered together, with dominos, darts and everything; entertainment. You could have a good damn weekend down there. Plus we got the big sports field. We used to have galas on there. All that's gone . . . My daughters used to be in the majorette band . . . all mining villages had one. We used to practise on field down at bottom, kids there, we had a trainer and learnt the drums and every-thing, raised money for them to get uniforms, and then they called it White Rose of Yorkshire. And the kids used to go in competitions against other mining villages, like Dodworth and Carcroft. And you could name them all. Goole, Stainforth, they are all mining areas.[48]

In the Dulais Valley, Hefina Headon, a miner's wife and postmistress of Onllwyn post office (until it was robbed in 1978), went back down the hill to a council house in Seven Sisters, where she had been born, and, as if to compensate, threw herself into volunteering in the community. She supported the pony club where her granddaughter Jayne learned to ride and the Dulais Silver Band in which she played, sat on the parent–teacher association of both the English- and the Welsh-speaking schools, raised funds to send the children to the Christmas pantomime in Porthcawl, and campaigned for the Labour Party. 'Nearly every evening would be taken up by a committee meeting of some type,' wrote Jayne. 'She had a different briefcase or bag for each committee's paperwork, and these would be lined up in the parlour to pick up and leave.'[49]

Within mining communities, the basic cell was the mining family. It was an economic unit, sustained by the income from the pit. Work at the pit was generally handed down from father to son. The father might not want his son to go down, and the son might not want to go down; but there was frequently no alternative. Fathers were injured, fell sick or died. Other workers went down the mine when they got married, in order to earn a better income, even a 'family wage'. Miners married early and often stayed with the wife's family until a Coal Board house or council house became available. Gender divisions were strict: the man was the authority outside the house and sometimes was rarely at home, dividing his time between the pit and drinking at the Miners' Welfare or working men's club. Husbands and wives went out together only at weekends. The wife ran the household and raised the children. In many cases, she also collected her husband's pay packet on a Friday, gave him pocket money for drink, cigarettes and the occasional bet, and controlled the budget – for a wage squandered on drink spelt doom for a working-class family.

Among the many miners who followed their father down the pit was Ronnie Campbell, born in 1944 in Glencraig and brought up on the new estate of Ballingry. 'All my family, all the Campbells were all miners, you know. My uncles were.' He went down the Mary pit until it closed in 1966, when he went to the Michael pit on the coast, until its reserves caught fire with the loss of nine lives in 1967. He returned inland to nearby Cowdenbeath, finding work as a furnaceman in the Coal Board work-shops.[50] Sean Lee, born in 1957 in Cowdenbeath, was the son of a Catholic Irishman from Waterford who came to Fife as an indentured worker in the mines and bored mineshafts. When he was injured, his seven children had to be taken into care. As Carol, one of Sean's older sisters, explained: 'My younger sister died in foster care, through cruelty. My dad had a nervous breakdown, and ended up in Stratheden [asylum] for the rest of his life.' Sean picked up the narrative: 'That was me the breadwinner, then, in the house.' He signed on at Seafield pit. Some of his sisters were working in local government but 'they were only juniors, and their money was very, very, scarce'. On his side, however, 'We beat the Heath government in '72 and our wages went sky high. We were the top paid in the country at that time.'[51]

The sickness or death of the father was clearly a major challenge for mining families, and was not uncommon. Cliff Jeffery, born in 1935, was the son of a pipe-layer from Hetton-le-Hole in County Durham who, during the Depression, went south in search of work. In 1940, he qualified as a shot-firer at Nailstone colliery in Leicestershire, but died the same year of kidney disease (possibly brought on by working in wet conditions), leaving Cliff and his younger brother. Their mother worked in a munitions factory during the war, and then at Precision Rubber. She did not want him to go down the pit and apprenticed him to an engineering firm in Coalville, but the pay was barely 'a copper a week'. 'Got to better myself,' he thought; he became a miner, first at Nailstone, then at Bagworth, earning a good wage.[52] David Potts (the cousin of Billy Potts, who married Josie) was born in Manton in 1953: 'I got three brothers and we all worked in the colliery, even though our father said you don't want to go down the pit, to each and every one of us, but we did.' His first job, after leaving school at fifteen, was at a wooden-handle manufacturing company. Then came the hammer blow: 'My father died while I was working there. And under tragic circumstances . . . He took his own life.' David had to stop work to grieve and the manufacturer sacked him. That was 'my first taste of capitalism being sort of wielded over the working class,' he reflected. 'I was unemployed for a while and I went along to the pit which I could do. Anybody could go. It was a pit. If you're coming at a job and nowhere else, you go down the pit and have a job. So, I went down to the pit.' One route out of the pit was to pass the 11-plus examination and go to grammar school. But this was stacked against working-class children. 'Looking back,' said David Potts, 'I can see the 11-plus was just there to cream off the best at the time and always has been . . . because if you failed the 11-plus, they're all shoved in the secondary education [sic] which wasn't up to much.'[53]

Paul Stratford, born in Horden in County Durham in 1950, was bright at primary school, but a bit of a rebel. Sent to Easington Boys' Modern School, he had ambitions to become 'a policeman or a fireman to do some good, thinking that, you know, them people did good'. When it came to choosing a job, a council careers officer came down to the school to lower his expectations. 'Me mum was there because you had to have a parent. Dad would be at pit. And he said, "Well, what you want to do?" And I said, "I fancy this. I fancy that." And he was writing his notes, he says, "Well, your choice is either the pit or the factories." '[54] It was not a question of intelligence, but of class. Even if they passed the examination, the family would rarely be able to afford the school uniform or the loss of an additional wage. Steve Williamson, born in 1953, the son of a Grimethorpe miner, recalled that

I did take the 11-plus. And I was sorely disappointed because for every year, prior to the 11-plus, I was top of the class in everything. And, the

11-plus, I still believe to this day, because the only people that went, that got 11-plus, went to grammar school, were teachers' children, bus inspectors. I can't recall any miners' children. And I know the children that went from my school, were nowhere near my level. I was absolutely heartbroken. But to say that, my father said if you do get to grammar school you're not going because we can't afford the uniform, can't afford the kit.[55]

Many of the former miners interviewed conveyed the straightness of the road to the pit by saying, 'I left school on the Friday and on the Monday I started at the pit.' It was not always as simple as that. All miners had a few weeks' training at a pit with a training centre, and would then work at the surface until they could go down the mine at the age of eighteen. But it was also possible to do a three- or four-year apprenticeship, sponsored by the Coal Board, with day release to a local college, to become a craftsman – usually a fitter or an electrician – trained to maintain the machinery and power in the mine. Paul Stratford went to Peterlee College and did his City and Guilds as a fitter, and might have gone on to become an engineer, but didn't want to become 'a boss'. Steve Williamson also took his City and Guilds as a fitter, moving between Yorkshire and Nottinghamshire as his parents broke up, and might also have gone on to become an engineer, except that his own personal difficulties intervened. 'I got into what you do as a teenager, drinking, womanising,' he confided. 'I put my first wife . . . my first wife was pregnant. She was seventeen, I was nineteen. We lasted about eighteen months, I think. And I had a son with her.'

Accidental pregnancy and early marriage were common in mining communities in the 1960s and 1970s. Young people were brought up together and had many opportunities to meet, whether at miners' clubs, rugby clubs or local dances. Betty Cook, a miner's daughter born in Doncaster in 1938, passed the 11-plus and went to Pontefract and District Girls' High School, 'a school for young ladies'. She did not feel at home there and left at sixteen to train as a nurse. All was going well, and she fell in love with a joiner called Colin; but then Colin dumped her, and her best friend arranged a date for her on the rebound with a young miner. 'I just didn't care what happened. And the usual story, working-class girl got pregnant, and in those days you got married. And so I got married. I had Michael when I was eighteen. Then I had Donny when I was twenty. And then I had Glyn when I was twenty-six. So I had three boys altogether.' Anne Harper, who met Betty during the 1984–85 strike, was born in 1941. Arthur Scargill came regularly to see her father, a trade unionist at Woolley colliery, about standing as a union delegate; then he started to ask Anne out. They went to dances at Barnsley swimming pool, which was boarded over for the winter, and then, she explained with some difficulty, they had to get married and live with Arthur's widowed father as well:

Yeah, yeah. I had to, uh [laughter] I had to, uh, yeah, and when I were twenty then . . . At that time it were, 'You've got to get married then.' Now they don't, but . . . me Mam went barmy. Me Dad went barmy. But, I had, and I went to live with Arthur. Well Arthur's mother had died. So his Dad were there. So I had to go there and live with him . . . And he said it's only going to be two or three year, two or three month. And Arthur, 'We're stopping with me Dad.' And then, when it come to two and three month, his Dad wouldn't go, so he lived with us all his life.[56]

There were some cases when, to avoid scandal, the baby was passed off as belonging to the grandmother. Even if the decision was consensual, it nevertheless gave rise to revelations at a later date, when the child learned who her real mother was. But if the decision was not consensual, family rifts could open up.

Hefina Headon in Seven Sisters had herself become pregnant at sixteen, married the unsuitable father, Johnny Smith, who joined the army and had affairs, and lost her first two children. She reset by divorcing after the birth of her third child, Jennifer, in 1952, and in 1958 married the more reliable John Headon, a miner who also ran a taxi service. At the age of fourteen, however, Jennifer herself became pregnant. Her baby, Jayne, born in 1968, was whisked off to Barnardo's Homes, before being adopted by Hefina and John as their own child. Jennifer left home and worked as a croupier in London's casinos and on cruise ships, before emigrating to America. Not until she was nine did Jayne discover who her real mother was.[57]

Meanwhile Pete Richardson, born in Askern in 1951, was a fighter – whether defending a friend at school against bullies or as a football supporter, passionately following Manchester United with the group of 'Doncaster Reds' that he helped to set up. On leaving school at fifteen, he worked as a welder in Doncaster and remembers whistling at Sue as she passed on her way to work at Tunstall Byers, a local electrical equipment factory. They started courting after a Valentine's Day dance, where he was a bouncer. Sue fell pregnant, but her parents thought that Pete was a 'wrong 'un'. She had also been raped around that time, so it was unclear who the father actually was. Her own father stepped in to control the women:

Me Dad was really strict, and when I was pregnant – we'd stopped going to church then – my dad said I couldn't keep her, he was having her. When I had her in hospital, they wouldn't let even me see her or look at her or pick her up or owt. Me mum and dad took her home, they named her, never asked me what to call her and didn't involve me. She didn't know that she was mine until one of the family blurted it out. She was about twelve.[58]

'We wanted to keep her,' Pete added, 'but in the light of what was going off, they volunteered to look after her. Then we wanted her back, but he wouldn't give us her back. Very hard to take. I challenged him down the pit, he said [we] had given her.'[59] The rift with Sue's parents was unbridgeable. But Pete and Sue stuck together and had four more children: Wayne in 1970, Lee in 1971, Vicky in 1973 and Mark in 1975. They were a family united by adversity and the injustices of the outside world. Pete, with his distinctive black beard, was always ready to 'stand his ground' – as he showed during the strike.

There was a strict division in mining families between men and women, although in the 1960s and 1970s this was becoming more fluid and was sometimes contested. Since the mid-nineteenth century, miners in Britain had been nearly all men: some women were employed above ground, picking stones from the coals until this task was mechanised. There were only 956 pit-brow women in British collieries in 1953, two thirds of them in Lancashire, and the last one left in 1966.[60] After that, the only women at a colliery were cooks, cleaners and office workers. The miner was expected to demonstrate his masculinity, whether as the breadwinner earning a 'family wage', as a fighter in the union and on picket lines or controlling the womenfolk in his home. The miner's wife was expected to give up paid work when she married, to stay at home, ensure that food was on the table for her husband when he came home from work, raise the children and ensure that the family stayed solvent.

That said, miners' wives (who were generally also miners' daughters) had to wrestle with the same challenges as their menfolk – or even more so. They also often had to deal with their fathers' sickness (or death) and with the lack of good parenting. They, too, faced the challenge of the 11-plus and the direction that their life then took. Some miners' wives gave up work for a while to bring up small children; others continued to work part time; and a third group made sure that they did not have too many children and kept going with full-time work. Resilience in all these areas helped to keep the family going; but that same resilience could also threaten their husband's self-esteem.

In Askern, miners' daughters Dianne Hogg and Jean Crane, born respectively in 1948 and 1949, became close friends during the strike of 1972, while their husbands were picketing. Jean had passed the 11-plus, but had not gone to the grammar school and was teased that her parents could not afford the uniform. She found a job on a market stall in nearby Doncaster, became pregnant at seventeen by Phil, a welder with Bentley Steel Supplies, and married at eighteen: 'so by the time I was twenty-one, I had all four of my girls'. Phil found a job above ground at Askern pit in 1969, after the third girl was born, but that scarcely made things easier. They were declared bankrupt in 1972, not least because of the strike, and had no access to credit for ten years. Jean found another job managing a newsagent's shop in Doncaster.[61]

Dianne had a very tough childhood, because her father, a miner at Bentley colliery, drank and gambled, while her mother had mental health issues; she and her sister were among 'the poorer kids in the street'. She went on: 'I left school Friday, and I started work in a newsagent's and tobacconist's on Monday'; she gave the family most of her wages. Then, when she was sixteen, her mother left home and she had to look after her younger brother and sister. She took a job bottling at Milton Dairies, where she met 'tall, skinny Pete'. She fell pregnant at eighteen, got married and 'I honestly told my husband more times than enough, the day I married him my life began'. Like Phil, he found a job at Askern pit top for the higher wage. 'He were a good father, he were a good husband,' said Dianne. 'He put food on the table, clothes on the back, holidays every year . . . Been skint, nearly, but never borrowed, never got into debt.' For the sake of appearances, she took great care when bringing up her four girls: 'If I went to the shops, my children would get hands and face washed, a clean dress on. I wouldn't take them out dirty. I didn't want people to think what I thought of myself when I were a kid.' She put the family first, although during the 1984 strike she went back to work part time at a newsagent's, to ensure that at least some money came in.[62]

In the Welsh Valleys, there were also strong women who had to deal with difficult family situations. Marilyn James, born in 1955, suffered because her father, a miner at Blaenant, was injured at the pit when she was twelve and her mother had to go out to work in a factory. After school,

Marilyn had various jobs in Neath – in a supermarket, betting shop and factory. She met Philip, whose brutal father had been sacked from the pit and had died of a heart attack when he was five, became pregnant and married when she was seventeen. Philip went down the pit at Treforgan to qualify for a Coal Board house, allowing her to give up work.[63]

Christine Powell, born in 1956, was in a similar situation when she was growing up, as her father, who worked in Blaenant pit offices, was off work for two years with tuberculosis and her mother continued working as a nurse. Christine was good at maths and science, passed the 11-plus, went to grammar school and Cardiff University, and qualified as a physics teacher. At the pony club she met Stuart, who became a fitter at Blaenant; as she recalled, 'he wasn't a better rider than me, but he had more bottle than I did'. Like her mother, she did not give up work, but continued teaching in Swansea and also coached Hefina Headon's granddaughter Jayne.[64]

Donna Jones, born in 1945 and brought up in the Afan Valley, also knew tough times. Her father, a miner at the Afan colliery, was invalided out at the age of fifty-five with a disease that locked his legs; but as he had not been injured, he was not entitled to compensation. 'We lived on national assistance, sickness benefit which makes me quite emotional,' she recalled. Full of grit, Donna passed the 11-plus, went to Port Talbot Grammar School and was offered a place at Bristol University; but she had to forsake it to earn money for the family. She found a job as a clerical officer at the National Insurance Office in Cymmer, ensuring that other sick miners got the payments due to them. Relatively late on, aged twenty-three, she married Gary, a fitter at Afan colliery, and had her children when she was twenty-seven and thirty-three. Asked whether she had ever thought she would give up her job on marriage, she riposted: 'No. I was quite determined that I wasn't.' This made it possible for Gary to leave the pit that had claimed his father's life for the building and haulage trade, where he earned less money, but where there was also less physical risk.[65]

In County Durham, there was a similar pattern of women continuing to work after marriage, but not always indefinitely. Kath Savory, born in

1949, wanted to be the 'best hairdresser in the world', but at fifteen took a job in a non-dispensing chemist in South Pelaw. She married aged twenty, had her first son at twenty-two and continued to work part time, leaving her son with her mother; her husband John left the Sacriston mine to work on the buses. Then, in 1967, 'when my second son came along', she said, 'I realised I couldn't put it on me mam to look after two'. She left work, and John made up the earnings shortfall by going back to the pit at Westoe, on the coast.[66]

Mary Stratford, born in 1955, had a good deal of childhood hardship to repair. She remembered her mother crying when she had an unplanned sixth child and the family had to move from their modern house in Peterlee new town and return to a back-to-back colliery house in Easington, because it was free. 'My dad was on low wages because he'd had an accident at the pit, and he was just a datal worker [i.e. paid by the day] then and the rents were going up.' She passed the 11-plus and went to a Catholic grammar school in Hartlepool, leaving at sixteen to become a library assistant in Easington, then a civil servant with National Savings, paying a quarter of her wages to her parents for board and lodging. She married Paul at twenty-one, moved to a new estate at Great Lumley, kept working and had children relatively late – Peter when she was twenty-five and Helen when she was thirty. Unlike many miners' wives, and despite being a Catholic, she was on the pill:

> I knew if there was one thing I didn't want, it was a baby before I was married. Not that I was rabidly having sex loads, but I just knew that that was something I didn't want to happen . . . I didn't want a baby, there was just no way; I've seen it destroy too many lasses' lives. I didn't want that. I think it was probably me mam had an influence on me on that, you know, given what she'd gone through. She used to tell me how hard it was for her . . . My grandmother was a devout Catholic and said to me when I was eighteen, 'Don't you go getting yourself pregnant. There's no need. I don't care what the pope says, he's wrong.'[67]

This book is an oral history of the Miners' Strike: it foregrounds the voices of those who took part in the strike. It is the first oral-history account of the 1984–85 Miners' Strike across the three nations of Wales, England and Scotland. It tells the national story through the voices of 148 men, women and children who took part in the struggle of that remarkable year. They weave together the personal and the political, the effects of the strike on their comrades, families and communities; and they tell the story of their lives before, during and after the strike. Following the distinction made by Lynn Abrams, it uses the interview as a source for a deeper understanding of the Miners' Strike from the 'bottom up', rather than thinking aloud about theoretical topics dear to oral historians – such as autobiographical memory, collective memory, and memory and trauma.[68]

The starting point of the project was to trace interviews that had already been undertaken with miners and their wives who had been involved in the strike. This made it possible to locate networks of miners, their wives and others who had played an active role in sustaining the strike.[69] The first port of call in 2016 was the South Wales Miners' Library in Swansea. After the strike, adult educator and activist Hywel Francis undertook dozens of interviews with both individuals and groups of miners and miners' wives in the Neath, Dulais and Swansea Valleys. He had intended to write a history of the strike, based also on interviews undertaken by Huw Beynon in Durham and Bob Fryer, principal of Northern College, Barnsley, but the project 'foundered', he recalled, 'because of conflicting perspectives mirroring the fragmentation of the strike itself'.[70] A small collection of 1986 interviews with miners and miners' wives in Askern was found in the Sheffield City Archives. The Nottinghamshire Archives held a collection of interviews with former miners at Manton colliery, Worksop, undertaken by former miner David Hopkins as part of a local millennium project. Further leads in Worksop were provided by local councillor Josie Potts, Natalie Braber of Nottingham Trent University and the cast of the 1984 documentary *Notts Women Strike Back*. In the County Durham Record

Office we found interviews from a Popular Politics project made in 2011 by David Connolly of the North East Labour History Society, which led to his contacts from the strike. Lynn Gibson of the Women's Banner Group in County Durham introduced me to interviewees in the Barnsley and Sheffield areas through the Orgreave Truth and Justice Campaign, while former Welsh miner Carwyn Donovan put me in touch with his old comrades from the Kellingley pit. In Fife, contacts were provided by Jim Phillips of the University of Glasgow, who was involved with former miners who had been mobilised by the independent review into police action during the strike (commissioned by the Scottish government in 2018). To compensate for the fact that my sample might be limited by a given address book, further connections were sought through the contacts of some of the former miners and miners' wives I interviewed for this project, particularly in South Wales.

The interviews for this book were conducted between 2019 and 2021 in six coalfields – South Wales, Leicestershire, Nottinghamshire, Yorkshire, County Durham and Fife. The few communities where extant interviews existed were prioritised, but the model of the 'pit village' (where the village adjoined the pit) was a rarity in the sample, except at Easington in County Durham, Askern in South Yorkshire and Manton in Nottinghamshire. Pit closures since the 1960s meant, as we have seen, that, in order to get to work, miners often had to travel long distances from villages where many or most of the working population may once have been miners, but where there was no longer a working pit. To gain a sense of what these communities were like, we focused on a few of them for each coalfield. These included villages in the Neath, Dulais and Swansea Valleys in South Wales; Askern and the villages around Barnsley in Yorkshire; Great Lumley outside Chester-le-Street and Leadgate outside Consett in County Durham; and Lochore, Ballingry and Lochgelly in Fife. In Nottinghamshire, there was a focus on Manton, the pit village of Worksop, Warsop near Mansfield and the pit at Annesley, where most of the miners continued to work. In Leicestershire, where the pit village scarcely existed, we highlighted the

'Dirty Thirty' of striking miners, mainly at Bagworth pit, who lived scattered over a number of locations.

Interviews were conducted in person – twice interrupted by Covid lockdowns – in the homes of former mining families or else in public spaces, such as community centres and church halls. Three interviews were conducted online: one with a miner's wife who had moved to France and two with American women miners who had come to Britain to support the strike. In Fife, five of the interviews were conducted by two people, Jim Phillips and myself. They were conducted mainly with individuals, but in sixteen cases former miners and their wives were interviewed together; in other cases, mothers and daughters, brothers and friends were interviewed. Interviews lasted for an average of two hours: some were shorter, while the longest took five hours. In the vast majority of cases, people were interviewed once; however, in one case a former miner was interviewed a second time with his wife and son, and in another case a grandfather was interviewed first with his daughters and then with two grandchildren. One miner's wife was interviewed alone, then with her husband and lastly with a fellow female activist. The interviews are available in the National Life Stories collection of the British Library and may be accessed online.[71]

Some may argue that after nearly forty years, people's memories are fading and becoming unreliable.[72] My own view is that while dates and names may be lost, the way in which the Miners' Strike impacted individuals, families and communities – ranging from the excitement of the struggle to the pain of defeat and its consequences – is not easily forgotten. Some may also argue that memories may be influenced by other interpretations of the strike, either in print, in film or on television. There is no doubt that collective experience influences individual experience, and the story of the strike is an interplay between individual stories and shared stories. It is also true that these interviews were undertaken at a specific moment, after mining communities had been devastated both by the closure of pits and other industries and by the policy of austerity. They were recorded after the Scottish and EU referendums, and – except in

South Wales – after the 2019 general election, which saw many 'Red Wall' seats fall to the Conservatives. Unlike interviews conducted soon after the strike – interviews that were coloured by the pain of defeat and a sense of betrayal – these conversations allowed former miners and their wives (and also their children and grandchildren) to reconsider the strike in terms of the consequences for their families, their communities and politics generally over nearly forty years. As the world changes, so interviewees, like historians, revisit and rethink their accounts of the past.

This study is heavily indebted to a large number of works that have gone before, researched and written over the forty years since the strike. These include general works about the coal industry,[73] militant works published in the immediate aftermath of the strike,[74] more recent contributions[75] and excellent regional studies of the strike.[76] The powerful role of women during the strike was recognised very quickly afterwards,[77] and has continued to form the subject of research;[78] but much less has been written about families[79] or the question of masculinity during and after the dispute.[80] There have been several studies of deindustrialisation and the decline of mining communities.[81] The decline of the British working class has been debated ever since Eric Hobsbawm's 1978 Marx Memorial Lecture on 'The Forward March of Labour Halted?', and has more recently been taken up by Ellen Meiksins Wood, Ross McKibbin and Selina Todd.[82] Much more, however, remains to be said about the ways in which the working class was 'unmade' or 'remade' after deindustrialisation.

The book is divided into sixteen chapters, which fall loosely into four parts. The first part (chapters 1–4) examines the outbreak of the strike, the picketing, the battle over the national ballot and the Battle of Orgreave. The second part (chapters 5–8) explores the infrastructure of the strike: support groups, the role of women, national and international connections, and the special case of Lesbians and Gays Support the Miners. The third part (chapters 9–12) returns to the chronological narrative with the state of siege in mining villages, hardship and Christmas 1984, the return to work and the continuing struggle. And the fourth part (chapters 13–16) looks at the afterlives of miners, miners' wives and children, and the stories that they share to give meaning to their struggle, past and present.

For many people, not least younger generations, the Miners' Strike may seem an event that occurred a long time ago, its purpose hard to understand. The organised working class, defeated by Mrs Thatcher, is largely a thing of the past, replaced as it has been by individual workers in the global gig economy. Meanwhile, a fossil-fuel industry that for two centuries contributed massively to carbon emissions in industrial Britain is regarded differently in a world facing a climate crisis. Boris Johnson provocatively attempted to run these two developments together, claiming in 2021 that Mrs Thatcher had had an environmental agenda: 'Thanks to Margaret Thatcher, who closed so many coal mines across the country, we had a big early start and we're now moving rapidly away from coal altogether.'[83]

There are, nevertheless, arguments for why what happened in 1984–85 should be of interest today. First, the brutality of the state used against the miners has become the subject of ongoing campaigns. In 2012, the Orgreave Truth and Justice Campaign was launched to demand a public inquiry into the police actions at Orgreave on 18 June 1984 and the subsequent cover-up. This was rejected by the British home secretary in 2016; but in Scotland, an independent inquiry set up in 2018 concluded that Scottish miners had disproportionately suffered conviction and dismissal. This finding led to a Miners' Strike Pardon Bill being introduced in the Scottish Parliament, and being passed into law in 2022.[84] Second, the legacy of the strike and its defeat is still with us. The closure of the pits hollowed out mining communities, leaving them with problems of unemployment, deprivation, poor health and education outcomes, family breakdown and endemic drug use. It is clear, too, that the conditions in those areas 'left behind' contributed to the Brexit vote of 2016 and the Conservative toppling of the 'Red Wall' in 2019.[85] Third, interest in the strike has been sustained in the media by a number of films: Mark Herman's *Brassed Off* (1996), Stephen Daldry's *Billy Elliot* (2000) and Matthew Warchus's *Pride* (2014); Janice Sutherland's Channel 4 documentary

Strike: When Britain Went to War (2003); and James Graham's BBC drama *Sherwood* (2022), set against the conflicted background of the Miners' Strike in Nottinghamshire. Lastly, the neoliberal project that brought in privatisation, undermined unions, and casualised and cheapened labour met a payback moment in 2022–23 when working people were confronted by a cost-of-living crisis, including rising food and fuel bills. Railway workers, dockers, postal and distribution workers, Border Force officials, teachers, lecturers, barristers, nurses and ambulance workers organised a rolling cycle of strikes. The situation was summed up by Mick Lynch, general secretary of the National Union of Rail, Maritime and Transport Workers (RMT), who said on 17 August 2022 at the Enough is Enough rally: 'We are the working-class, we are back. We are here, we are demanding change, we refuse to be poor, and we are going to win for our people on our terms. Our message is this, straightforward. The working class is back. We refuse to be beat, we refuse to be humbled, we refuse to wait for the politicians and policy drivers and we refuse to be poor, anymore.'[86]

1

STOP-START

Asked whether they had seen the Miners' Strike coming, former miners and their wives say that they had, but they were not sure when it would be upon them. 'It had the inevitability of a train wreck,' said Siân James.[1] It was inevitable, because the battlelines had long been drawn. The miners' strike of 1974 had brought down the Heath government, and the Conservatives were not going to allow that humiliation again. In 1977, Nicholas Ridley MP, son of a Northumberland landowner and chairman of Northumberland County Council, famed for his chain-smoking and air of disdain, chaired a committee which reported to the Conservative Party on plans for an incoming government to privatise nationalised industries and defeat strike action. This was leaked by *The Economist* in May 1978. The report's confidential annex on 'Countering the Political Threat' envisaged picking a fight with the coal industry over (a) an 'unreasonable wage claim' or (b) 'redundancies and closures'. In order to ensure victory, the plan was to 'strengthen our defences against all-out attack in a highly vulnerable industry' by building up coal stocks, measures to 'cut off the supply of money to the strikers' and a strategy to 'deal with the problem of violent picketing'. The report concluded that the government would need 'a large, mobile squad of police who are equipped and prepared to uphold the law against the likes of the Saltley Coke-works mob'.[2]

When Mrs Thatcher became prime minister in May 1979, a confrontation with the miners was only a matter of time. The reasons were both
economic and political. In order to prepare the way for privatisation, the
Coal Industry Act 1980 cut subsidies and required the Coal Board to
become self-financing by 1984. This would mean shutting so-called 'uneco-
nomic' pits and making the industry leaner, fitter and more attractive to
buyers. If the miners resisted, Thatcher would be ready for them. 'The last
Conservative government was destroyed by the Miners' Strike,' she told
Willie Whitelaw, her home secretary and deputy prime minister. 'We'll
have another one and we'll win it.'³ The Employment Act 1980 outlawed
secondary picketing, so that striking miners could not be supported, for
example, by dockers or railway workers, and a code of practice limited to
six the number of pickets who could be sent in to prevent non-strikers
working. The thumbscrews were already on.

On the other side, the NUM was in the hands of Joe Gormley. From
a mining family near Wigan and general secretary of the Lancashire and
Cumberland miners before he became NUM president in 1971, Gormley
had been in charge during the strikes of 1972 and 1974. What he wanted, he
said in the traditionally gendered way that characterised the trade union
movement, was for miners to have 'a good education for the children, a Jaguar
at the front and a Mini at the back to take the wife shopping'. He was a
patient negotiator and, in the words of one Coal Board official, 'Joe could
bargain the buttons off your trousers.'⁴ But the retirement in the 1970s of
an older generation of miners led to a new intake of young miners, some of
whom had enjoyed NCB- or NUM-sponsored education and were more
politicised. Historian Jim Phillips described them as 'the cosmopolitan colliery
generation', since they travelled long distances to work in pits that were still
open.⁵ This workforce was becoming more combative, its vanguard joining
either the Broad Left or – in South Wales and Scotland – the Communist
Party, and it was looking to elect a more pugnacious NUM president.

Dave Douglass, discontented miner that he was, took three years off in
1976 from Hatfield Main, Doncaster, to study history, industrial relations

and law at Strathclyde University. He threw himself 'lock, stock and barrel' into the student movement and had eight girlfriends. 'The scene back in Donnie had been developing while I was away,' he noted on his return in 1979. 'Our political attitude of social revolution and union militancy were already fairly common among the young folk of our generation and the sexual revolution had taken off quite on its own.'[6] In June 1981, aged thirty-three, he was elected NUM branch delegate at the pit, 'perhaps the proudest moment of my life'. 'I will represent these men through thick and thin,' he promised. A year later, with the support of 'militant collieries' such as Askern, Frickley, Goldthorpe and Yorkshire Main, he was elected to the Yorkshire Area Executive Committee.[7]

The experience of David Potts at Manton colliery was similar. He was sponsored by the NUM to do courses in industrial relations, economics and politics at the University of Sheffield from 1978 to 1979, and 'found the economics one exceptional. I sort of took to it like a duck to water and the stuff that we read was meat and drink really to us.' This equipped him to become an NUM delegate at Manton pit, aged twenty-six, attending the Yorkshire Area delegates' meetings.[8]

In South Wales, Ian Isaac, the son of a miner at Duffryn colliery in the Afan Valley, worked for British Leyland in Cowley before he became a miner at St John's, Maesteg, in 1974. He went to Oxford's Ruskin College in 1977–78, writing a dissertation on 'The History of Mining in the Llynfi and Afan Valleys'. Returning to St John's he was elected secretary of the lodge; he, too, was aged twenty-six and was the youngest secretary in South Wales. A photograph of the St John's committee that year showed him in the centre, looking like a schoolboy among ranks of middle-aged men: young men linked to the Broad Left would replace them over the next three years.[9] One of these was Phil White, a miner of Irish Catholic stock at Maesteg, who was two years younger than Ian. When he came to St Johns, 'I became a friend of his, a personal friend,' said Phil. 'It was through Ian that I became more politically agitated.' Ian advised him, 'Phil, you should be reading Engels and a bit of Marx.' Within a year or so,

Phil was on the lodge committee, specialising in issues of miners' injury and sickness compensation.[10]

Alongside the Broad Left in South Wales was a small network of communists, who drew inspiration from the interwar communist leadership of Arthur Horner and who were dedicated to educating the miners in an understanding of class struggle. Hywel Francis, born in 1946, the son of Dai Francis (general secretary of the South Wales Miners' Federation between 1963 and 1976), graduated in history from Cardiff in 1968 and secured funding for a Coalfield History Project to rescue the archives and libraries of NUM lodges from collieries that were being closed, and to set up a South Wales Miners' Library within the University of Swansea in which to house the material. When it opened in 1973, a Swansea professor asked, incredulous, 'Do miners read Dickens?' Appointed lecturer at Swansea's extramural department in 1974, Hywel educated young miners such as Des Dutfield and Tyrone O'Sullivan on NUM day-release courses in labour history, and indeed did encourage them to read Dickens's *Hard Times*. Meanwhile, he cofounded Llafur, the Welsh Labour History Society, and joked that its thousand members were 'the political wing of the Miners' Library'.[11]

The Broad Left presence in South Wales was reflected in County Durham, while the communist presence was taken up in Scotland. 'We would travel all the time to Midlands, Scotland, Kent,' recalled Phil White. 'Not so much in the Midlands. But the North East was good.'[12] One of the militants there was Paul Stratford, a natural rebel who had been active during the 1972 strike, picketing on Teesside to prevent coal deliveries. After that he spent a week at Ruskin College, learning

> TUC policies; there was a lot of trade unions. There was a jewellery makers' trade union. There was the printers' trade union in Glasgow, definitely left-wing. Again, it was more education for me, just listen to these lads talking, because you don't have much. In the pits you don't have much.[13]

Returning to Easington, he was elected lodge secretary of the Durham Mechanics, which he said has 'always been a right-wing organisation', but now it was time for change. The driver of much of that change was David Hopper, a miner at Wearmouth who became secretary of its lodge and, with the support of the Broad Left, made elections to the Area Executive more democratic, paving the way to be elected to it himself in 1982.[14]

In Fife, the Communist Party had a powerful influence on older miners, who then transmitted their political awareness to younger ones. Ronnie Campbell, by that time a furnaceman in the Coal Board Workshops, was elected to the Workshops' NUM Committee and in 1976 joined the Communist Party. His wife Elizabeth came from Lumphinnans, nick-named 'Little Moscow'. Ronnie acted as election agent for Willie Clarke, who was NUM secretary at Glencraig (before it closed) and then at Seafield colliery, and who in May 1973 was elected to Fife Council as a Communist councillor for Ballingry, Kelty and Lumphinnans. Clarke imparted disci-pline and socialist thinking to raw younger miners. Iain Chalmers, born in 1952 and brought up in Lochgelly, came from a long line of miners; but he reacted against this, left school at fifteen and toured pop festivals. He claimed to have 'had a joint with Hendrix' (albeit a discarded one) at the Isle of Wight festival in 1970, lived in a hippie commune and did time in a youth detention centre for theft. He met a US veteran who revealed the horrors of the Vietnam War and a Chilean fleeing the coup of 1973 and joined the International Socialists. Eventually, with a wife and daughter to support, he took a job at Seafield pit, where Willie Clarke and his comrades calmed him down:

> I was young, I was idealistic, I wanted to shoot the bankers, abolish the royal family, you know, create a Trotskyist model state, but they kind of took me aside and took me under their wing and said, 'No.' What they did was they calmed the flames down a wee bit and said, 'No, this is how it works.' And 'do this and do that'. And took the edge off it.[15]

Willie Clarke also educated Sean Lee, who was five years younger than Chalmers and who, as we have seen, had become the family breadwinner when his father was injured, had a nervous breakdown and lost both his job at the pit and the coal allowance that kept them all warm. Sean and his sisters appealed to Willie, as a councillor, to help their family and then, when Sean found work at Seafield in 1973, Willie gave him a political education, sending him to the hotel in Perth where the NUM ran weekend training courses:

> He's a very tall guy, he's very imposing, and the first time we met him was when my father got invalided out the pit. We had no coal, and we were freezing, and he was a union rep that came to the house and managed to fight the case, which allowed us to get coal from the Coal Board. [He] encouraged me to go and learn about politics. I used to go to the Salutation Hotel in Perth and learn about, well, communism, basically Marx, Engels.[16]

Pressure was building and the strike might have happened in 1981, but on that occasion the government blinked. On 10 February 1981, NUM leaders were summoned to the NCB's London headquarters at Hobart House, Grosvenor Place, to be told by chairman Derek Ezra that because of the Coal Industry Act, they would have to cut production by 10 million tons. Pressed as to what this might mean, he conceded that twenty-three pits would be closed. The miners' leaders were aghast. 'We have been here before, Mr Ezra, to discuss a colliery closure,' said Emlyn Williams, president of the South Wales Miners' Federation, 'and for our part we have always done our best to be reasonable and constructive. *But twenty-three collieries!*'[17] When news got out, the miners reacted swiftly. A contingent from South Wales demonstrated outside the London headquarters of the NUM on Euston Road to demand strike action. The NUM Executive responded by ordering a national ballot and national strike action if the closure plans were not withdrawn. They were not, and delegates at Area conferences in South Wales and County Durham on 14 and 16 February – demonstrating the newfound muscle of the Broad Left and the anger of miners in the threatened pits – endorsed the call for a national strike.[18]

Despite having prepared for a strike, this precise moment was not good for the government. The economy was in crisis: there had been sixteen consecutive months of negative growth; unemployment was rising (it would reach 2.5 million in June 1981); inflation stood at 12 per cent; and there was a government deficit of £22 billion (3.8 per cent of GDP). IRA prisoners were on hunger strike in the Maze Prison (and Bobby Sands was to die on 5 May). Racial tension was building in inner-city areas and would explode in Brixton in April and in Handsworth and Toxteth in July.[19] Mrs Thatcher met the energy secretary, David Howell, and was told that coal stocks were not yet sufficient to withstand a national strike. In her hands she had a copy of the *Evening Standard* with the headline 'Government dithers'. 'Bring it to an end, David,' she told Howell. 'Make the necessary concessions.'[20]

'Surrender to King Coal' was the verdict of much of the press.[21] The miners were cock-a-hoop. Joe Gormley was due to retire as NUM president in 1982, having held on long enough to ensure that the Scottish miners' communist leader Mick McGahey was too old to stand. The favourite was Arthur Scargill, the hero of Saltley Gate, who had attended the 1959 World Youth Festival in Moscow as a Young Communist and had allegedly criticised Khrushchev for criticising Stalin.[22] He left the party in 1963 (perhaps as a condition of rising in the union), became a delegate at Woolley colliery and in 1974 Yorkshire NUM president. He was nominated for NUM president in moderate coalfields such as County Durham and the Midlands, as well as more radical ones such as Yorkshire, South Wales and Scotland, and was elected NUM president in December 1981 on a programme of resisting mass pit closures, gaining an astonishing 70.3 per cent of the vote.[23] He took office in April 1982, and at the annual NUM conference a few months later, in July, linked the victories of 1972 and 1981 to a fighting future:

Ten years ago we achieved possibly the greatest triumph in the long history of the Miners' Union. The spirit, determination, unity of purpose and involvement which marked the great 1972 strike must characterise our every-day activities in the Union . . . The Union showed in February 1981 that a programme of closures could be stopped . . . The first priority for the Union is to protect the Coal industry from the ravages of the market mechanism, the short-sightedness of politicians and the deliberate political decisions designed to destroy our industry, jobs and communities. If we do not save our pits from closure, then all our other struggles become meaningless.[24]

By this time, however, the fortunes of Mrs Thatcher had improved dramatically. She had sent a task force to the Falklands in April 1982 and had ended Argentinian occupation on 11 June. Three weeks later, she gave a victory address to a Conservative rally in Cheltenham:

[W]e have learned something about ourselves – a lesson which we desperately needed to learn. When we started out, there were the waverers and the fainthearts. The people who . . . thought we could no longer do the great things which we once did, [who] had their secret fears that it was true: that Britain was no longer the nation that had built an empire and ruled a quarter of the world. Well, they were wrong. The lesson of the Falklands is that Britain has not changed and that this nation still has those sterling qualities which shine through our history . . . What has indeed happened is that now once again Britain is not prepared to be pushed around.[25]

The lesson that Britain was 'not prepared to be pushed around' was meant for both an international and a domestic audience, and it signalled a hardening of Mrs Thatcher's attitude to the miners, who would soon be denounced as 'the enemy within'.

The strike might also have happened in 1982, but this time it was the miners' leaders who hesitated. Attention moved to Scotland, where Albert Wheeler, the tough new Area director of the Coal Board in Scotland, had been appointed in 1980. He told David Hamilton, NUM delegate at Monktonhall colliery: 'I'm going to break you.'[26] The Kinneil pit in West Lothian, on the south bank of the Firth of Forth, near Bo'ness, which employed a thousand miners, was scheduled for closure. Instead of a strike, the miners tried a new tactic – the stay-down. Just before Christmas 1982, twelve miners, who became known as 'the Dirty Dozen', went down and organised their protest from the pit bottom.[27] After Christmas, Kinneil miners picketed other Scottish pits in order to bring out as much of the Scottish coalfield as possible. Bogside, Castlehill, Comrie and Frances on the coast of Fife were among those to come out. A meeting of Scottish NUM delegates and secretaries of the colliery branches on 28 December was attended by a group of miners from Lewis Merthyr colliery in the Rhondda, who were also threatened with closure and were keen to rally support. However, the Scottish NUM leader, Mick McGahey, decided that strike action was premature and possibly illegal. McGahey told the meeting that 'the hearts and minds of the Scottish miners had not been won for the action on Kinneil'.[28]

The Welsh miners were galvanised to act, but their leadership also hesitated. The Lewis Merthyr pitmen went back to their colliery and twenty-eight of them staged a stay-down from 21 February 1983. It was led by Des Dutfield, a lodge official there and vice-president of the South Wales Miners' Federation. He argued that they were 'fighting the government, fighting the Board, staying loyal to the union'.[29] Collieries in South Wales, such as St John's, Tower and Maerdy, came out and Welsh miners fanned across England to lobby for support. The idea was to develop a national strike from the bottom up.[30] However, they were disappointed by the reception they received. One of them, who went to Nottinghamshire, was bluntly asked, 'what are you doing up here?'[31]

The Yorkshire miners were sympathetic, but there was also a feeling that if there was a national strike, it should be led by Yorkshire. Emlyn Williams later complained that the 1983 strike 'didn't escalate because certain national leaders thought that South Wales should not be in the vanguard of the struggle against pit closures'.[32] Williams called off the strike action in favour of a national ballot to decide the issue, which sent out a very negative message. Dave Douglass, the delegate for Hatfield colliery, affirmed that the Yorkshire Area was due to meet on Monday 28 February 1983 to vote to strike in solidarity with Wales. But before this happened, the South Wales Executive called off the action:[33]

> We were anticipating them coming to Hatfield. We had an emergency panel meeting of the twelve Doncaster pits, and said we would strike, as soon as the Welsh pickets arrived. And we'd call an Area Council meeting for the following Monday, where we expected to get the Yorkshire Area on strike. So they were sweeping all in front of them, when they made the ridiculous decision, their Executive, to call for a national ballot . . . the Welsh Executive . . . Anyway we had the ballot and we lost. We lost the ballot. It was a mistake.[34]

The national ballot held in March 1983 required a 55 per cent majority to trigger a national strike against pit closures. The South Wales miners voted 68 per cent for strike action, Yorkshire 54 per cent and Scotland 50 per cent. But the Durham miners could muster only 39 per cent for strike action and Nottinghamshire a paltry 19 per cent.[35] It seemed that miners were not going to come out to defend the jobs of other miners in coalfields far away, if their own jobs felt safe. It was not clear either that a national ballot would be won the next time there was a call for strike action, or that a national strike would be supported across all coalfields.

Three months later, the balance of power changed again. In the general election of 9 June 1983, the Conservatives increased their tally of seats from 339 to a heady 397, giving a majority of 117. Mrs Thatcher was now emboldened and had her hitman in place. Ian MacGregor, a union-busting Scot who had made his career in the USA, had been brought back to the UK in 1980 to wind down British Steel, where he crushed the resulting steelworkers' strike. On 1 September 1983, he took up his appointment as chair of the National Coal Board and drew up plans to close seventy-five mines over the next two years, reducing the workforce by 55,000 (out of 200,000); that was to be followed by the closure of another eleven mines, with the loss of a further 9,000 jobs. The small Kent coalfield would be closed, and a third of the Scottish miners would be laid off, along with half of the Midlands, South Yorkshire and Durham miners and two thirds of Welsh miners. A secret meeting was held in 10 Downing Street on 15 September involving the prime minister, Chancellor of the Exchequer Nigel Lawson, Energy Secretary Peter Walker and Employment Secretary Norman Tebbit to endorse these plans. The account of this meeting was not published until 2014, and when Scargill claimed that the government had seen a hit list with seventy-five collieries to close and 60,000 miners to go, the media were briefed that this was pure invention.[36]

The government proceeded by stealth and was keen not to provoke a national strike during the winter of 1983–84, when the miners would be able to exploit dwindling coal stocks. Closures began piecemeal in Scotland, under the iron fist of Albert Wheeler. In May 1983, he announced the closure of Cardowan, the last pit in Lanarkshire, with 1,400 men. Miners from Polmaise were told to accept men from Cardowan on 6 July; when they refused, Wheeler locked them out. MacGregor visited Scotland on 15 September, and in Midlothian he called Bilston Glen 'the jewel in the crown' and Monktonhall 'second division'. The manager at Monktonhall literally tore up joint agreements, sacked men who were late for work after attending a pithead meeting and imposed a lockout.[37] The Monktonhall miners went on strike, the Scottish Area Executive made it official, and a special delegates' conference in Edinburgh on 11 October called for a one-day Scottish strike in defence of Monktonhall. Tom Adams, who had become a miner at the coastal Frances pit in 1980, having previously worked as a ship's stoker and tarring roads, remembered a packed miners' meeting in Edinburgh in November 1983 that was addressed by a charismatic Arthur Scargill. 'Honestly,' he said, 'everybody coming out of that meeting would have just walked into the Clyde for him. They'd have done anything for him.'[38] For many miners, Scottish ones included, Scargill was going to be their saviour.

The Coal Board in Scotland did not interrupt its plans. In January 1984, Wheeler announced the closure of Polmaise, which in turn went on strike on 21 February, calling for wider support.[39] The Bogside mine flooded for want of maintenance during an overtime ban. 'What the Coal Board did,' as Iain Chalmers recalled, 'was to instigate industrial strife at Seafield. We were out on strike for a month. It was early in February '84. We were out on strike for a month before the big strike.'[40] Because the coal from the Frances pit came up at Seafield, the Frances miners had to stop work, too. Thus, in the first week of March 1984, as the strike was breaking out in England, according to Jim Phillips 'a majority of Scotland's miners were locked out, on strike or otherwise engaged in dispute with local management'.[41]

As winter drew to a close, the government felt ready to provoke the strike that was intended to be the final showdown with the mineworkers. Because of the defeat of 1974 and the humiliation of 1981, losing was not an option. The plan was to inform the miners' leaders on Wednesday 6 March that twenty pits were going to close, with the loss of 20,000 jobs. Although a gross underestimate, it was considered enough to provoke a national ballot on strike action that the NUM would lose, as it had a year earlier. In the event, however – as Dave Douglass, who was on the Yorkshire NUM Executive, recalled – the bombshell went off almost a week early, on Thursday 1 March:

> They jumped the gun. The Area director, Hayes, in Yorkshire, told, on the side, the manager at Cortonwood that his pit was going to close. The manager sees the union official walking up the pit lane, threw the window open, says, 'Hey, they're shutting the pit!' so the cat was

out the bag. The Cortonwood miners went on strike then and there. Picketed the Barnsley offices and the Yorkshire Area was on strike.[42]

The way it happened was as follows. Furious, the Cortonwood miners lobbied the Yorkshire Area Executive meeting in Barnsley, and the Area Executive recommended to pithead meetings in Yorkshire that a strike should begin from the last shift on Friday 9 March. Across Yorkshire, miners held mass meetings at their pits on Saturday 10 March and overwhelmingly supported the strike. The National Executive Committee (NEC) of the NUM now called on other Areas to join the strike, hoping to launch a great showdown with the Thatcher government.[43]

In the event, the Miners' Strike of 1984 was a national strike only in name: a national ballot was never held. Some miners' leaders argued that the national ballot from March 1983 was still valid in their Area, while others argued that a fresh ballot was needed. There was a series of regional strikes, as coalfield followed coalfield. But not all coalfields followed in the same way, and the 'unity of purpose' that Arthur Scargill had called for in 1982 was never fully recognised.

In County Durham, where the Broad Left had made significant progress, the moment of truth came on Friday 9 March 1984, when the Durham Miners' Association Executive met in the committee room at Redhills, chaired by the risk-averse Harold Mitchell, in order to respond to the call by the NEC to make strike action in the coalfield official. By a majority of five to three, it recommended strike action.[44] The decision of the Executive was sent to the Area committee of lodge secretaries from the various pits, also chaired by Mitchell, which met in the Grand Council Chamber at Redhills, its walls hung with exquisite colliery banners. According to Dave Wray, a miner from Sacriston, 'Davey Hopper said, "I propose that we come out on strike in support of Yorkshire." And it was a tie, right? And the president of the Durham Miners' Association – in the case of a tie – has to go with the proposer. And the story is that it took him three minutes [to decide].'[45]

This decision to strike had to be ratified by each colliery, and there was some hesitation there, too. The Easington miners initially voted against the strike, but the mechanics, including people like Paul Stratford, threatened to picket them out, so they fell into line. Murton, threatened with closure, also voted not to strike, as did Seaham, Vane Tempest and Dawdon, where the 'feudal' influence of Lord Londonderry still counted for something. The Area's decision was nevertheless applied to all the County Durham pits by Monday 12 March.[46]

While County Durham havered for three days, South Wales wavered for a week. Under the leadership of Emlyn Williams, the Area conference voted that same Friday 9 March for strike action to begin the following Monday; but in the coalfields, the lodges did not all feel the same way. Thirteen voted to strike, but eighteen were against.[47] One of the latter was St Johns, Maesteg, where Ian Isaac, as secretary of the lodge, recommended strike action to a meeting of 600 miners on Saturday 10 March. There was, however, a feeling that Yorkshire had not supported them in 1983 and, besides, their pit was not among those scheduled to close. The men voted by a majority of thirty not to support the strike.[48] At Blaenant, in the Dulais Valley, there was a similar apathy. Lyn Harper, a fitter and craftsmen's representative on the lodge, said that of the 750 miners, only 250 turned up and voted by a majority not to strike. 'Yorkshire owed us a fortnight' was the general opinion.[49] The lodge chair at Blaenant, Phil Bowen, was of the opinion that because the pit was doing well, there was less incentive to strike:

> It was a well-mined pit. There was good money being earned. The addition of the wife going out to work made them less militant. Because they had bills, bigger bills because they were having more things. You had a situation where extra money was coming in. I remember the production manager looking out of the window one day when he was talking to me and he said, 'See that carpark out there, I wish all that carpark would be full. The housing estate up there, brand new houses,'

he said. 'Get them in now. You'll never see any more strike action or militancy in your life.' And there was a message behind that. How society was changing![50]

The South Wales leadership had to act quickly in order to save face and unity, and to avoid being picketed out by Yorkshire miners. Emlyn Williams turned to Kim Howells, who had been brought up in Aberdare, in the Cynon Valley. He had gone on to Hornsey College of Art, where he had led the student occupation in 1968, before returning to become research officer at the NUM office in Pontypridd. Hywel Francis, who had employed Howells in the South Wales Miners' Library in 1979–82, and who was close to Arfon Evans, chairman of the lodge at Maerdy, recalled:

That critical weekend I was trying work out what was happening. I was speaking to Arfon Evans in Maerdy, which had voted for strike action, and to Kim Howells, who was the research officer for the NUM. He had gathered together all the pits that had voted for strike action for a secret meeting in Hirwaun. The intention was – it was a relationship between Kim and the president [Emlyn Williams] – that even though the coalfield had voted against, they were going to use the mandate they had from the previous year [1983] to call the coalfield out. They had an Executive meeting that Monday, they were picketed by the pits that were on strike, and they made the call to come out. And then they unleashed the striking pits onto the ones that were not.[51]

The 'secret meeting' of delegates from militant pits was held at the Ambulance Hall in Hirwaun, partly because of its location at the head of the Neath Valley (running south-west) and the Cynon Valley (running south-east), and partly because its Tower colliery was a fighting pit. Heading the fighters was Huw 'the Red' Edwards, chair of the lodge, his wife Barbara, her friend Ann Jones and her husband Dai John. Ann took her cue from her grandfather Dai Griffo Jones, who had been sacked from the pit in the 1920s for militancy and had worked for the council, while acting as a 'poor man's lawyer', advising mining families that were in trouble with the authorities. Personally, too, 'I think I was a bit of a rebel,' she said. 'I didn't like conforming, I never listened, it didn't pay in that school, run by cane and the dap [a plimsoll, used on the backside].' Dai John was among the Tower miners who, from first thing on Monday 12 March, picketed out reluctant miners from other pits:

> We'd send delegates down to these different pits that were still working and tell them, 'Listen now, we've already had our votes, to stick what you've already said you were going to do.' Each pit would then start coming out. They would send delegates to other pits. If they were a bit unpersuaded, you'd send your pickets. Some areas down the west were a bit slower to come out. To get 'em out took a little bit of persuasion.[52]

Militant pits like Tower and Treforgan thus picketed out less-militant pits, including St John's, Maesteg and Blaenant. Formally, though, the decision to strike was taken by a meeting of all the delegates of the Swansea district at Pyle, near Bridgend, on Tuesday 13 March. Hywel Francis travelled with the Blaenant miners to observe, and was impressed that a young miner with Welsh roots from the small Kent coalfield seemed to make a huge difference. Kent miners were at the top of the closure list and could only win by persuading miners in other coalfields to come out:

> I was at the back of this leisure centre, the sports hall in Pyle. It was very demoralising because there were hardly any pits that had voted for strike action. But there was a speaker there from Kent – a young miner whose parents were actually from South Wales – and he called on them to support the Kent miners. It was very powerful, probably the best speech in the conference. They had to accept the diktat of the [South Wales] Executive that this was the recommendation, there must be

strike action. By the end of the week they got them all out, because men would not cross picket lines.[53]

Even more hesitant than the South Wales coalfield was Nottinghamshire. Notts miners were also doing very well, benefiting from the 1977 bonus scheme, which rewarded productivity. They did not have a strong tradition of sons following fathers into the pits, because other employment opportunities in the Midlands – such as textiles, engineering and the car industry – meant that many miners came to the pits relatively late in life and might move out again. Only rarely did they live in mining villages, instead being scattered through villages and towns across quite a wide area; they thus socialised with each other much less. Lastly, they had a weighty tradition of 'Spencerism', having formed a breakaway union under George Spencer in 1926 that made peace with the employers.

That said, Nottinghamshire was not monolithic. Manton, exceptionally, was a mining village attached to Worksop. At the northern tip of the county, it was also officially within one of the four panels, or districts, of the Yorkshire coalfield, and took part in its decision making. David Potts, the NUM branch secretary at Manton, attended the Doncaster Area panel of branch secretaries and delegates from twelve pits on Monday 12 March. Miners from Cortonwood had come to besiege it, demanding that they join the strike action. Potts was torn. The Nottinghamshire part of him prompted him to argue against the strike, saying that it was not a good time; but the Yorkshire part of him went with the majority in favour of the strike. On Saturday 17 March, Potts told the Manton men that he now backed the strike. This was endorsed by a heavy majority.[54]

A minority of Manton miners opposed the strike. One of these was David Hopkins. He was neither local nor of mining stock. His father was from Gloucestershire, the 'black sheep' of the family, who had run away to fight in the war and then found a job at Staveley ironworks in Derbyshire. David had wanted to become a footballer or an engineer, but his father – a drinker and often 'on the club' (sick) – persuaded him to go down the pit to support the family. Just after he began training his father died. 'I was tiny,' he remembered. 'I looked about thirteen. My dad had died, I can remember suffering from anxiety, I was really scared.' Things looked up when the productivity bonus kicked in, and he enjoyed holidays with mates in Italy. When he got married in 1982, he and his wife bought (and then sold) a Coal Board house; and just before the strike, they bought a private house on an estate in Worksop, two miles from Manton village. He was thus scarcely part of the mining community. He suggested that, despite the pressure to go on strike, there may well have been a silent majority of miners opposed to strike action. Disgruntled, he did not cross the picket line, but neither did he go picketing.[55]

The leaders of the Nottinghamshire miners were in a quandary. Indeed, they, too, were divided. Nottinghamshire General Secretary Henry Richardson and President Ray Chadburn, both members of the NEC, were more inclined to follow the Scargill line, while Roy Lynk and David Prendergast, Area officials but not on the NEC, sided with the moderate rank and file. The dynamics changed when flying pickets from Yorkshire poured over the border on Monday 12 March, in order to picket out the Nottinghamshire pits. Faced with this incursion, all four officials signed a letter on 13 March denouncing the 'mass blockade' imposed by the Yorkshire miners and 'the type of intimidation that has taken place', and urging them to withdraw until the Nottinghamshire miners had held their ballot. 'Give the men a chance because there is a strong indication they may support us,' Richardson wrote in the *Mansfield Chad* on Thursday 15 March. 'This sort of picketing is alienating men and is counterproductive, that is the tragedy.'[56]

Among those who felt alienated by the aggression of the Yorkshire miners was Steve Williamson, NUM branch secretary at Annesley and, paradoxically, a Yorkshireman. In the union, he used his mathematical and negotiating skills with the bonus system to increase his men's pay from £7 to £10, £11 and then £12 per shift. His success as what he likes to call 'a militant moderate' was threatened in the early days of the strike, when pickets arrived from Yorkshire to force them out of work before they had held a ballot. For him, these men were no longer comrades:

> They were thugs, drunken thugs. I'll give you one example. At Bentinck colliery the pickets came down and their telephone exchange man – they usually went to people who had been injured in the pits – was a disabled man in a disability car, through a mining injury. And he was going to work and they turned the car over. They were punching people, a couple of my lads had broken noses. So when it came to deciding to have a vote we said 'we're not going to be kicked out on strike'. We knew what Arthur [Scargill] was on with. He was trying to get us out on strike without a ballot. He'd had two ballots and lost. And basically he wanted to kick us out [on strike].[57]

A similar view of the Yorkshire miners was held by David Amos. Unlike Williamson, he was a local boy. His father had been a miner, his mother had been in service, and they lived on an estate in Kirkby-in-Ashfield. He had not really wanted to be a miner, but the pay after the 1974 strike could not be sniffed at, and so he trained as a pit electrician at Annesley. He had been mentored by Williamson, and was elected onto the branch committee in 1983. When the strike broke out, he was likewise horrified by what seemed to be an invasion by Yorkshire pickets, in defiance of union democracy. He portrayed them as completely alien:

> I do clearly remember the first day when they came down, on 12 March – the Yorkshire pickets, Doncaster pickets particularly. They just descended on the Notts coalfield. At the time there were the *Star Wars* films and, you know, the Stormtroopers. They resembled them without the uniform. They were walking down to the pit and without a word being said they'd come to do a job. They wasn't asking, they was telling. Some of them were openly hostile and making references to 1926, to the Spencer Union. You've got to bear in mind that Notts had agreed at

the NEC meeting that they were going to have a ballot later that week. Whatever happened the ballot was going to take place, but there were one or two who let their political bias get the better of them – were saying, 'You scabby bastards need to come out now.'

Interestingly, when the Notts ballot was held on 15–16 March, Amos voted in favour of strike action, but then went with the majority of 73.5 per cent against. In retrospect, he judged, 'I think that the strike was lost on the first day.'[58]

Nottinghamshire was not the only coalfield where a majority of miners refused to come out on strike: Leicestershire was even more dead set against it, with only 30 out of a workforce of 1,500 staying out for the duration. The Leicestershire coalfield was concentrated in the north-west of the county, around Coalville. The biggest pit was Bagworth, but there was no mining community. The miners were scattered through villages and towns across a forty-mile radius, including Leicester and Loughborough. Many, as in Nottinghamshire, had migrated from Scotland and the North East. Nor was there a strong tradition of mining families. As in Nottinghamshire, there were many other job opportunities – the hosiery and boot and shoe industry, quarrying, brickworks and engineering. Workers moved between them as wage differentials changed, and if they went into the pits, it was because wages rose after the 1974 strike, and they subsequently did well out of the bonus scheme.

In the light of this, from the outset the Leicestershire Area leadership under Jack Jones urged caution. Miners continued to go to work while a ballot was scheduled for Monday 19 March. Ahead of this, on Wednesday 14 March, two coachloads of Kent miners arrived at Bagworth pit to persuade their comrades to join the strike. They were allowed to address the Leicestershire men in the pit canteen the next day, and overwhelmingly the miners voted to come out. This was not to the taste of the branch committee, and one of them, Trevor Hines, went to see Jack Jones in Coalville. Jones rushed to Bagworth to inform the miners that until the ballot was held, any strike was illegal. When Yorkshire pickets arrived during the night of 15–16 March, he told his men to cross the picket line. Scuffles broke out. When the ballot was finally held, 1,441 of the miners voted against strike action, with only 173 (11 per cent) in favour. Jack Jones warned the NUM Executive:

> If we are attacked we shall defend ourselves. If they come here they can expect war conditions. We are not violent people but we will not be intimidated. We have voted to work and even if we are operating the last four holes in the country, we will work.[59]

Of the 173 in Leicestershire who voted to strike, in the event only 30 came out and remained on strike to the end. Their enemies called them the 'Dirty Thirty', a name they embraced with pride. Very little distinguished them from the average Leicestershire miner: they lived scattered over a wide area and had had other jobs before mining. What all the Dirty Thirty had in common, however, was some connection to the mining tradition (sometimes through marriage), and they refused to cross the picket lines.

Malcolm Pinnegar, known as Benny, emerged as the leader of the Dirty Thirty. His father had been a quarryman at Stoney Stanton, and he was working in a boot and shoe factory in Barwell when he met his wife Margaret, who was in the wages office. Subsequently they both moved into the hosiery industry, and then he went to Imperial Typewriters in Leicester, where he gained experience of strike action in 1974. Both sides of Margaret's family had been in mining, and after 1974 Malcolm went to Bagworth pit because the pay was better. As Margaret explained, when the Kent miners appeared and he came up from the pit, he did not hesitate:

> They were there and obviously he were talking to them, and he said, 'Well, okay mate that's me, I'm done. I shan't be going back.' And my words to Malcolm were, 'Please don't be the only one.' Because I was

convinced that there wouldn't be hardly anybody out, because it did come back to the Spencer, Spencerism and what have you.[60]

Fortunately, he was not the only one. Mick Richmond, known as Richo, became Benny's second in command. Richo's grandfather had been a miner at Ibstock, and his father had been down the pit briefly there before he left to become a power station engineer in Lancashire. Mick was sent to a Catholic school there, which he did not enjoy, and was in hospital with rheumatic fever when he should have been taking his 11-plus. Back in Leicestershire at sixteen, his main passion was his band, the Merlons, but it folded when the lead guitarist left. He got married at eighteen, had two daughters and worked at Ibstock brickyard before going to Bagworth pit, aged thirty-two, in 1979.[61] He was trained by John Brearley, the NUM delegate at the pit, who had taken part in the 1972 and 1974 strikes and who opposed the bonus system, because, he said, 'It'll kill the pit, because it will put one pit against another.' Brearley passed on his union commitment to his daughter Kay, who made sure that her husband Phil Smith, who became delegate at the pit, went on strike in 1984. 'Thank God for that,' she said, recalling his decision to come out. Striking her breast, she went on: 'I knew what I believed, what I felt in here.'[62]

At the coal face, where they operated wickedly toothed shearing machines, Richo's best mate was Cliff Jeffery, who was into science fiction. Nicknamed 'the Geek', according to Richo he was 'nuts, just like me'. When Cliff went on strike, he came out with his son Nigel. He had suffered from his parents' breakup, had been expelled from school and had started training at Bagworth pit in 1977, aged fifteen. Under the bonus system, he was earning '£50 a shift then. So that's £250 a week on top of your wages'; but family loyalty came first.[63] Through his second marriage, Cliff had gained five stepchildren, two of whom – Mark and Alan 'Chump' Findell – were miners at Bagworth. Cliff Jeffery thus accounted all on his own for four of the Dirty Thirty. As he put it, 'That's the reason why I come, one of the reasons I come out, because I thought, well I've got Nigel, I've got three lads now working at the pit. So how can I not try to stop them closing the bloody pit?'[64]

Richo was a charmer, while Benny had the gift of the gab. Richo found the Kent miners 'awesome' and became great friends with one of their leaders, Terry French. He rounded up other comrades to join the picket line, notably Bobby and Sam Girvan, who had been brought down as teenagers from Scotland to Coalville by their father, who had once been a miner at Kinneil. They were bullied as kids because of their Scottish accents and had had to learn to 'speak Coalville' and support Leicester City. They did apprenticeships in, respectively, engineering and bricklaying, but after work dried up Sam found a job at Bagworth in 1979. Bobby followed. Sam said that the Kent miners were 'just like them' – not locals at all, but economic migrants from Scotland, County Durham or Wales.[65] Richo also brought in Mel Elcock, whose father had been a Yorkshire miner who, during the war, had married a woman from Loughborough employed in the hosiery trade. Mel himself had worked as a fitter in a hosiery machine manufacturer until he was made redundant in 1974; he would have become a soldier, had the recruitment office not been closed. Instead, he found work as a fitter at Bagworth. He valued the unity that the miners had enjoyed before the bonus system was introduced, reflecting that 'if everybody's getting the same money, people stand together better'. He was particularly hostile to Jack Jones and to those who did not have mining in the blood:

[Jones] said he would lead them through the pickets, with a pickaxe if necessary . . . There's an old saying, and I'm sure you've heard it, miners will not cross picket lines, and for the first time . . . well not the first time actually because it happened in Nottinghamshire in the general, in the '26 strike. You've probably heard about the Spencer Union . . . They were a different type of miner; I would say, at Bagworth. Many of them had no mining history at all, they'd come from jobs, just like me, but I'd got the history. I don't think they actually grasped what it meant to be a miner.[66]

The youngest member of the Dirty Thirty was Darren Moore, born in 1961. He did not come from a mining family – his father was a car worker and his mother was in hosiery – and he himself had wanted to be a journalist, except that he got into punk rock and messed up his A-levels. However, he was political, demonstrating with the Anti-Nazi League against the National Front in Leicester in 1979, and then joining the Young Socialists. He found a job at Bagworth in 1979 and was doing his City and Guilds to become a pit deputy. He was on day release at Coalville Technical College the day the Kent miners arrived. He was amazed that the convention did not seem to exist in Leicestershire that men should not cross a picket line, because they drove through it day after day. He attached himself to Benny as a sort of adjutant and recalled the battle they had at an NUM meeting in Coalville when they tried to explain why the men needed to join the strike and found themselves dangerously outnumbered:

> I remember Benny getting up and saying, you know, the national rules supersede the local Area rules. If you read the Leicestershire rule book, it says, where there's a dispute the national rules will overrule the Area rulebook, but they were having none of it. So, you know, we were just heckled and shouted down, I was just looking where the exits were, thinking we might need to get out of here fast! . . . After the second meeting, we knew that then it was almost a lost cause; they were not going to come out on strike. You know, it did become polarised would be the word. People had become polarised.[67]

Although the Miners' Strike is generally portrayed as a national strike that roared into life in March 1984, the process had actually been spluttering along since 1981 – stopping, starting, stalling and then taking a good two weeks in March to get properly under way. In 1981, the government had not been ready for the fight; in 1982, it had been the NUM leadership. The strike began in Scotland two weeks before it was triggered in England, and there was then an attempt to coordinate the coalfields.

Each, however, had its own history and traditions, migration and employment patterns, and degrees of radicalism or moderation. So each was
more or less enthusiastic about strike action. In Nottinghamshire and
Leicestershire, only a minority of miners answered the call to strike. It was
this that ushered in the most spectacular – and also the most divisive –
practice of the strike: picketing.

2

PICKETING OUT

At the outset of the strike, Dave Douglass, branch delegate of Hatfield colliery and member of the Yorkshire NUM Executive, was given the job of organising pickets in the Doncaster area to ensure solidarity behind the strike. Yorkshire was basically solid, but Nottinghamshire was not, and flying pickets were sent over the border to persuade Notts miners to join the strike. Very soon, however, the police were blocking roads leading into Nottinghamshire. Based at Brodsworth colliery, he approached the task as a guerrilla leader:

> I was immensely proud that the Doncaster branches had elected me to coordinate and plan the picketing operations for the area . . . We were in a situation where we were fighting a better-equipped and usually more numerous enemy. So, of course, we used classic guerrilla tactics: secrecy, hit and run, mass pickets switching from one site to another, one county to another, or spreading out to hit all parts of one region, then regrouping to take all the pickets to one target.[1]

Interviewed in 2020, he claimed that he had been a 'right-hand man' of Arthur Scargill, but disagreed with him about how to organise picketing. Whereas Arthur had in mind Saltley Gate, the triumph of the mass picket, Douglass favoured the mobility and secrecy of the flying picket:

The only way we were ever going to get the drop on the cops, was by them not knowing where we were going, or what we were doing. So we made a huge elaborate plan of where the picketing targets would be. We only used codes on the phones, changed the codes every week, sealed instructions were given to different pits on the night time, not opened until the following morning, early in the morning, so the police wouldn't know where we were going to go. The whole operation had to be kept secret.[2]

The government had measures in place to respond to this. A group of senior ministers, named MISC 101, was set up by the Cabinet on Thursday 8 March to keep a close eye on the strike situation. The following Wednesday (14 March), Margaret Thatcher complained that 'the police were not doing their job'. One problem was that each constabulary was under its own chief constable, who exercised operational control over it. There was no national police force in Great Britain, and the Home Office was not supposed to give orders to the police. And yet the government was committed to protecting the principle of the right to work, and it needed to ensure that laws restricting picketing were enforced and that forces could be sent from one part of the country to another where disorder was breaking out. One solution was offered by the national reporting centre at Scotland Yard, which reported to the home secretary: it could offer overall coordination and might respond to 'prodding' about what the police needed to do.[3]

A first manifestation of the violence that was going to ensue occurred the day after Mrs Thatcher's complaint, on Thursday 15 March. It was triggered by Yorkshire miners picketing the Nottinghamshire colliery of Ollerton. David Jones, a twenty-four-year-old picket from Ackton Hall colliery near Featherstone was picketing there when he was hit in the chest by a flying brick. He died later that day. His funeral in Wakefield on 23 March was attended by three thousand miners from all over the country. The Miners' Strike had its first martyr.

The miners of Askern were in the vanguard of the pickets. Their head-quarters was the Miners' Welfare, whose secretary was a former miner, Councillor Mike Porter. He reported in 1986 that 'as many as eighty or a hundred would arrive as early as two o'clock in the morning, use the side door, we did it very quietly. They were given instructions and off they'd go, as far as Coventry, mainly Nottingham.'[4] One of those pickets was Pete Richardson, who was not afraid of a spot of bother; in fact, he embraced it. Interviewed in 1986, he confessed: 'I'm a big football supporter and I've come across a lot of police violence. I've always hated them. I was arrested at seventeen and they gave me a good hiding, and since then I've been at war with them.'[5] He said that the day the strike was called in Yorkshire, Askern was already on strike, responding to the sacking of four chock fitters, one of whom was his father-in-law, Jimmy Murphy, who died of a heart attack during the strike.

Richardson gave a graphic account of his first picketing at Bilsthorpe colliery in Nottinghamshire. First, shouting at the strike-breakers, then the push against police lines to get at them, and finally his grab to help a fallen comrade, which led to his arrest:

It were a bit hectic at first. Everyone wanted to get down, get them out. We were shouting to them, 'scabs, support the union, stand up and be counted!' . . . We were all stood there together to stop 'em coming through in cars, and we'd shove, and the police would shove us back, to-ing and fro-ing. Then I spotted the police rough-handling one of the lads, he were on the floor, and I just jumped in, give them some of their own medicine, sort of thing, and I got arrested.[6]

Taken to court, he was bailed and told that he could no longer picket in Nottinghamshire; so the next day he went picketing in Staffordshire. Later Richardson was arrested again, tried and sent to Durham gaol; out for Christmas 1984, he was back inside for Christmas 1985. There he wrote his 'Confessions of a Picket' in three school exercise books. He dealt less with police violence than with the camaraderie that motivated him and told the same story of his arrest with a laddish bravado, as if he were recounting it in a pub:

It was then I spotted Tommy McLoy on the floor with some cops. They were trying to re-arrange Tommy's clothes by the look of it, and must have been tickling him, as he was struggling. I could see Tommy's point of view and jumped in and started tickling some of them. Anyway, I was arrested.[7]

Other Yorkshire miners were victims of violence, rather than violent themselves. Charlie Hogarth, born in Newcastle in 1956, suffered from the fact that his parents had broken up; his father had been 'a bit of a drunk' and his mother had been jailed for perjury – for claiming that she was not living with someone when she actually was. Charlie was brought up in a children's home, dreamed of becoming an electrician in the RAF, but resigned himself to going to Bentley pit near Doncaster. During the 1972 strike, he witnessed the death of Fred Matthews at Keadby power station, near Scunthorpe, when 'this lorry come down and the back wheels caught him, you know, he were like bent over and went under the back wheels'. Then, in 1978, he was underground on a paddy or workmen's train which went out of control, killing seven miners:

I knew all the people, like Ken Green, Don Box, there was Tony Hall, Jim Mitchell, who were quite, well he were one of oldest, Jim. Bob Aitchison, he were another . . . One of them got decapitated and his parents didn't find out till years later, because no-one'd tell 'em. And there was another one, scraped all his face off. And then there was a couple . . . you'd think they were just asleep.

This horror came back to haunt him during the strike of 1984–85. Only this time it was the violence – amounting to torture – that police used on one of his mates and the lack of accountability that shocked him:

We were at one of Nottinghamshire pits, and they'd been corralled into this space and the police were taking someone off. And I said, 'Hey, you can't fucking do that.' Then I'm arrested. They take me to this car park, and they put me in this van, and they'd got this kid, I had no idea about age or owt, and there were about four or five coppers had got him at side of transit van, holding him up, and there was one really squeezing his testicles, and I mean squeezing, and they were knocking the hell out of him. And I says, 'You can't do that.' 'Shut up or you'll get some.' And prior to that I just never believed police did that. And there was not one copper was convicted of any violence throughout the strike.[8]

David Potts, the NUM branch secretary at Manton, was himself the victim of police violence in Nottinghamshire in April 1984. In his case, it was caught on TV and the local MP intervened, but there was no redress:

There was an incident at Babbington colliery. Outside the colliery gates was a dual carriageway, and we got pushed away up onto the side of this dual carriageway, which went up a steep hill, the bank. And the police were using new tactics, snatch squads, that would come into an arrow-head formation, into us, which put them behind our front lines. I turned round and saw them carrying one of our lads, arm and a leg each, four of them. I stood in front of them to stop them. Another one came behind me and cracked me on head. I fell to the ground and they just carried on, walked on top of me. It was pretty bad, I finished up with seven stitches on the top of my head. The blood was pouring down. I had to go to hospital, get stitched up. Next day Joe Ashton, the [Bassetlaw] MP at the time, got to know about this. There was uproar, it was on TV, all over the papers, with all my face bloodied. The head-line was '1984 Great Britain' and my picture.

As a result of the MP's intervention, the chief constable of Nottinghamshire came to see Potts in hospital. He assured him that the use of force was not their policy and that they would try to find the guilty policeman. 'Load of rubbish,' concluded Potts.[9]

Other miners, while not suffering violence, were still arrested simply for going picketing and finished up with a criminal record. Paul Winter, a twenty-year-old Yorkshire miner at Dodworth, was part of a four-man flying picket trying to get into Nottinghamshire in the dead of night on 14 June. Their car was stopped by the police on the A1 and they were told to turn around or face arrest. Dave, the driver, refused, so they were arrested, thrown into a Black Maria and taken to Mansfield police station. 'Jimmy set off singing in back, "I want to break free", you know, that Freddie Mercury,' said Paul; but he was not amused by the arbitrary arrest, the humiliation of the cells and the fact that the NUM solicitor advised them to plead guilty:

> You can call it a cell, but it was a room with an open toilet in one corner. And we were left there all day. They flushed toilet from the outside. They pressed the lever on the floor outside to make toilet flush so you can't flush it yourself but they won't flush it. They just left it all day, full of piss and shit for us to sit in. And then we were taken out one by one and interviewed and whatever. We saw the NUM solicitor. They flushed the toilet about ten seconds before he went in but anyway, NUM solicitor said, 'We're going to ask you plead guilty to obstruction. And if you plead guilty to obstruction, you'll be let go today and you'll get a fine that NUM will pay' . . . I pleaded guilty and I was given a seventy-five quid fine which NUM paid. But I was told then, this was on 14th of June, that part of conditions for me being released were that I could only now picket, peacefully picket me own place of work, I couldn't go anywhere else.[10]

Picketing collieries where miners continued to go to work was only one aspect of the miners' effort. They needed to stop coal being imported from abroad, being delivered to coke works, steelworks and power stations. To achieve this, the Triple Alliance between miners, railwaymen and transport workers would have to be activated – and an alliance forged with steel-workers, too. This was problematic, because the steelworkers' strike had been crushed in 1980, and Scargill was opposed to the South Wales miners' idea of 'sweetheart deals', whereby steel plants would be supplied with enough coal to keep the furnaces alight, but not enough to produce steel. Steelworks such as Port Talbot and Llanwern in South Wales and Ravenscraig in Scotland were thus picketed. The National Union of Railwaymen (NUR) and the engine drivers' union ASLEF helped the miners by refusing to transport coal; but fleets of lorries belonging to private haulage companies were mobilised to take coal by road along the new motorways.

A major setback occurred early in July, when iron ore was unloaded at Immingham on the Humber. Strike-breaking dockers had been brought in by the British Steel Corporation to do this, and that provoked a national dock strike by dockers, who regarded this as a violation of the 1947 National Dock Labour Scheme that protected their jobs. The situation was so grave that on 16 July the Cabinet discussed whether a state of emergency should be declared to enable the army to drive lorries to shift coal and foodstuffs.[11] Dave Douglass explained that the Yorkshire miners managed to persuade the railway workers not to unload from the port and mobilised the unionised dockers (traditionally part of the Triple Alliance) against the strike-breaking dockers who had been brought in. The support of the dockers, however, did not last. The villain of the piece was not Keith Joseph, as Douglass remembers, but Nicolas Ridley, the secretary of state for transport, who, after consulting with the Cabinet, informed the House of Commons that the government was not considering the abolition of the Dock Labour Scheme:

We had picketed down at Immingham, a railway bridge, which was transporting, underneath which coke and iron ore were being deliv-ered. And we hung a banner over that bridge calling on ASLEF and NUR not to cross the picket line. Which they did. The driver of the first train got out of his cab, walked up to the bank, said 'right there's no more' and left his train on the line, and it never moved, nothing moved. So they had to transfer the deliveries to road transport. I remember it was 2,800 lorries to replace one of these train loads of stuff. We asked the dockers not to unload it. First of all the company brought in scabs to unload the ships at Immingham, and the first national dock strike started. Not in support of the miners, but in defence of the Dock Labour Scheme, which said that only registered dockers could unload at registered ports. Thatcher goes to Keith Joseph and says, 'You need to concede anything the dockers want, because we're going to lose this.' Keith Joseph goes to the dockers' leader, Ron Todd, and says, 'Right, what do you want?' and they says, 'Well, we've got a National Dock Labour Scheme, registered dockers have to move cargo at registered ports.' So, 'Alright, concede you that.' Threw the ball back at the dockers' union. Now, that should have clinched it, Thatcher said she was ready to surrender, she was ready to call the Cabinet together. The dockers at Immingham, who were in the union, unloaded the scab fuel. So they were breaking our strike, although they were members of the union . . . If we lost the strike anywhere, that's where we lost it. We lost it at Immingham.[12]

Trusting that the government would not abolish the Dock Labour Scheme, the dockers thus ended their national strike, breaking the Triple Alliance and depriving the miners of their support. Despite the government assurance, the Dock Labour Scheme was abolished in 1989.[13]

The ambition of Dave Douglass was to develop mobile and targeted picketing by Yorkshire miners; but they acquired a reputation for mass picketing and for violent confrontation that alienated public opinion and failed to bring out the strike-breaking miners in Nottinghamshire and elsewhere. Hywel Francis was very keen to draw a distinction between them and the Welsh miners, arguing that the latter's picketing was more strategic, cast the net wider and was more effective:

At one point, the South Wales miners were picketing two thirds of the land mass of Britain. All that Yorkshire did was cross the border into Nottingham and cause mayhem. There was a debate as to the difference between mass picketing and strategic picketing and this was strategic picketing from South Wales. They were picketing the other coalfields in small numbers, two or three men or a group of six would go to one pit. You wouldn't have any mass picketing, but you'd also then be picketing power stations, coal-fired power stations, nuclear power stations and nationally the union wasn't doing that. South Wales was doing it. So South Wales took on a national role.[14]

As for the Welsh miners' own accounts of picketing, they were less epic and more picaresque than those of the Yorkshire miners. They highlighted their powers of diplomacy when speaking to working miners and distanced themselves from Yorkshire miners with their sense of humour and desire to subvert the brutality of the police.

Although the Blaenant miners had been reluctant to come out on strike, once out and their coalfield secured, they threw themselves into picketing: first at the pits in Nottinghamshire, then at power stations in North Wales. On Monday 19 March, Phil Bowen, the chair of Blaenant lodge, was sent by Kim Howells at NUM headquarters in Pontypridd to Nottinghamshire with a group of young pickets. They went in four hired Cortinas and Phil's red car. This had a Nottinghamshire number plate, because his brother-in-law had bought it there, and they hoped that this would help them to get past the police. They arrived at Bilsthorpe at 6.30 a.m., but a lone policeman raised the alarm. Phil's story highlighted the terror of that moment, especially for the young men:

Within about half an hour there was a stream – have you seen that Coca-Cola advert where they have lorries going down and big lights? Well, this big thing like a snake was coming over these mounds, hills, things like that, and in they started coming. And [the policeman] came

out, opened the gates, and stood by the gates and police came in with
Transit, double-wheeled Transit vans at the back, covered in all hard,
almost armour type of thing. I had boys who were young chaps, eighteen, seventeen. And I said, 'Look boys, this is the day that we all grow
up, alright?'

Having failed to picket Bilsthorpe, they took the A38 to Staffordshire,
where the police presence was weaker. Then they returned to Ollerton,
where Bowen managed to address the miners in their canteen and persuade
them to come out on strike. He told them that their pits were threatened,
too, and played on the fact that their lodge officials were happy to speak to
Welsh pickets, because they were 'worried about the fact that Yorkshire
miners would be down here and they would create havoc with us'. Bowen
tried to manage hostility towards Arthur Scargill by playing the patriotic
card, arguing that a pithead vote was one of the freedoms secured in the
Second World War:

I remember one chap getting up and he was a Pole, and he said, 'I've
come from a country [where] we fought Nazism, and this Arthur
Scargill is a fascist' . . . And I said, 'Look, I've got uncles that have been
in the last war. My father-in-law was in the Glider pilot regiment at
Arnhem and on D-Day.' And I said, 'These people, you're right enough,
fought for freedom. And that's what this is about – that's what we're
doing!' So we just said, 'Nobody's forcing you. You have a vote like
everyone else out here, and rightly so.' And when I finished I said, 'Oh
by the way, I've forgotten, welcome to Britain?' Had a bit of a laugh
and they went straight to a vote, and they all voted to go out on strike.[15]

It is unclear what the status of this vote was, as the Nottinghamshire miners
had already balloted on 15–16 March not to strike. But it suggests that
debate about whether or not to strike went on into the third week of the
strike.

One of the older Blaenant miners, on a different mission, was Alun (Ali) Thomas. Born into a mining family in Onllwyn in 1940, he was the eighth of ten children, and the family also welcomed evacuees from London during the war. He joked that the family only had three school caps, so that the boys had to take it in turns to go to school. Prospects were limited and six of the seven boys went into the mining industry. Ali suffered an arm injury when a coal-cutting machine came loose – 'was idle a long time'; when Onllwyn closed in 1964, he moved to Blaenant, where he ran the weighbridge. Early in the strike, he was sent with a handful of miners to picket Wylfa nuclear power station on Anglesey. When they arrived, he realised that the manager was a former rugby player from back home. This comradeship was used to defuse the standoff:

All of a sudden I recognised Eddie Burford. Eddie Burford was an outside half, played for Seven Sisters. I played under him. Outstanding player. Could have gone anywhere. He had left Seven Sisters to go to North Wales and was one of the top men there. He came out to ask me a favour. 'Can you get these guys away?' It wasn't a case of obeying.

Later, Ali and his comrades were arrested for stopping vehicles going through to the power station and taken to the police station in Holyhead. Now he disrupted the interrogation by playing a practical joke on the officer:

We were being interviewed now. 'What's your name?' I said, 'Ali.' 'Listen now, never mind the jokes, what's your name?' I said, 'Ali.' He said, 'You're the same bloody colour as me, son.' Can you imagine him saying that now? He finished taking everything down. He said, 'Anything else loose on you now? Keys? Money?' So I took my dentures out. And I put one on each end of his desk. 'Oh it's games is it? It's fucking games you want is it?' You should have heard him . . . 'Lock these up,' he said. 'There's seven comedians here by the look of it.' And they locked us up.

The miners had the last laugh, though: next morning, when they were up before the court it transpired that the chief magistrate was the wife of the Labour MP. 'She was brilliant,' said Ali – she simply told the miners to behave themselves.[16]

There was another dimension to the roguish Welsh tales that is not often talked about. Striking miners had a courageous, manly profile that attracted the attention of both men and women. Travelling a long way from home, often relying for sustenance and shelter on local sympathisers or political activists, they sometimes ventured into amorous relationships. Phil Bowen remembered being asked by Kim Howells to go to the nuclear power station of Trawsfynydd in North Wales to deal with a romantic encounter that had gone wrong:

Kim phoned me and said, 'Your men are up in Trawsfynydd picketing?' And I said, 'Yeah we've got a group going up every week.' He said, 'I've had an irate husband on the phone saying there was an affair going on between a picket and his wife. They're up here and disrupting everything.' 'Right ho,' I said, so I went up there to sort things out.[17]

One of the places picketed by Welsh miners was Leicestershire. Here, picketing was extremely difficult, because there were only thirty strikers endeavouring to stop 1,500 miners going to work. There was an additional problem, in that whereas pickets from striking Areas were paid a pound or two a day by the local NUM, the Leicestershire NUM did not recognise the strike, and so they got no pay. So first, they were on a hiding to nothing; and second, they were not paid for their trouble. Fairly soon, it became clear that the priority had to be to raise funds to keep themselves out on strike. As Darren Moore, the youngest of the Dirty Thirty, remembers,

I think we had six weeks picketing. We'd picket the day shift, we'd picket the afternoon for six weeks, we're doing days and afternoons and people were not turning back, you know, they're just driving through. You weren't getting to even communicate with people. You know, people were not stopping, most of them were not even stopping to take leaflets anymore. So we spent six weeks doing that so, you know, we decided we needed to raise some money.[18]

Nigel Jeffery, a few months older than Darren, had a similar story of futility. On the plus side, he pointed out, pickets turned up in Leicestershire from other parts of the country, in order to help them. The Dirty Thirty acquired the status of heroes among striking miners in other coalfields, but for them the most valuable thing was the show of solidarity from other striking miners in the teeth of the isolation they faced:

We picketed in vain. I can remember the cameras, the local the BBC and the ITV, the cameras had come out and filmed us on this picket line. We stopped nobody. It was after I think a week, no lorry ever turned back, and it was just a waste of time . . . The thirty of us wasn't paid whatsoever by the Leicestershire NUM, so our main source of income was collecting, collecting money and collecting food. When the lads from the North East or from Wales came down, which we actually housed here at times, they would go off picketing, Wendy would go off to work because she was still working to pay the mortgage and I'd go off collecting.[19]

One of the striking miners who came to Leicestershire from County Durham was Bill Frostwick, an electrician from Herrington colliery. He was a member of the Colliery Officials and Staffs Area (COSA) and not technically involved in the NUM strike. But, like Cortonwood, Herrington was one of the pits scheduled to close and, he said, 'having been involved with union activity since I was an apprentice it was something that was instilled in you, and I would never, ever cross a picket line'. Nodding to his wife Elspeth, he added: 'In fact, if I would try to cross a picket line I would have to deal with you!'[20] Bill went even further: because he could not get through the police cordon into Nottinghamshire, he went to Leicestershire as a flying picket. 'As soon as you went to Nottingham,' he said, 'the police stopped your car, they asked where you are going and as soon as they heard the accent, "Turn around, go back." We heard it was easier to get into the Leicestershire coalfield.' There he struck up a close relationship with Nigel and Wendy Jeffery, slept on the floor of the house they had just acquired, used it as a base for picketing and often cooked their evening meal. After the strike, when Nigel and Wendy got married, Bill was Nigel's best man.

Meanwhile, Mel Elcock, the Bagworth fitter who lived in Loughborough, struck up a relationship with a group of Welsh miners from Tredegar, the birthplace of Aneurin Bevan, former miner, Labour MP and the brains behind the NHS. The importance of the link was not so much that together they would get more miners out, but that it provided a source of food for the hungry Leicestershire miners and their families:

A chap called Howard Miles from Tredegar said, 'If you send a car down, we'll fill the boot with food.' Because we'd got nothing, and nothing organised at that time. So I went down, I met Howard, he'd been picketing up here, Howard with the Tredegar boys. And yeah, I had to borrow me dad's car because I ain't got one, and they literally filled the boot with everything you could think of.[21]

This comradeship between miners from different Areas was important for the survival of the Dirty Thirty, who in some ways were like a large family. The biggest actual family among them was the Jeffery family: Cliff, his son Nigel from his first marriage, his second wife Barbara and her two sons. Sometimes they picketed at various hotspots outside Leicestershire, notably at Rawdon in South Derbyshire. Cliff, aged forty-eight at the time, was coming up for retirement and did not want to lose his pension by getting arrested on the picket line. But, said Nigel,

He would go, and he had a caravanette, and he would run a breakfast from there for everyone. Him and Barbara would do the drinks and the sausage cobs. He charged a very minimal amount so that he could next day go to the Co-op and get more ready for the next breakfast.

While Cliff dodged trouble at Rawdon, Nigel became involved and was arrested while shouting at strike-breakers who were driving through the picket line, where the Metropolitan Police had taken up position and were looking to deal with troublemakers:

I'd been most verbal throughout the half an hour . . . I was probably there because I was shouting trying to make them hear, 'Turn around, turn round, come on.' You know, and if they carried on driving, then I would shout 'You scab!' and so forth. And then for no reason two police officers come walking across the road and stood behind me. So the next time I shouted at a car that was going into work my arm was twisted around up my back, the other guy had got my shoulder, up me other arm, marched me across the road. Of course, me step-mum was screaming, me step-sister was screaming, me dad was shouting, 'Let him go, let him go!' And I think the other police was like holding him, holding everybody away from getting near me. I was bundled, chucked, literally forcefully thrown in the back of this minibus.

He was taken to Coalville police station and charged with 'disturbing the peace, unruly and threatening behaviour'. He was bound over not to picket outside Leicestershire and later went to court, where he was acquitted.[22]

The unity of this family was not necessarily replicated elsewhere. Because the strikers were so few in Leicestershire, families were divided by the strike. Margaret Pinnegar came from much more of a mining family than her husband Malcolm, and doted on her older brother, George, calling him 'my hero'. Unfortunately, George continued to work, which made family and social occasions very difficult and forced her to choose between those she loved:

We always used to go out on a Saturday night, and when the strike kicked off and Malcolm was on strike and George wasn't, I said to Malcolm, 'I don't want this family all to disintegrate.' And he said, 'No, I'll be civil.' Anyway, we went out this particular night and another miner come into the pub and he said to George, 'Oh hey up, George,' you know. 'Do you want a drink?' And George says, 'Ah, right-o.' And [George] said to Malcolm, 'Do you want to drink, Malcolm?' And Malcolm turned and looked at me. He said, 'I'm off. Can't do this. Can't do it. Cannot take a drink off of him. I can't do it.' And he got up and, and he walked out. That was it. And I went, I went over and saw my brother and said, 'This is the situation, and if I've got to choose between you and Malcolm, then I'll choose Malcolm every time.' I said, 'Until whatever this is, you know, we're done. We're done.'[23]

In County Durham, as in South Wales, picketing did not happen on the same scale as in other coalfields, because the strike was solid, so the more active miners, like Bill Frostwick, picketed in other Areas. Paul Stratford likewise picketed far away, at Wivenhoe, the port of Colchester, to prevent coal being unloaded, and Rugeley in Staffordshire, which had not only a pit, but also two power stations.[24] Other Durham miners recalled that they did very little picketing, because there were few opportunities. As Peter Byrne, an electrician at Wearmouth, said:

We just went to local places. Up at Butterknowle there was a depot up there, it was just to stop movement of any coal to smaller places. We didn't get to the big collieries where there was trouble and that; we never got across to those. It was just a way of getting a little bit money that would subsidise and keep you going.[25]

And as Dave Wray, his 'marra' (mate) and an electrician at Sacriston, recalled:

> The people that I was involved with in the strike, we didn't picket outside of Durham. And we only picketed when we were asked. We were not everyday picketing . . . I'm trying to think where we went; it was mainly opencast sites. I can remember sitting in my car with the television plugged in and it must have been the Olympics or something big. Watching the [Los Angeles] Olympics outside a coal depot. I don't know why I was there. There were four of us in the car. We were just asked to go there, to sit outside, I mean it was stupid.[26]

Over the border in Scotland, on the other hand, the miners were geared up for war. Fife was divided into two for the purposes of strike organisation, with the East Fife Area strike centre at Dysart, close to the Frances and Seafield pits, under the chairmanship of Willie Clarke. Communists transferred their control of the union branches to control of the strike committees. Under Dysart were eight local strike committees, each of which sent two representatives. At Cowdenbeath, Iain Chalmers was on the committee which met in the Welfare Hall, and he was also a representative at Dysart. At Lochore, the committee met in the Miners' Institute and the chair was 'Red Ronnie' Campbell.[27]

As in Durham, some miners travelled long distances to picket in other coalfields. Iain Chalmers went to the funeral of David Jones in Wakefield on 23 March on a bus chartered by the Scottish NUM. After the funeral, he was invited for refreshment at Askern Miners' Welfare and was enjoying the free beer and sausage rolls when a picket organiser came in and said, 'two seats left to go picketing at Nottingham if any of you Scots guys want to go'. Chalmers volunteered and went by car to Bevercotes, in the northeast of the county, where they were stopped 300 yards from the pit. Like other miners from elsewhere, he was overwhelmed by the police presence, and already there were rumours that the army was involved:

I was half expecting to get arrested to be honest with you . . . I mean, to read about it, you know, and to see snippets of it on the TV, but to actually be there and see the amount of police. And it's like, there's no way they're police. Absolutely horrendous . . . And on the way back, we got talking to the guys and they were telling us what it was like down there. And by the way, we never had it easy up here, no stretch of the imagination did we have it easy up here. But when you were talking to these guys they were literally living in a police state. It was as bad as that.[28]

Unlike in Durham, however, in May the Scottish miners were picketing at major sites, in particular to stop the supply of coal to the Hunterston power station on the Firth of Clyde and to the Ravenscraig steelworks near Motherwell. There they came up against a huge police presence that was prepared to use violence and was intent on making large numbers of arrests. Tom Adams, NUM branch treasurer at Frances, came to Hunterston with a mass picket of 600 miners from Fife and Midlothian, all in high spirits, to stop the lorries getting through. The police nevertheless intervened in even greater numbers, and in retrospect Tom saw the invitation for the pickets to come to a preordained site and the subsequent police cavalry charge as a prelude to Orgreave:

We went in and they were all laughing and joking. And the next thing, the police buses arrived. And they must have had about 800 police, coming off the buses. They all lined up like an army squad and they marched up the middle of the road. The whole lot of them just marched right up. And then they formed lines at either side of the banking. When the first lorry came, the horses then came as well. As we were pushing down the banking the horses just charged into the miners. They just charged right into them. And Davie Hamilton, who then became the MP in Midlothian, got knocked out. He was taken away in an ambulance and I think he was out cold for about three days.

He was in a coma. I never got arrested there. It wasn't for the want of trying, I'll say.[29]

Meanwhile, Ronnie Campbell and Sean Lee, the Seafield miner who lived in Lochore, had a similar experience at Ravenscraig, where the police were ready for them. Both ended up getting arrested. For Campbell,

Ravenscraig was a massive picket line, it was massive. Well, when the lorries came into Ravenscraig, of course everybody started shoving. We were fighting, more or less fighting with the police, and the police were just grabbing anybody. I spent the night in the cell, and then I was taken to Hamilton Sheriff Court, and I got fined £80.[30]

For Sean Lee, whose family had Irish republican origins, the odds were stacked against them not just by the police presence, but by infiltrators and what he thought were soldiers camouflaged in police clothing:

We had been infiltrated. There were agents provocateurs in amongst us, in the ranks. They were trying to direct us into a certain area where we could be penned in, so some of us broke free and, well, I mean, we saw the police and we knew they weren't the police. We believed they were the army. Anyway, a part of us broke free and when the lorries did come in, I picked up a cone, one of those traffic cones, and hoisted it at the lorry and got arrested.[31]

Miners clashing with the police on picket lines provide many of the iconic images of the strike. They highlighted an aspect of the miners' masculinity, prepared as they were to fight for their pits and their jobs, to risk injury and arrest – even though that could lead to them having a criminal record and being sacked. But not all miners picketed. Some wanted to avoid violence, or getting a criminal record, or simply wished to make ends meet by working on the side. In Manton, for example, Dave

Potts, who was bloodied at Babbington, was in a minority. His cousin Gary Fisher spent most of the strike at the Manton Miners' Club, pulling pints and tending the bowling green.[32] Kevin Greaves, whose mother was Italian – brought back by his serviceman father at the end of the war – used the strike to set up a new business making Italianate decorative plasterwork for home interiors. 'I wanted my two boys to have something better in life,' he confessed.[33] Frank Holmes, a hydraulic chock fitter at the pit, was a notorious tough guy, the son of a miner nicknamed 'the Askern bull'. He himself was reputed to have floored the local 'Gypsy King'. He did not, however, join the picket line, because he had given up his violence and marital infidelity to become a born-again Christian:

> I didn't go on picket lines because I had a reputation. I was never a bully or a trouble causer but I had quite a reputation if things went a bit wrong. And I knew from some of the experiences that me mates were telling me about the police pushing them around – and I'd just become a Christian then – and I thought, how will I handle this if some person starts pushing me around? I would have retaliated and I thought, I need to take control of myself.[34]

Women – above all, miners' wives – were seen regularly on picket lines. It was often said that miners' wives 'stood by their men' and this was one of the main reasons for the long duration of the strike. Where the women did not support their men, those men very often went back to work. More than this, however, some women actually took the place of their men on picket lines. Police blockades targeted cars full of miners, whereas women in a car were less obviously pickets: they often made up stories about going shopping or meeting friends. If the menfolk were arrested, sent to court and bound over to keep the peace, their wives might picket in their place. That said, women were becoming active in their own right, fighting for their families, for the jobs their children would need, and for their communities, which risked being devastated if the pits closed. Some were inspired by the women who gathered at Greenham Common in Berkshire after 1981 to protest against the cruise missiles that were being held there for a potential attack on the Soviet Union. Those women later came to support the miners' wives. Outside the collieries and steelworks, they themselves underwent a rite of passage, realising that the police were far from being the local 'bobby'. They came up against police intimidation, taunting and violence on behalf of a state that was out to break their resolve.

In Askern, South Yorkshire, short, stocky Phil Crane and 'tall, skinny' Pete Hogg were often on the picket lines; but that did not stop their wives, Jean and Dianne, from wanting to go, too. The Askern NUM secretary initially told them that 'it would be too dangerous and, anyway, it was no place for women'. Eventually, however, the union lent a minibus and gave them petrol. They discovered that they could get through the police lines – unlike cars full of men. They went to Creswell to challenge the masculinity of the Notts miners with a banner reading: 'Askern women will fight for your jobs, why won't you?'[35] Interviewed in 1986, Jean said, 'The men really thought that what we were doing were great.' She added, 'We got through to Annesley. Men didn't. There were next to none on strike at Annesley.' They were given breakfast by the few striking miners and left the £1 they had earned on the picket line for the miners' breakfast.[36]

Jean and Dianne nevertheless soon encountered a police violence that seemed to draw no distinction between women and men. This happened on a trip to Calverton in June. According to Dianne,

It were laughable, really. We didn't know where we were going. Not many women there. The police came out of the social club. They'd been drinking. You could smell it on their breath. I'd stake my life on it. They got behind us and this inspector asked us to move. We said, 'We're not moving.' He said, 'You don't treat these like women. You kick 'em and you nick 'em.' They started pushing. It were really scary. Women were falling over. They threw me over and I landed on the road. I kicked this car, and the cops said, 'You're nicked.'[37]

Dianne later explained that she had kicked the car because she was frustrated, but did not allow herself to swear. Thirteen women were taken in a 'meat wagon' to a police station, interrogated, kept in the cells until the following afternoon and later fined. 'Never went on another picket line,' she confessed. 'Pete wouldn't let me.'[38]

Jean herself was not arrested, but she was deeply shocked. 'I was flung across the road and dropped my handbag. Somebody else had to scoop it up. My next-door neighbour was actually crying. We were penned in . . . After Calverton, none of us ever went again. We were really shook up.' She reflected that this was a turning point:

> Always brought up to respect the police. We respected the law as well. We were brought up to know right from wrong. But after seeing the things they did, they were vicious, really evil. When they opened ranks to let them out at Calverton, they said, 'We've really enjoyed this, ladies.' And there was this girl, they dragged her right through all of us. She's saying, 'Please stop, I've hurt my foot.' I wouldn't let my husband treat me the way they treated her.[39]

Police violence involved the deliberate humiliation of women who were arrested for picketing. Anne Scargill, Arthur's wife, who worked at Brook Motors in Barnsley, and Betty Cook, who was a shop steward at Empire Stores, Wakefield, were involved in Barnsley Women Against Pit Closures. They went in a minibus with other Barnsley women to picket Silverhill in Nottinghamshire. Arrested, Anne suffered brutal and degrading treatment from policemen and policewomen – something that attracted huge publicity at the time:

> They took me and Lynne Hathaway and them other two in a Black Maria and they took us to police station. I wanted to go the toilet so I was running into the police station and they grabbed me and pulled me back. I said, 'I'm not running away. I want to go to the toilet.' I was

dying to go to the toilet and they put us in a dog compound and it were raining, and there were dog muck all over. I started kicking the bottom of the door and they opened it, took us into a room with a toilet . . . And they said, 'What's your names?' And we wouldn't tell 'em . . . I says, 'Tell me what I've done this morning and I'll tell you what to call me.' So anyway, after a bit they fetched me in a room. There were four of us. I can remember this, it is etched on my brain. There were a bath and all. And [the policewoman] said, 'Come on, get undressed.' And I said, 'You what? I'm not mucky.' She said, 'Get undressed.' I thought, she's serious. They strip-searched me. She said they were looking for drugs and weapons. She did it to all four of us. Strip-searched us.[40]

In Nottinghamshire itself, there were few striking miners and few wives of striking miners; but of those few, many were very committed. Anne Heaton was a Lancashire woman who had worked in a cotton mill and married Harry, a Lancashire miner. After a spell in South African mining, he moved them to Welbeck colliery in Nottinghamshire, where he became a training officer and she became a cleaner at the pit. She initially voted against the strike, but then, fortified by involvement in the Welbeck Women's Action Group, tried her hand at picketing, only to be foiled by the police:

We used to have a motor home, Harry and myself. We could fit quite a few people in it. So the Women's Action Group decided they were going picketing at Mansfield Woodhouse. The police stopped us just going out of the village and asked us where we were going. Quickly I said, 'We're going to see how the women in Derbyshire work their soup kitchens.' They said, 'Right, we'll escort you.' So they escorted us into Derbyshire, quite a way, and then said, 'Right, we'll leave you.' I bet they were really laughing them policemen. I bet they knew really what we were doing and said, 'Let's get them lost.'[41]

She did not personally experience police violence, but her son Gary, a miner aged twenty-two, was arrested. Interviewed in 1984 for the documentary *Notts Women Strike Back*, she explained how she took it out on her mother, back in Lancashire, who was married to a working miner, one of those who forced her son to picket and risk arrest:

> I couldn't understand violence until my son was arrested. That day I wanted to go out and murder everyone. I wanted to strangle everyone who was going to work because if they weren't, he wouldn't have got arrested. My daughter was screaming her head off. I took it out on my mother at the end of the phone.[42]

She later clarified that 'I must have rung my mother. I knew her husband – not me dad – was going to work, he worked in pit. I said, is John working? I said, For God's sake, tell him to stop working. Do you know Gary's been arrested because he's [John's] working?'[43]

In South Wales, Dai John Jones, a miner at Tower, had been involved in picketing out reluctant Welsh miners at the beginning of the strike. His wife Ann said that, to begin with, the men – unbending in their traditional masculinity – had not even wanted women on the picketing buses, and sometimes refused to give them a seat. But, she observed, this changed over time:

> In the end we were organising the picketing buses, as so many of the boys had been arrested. They were watching them so much they couldn't move. For every man the police took off the picket line, a woman would take his place. The motto was, 'We're standing shoulder to shoulder not behind.'[44]

Interviewed some months later with her friend Siân James, Ann was more forthright about the fact that some men had started to lose the will to fight; and in giving up, they had surrendered their masculine pride to the women:

Sometimes I'd get so frustrated that I'd say to them, 'Aren't you going picketing then?' And the classic one that sticks in my mind today, 'Can't you see, love,' he said, 'I've got a hole in my welly.' I mean, to that man that was a genuine excuse why he couldn't go picketing. And the other one was, 'My wife won't let me.'[45]

The most brutal picket lines were at the Port Talbot steelworks and involved both men and women. On 29 August 1984, a hundred more intrepid miners infiltrated the steelworks by night and occupied three wharf cranes to prevent the bulk carrier *Argos* unloading coking coal. They remained there for three days until the police persuaded them down, then charged many of them with trespass and criminal damage.[46] Miners' wives and Greenham Common women were also badly treated. Ann and Siân described how they were subjected to both verbal and physical abuse that questioned their female virtue. Siân aimed her criticism at the women police officers – whom she calls 'Juliet Bravos' after the 1980s police series – while Ann recalled the ways in which male police officers would flaunt the wages they were being paid and offer the hungry women a cut for sexual favours:

Ann: The worst case of that which I've told you about was Port Talbot. Absolutely horrendous with those women that walked down from Greenham. Absolutely horrendous.

Siân: The way they treated people. I was saying about the Juliet Bravos, remember? What they would do is you'd be chest to chest here. You know, we'd link arms and then you'd feel a hand coming up at the side of your breast and they would grab a lump of flesh and twist.

Ann: You see, Siân, they used to stand outside the furnace site in front of their lorries with £5 notes pasted to the windows and saying, 'Thanks for our holiday. Thanks for this. If you're really short come behind here and we'll give you one of these.' And that was every morning of the week that was.[47]

Dorothy Wray, whose husband Dave was at Sacriston in County Durham, picketed the pit in the winter of 1984, when the miners were starting to go back to work. She had a similar view of the threatening and taunting behaviour of the police, which was particularly difficult to bear because they had so little for Christmas:

I can remember being at Sacriston and there was the Metropolitan Police and they were bastards ... I remember them saying to me, 'If you step up that kerb I'll arrest you.' And I was like, 'Really? It's a public path. You cannot tell me not to step on a public path.' He says, 'Do you wanna try it out?' So I stepped and he made me sit in the van for an hour. And I say, 'You know what, mate? It's all nice and warm in your van here. It is freezing out there.' And then they would say things like, 'What are your kids gonna get for Christmas? My kids are gonna get that.' 'You bastards.' But then don't let them get you.[48]

In Scotland, where things became violent much earlier, there were both macho male flying pickets at Hunterston power station and Ravenscraig steelworks, and also women and children involved in community picketing at local sites. One of these was Cartmore, an opencast mine on the outskirts of Lochgelly, from which lorries from a private haulage firm were taking coal for various industrial purposes, speeding through the town with scant regard for the safety of the population. To prevent this, a mass picket was organised on 7–8 June. The usual male suspects were there, but so also were women and children from Ballingry High School, in front of which the lorries charged down the hill. Without permission from the school, but with some approval from their parents, the children filed out of their lessons to show solidarity.

Tom Adams, the Frances miner who had avoided arrest at Hunterston, told a bravado story of again flirting with arrest by trying to stop a lorry coming out of the Cartmore dump:

When the lorry came through with the coal on it, I managed to get up on the passenger side to . . . I was hanging on the wing mirror, banging on the window. And suddenly this reality hit me and says, 'What the fuck are you doing up here? What are we going to do here? I can't stop anybody. The driver's not stopping, he's just keeping on going.' And I'm hanging off a wing mirror. I couldn't even do anything. And I went, 'Ah, just get off.' So I jumped down. The minute my feet hit the ground, I got picked up and I'm getting marched down the road. With two policemen. I was about halfway down. And one of my pals came running up and jumped on the two of them. He got lifted and I got away.[49]

A similar account was given by Sean Lee, from Seafield, who had been arrested at Ravenscraig in May and was now arrested again:

When the lorries filled up and they tried to come back out we were there in numbers. And this time we closed the road, we ran across and stopped the lorries coming up the road. So after about a ten-minute standoff, we weren't going nowhere and the police couldn't do very little about it, so they decided to start making arrests. And I was just as it happened nose to nose with the inspector at the time, so I was first in the van. Probably just unlucky. Aye. I was pretty militant right in his face anyway.[50]

One of the women present was Margaret Coll, a miner's wife from Crosshill, between Lochore and Glencraig. She was a fiery redhead and chair of the Lochore Women's Support Group. Her first husband had abused her, and her second later came back from Orgreave 'with all his head burst open with a baton'. She was at Cartmore that day and was abused by the police, too, but also remembered the successful action by the Ballingry high-school students, who stood outside their school to prevent the lorries getting through on the main road to Cartmore:

We stood for about half an hour and they couldn't move. Then all of a sudden there were hundreds of police cars came and they just grabbed us by the hair of the head too and just flung us against the wall so they'd get by. But we'd already planned – the high school in Ballingry – to stand in front outside the school. And we said, 'They can't touch you because you're under age and they'll not be able to touch you.' So every bairn in that school stood in front of those lorries and the police were trying to intimidate them but they didn't move. So they had to back away and never got through at all.[51]

One of those high-school children was Margaret Campbell, daughter of 'Red Ronnie', who had already been arrested at Ravenscraig. She recalled that the high-school children not only stood in the road outside the school in Ballingry, but then walked the two or three miles to Cartmore to join the picket there. Thirty-six years later, she remembered with her father the moment parents and children joined together to defend their jobs and their community:

Margaret: My dad's out there, fighting, up there on the front line, taking the consequences, taking the responsibility, taking whatever it took, for somebody to listen. 'We're here, I've a family, I've a wife, we're villagers, this is our life, this is our bread and butter, and you're taking that away.'

Ronnie: And there was a massive picket line there, oh for about two or three days we were up there, arguing and fighting with the police, you know.

Margaret: All the pupils from Ballingry Junior High were involved. Because I was there. I was one of them.

Ronnie: We were all there waiting on these lorries coming, and all the schoolkids marched out the school, and they came right down the brae.

Margaret: You had the miners, all the men, and you had the women, but you actually had a part of Benarty kids taking control of things, and going, 'Well, we'll just go and join them.' And we were brought back to the school. We all got into trouble for it. I think all the parents were all involved.[52]

The picketing of other pits and of other industries demonstrated both the solidarity and the lack of solidarity of the Miners' Strike. Solidarity, because miners travelled long distances to picket out working miners in Nottinghamshire, dockers at Immingham and steelworkers at Ravenscraig. South Wales and Durham miners bonded with the isolated Dirty Thirty. But there was also a lack of solidarity, because so much effort was expended on trying – and failing – to construct a united front of striking workers. The majority of Notts and Leicestershire miners did not come out; the steelworkers and dockworkers were prevented from secondary picketing (and in any case, defended their own interests); and communities and even families were divided. Picketing was a display of the traditional masculinity of the miners, fighting to protect their own jobs. But many miners did not get involved in picketing, preferring to make a living on the side and to avoid arrest. Alongside them – and sometimes in their absence – miners' wives also volunteered to picket and had brutal encounters with the police. Meanwhile in Fife, men, women and children battled together to save their pits and their community.

3

THE BATTLE FOR THE BALLOT

Early in the strike, Steve Williamson, NUM branch secretary at Annesley colliery, was invited onto *Newsnight* to debate with the NUM president, Arthur Scargill. The programme was broadcast from Sheffield University in front of two or three hundred striking miners, and Williamson confessed that it was 'a little bit intimidating. I was set up actually.' The debate was about whether or not the strike was legal and democratic under the rules of the NUM. Scargill went first. As Williamson recalled,

He said, 'We've got 80 per cent of our members out on strike and you're saying we're not being democratic.' I said, 'Arthur, give us a ballot, and I'll vote for a strike. And if you get 50 per cent I'll be with you. But let's run it by the rules. They've been running for forty years, these rules. They've been fought for by everyone before us. Give us the chance of a ballot, and I will vote for a strike and I will campaign for a strike. You cannot kick a man out on strike. We don't accept that we can be on strike without a ballot. All we wanted was democracy.' And what did he say? 'I don't trust you.' And I said, 'I don't trust you.'[1]

Williamson did not trust Scargill not to bully the Nottinghamshire miners, and instead to respect the different tradition of their coalfield and the autonomy of the Nottinghamshire NUM. Scargill did not trust

Williamson to vote for a strike if a national ballot were held, given that his members had voted against strike action by 81 per cent in March 1983 and by 73.5 per cent in March 1984, and that their tradition included founding an anti-strike, breakaway trade union in 1926.

The NUM was a powerful body, which in 1984 represented 184,000 miners.[2] It had immense industrial muscle; and when it chose to flex that muscle, the country trembled. But it was also a bureaucratic organisation that had made its gains incrementally, so that precedents and rules were very important. Unfortunately, strike action was governed by two rules, which were not necessarily in harmony. Rule 41 said that

> In the event of a dispute arising in any Area . . . the questions involved must immediately be reported by the appropriate official of the Area in question and to the National Executive Committee (NEC) which shall deal with the matter forthwith, and in no case shall cessation of work . . . take place without the previous sanction of the National Executive Committee.

However, Rule 43 said that

> A national strike shall only be entered upon as the result of a ballot vote of the members taken in pursuance of a resolution of a Conference, and a strike shall not be declared unless 55 per cent of those taking part in the ballot vote in favour of such a strike.

In early March 1984, the strike broke out because of a local dispute in the Yorkshire Area. This was rapidly sanctioned by the National Executive Committee, presided over by Arthur Scargill, and other strikes in Scotland, County Durham and South Wales were also approved. However, the miners of Nottinghamshire, three quarters of whom had voted against strike action, insisted that a national ballot be held to ascertain whether the miners of Great Britain would support the strike. Moreover, in County

Durham, pits – including Sacriston, and along the coast at Murton, Seaham, Vane Tempest, Westoe, Horden and even Easington – petitioned for 'the democratic right for an individual vote of the membership in a cessation of work situation, either by area or national ballot'. A Durham Area conference of all the chairs, secretaries and delegates from each lodge met at Redhills on Wednesday 21 March, and duly requested an emergency meeting of the NEC, in order to implement NUM Rule 43.[3] Fears then arose that a national ballot might be lost, and so a second Durham Area conference, held on 13 April, voted to reduce the majority of 55 per cent required under a national ballot to a simple majority; those Areas still working should show 'good faith' by immediately ceasing work while a national ballot was held.[4]

The legality of the strike was now in question. It would be impossible to form a united front if the Nottinghamshire miners refused to join the fight and if the Durham miners got cold feet about the lack of a national ballot. The question had to be resolved, and so a special delegates' meeting, with representatives from every coalfield, was convened in Sheffield on Thursday 19 April. The Durham miners put their resolutions to the conference. They secured approval for a simple majority in any national ballot, but not for a cessation of work while a ballot was held. Hostility to any form of ballot that could undermine the momentum of the strike was overwhelming. Dave Douglass, flying picket organiser for the Doncaster Area and delegate for Hatfield colliery, found the Durham motion faintly ridiculous, since most miners were already on strike:

The Durham Mechanics proposed that we have a ballot, but if we lose the ballot, we respect picket lines. So you'd be on strike whatever you did. Now when it went to the vote, 'no ballot' won. Because we were already on strike. They were saying, 'Why do you need confirmation in a ballot?'

The conference then voted to endorse the NEC decisions of 8 March and 12 April which had sanctioned industrial action in different Areas under

Rule 41, and then called on all Areas to join the 80 per cent who were already on strike and thereby ensure maximum unity in the union.

The delegates' conference in Sheffield did not take place in a vacuum. Striking Yorkshire and Welsh miners turned up in force to lobby for the strike action to be endorsed. Douglass probably exaggerated the numbers, but not the sentiment: 'There were 20,000 men outside, singing, "Stick your ballot up your arse" to the tune of "Bread of Heaven".'[5]

One of those striking Yorkshire miners was Pete Richardson from Askern, who had already been arrested while picketing working Nottinghamshire miners at Bilsthorpe. He had a particular gripe about Ray Chadburn, the Notts miners' president who had stood against Scargill for the NUM presidency in 1981. Along with his usual activity of rescuing comrades from the police, he was accused of shouting 'Kill Chadburn!':

> I got arrested but I didn't do nothing. This Welshman had gone down and I went to help him. But the police were six deep and one of them did me in the kidney. I protested and they said, 'Get him.' As I went into them they were kicking and punching me. If I were on the floor they'd have kicked me to death. They arrested me for police assault, for threatening Ray Chadburn's life. Gave me two months in Durham. It was all trumped up.[6]

A different impression of the Sheffield meeting was relayed to Mrs Thatcher by a flamboyant and rather sinister character who had ingratiated himself into her inner circle and who saw it as his mission to steel her against the striking miners. David Hart, the Eton-educated son of Louis Hart, founder of the Ansbacher Bank, made a rapid fortune in the 1960s as a property developer, but bankrupted himself in 1975 by spending it equally quickly in buying a country house, travelling by chauffeur-driven car and helicopter, and keeping two mistresses. Saved financially by the death of his father in 1978, he reinvented himself as an *éminence grise*, and sent the prime minister some 'Impressions from the Coalfield' at the end of April. These highlighted the rift between the Nottinghamshire miners and Arthur Scargill, whose rabble-rousing methods he equated with Nazism, while painting a portrait of an 'immaculate' police that Pete Richardson would not have recognised:

> The Notts miners are very angry with Scargill. They do not like the way he is playing with their right to vote on important union matters. The present determination in Notts to continue working is not simply because they want the money. Though many do, if they were offered an honourable reason to strike, many would. For some, possibly most, a positive ballot would provide such a reason: loyalty to the union. This does not mean that they will vote for a strike. The longer they are not given the opportunity to ballot the less likely they are to vote for a strike.
>
> Sheffield was different. Standing in a crowd of miners – not the seven thousand of the press reports, more likely three thousand – I could not escape thoughts of Nuremberg. Though they were better humoured the other elements were there. The stink of fascism. Admiration bordering on adoration for their leader. A scaffolding plat-form at the head of the square. Quantities of free beer financed by the union. Speaker after speaker making extravagant personal attacks on you. And on the police. Flannery MP saying that the police had broken the 'Law of the Land' and that the miners should make up their minds what they were going to do about it. The next speaker urging the crowd to 'get stuck into the police'. The police behaving immaculately despite grave provocation.[7]

After the Sheffield meeting, Arthur Scargill and the Nottinghamshire miners came into direct conflict. He took the delegates' vote of 19 April as a collective decision to make the Miners' Strike official. With NUM General Secretary Peter Heathfield, he went on 25 April to the Nottinghamshire miners' headquarters at Berry Hill in Mansfield to inform the Notts leaders that they must now bring their men into line. They won over Chadburn and Notts General Secretary Henry Richardson to their view, but not the rank and file of Nottinghamshire miners. David Amos, who was on the union committee at Annesley, said that 'by the April Richardson was openly coming on the television to tell Nottinghamshire miners to get off their knees and stop scabbing'. When he and his mates were called out of the pit to attend the Berry Hill meeting, Amos argued that they were now defending democracy against dictatorship:

> I said, this is Scargill coming down with a 'You will.' He came to this meeting which followed the special delegates' meeting and said, 'This is official. You as elected members will go back and tell your men.' And of course there was a split in the union. We refused. At the Annesley branch we refused. This is not trade union democracy. So we refused.[8]

Steve Williamson, who was one of David Amos's mentors at Annesley, organised a powerful response to Scargill and Heathfield. He had had enough of being called a scab by striking miners at Annesley and wanted to demonstrate to Chadburn and Richardson, who had gone over to the NEC official line, the feelings of the 73.5 per cent Notts miners who had voted not to strike. To this end, he brought together like-minded officials in other pits for a 'right to work' protest rally at Berry Hill on 1 May:

> I organised that. The reason I organised that, I used to walk up to the canteen on the day shift and everybody used to speak to me. [Now] I was getting death threats at twelve o'clock at night saying that they were going to kill my children, and I went to the canteen, I said, 'I'm fed up to the teeth with all this flak. We've got two leaders at Berry Hill who represent us, Chadburn and Richardson. It's about time that we went there to tell them what we think about it.' I said, 'We ought to go there and picket them.' Then I started to bring round the branch secretaries. I started to see them at a place called Kirkby Hall. I did a left-

wing policy, I started to organise the moderates. It snowballed. We finished up with 17,000 people there, which wasn't a bad turnout.

The only trouble with the meeting, said Williamson, was that, in advance of it, he had consulted the police and they had informed Chadburn and Richardson. The outcome was that when the 17,000 working miners arrived at Berry Hill, they found that two or three thousand striking miners had occupied the NUM offices and surrounded the building. The working miners were kept at a distance by a police cordon:

We instructed the police that as branch officials we wanted to go into the HQ and address them. They had loudspeakers and they were talking down to the men. And we said, 'We're not having this. We want our say.' So the police bundled about a dozen of us officials. You could imagine, trying to get a dozen people through. They were on the roof, throwing bottles at us, throwing bricks at us. The police shoved us inside Berry Hill and left us. There wasn't a policeman inside. We were faced with mayhem. I went to speak. And Jimmy Hood said, 'If you go out there, I'll throw you off the balcony.' I said, 'If you do you're coming with me.' And when I got up to speak something was thrown up at me. We weren't allowed to speak. To be honest we were glad to get out. We feared for our lives.[9]

David Amos, who was one of the dozen bundled into the building, recalled that 'I got covered in spit coming out. Somebody shouted, "There's the little bastard, we'll kill you!"'[10]

At the same time, however, cracks were appearing in the Nottinghamshire NUM leadership. Roy Lynk, the Notts Area agent who had lost out only the previous December to Henry Richardson in the race to become general secretary, never forgave him and was already preparing a challenge.[11] Mick Marriott, a working miner at Annesley who was kept behind the police cordon, said:

I was there. I can remember the two Notts officials [Chadburn and Richardson] trying to talk us into going on strike. And then Roy Lynk came on, he grabbed the mike, and he says, 'We've got a right to work until there's a national ballot.' But it never happened. There was a lot of stone throwing.[12]

Indeed, the national ballot did not happen. The Nottinghamshire miners placed themselves at the vanguard of a National Working Miners' Committee, which was to be the embryo of another breakaway union. Steve Williamson was heavily involved in this and remembered a visit to Monkwearmouth, in Sunderland, where he addressed a meeting of 700 sympathetic miners:

We didn't want anything else, we wanted to make sure that we weren't going to be victimised, that we were going to carry on. We were going around advising other Areas, because that's not right what they're doing to you. It's not legal, it's not right. You're being bullied out of work. That's not what the rule book is about.[13]

The secretary of the Working Miners' Committee, Bob Copping, a winder at Houghton Main, near Barnsley, later resigned and told *Mirror* journalist Paul Foot that in August 1984 he was introduced to David Hart at a guest house in Castle Donnington, and then met him at a luxury restaurant near Oakham in Leicestershire, owned by David's brother Tim. Hart was making frequent trips from his London base at Claridge's to the East Midlands to help organise the working miners, and was reporting back on a regular basis to Downing Street.[14]

Long before that, though, the striking miners decided to put on a show of force as a riposte to the 'right to work' demonstration, held in Mansfield on 1 May. They organised their own pro-strike rally there on Monday 14 May. The police presence was heavy and well-trained and, unlike on 1 May, was designed not only to contain the striking miners, but to teach them a lesson. Demonstrators were told that the meeting was to be held somewhere they could easily be corralled and softened up, with snatch squads on hand to arrest militants.

Pete Richardson, always game for a fight, went down on a bus with a number of his mates from Askern. They marched behind their Askern NUM banner and then decided to get some refreshment:

Had a good drink, like, we were on our way to Berry Hill. The policeman on the corner said, 'Are you pickets? The plans have changed. It's at the Leisure Centre.' And when we got there, there were bricks and bottles flying. It had started. The police were arresting pickets, so we went in and helped them out. We did it again, four or five times, like a snatch squad in reverse. We got split up, there were 200 police and only a few pickets with Frank my mate in the middle. He thought he could make it alright. I walked up to Frank and the pickets started cheering. This time they regrouped. They advanced real slow, swallowed him up, and then started running. There were ten cops chasing four lads. I said, 'Stop chasing them, they've done nowt.' They just turned round, I'd done nothing. I got a fairly rough ride.[15]

In his 'Confessions of a Picket', Pete took a relaxed view of police violence and the arbitrary justice of the courts. Everything was a bit of a laugh. At the core of the story were 'the damn good bunch of lads' from Askern, with their camaraderie and bravado, workmates, drinking companions, Manchester United supporters and now flying pickets. They were committed to the strike and willing to accept the consequences. Morally, they would come out on top. In this account, 'little Frank' is described as being at the head of a hundred pickets, 'facing a wall of two or three hundred police'. Pete said that he looked as if he was leading the 'Abide with Me' song at Wembley. When he went to rescue Frank and they were both arrested, Frank started to sumo wrestle with some of the cops. The ones round me started to dance on my face. Anyway, one of the cops must have pulled a banana out and tempted Frank to stop monkeying about, then threw him into the back of the van.

Pete adopted the same nonchalant tone when describing their arrest, their confinement in two police stations (which he ironically calls 'our hotel' and a 'four star hotel') and their interrogation for up to two hours each. His humour expressed defiance of authority. 'Dave McLoy was gone for about 2½ hours, he must have got a cup out of them, the crafty sod,' he joked. They were brought to Nottingham Crown Court on the evening after the incident, and the charges were read out to each of them in turn:

> There was the rest of the Askern pickets, always in there where it counts, a damn good bunch of lads they are. I pulled a face at Frank and he started to giggle. After that, he just had to look over and catch my eye and he was all a giggling.[16]

Rather different was the account of Steve Walker, a young miner from Scargill's home pit of Woolley, who hadn't been picketing before. He had put his name down, but hadn't been called. Then a mate urged him to go to the Mansfield rally, where there would be 'people coming from all over the country, Scotland, Wales, Kent, coming with their banner and bands' and some pocket money from the NUM for a drink. It is the story of a party that went disastrously wrong and provided a callow youth 'scared to death' with a baptism of fire:

> As we walk round Mansfield, with banners, bands were playing, great atmosphere, like a party, brilliant, fantastic. When it finishes, I can only describe it, there were like a big car park, I don't know if it were like summat municipal, swimming baths, or summat like that, or sports centre, with a big car park there. They had all the speakers there, politi-

cians, NUM men and all that. Well, we weren't interested in that. We're off down into Mansfield for a few beers, like all young people. We trots down into town centre, still a great atmosphere, everybody were like in a market square with pubs round it. Everybody having some beers and that. Bit of singing, bit of chanting, nowt nasty, nowt malicious, everybody's having a good time. They sent a couple of bobbies in on their own, sticks out, prodding people. 'C'mon. Move on, Get yoursens back up there. We don't want you around here causing trouble.' It was bound to get nasty and it did, right quick. And soon coppers coming from every street, they were waiting. So we managed to get out of way, make our way back to the rally. That had all finished, people were making their way back to buses.

At that moment, he said, everything changed. The police began to attack the miners and even their families. His description, recorded in 2020, recalled John Harris's famous photograph of Lesley Boulton being attacked by a mounted policeman at Orgreave and miners jumping over walls to escape in *Billy Elliot*:

Police come, line of coppers, five or six deep, just marching across the car park, shoving everybody. It got nasty, bottles and bricks flying. There were women with kids in pushchairs, getting knocked all over. The coppers were just beating folk up here, randomly, setting about them for no reason. I'm there trying to get back to me bus, trying to get out of the way, thinking fucking hell, what's happening here? Christ almighty. I've never seen owt like it. It was just like being at war, like a war without guns. They started charging in with horses, cavalry came, then with dogs on great long leads. I'm trying to get back to bus and this bloody copper on a horse charged straight into the back of me, flattened me. Gravel all over me arm, arm ripped to bits. I jumps up, I saw him wheeling his horse round with a stick out, coming back for another go. So I ran and jumped over this wall. I didn't have a chuffing clue what was on other side of it. I was straight over it and I got away. I managed to get back on me bus. That was me first experience of going with the union. I shit meself. Anyone who says they're not scared is lying. I were only nineteen and that scared me to death.[17]

The battle for the ballot opened up a front between striking and non-striking miners, which snaked along the Yorkshire/Nottinghamshire border and found a hotspot in the town of Mansfield. These coalfields had different mining conditions and traditions, and the Coal Board and government sought to widen the division by not scheduling any pits in Nottinghamshire for closure. Within this, however, different choices about striking and not striking were made by individuals. Is it possible that they had different family histories, whether in terms of relationships or mining? That they came from different kinds of community? It may be that strikers set more store by solidarity with their comrades, while for non-strikers it was about principle, doing things by the book, having a democratic vote. The first saw the enemy as the employers and the state, which was prepared to use violence to take away their jobs and their way of life; the second saw the enemy as Arthur Scargill and his henchmen who were prepared to use violence to 'kick them out of their jobs' which afforded them a good standard of living.

Dave Douglass, a Geordie in Yorkshire, was very clear about his family and community identity. 'I come from eight generations of coalminers,' he said proudly, while Hebburn, 'the community I grew up in on Tyneside was part of the Tyneside Irish community. My sisters were both champion Irish dancers, my mam had been an Irish dancer.' He left Tyneside when he married Maureen, who was a grammar-school girl, but whose two grandfathers had been miners. They went to Yorkshire, so that she could pursue a fine art degree at Hull, while Dave went down the pit at Hatfield. 'This was the old-fashioned pit house, outside toilets, no inside toilet, we went back in time.'[18] They were defined by their membership of the Beat Generation in Newcastle and by their joint radicalism, committed as they were to the Campaign for Nuclear Disarmament (CND), freeing Vietnam from the Americans, Palestine from the Israelis and Northern Ireland from the British army. Maureen visited the Palestinian refugee camps of Sabra and Shatila in 1977 (some five years before the massacre by a Lebanese militia under the eyes of the invading Israeli forces). Their profile as hippies and activists meant that they did not fit easily into the mining community in Dunscroft. Maureen recalled 'somebody shouting "gypo" at me in the street, which is for Gypsy, of course, you know, meaning insultingly, you know. I was more insulted on behalf of "gypos" than I was on behalf of myself.'[19] Lack of understanding in the local community, though, was compensated for by the fact that both Dave and Maureen were networked into national and international political activism.

Pete Richardson was committed to the strike because of much more local ties. Brought up in Askern, he described it laconically as 'close-knit really. I mean, the average for a mining village.' The mining heritage was strong: 'My dad worked at the pit, my granddad worked at the pit. He got a badge for working twenty-five years.'[20] He had issues with his father-in-law Jimmy Murphy, who had forcibly adopted Pete and his wife Sue's first child, but this did not affect his grief when Murphy died of a heart attack. 'The worst thing by far that happened to me in this year was the death of my father-in-law James Murphy,' wrote Pete in 'Confessions of a Picket'. 'One of the four chock fitters sacked . . . He was a very staunch union man was Jimmy.'[21] Pete and Sue stood together and raised four more children. Pete's dedication to his family and the community is exemplified by a letter he wrote in 1985, asking a football coach to 'come down and have a look at my lad Wayne play football for his club. He is 15½ and plays on the wing. He has been the club's top scorer for the last two seasons. I have big hopes for him, as have lots of others . . . He had a season with Doncaster Boys as well as trials for South Yorkshire Boys.'[22]

Fourteen years younger than Richardson, Steve Walker was brought up in Kexbrough, on the north-west border of Barnsley. He described it as a semi-rural, semi-industrial village, mainly council houses. Most people I knew or associated with – [their] parents worked in coal mines or associated industries. There were probably about three or four shops, two pubs in village and a working men's club.

He underscored the closeness of family and community by talking about his father: 'Harry Walker were a coalminer all his life. Started work at Pummer pit at age of fourteen I believe. Pummer pit were in Mapplewell, where I'm now living, and ironically I'm living on the street where he were born.' His three siblings managed to escape from the pull of the pit. One brother worked in a paper mill and a second was a welder, while his sister worked in sewing factories and woollen mills and went out with the lead singer of Barnsley-based rock band Saxon. Steve, hit by the wave of unemployment in 1981 as he left school, was the only one to become a miner, at Woolley colliery. He waxed lyrical about the camaraderie of the pit, below ground and above, inevitably fuelled by beer and sometimes becoming physical:

Friendship, looking out for each other and I mean looking out for each other because it were dangerous. Especially, well, underground it were very dangerous, so you, you've got to look out for each other. It's a bond, innit? . . . Pubs were handy, it were like Wild West at times. We were out three or four times a week, every week . . . Some at the older end you'd have to watch them if you were on nights because they were nasty buggers, because they'd been out in afternoon, and they'd come home, have their dinner, go to bed, get up feeling as rough as a bear's arse and go to work. And young lads then, if they got in their way, well [laughs] they wouldn't be adverse to giving you a clip if they got chance . . . There were always folks scrapping and carrying on, but they were still mates after it. Still went to work on a Monday morning and it were all forgotten. Didn't make any difference, some folks had a black eye and that but . . . [laughs].[23]

Paul Winter, a year older than Walker, was brought up on the other side of Barnsley, on the Kendray estate, built in the 1930s and 1940s as the town's slums were cleared. There miners lived side by side with steelworkers and glassworkers. As with Walker, mining was in the family: his grandfather had been a miner at Dodworth, as had his father and his three uncles. His mother worked at the bar of the working men's club, and her father, Jack Woofinden, was president of the NUM branch at Dodworth. While Walker described Dodworth as 'very militant', Winter called it a family pit, where you were known because your father was (or had been) there. On his first day, the training officer asked, 'Which one is Winter?' I said, 'That's me.' He said, 'Whose lad are you, John's, Walt's, Arthur's or Colin's?' I said, 'I'm John's.' Paul was also lyrical about the camaraderie in the pit, focusing on its black humour. His favourite story was of a mate who

had a shit on the floor and he dipped telephone earpiece in the shit. He put the handle back on and walked half a mile to ring me up. So, I picked this phone up and say, 'Ay up.' And I could hear him laughing and I got shit all in my earhole, right?

The camaraderie of the pit did not, however, transfer across coalfields, and especially not to Nottinghamshire. Paul traced this back to the bonus scheme introduced in 1977 which paid pits according to their productivity. This was higher in Nottinghamshire, which had twelve-foot seams, than it was in Yorkshire, where they were only four feet high. The inequality of pay and the decision to close pits in some coalfields but not others was part of a divide-and-rule policy that ensured that Notts miners would not come out on strike:

A face worker at Dodworth ended up on less money than a canteen worker in Nottingham. That's how incentive bonus scheme worked. And that slowly started to drive that wedge. So, you only need to sow that seed that's already there because people forget that in the '26 strike when they formed Spencer Union, it was Nottingham that broke. So you've got an Area that's notoriously moderate that's on tons and tons more money than anybody in any other coalfield . . . You've got Coal Board leadership saying, 'We want to shut twenty pits, they're in Durham, they're in Scotland, they're in Wales, they're in Lancashire, they're in Yorkshire but Nottingham is alright. You'll be alright. You're on this good money. You're productive colliers, you're making most brass. You'll get looked after if you keep working, it's all these militant awkward difficult pits that we're shutting.'[24]

Turning now to some of the working miners in Nottinghamshire, one of the most outspoken was Steve Williamson, born in 1953 and brought up in Cundy Cross, just east of Barnsley. His family life was disrupted and forced him to move between Yorkshire and Nottinghamshire. He explained that 'my dad, being a miner, like to go out Friday night, Saturday night, and Sunday night. My mum was a non-drinker, she would never go out. And every time he came in, it was World War III.' He was very close to his older sister, Pat, and used to sit on her knee as a child. Before she died, 'years, years afterwards', she told him, 'We never had any love when we were children.' His parents broke up when he was at school, and he moved with his mother down to Kirkby-in-Ashfield; then with his father back to Yorkshire; and then back to Nottinghamshire again. He never got the chance to become the motor mechanic he wanted to be, and instead followed his father down the mine. Nor was he able to keep his own life together, until he found both his best comrade (Area agent Roy Lynk) and a new wife (Tracey) in the same pub:

Second wife, seven or eight years [we were together], I think. We had twin boys. Plus I was going through a romantic entangle. I met my [third] wife through drinking where Roy Lynk went, and she worked behind a bar . . . I was playing the field to be honest. I was a poor husband, a poor father, I'd never had time for them. If I could go back,

I would apologise to my ex for what I put her through, because she went through the strike with me as well.

Steve's real home was the union, where he saw himself as 'a militant moderate'. 'The men at my pit wanted to get a fair day's pay for a fair day's work', and it was his job to see that they got it. He believed in negotiating with the employers and had no time for the militant NUM leaders. The fixed point in his universe was the NUM rule book and, he said, 'I used to train all my committee members and I would say that is your Bible. If ever you need any information, it's there.' The danger was that he isolated himself in a group for whom Rule 43 was the gospel and they would brook no compromise, even if their former comrades turned against them and their families:

I used to socialise with Roy Lynk and we used to go out with two policemen every night. Wherever we used to drink, there would be a couple of hundred strikers. We were never assaulted but when you've got two hundred [sic] eyes staring at you and when you go to the toilet and they all come in and try to intimidate. It's what they did. It's like they used to ring me up and say they were going to come and kill my kids . . . They never came and I knew they wouldn't come, but you know, when somebody rings up at twelve o'clock and says they're coming to get your kids, you don't sleep, do you?[25]

David Amos, four years younger than Williamson, was very much in his orbit at Annesley and had a similarly disrupted background. 'Generation wise, there's three generations of the Amos family worked in the pit. I was the last.' And there were three generations of miners on his mother's side, too. His parents divorced when he was ten, and both remarried when he was thirteen, 'so they'd not got a lot of time so basically, as I say to my daughter now, I had to make my own way in life as best as you could'. He moved away from the village of Nuncargate, near Annesley, to a council estate in Kirkby-in-Ashfield, where there was little sense of community. His neighbours were basically 'Jocks and Geordies' who had come down to work in the Annesley–Newstead–Bentinck group of mines. This enforced self-reliance and lack of trust in others perhaps explained Amos's attitude during the strike, when in any case he was living alone. Although he voted to strike, three quarters of Notts miners voted not to, and he now considered that he had a mandate from that majority. He became a target for intimidation by striking miners, but this only made him more obstinate in defence of democracy. At Annesley, only 50 out of 950 miners went on strike, but they were highly militant and Amos saw some justice in the fact that the worst of them met a brutal end:

> They made a beeline for me because they knew I had voted to strike, and then wasn't carrying what they deemed I should have been carrying, their strike mandate. And I said, 'No, it don't work like that' . . . They put extra pressure on me to try to conform to them, which had the opposite effect. I've lived in a rough area and that, I've never been one for scrapping for its sake. If you have to defend yourself, you will. But, I'm also one, that if anybody threatens me, and they start putting pressure, I do exactly the opposite of what they want. And that's what happened in them first few weeks of that strike, and how it played out eventually. There was one of the strikers got dismissed at Annesley, who later, twenty years after the strike, got murdered. He was an Annesley miner, his name were Keith Frogson. And, when I think of Scargillism now, I think of him.[26]

Mick Marriott, born at Kirkby-in-Ashfield during the war, had a similarly troubled background: 'I've got no father, I never knew who my father was. My mum struggled to keep the family together. Life was very hard at the time.' One of five sons, he was farmed out to his grandfather, a miner who had come to Annesley from Derbyshire, and then to an aunt. He described his family as 'a bit scattered and a bit at loggerheads at times'.

He married his brother's girlfriend, Christine, and the marriage lasted. At Annesley, he resented the 1966 National Power Loading Agreement, because 'you were more or less brought into line with all the collieries. And we lost a lot of money but they gained quite a bit.' He favoured negotiation, rather than confrontation, and argued that in the 1970s 'we had a good leader, Joe Gormley. He was a brilliant man. He was a negotiator. And he could sit down and negotiate a deal, unlike Arthur.' During the strike, he also came up against Frogson, but was more concerned by the dishonesty of another striker, who was said (although it was never proved) to have raised money in Australia for the miners and then kept it:

I used to work with [Frogson]. He was a staunch striker he was. And would just call everybody scabbing bastards. He was a bit of a fighter. Some people were frightened of him, intimidated by him . . . Another man on strike went Down Under doing the collection. He was collecting money for the miners. But the miners never saw any [laughs]. It was going in his pocket.[27]

A fourth working miner was Trevor Taylor, also born during the war, at nearby Sutton-in-Ashfield. His father worked at the nearby Teversal colliery, as he explained, 'I come from a split family where we've got two fathers. Me and my sister came from the first father. Then the others are like my half-brothers.' He married Susan, who had an office job at a hosiery company, when he was twenty-two, having bought his grandmother's house for £1,200. 'I was getting just under £9 a shift,' he recalled. 'I was walking home, after stoppages, with about £40 per week, which . . .' At this point Susan chipped in: '. . . was a lot of money'. Trevor said that he was a supporter of the interwar Spencer Union, because Spencer had set up a Nottinghamshire pension scheme under an agreement whereby 'for every ton of coal that turned in Notts, the coal owners paid an old penny into the Notts Miners Pension Fund'. By the 1980s, this was worth £90 million. 'We always said,' he quipped, 'that our friend Mr Scargill was after Notts to get his hands on the £90 million. And that continued until about 1994.'

Trevor and Susan's joint hatred of Scargill was patent. Speaking on the right to work rally at Berry Hill on 1 May 1984, Trevor remembered that 'They'd got effigies of Scargill on gallows, hanging him.' The working miners drowned out Chadburn and Richardson, 'Because they were Scargillites. If Scargill tell them to jump, they jump.' Susan again chipped in: 'Or they'll say, "How high?"' As the battles over the strike intensified, Trevor and Susan fell back on what she called 'our circle of friends', which included Mick Marriott and David Amos. 'We'd perhaps go out for a meal. For somebody's birthday or a wedding anniversary.' This did not include one family friend who was on strike – not, claimed Trevor, out of principle, but because 'he don't like work, so any excuse he could have, any excuse not to go to work. And he only stuck it for about half the time.'[28]

The question of the ballot was the rock on which the hoped for united front of the NUM foundered. It was exploited by the Coal Board and the government, through agents like David Hart, to form the embryo of a breakaway working miners' union, along the lines of the Spencer Union of 1926. This approach played on real differences between the coalfields and the relative autonomy they enjoyed within the NUM, but also increased divisions by not scheduling pits in Nottinghamshire for closure.

There were also differences between individual miners, although these are difficult to characterise. The four working miners portrayed above had disrupted family backgrounds, but so did striking miner Pete Richardson. The mining tradition was strong in striking miners' families, but the working miners' fathers were also miners. The striking miners underlined the importance of their close-knit communities, whereas Steve Williamson was shuttled from Yorkshire to Nottinghamshire and David Amos was critical of 'Jocks and Geordies' on his estate and Kirkby-in-Ashfield. On the other hand, the Dirty Thirty in Leicestershire also lived scattered between many communities, and the Girvan brothers were Scottish. The striking miners underlined the importance of camaraderie, while the working miners found themselves on the receiving end of hostility and even threats from striking colleagues. What united the working miners was an appreciation of the autonomy of the Nottinghamshire coalfield and the benefits of the bonus system, and a hatred of what they called Scargillism, which they regarded as interference by an alien radicalism, kicking them out of their jobs.

4

ORGREAVE

'I was at Orgreave' is a proud claim of many former miners, as if they had been at the Battle of Agincourt or Waterloo. It was indeed a battle, but one fought on unequal terms between T-shirted miners and highly organised police – some miners say together with soldiers posing as police. The mass picket of the Orgreave coke works near Rotherham was billed as a reprise of the Saltley Gate mass picket of February 1972, which had brought in 15,000 trade unionists and catapulted the young miners' leader Arthur Scargill to fame. The simultaneous blockade of power stations in 1972 had forced the Coal Board and the Tory government to capitulate to the miners' demands on pay, and in 1984 the government and the police were adamant that this must not happen again.[1]

The victory of 1972 was indeed not repeated. The strategy of the mass picket was criticised by many miners' leaders as erroneous, as it played into the hands of the police, who could dictate the terms of engagement and who had gained experience of corralling and softening up miners at the Mansfield rally of 14 May.[2] Subjected to extreme police brutality on the day, miners suffered a blow to their conventional masculinity and came away profoundly shocked and intimidated. This shock was also felt by their wives and families, who saw events unfold on the television news. Few made the connection that 18 June 1984 was the 169th anniversary of the Battle of Waterloo; but this time the miners were the French and Scargill a beaten Napoleon.

Orgreave, between Sheffield and Rotherham, was selected as the site for a showdown because it was producing coking coal for British Steel and notably its works at Scunthorpe. Since the rail unions, in support of the miners, refused to move coal, it was supplied by private haulage companies, which brought in coal from as far afield as Poland and South Africa, arriving in convoys of thirty lorries, three times a day.[3]

A great deal of support came from Sheffield, whose Trades Council called for a mass one-day strike and picket of Orgreave on 6 June. The president of the Sheffield Trades Council was Blanche Flannery, who had been converted to communism in the 1930s, after being taken to an open-air meeting on Attercliffe Common to hear the general secretary of the Communist Party of Great Britain, Harry Pollitt. Her schoolteacher husband, Martin, had been politicised by the Spanish Civil War and was elected Labour MP for Sheffield Hillingdon in 1974. He had addressed the Sheffield NUM delegates rally on 19 April and allegedly accused the police of breaking 'the Law of the Land'.[4] Their daughter Kate, who had just found a clerical job with Sheffield social services, had herself gone to a youth festival in Cuba in 1978 at the age of eighteen and had come back a Young Communist. She pointed out that

the Trades Council were very heavily involved in trying to get people out to Orgreave, to picket Orgreave, because the NUM had asked for people, from not just the NUM, but from the wider movement to go and try and persuade the lorries not to export the coke to Scunthorpe. And the railway workers were very heavily involved, because they were refusing to transport the coke, so that's why they were using scab labour in lorries. We were all part of that call to try and get people out to Orgreave. My mum was there, and she was involved in trying to get people there.[5]

On 18 June, however, the mass picket was mounted solely by the NUM. It was to be Arthur Scargill's day, a victory for the miners that would put the Thatcher government on the ropes. A great deal of organisation went into it, with miners being bussed in from Kent, Wales and Scotland, as well as from more locally. That said, many militants who might have been at Orgreave were not there on the day. Miners who had been arrested and taken to court were generally bound over to keep the peace and were not allowed to picket, except at their own pit. Other miners did not turn up for fear of arrest and jail.

Two who did not make it from Fife were Sean Lee and Tom Adams. Sean, a miner at Seafield, had been arrested at Cartmore in early June and sent to court in Dunfermline, where he was held over to prevent him going to Orgreave.[6] Tom Adams, from Frances, had avoided arrest at Cartmore, but had then been grabbed by a snatch squad at Perth, where a picket was trying to stop coal coming into the harbour. He was admonished by the sheriff court in Perth, which put him off the idea of going to Orgreave:

Part of this getting admonished was if we got caught on a picket line, arrested again, we would be immediately jailed. And that's why I never got to Orgreave, because I then says that I'm not going down there because if I get caught I'm gone. I'm in the jail. Bearing in mind I had two kids to feed on £13 a week.[7]

Meanwhile, in Yorkshire itself, Askern picket Pete Richardson had been arrested at the Mansfield rally on 14 May and sent for trial: 'I'd been banned from going then. I couldn't go. I had to stop at me own pit.'[8] Others who had already been beaten or intimidated or had heard of similar events did not wish to repeat the experience or to put themselves in danger. 'My boyfriend at the time was meant to be going up,' said Kate Flannery, but

he'd heard that people had been assaulted by the police at previous pickets and he set off to go and he was frightened. He set off and he thought, 'I just can't face this.' And so I was at work all day worrying about him, because I thought he'd gone to Orgreave. I didn't know that he wasn't there.[9]

Those who came to Orgreave recalled that there was indeed a great deal of organisation, with the ambition to repeat Saltley, but that the plans were far from secret. There was also doubt among some as to whether this mass picket was the best strategy. As Dave Potts, the NUM branch secretary at Manton, recalled:

The only time we got instructions where to go and what to do were at Orgreave. We got a letter on the Monday night, which we were told we shouldn't open until the Tuesday morning. Read it out to your men on Tuesday morning before you come to picket. They said it will be Orgreave, it will be very tense, with a lot of police and police dogs and horses. Told us what to expect. That was the only time we got leadership instructions from Arthur. It was at Saltley Gate, wasn't it, when the guy got killed? It was a success, apart from the death of a picket. He won with that. He thought would do it again.[10]

Dave Douglass, the branch delegate at Hatfield colliery, was a specialist in organising pickets that flew under the police radar. Although he was on the left and close to Scargill, he thought that the attempt at a Saltley Mark Two was a strategic error, referencing disputes at the Grunwick film-processing factory in 1976 and the Warrington printers' dispute of 1983:

Many thought Orgreave was Lourdes: all our sins would be cleansed there . . . It was in my view however a monumental mistake. Since Saltley we had lost just such showdowns, at Warrington and Grunwick. The police, knowing where we would be and how we'd got there, could move all their forces into pre-planned positions and reinforce them and change them at will. We on the other hand would be permanently tied down.[11]

Interviewed in 2020, Douglass reiterated his criticism about

> Centralising all of the pickets in the country at Orgreave . . . which the
> cops knew for weeks in advance, so they were able to assemble their
> cavalry, their dogs, rat squads and snatch squads and all the rest of it.
> So I totally disagreed with him about that.

That said, he admitted, he was 'in on the plan, I've actually still got the
drawing I did of the plan'. He and his 'anarchists' were given instructions
to try to take the Orgreave plant itself – 'We'd go in the back and seize the
plant while they were battling it out at the front.' They did, indeed, get
into the plant and were briefly in a position to tip the balance of power
against the police; but then the moment was gone:

> I led the assault into the back. There were no cops on the back, so we
> got in there. A handful of riot cops with short shields came up and told
> us to disperse. And one of the guys from Goldthorpe, which was a very
> militant pit – there was a stack of gate posts, railing posts – told
> everyone to grab one of these, so we all grabbed a big railing post. He
> said, 'Look we outnumber you fifty to one, bugger off.' So they
> buggered off. And we actually got to the loading bay, and there was a
> lorry, standing with its engine running, and a guy got out the cab and
> ran away. Now I didn't drive at that time. I said to one of my right-
> hand guys, 'Get in that lorry and drive it into the loading bay, smash
> it into the loading bay.' And we had the plant when, next thing we
> know is, all these riot cops sort of came back again. And the guy Barry
> Miller says to them, 'I warned ye, fuck off.' He said, 'No, you fuck off.
> The odds have changed.' And we looked around, and there was about
> twenty-five of us. The men had melted away.[12]

Meanwhile, in front of the plant, miners had gathered in their thousands, having come from all over the country to answer the call to fight at

the battle at Orgreave. The sun was shining and spirits were high, and this time, far from blocking their way to the plant, as they had been doing for three months on the borders of Nottinghamshire, the police were ushering them in, guiding them to the site. A few miners smelled a rat. As Bill Frostwick from Durham confessed:

We should have really known from the start, 'cause, as I said earlier, if you were trying getting to Nottingham, the police: 'You get back.' But they were advising us if we wanted to go to Orgreave, 'Just go down that road there.' And they were herding us to Orgreave because it was all planned. And you've got trainers on, shorts on and your T-shirt, up against someone in riot gear you haven't got a chance really. They were so well organised, man, it was a trap. And we fell for it, went straight in.[13]

A similar observation was made by Pat Egan, a twenty-three-year-old miner from Twechar, on the Lanarkshire/Dunbartonshire border, who had gone to work at Frances because all the pits in Lanarkshire had closed. When the strike broke out, he was sent back home by the NUM to organise the Cardowan Central Strike Committee to rally the miners who still lived in the area. Having just experienced the mass arrest of Scottish pickets trying to get to Hunterston power station, he was astonished that when they got to Orgreave they were not turned back by the police. He also emphasised the calm – even bonhomie – there was before the police attacked:

We travelled down the day before and we stayed at Whitley Hall, just outside Sheffield. And we didn't even know where Orgreave was. And the rest of the Scottish miners were staying at Northern College. So we got up in the morning, got our breakfast, got on the bus . . . So we were heading for Rotherham and the police stopped us. And, of course, we thought, oh well, here we go. We're getting turned back. 'Are you miners going to Orgreave?' 'Yeah.' 'Do you know how to get there?' 'No.' 'Follow us.' Now at the time we thought, 'That's weird.' We were on the bus and the police took us there and we got out. Again a glorious day. We went down and at the start it was just banter, in fact I think we were playing football with some of the police at the start, seemed to be the thing. And then you just seen crowds gathering and all of a sudden policemen in this field. The coal plant in front of you, you come down a hill and there was fields to that side and the railway to that side . . . Up here at the railway side was all police on horses . . . just along the side policemen with dogs. And then the next thing they just opened up, chased us all and you were running.[14]

Although Sean Lee was not himself at Orgreave, his brother-in-law Robert (Rosco) Ross was. A fitter and turner at the Cowdenbeath Workshops, Rosco was also branch secretary at Cowdenbeath of the Scottish Colliery Enginemen, Boilermen and Tradesmen's Association (SCEBTA), which was affiliated to the NUM, and on the Cowdenbeath Workshops strike committee. As such, he organised a busload of pickets from the Workshops to go to Orgreave. Like Pat Egan, he was struck by how easy it was to get to Orgreave, the relaxed demeanour of the police and the atmosphere of a miners' jamboree:

We got to Orgreave. Alexanders [the bus company] gave us a double-decker bus from Cowdenbeath Garage. We filled that bus, and we could have filled it twenty times over . . . We drove during the night, down to Orgreave. We got directed by the police, where to put the buses, to the picket line. All the buses were parked up. We then had to walk through where the police were. The police had ice-cream wagons, ice-cream salesmen. It was a scorching day, it was like going on a picnic . . . We were sitting on the top of this grassy mound, like a summer's day. We were roaring and shouting, and you can see the police presence was getting bigger, and bigger, and bigger. You could sit and talk to your mates, I mean, we met guys from Yorkshire, we met guys from Kent, and you're just sitting chatting saying, what's happening in your Area? Blah, blah, blah.

Rosco described a transition when the police line began to form, wearing full riot gear. For a moment, one miner thought that it would still be possible to continue the bonhomie, to jest with the police as a way of disarming them. But the mood had changed, and violence now broke out, with snatch squads arresting and beating up miners, and with the miners responding with bottles and stones:

You could look down to the bottom of the hill again and go, 'Holy hell, where did they come from?' Because the black line just got wider, broader, thicker. And then, when the riot shields came out, the front rank had the riot shields. And I'll never, ever forget the local comedian – every pit has got one, there's a character – he walked down the hill, and he started walking along the line of police going, 'Straighten up your tie, fix your hat.' And he's walking along the line, giving them all this, and he got halfway along the line, and the two shields opened up, and he got pulled in. And you could see them kicking him. Honestly. And that's when it got dirty. That's when the bricks started coming from the back. Bricks were hitting our own boys . . . I thought, 'Holy hell, this is going to kick off' . . . The shields would open up, ten, twelve of them would rush out with their batons, flail at everybody. Then they would grab a guy and pull him in. And once he's behind that shield, you could only bloody hazard a guess of what was happening. It was horrendous. When the police charge came, honestly, I'm a guy, I'm thirty years old, I'm in my prime, I play football, I'm pretty fit – I was terrified, I was shitting myself.[15]

Durham and Scottish miners were joined at Orgreave by Welsh miners. One of these was Philip James, a thirty-four-year-old picket from Seven Sisters in the Dulais Valley, who worked at the Treforgan pit. Like Egan and Ross, he was bemused by the fact that the police had not only let them through, but directed them where to go:

> We went up to Orgreave, stayed at Ripley in a house with no furniture, sleeping on the floor. When we got to Orgreave, the police were there. 'Park your van by there, boys.' Well, we assumed that the police were the same up there as they were down here, but they weren't. We parked the van, they said, 'Go up by there on that patch, by that cornfield.' Everyone was happy-go-lucky, tidy. Pretty much the same as being in Port Talbot at the time. We'd been up early so someone said, 'Let's have breakfast.' Someone said go over the [railway] bridge and on the industrial estate there's a café. So down we go.

Philip was impressed by the fact that miners had come from all over the British Isles, to the extent that he could not understand some of them. On the trip to the café, he said, 'This Scottish guy came with us. I tell you what, he had a real Scottish accent. Out of every ten words he said I could only pick up about three or four. He could have been talking another language.' But he, too, witnessed the sudden shift that turned a peaceful gathering into a battlefield:

> We had our breakfast, came back. Things had changed. You know when they time travel, they walk through a mist into a battlefield, with armies and swords and things like that. Ooof. It had erupted. They were all pushing, the miners up against the police shields, because the lorries must have been coming in by then. We got into the push, like. There were stones being thrown but they were falling short. The chap in front of me cut his head so we all started pulling back. During the trial one of the chief police officers said the sky was black with stones.

He became suspicious that police had agents provocateurs in the crowd, deliberately throwing stones short, so that the picket line would pull back, allowing the police lines to open up to allow through the horsemen and snatch squads. Going to the help of a comrade who was being hit, he was himself arrested and beaten:

> They opened the line, sent these horses out, snatch squads out. There was one policeman hitting hell out of the sky. So I thought, 'Shall I go in and pull him off?' I thought, 'You're going to get into trouble basically.' This policeman came up. I said, 'Here you better get him off him, he's going to bloody kill him.' He said, 'You're nicked you are.' That's how I got arrested. He had his arm round my neck, leading me towards the police line. I put my arm up to protest and he hit me on the head with a truncheon.

Philip was taken to a holding pen, and that evening to court at Rotherham, where he was granted bail ahead of a trial. His wife Marilyn was also appalled by the violence, but received little sympathy at the time. 'I saw him being arrested on the telly. I was watching the news. I phoned up the lodge at Treforgan. They told me I was a hysterical woman.'[16]

Meanwhile, back in Chester-le-Street, Elspeth Frostwick was also watching the lunchtime news and was confused and frightened by what was being shown:

> It came across that the pickets started throwing stones and being violent and then the police charged . . . I didn't know until the night time if [Bill] was alive or dead or in the hospital, or anything. But I saw that charge with the truncheons, and I thought 'God, they are all going to end up with broken skulls.'

The violence did not finish there. Around lunchtime, many miners went back over the railway bridge, away from the police lines, to find something to eat in the village or on the industrial estate. There they found themselves subjected to another wave of police attacks. Pat Egan gave an account of what seemed a gratuitous attack. Like Elspeth Frostwick, he described how the television images broadcast gave the impression that the police were responding to violence initiated by the miners:

We came away from that and we were sitting. There was a place where we went, it was like a wee Tesco's Local type thing. A wee place with sandwiches and maybe about eight or nine shops with a big grassy bit outside. And we were lying there eating our lunch, so to speak. And the next thing, the boy says, 'You'd better run.' This time the police came right up through the village and we'd just to run up the road wherever we could. They were just taking out everything in front of them. And then what made it worse was, when we got back up the road, and people are asking us, 'What were you doing attacking the police?' Because of how the BBC had reversed the tapes. We didn't know till we got home. A lot of mining villages were saying, 'What actually happened down there?' And people didn't believe us.[17]

Bill Frostwick, like his wife Elspeth, had the same impression that the media had cut and spliced the tapes to make it seem as though the violence was initiated by the miners. 'After that came out on TV and a lot of people saw violence,' he said, 'the story was the wrong way around. The miners got all the blame for starting up the trouble and when it all came down it was the other way around. It was the police.'

Faced by this violence, and wearing only T-shirts and jeans, the miners had no alternative but to run. Bill Frostwick admitted that he had to accept the humiliation of defeat on the battlefield, throwing himself on the mercy of local residents:

I ended up hiding in somebody's garden shed. Because if I kept on the road, the police was hitting everybody with truncheons and I said, 'This is not for me. I could get killed there, it's not worth it.' When I opened the shed door I says, 'Is there room for another one?' and then we all squashed in. But the residents of where we were, honestly, they were great. They kept coming out, and people who had been injured they were looking after them. They were offering us – it was a red-hot day – 'Do you want a drink of pop?' and I couldn't believe it.[18]

Rosco Ross was with a pair of brothers – also extremely tough; but they all ran. As it happens, the brothers were the sons of Alex Maxwell, the manager of the Cowdenbeath Workshops, who was also a local Communist councillor. According to Rosco, Maxwell seems to have contacted his opposite number at Orgreave to get them out of trouble:

There were mounted police, with three-foot long batons, just battering guys over the head . . . I was with two brothers, who both were black belts in karate, two of the hardest guys I've ever known in my life, Alex Maxwell's sons, Harry and Gordon. I quite believe they could take on six policemen and destroy them, but they ran with me. We ran through a cornfield, to get away from them. There was a police helicopter up above us, following us through the field, we hadn't a clue where we were. We didn't know the lay of the land, we didn't know how to get back to the buses, or anything. We got through the cornfield, and lo and behold, we came onto a road, a tarmacked road, that leads into Orgreave coke plant . . . Just then, a car drew up, the guy shouted, 'Get in lads.' We jumped in, we didn't have a bloody clue who it was . . . He said, 'I'll take you to the buses.' That was the manager of the coke plant.[19]

Although Orgreave was overwhelmingly a miners' affair, some women were also there. As we have seen, Kate Flannery's mother Blanche, president of the Sheffield Trades Council, was there as an observer, but Kate's boyfriend had bottled out. Perhaps the most iconic picture from Orgreave is of Lesley Boulton about to be struck by a mounted policeman wielding a baton. Dianne Hogg, a miner's wife from Askern who had herself been arrested for picketing in Nottinghamshire, travelled the twenty-five miles to check that her husband Pete – of whom she said 'the day I married him my life began' – was alright:

Dianne: And I went to Orgreave, and you see I weren't driving, I didn't know we were going to Orgreave, and you saw the row of the police, it was solid row after row. And the miners were just on the field then. The lorries hadn't come in. I found my husband straight away, out of all them.

Q: How did you find him?

Dianne: I don't know! Well, he's tall, good-looking [laughs]. But I saw him straight away. Of course he wasn't pleased.[20]

Elsie Potts's husband Bill, a miner at Warsop Main in Nottinghamshire, belonged to the small minority of Nottinghamshire miners who went on strike. Elsie and her daughter Lisa told the story of how she followed Bill to Orgreave and became separated both from him and from the other women. She then found herself being charged by horses:

Elsie: I'm stood there. I was looking for him and looking for Bill and then this hand comes on me shoulder. And I turned around and it were this chap and he said, 'Get out road, duck. They'll be letting them horses out now.' And he says, 'Come up here, I won't hurt yer.'

Lisa: He helped you into a tree, didn't he?

Elsie: And he got me up a bit of a wall and into a tree and horses were 'psst'.

Lisa: They charged, the police horses.

Elsie: I couldn't count. There were about eight horses.

Lisa: Big ones as well . . . You're still terrified of horses, aren't you?[21]

Even more striking is the story told by Dave Potts of Manton – no relation to Elsie – about the retreat of his young miners into Orgreave village in the afternoon. He had trouble rallying them, because all they wanted to do was to beg water from the inhabitants. Then their lack of courage was exposed in public by the theatrical gesture of an elderly female resident:

As we came down from the pit tip into Orgreave pit yard, that left us at the bottom where the houses were. There was a funny incident when we got down there. We'd got a bit battered by the police, the horses chased us through the fields. It was a hot day. Lots of lads had shirts off. They pushed us back against the bungalows, old people's bungalows. It was a hot day and they were knocking people's back doors saying, 'Can you give us a drink of water?' I said, 'We're not doing that. Get out lads.' The police came in their line. We lined up in front of the police. And an old lady came out of her bungalow, and she walked down the middle of the two of us – us on one side, police on the other – with her back to us and looking at the police all the time. And she'd got on her arm a handbag, I don't know what were in it, summat heavy. And she said [laughs], 'Have they been hitting you, lads?' And we said, 'One or two.' And she went [swipe] and she took out three policemen. She were about eighty-five, this woman. We loved it because the police didn't know what to do with her.[22]

The miners who went to Orgreave were left with a story that would remain difficult to tell. They had been subjected to brutal police violence, pitting riot shields, dogs and horses against their T-shirts or bare white chests on a bright June day, and were now being accused of triggering the violence that obliged the police to impose law and order on behalf of the great British public. They had travelled to Orgreave to repeat the victory of Saltley, but had been lured into a trap and comprehensively routed by a police force that many believed was reinforced by the army. About ninety of the miners were arrested and charged in exaggerated fashion with unlawful assembly and riot, which could carry a prison sentence of fifteen years. The trial opened in Sheffield after the end of the strike, in May 1985. The defence, led by Michael Mansfield QC, tore the fabricated police evidence to shreds, and the miners were acquitted on 17 July 1985.[23] About forty of them, among them Philip James, sued for compensation and were awarded the sum of £425,000, about £10,000 each. For Philip, this gave him a small triumph over the police who had been paid so handsomely during the strike and who had rubbed the faces of the hungry miners in it:

> This was about 1991 now and I'd had the money by the time this had come out and I told [Marilyn] what I'm going to do with this money. I'm going to buy a car and a caravan. When I see the policeman and he tells me, 'I had a car and holidays out of you,' I'll be telling him, 'I had a car and holidays out of you.'[24]

This quip illustrates how, in their story-telling, the miners who had been at Orgreave strove to recover a masculinity that had, in many ways, been left in tatters on the field. A trap had been set for them. They had fought against impossible odds. The bonhomie and bravura of the pickets was slapped down by a state that was determined to administer a beating they would never forget. This was followed by a show trial of miners indicted for medieval crimes and with false evidence. The miners recovered their honour and humour and turned the tables on the police and the state. Maybe Orgreave was the Battle of Agincourt, after all.

5

'CLOSE A PIT, KILL A COMMUNITY'

'Honestly, it never occurred to any of us that we could run a soup kitchen,' said Jean Crane, a miner's wife at Askern, even though at the time she was managing a newsagent's in Doncaster.[1] The NUM branch at Askern had set up a soup kitchen for striking miners in the Miners' Welfare, but it needed food and funds to sustain it and decided that this was something for the women. To begin with, the women went with collecting tins around the pubs and clubs of Doncaster and other nearby towns on a Friday night, when people had just been paid. Then Branch Secretary Pat Hewitt told Jean that there was a meeting in Doncaster about setting up women's support groups. 'I went in my lunch hour,' she said, 'and stayed two-and-a-half hours.'[2] She called a meeting to set up a group in Askern one Tuesday in May 1984 and invited her friend Dianne Hogg. Dianne had just lost her father to pneumoconiosis and was grieving, but she decided to get involved in order to take her mind off things. Jean became the secretary of the Askern NUM Women's Support Group and Dianne the treasurer.

A month or two into the strike, it became clear that the miners were in for the long haul. They had failed to bring out most of the pits in the Midlands because of the police blockade, the stubbornness of the working miners and limited success in preventing the transport of coal to steelworks or power stations. No income was coming into mining families, apart from the meagre pound or two per day provided by the NUM for pickets, which the government then deducted from any supplementary benefit due to a miner's dependants. The Easter holidays at the end of April and beginning of May meant that school meals were suspended and there was precious little in the larder at home.

The men of the NUM increasingly turned to their women for help. Many of them, like Dianne, were at home, running the household and raising the children; others, like Jean Crane, worked outside the home to support the family income. In some households, the men controlled the money; but in others, the women held the purse strings as the safest option, allowing their men pocket money for drink, fags and the betting office. The colliery was a male space, with women employed only as cleaners and canteen workers, and in the Miners' Welfare women were not supposed to buy drinks at the bar. Now things were changing. Miners' wives were increasingly becoming part of the struggle. They went picketing in minibuses provided by the NUM, and Jean and Dianne were at Calverton in June, where Dianne was arrested.[3] But they were also active on the home front, raising money, running soup kitchens and organising food parcels. Sometimes they worked with union men on the committees of support groups, and sometimes they organised their own women's support groups. Generally, the men and women cooperated well. They were fighting the same battle. But women were also enjoying a new autonomy, coming into their own, finding a new purpose and identity, and increasingly questioning the gender hierarchies that characterised mining families and mining communities.

In County Durham, Heather Wood had a rather different attitude to this question. 'There's a common misconception that women in mining communities are held down,' she said. 'Well it's the opposite actually. Mining women have always been the backbone.' She might have been speaking about herself. Her father's family was Scottish in origin and had come to Durham to work in the mines. Her father's father had died in the pit in 1928, the year her father was born, and he himself had narrowly escaped death in the Easington colliery explosion in 1951, the year she was born. Her mother's family was Welsh, and her mother Myrtle, intensely political, took Heather campaigning from a young age for better housing, education and the NHS. Heather was also highly combative: she gave up nursing because of the oppressive live-in regime, formed a union at a mail order firm in Sunderland when she was eighteen, and later became chair of the Constituency Labour Party. In October 1983, the year before the strike, she chaired a meeting at the Easington Miners' Welfare Hall which set up Save Easington Area Mines (SEAM).

Women may have been the backbone, but at its head SEAM was dominated by male councillors, miners and tradespeople. 'We need to get to the women,' declared Heather, since their support for the strike was crucial.[4] She took matters into her own hands, mobilising friends and family to leaflet all homes in the Easington district in order to contact miners' wives. The message was that pit closures would lead to school closures, shop closures and no jobs for their children as they grew up:

What future will there be for our children when they grow up? They will be forced to leave the area in their droves to find work, leaving behind an ageing population with no-one to take care of them. As the population falls and job prospects dwindle, schools will close, there will be a surplus of empty houses with the consequent reduction in values (as witnessed in the Consett area). There will be an upsurge of bankruptcies particularly amongst small businesses and local shopkeepers, and so the inevitable decline will continue in a sickening and depressing spiral, UNLESS WE CAN RALLY TO SAVE THE PITS through a vigorous campaign uniting all sections of the community in protest. While the NUM is fighting pit closures, we feel as women we should be giving our active support in many ways to protect the long-term interests and welfare of the community.[5]

Interested women were invited to a meeting in the council offices at the beginning of May 1984. The immediate task was to set up a soup kitchen in the Easington Working Men's Club, for the striking miners first, then for their families. Myrtle, who had just retired as a school cook, would teach the women how to make meals on a large scale. There was one obstacle standing in the way: they needed the permission of Easington lodge and its secretary, Alan Cummings. No woman had ever attended any of its meetings, and Heather was kept waiting while it was decided whether she could come in:

> When you opened the door there was Committee room table straight ahead of you. At one end was Alan Cummings and then all these men sat round. All round the walls were portraits or photographs of men, the only woman being the queen, the head. The picture in my mind is so vivid. There was a wooden threshold and I lifted my foot like that and I said to Alan, 'Are you sure? Because once it comes in it's not coming out.'[6]

Many of the miners who worked at Easington did not live there, but commuted from villages in the interior. Paul Stratford, a colliery mechanic at Easington, moved in the late 1970s with his wife Mary – the sister of his mate, Michael Hunt, secretary of the Durham Mechanics at Easington – to Great Lumley, near Chester-le-Street, where Michael and his wife Dorothy had already bought a house. In order to sustain the strike in County Durham, the union advised miners and mechanics who were no longer going to the pit to set up support groups in the villages where they lived. Michael called a meeting to establish a Great Lumley support group, which he chaired. Mary was elected secretary of the group, while Dorothy became treasurer. In this mining community, reflected Mary, it mattered 'whose wife you were, whose partner you were, whose sister you were'. But with the strike, miners' women were assuming responsibilities outside the home, in particular at soup kitchens and for the filling and distribution of food parcels for striking miners' families. This began to challenge the traditional rule of men in the public sphere. Until the strike, as Mary observed,

It was very matriarchal in the sense that my mother and grandmother all took care of the money in our family. There was never any idea of 'housekeeping'. My mum collected the wages, took all the responsibility and 'nurse-fed' the men. But the power lay in the hands of the men outside the home. The home was the women's domain but outside that – the Labour Party – the women's section had to defer to the NUM quite a lot.[7]

The Great Lumley operation was centred on the weekly delivery of food parcels. Mary was keen to establish the principle of self-help, rather than dependency, 'because it was about miners and their families doing it for themselves and supporting each other in the process'. In order to get a parcel, people had to come to the weekly meeting and volunteer to do something in return:

So whether you organise a raffle, or go street collecting, or you ask your brother-in-law who was a union rep to have a collection at their place, or you run a jumble sale or you do a quiz night. Whatever you do, you got to do something.

In addition, as in the case of herself and Paul, there had to be cooperation between the miners and their wives. 'There was no way it was ever going to be all women or all men because there weren't enough of us. And we were in it together. It was men and women together.'[8]

Still further inland, on the outskirts of Consett, was the mining village of Leadgate, where miners at local collieries such as Crookhall or Eden historically supplied the iron and steelworks. The initiative for a support group was taken by two union men, Dave Wray, who had been secretary of the Durham Mechanics' Association at Eden colliery, but who moved to Sacriston pit when Eden closed in 1975, and Norman Henderson, secretary of the Durham Miners' Association at Eden before he, too, moved to Sacriston:

Norman and I decided to have this meeting in Leadgate club and try to organise something. And it became obvious that we needed somewhere not to give people food, but to feed them. As I said, we lived in streets of miners' houses; we still live in it. And at the top of the street there is a Methodist chapel. So I called the minister and, I don't remember the conversation, but I said, 'We are looking for somewhere where there is a kitchen; do you have a kitchen that we could use?' He said, 'Yes, there is a kitchen; there is a big room where you can have food. You can have it Monday, Wednesday and Friday.'[9]

The support group included Dave Wray and his wife Dorothy, who, when their daughter Sam was little, took a part-time job at the Post Office, and then, during the strike, at a corner shop, 'because the Post Office were not keen on anybody who was a bit mouthy'. She hated cooking, but would peel potatoes and do the washing up. During the school holidays they were able to use the school kitchens, and miner's wife Mary Clark 'was in seventh heaven, because it has all these cooking facilities, so big-style cooking, you know. Mary was making pies and she was over the moon.'[10] They had trouble from the local greengrocer, who told them, 'Get yourselves back to work,' but they enlisted the help of the Chinese restaurant owner (who had a potato peeler) and the Young Men's Christian Association, which had a van with which they could do the shopping at a local cash-and-carry and bring in striking miners from down the valley for the soup kitchen.

The miners' unions in County Durham decided to set up a federal system that would bring all the support groups together to decide aims and strategy; this became known as the Durham Area Miners' Support Group. The initiative came from Billy Etherington, the general secretary of the Durham Mechanics' Association, who 'lent' his secretary, Anne Suddick, a woman of huge commitment, to set this up. There was, according to Mary Stratford, the danger of a 'power grab' by the leadership of the Durham Miners' Association. To 'stop the union, ergo men, from dominating the whole thing',[11] she contacted Heather Wood at SEAM, as well as her Labour Party friend Pat McIntyre (who had recently been pipped to the selection at Sedgefield by one Tony Blair) and her husband Vin, careers officer at the university:

> So they came and we had a meeting, quite a lively meeting, actually, and we eventually thrashed out that there wouldn't be a committee . . . Every support group could send anybody. If you went to the meeting you got a vote, and it would be the decision of the meeting as to what you would do. So it was very much about not letting any particular group take control of the whole thing.[12]

In addition, meetings were moved from the Durham miners' headquarters at Redhills to the Crossgate Club in the city. This opened the support group movement to a whole host of other activists outside the miners' union – and above all to women.

The women of County Durham had their struggles with the union men, but generally managed to get the better of them. In Fife, these disagreements were, if anything, more acrimonious. At the beginning of the strike there were soup kitchens, run by women, but only for striking miners. It was assumed that miners' wives would feed themselves and their children at home. But miners' wives had no more resources than their husbands, and when the Easter school holidays arrived matters became pressing. Conventional, sexist attitudes were reinforced by the dominance of the Communist Party in the union and the strike centres – and not least by the chairman of the central Dysart strike centre, Communist councillor Willie Clarke.

In Lochgelly, three women (two of whom had done the same in 1926) would cook a midday meal at the strike centre for miners returning from the picket line. For Linda Erskine, this approach was problematic. Her husband George was a turner-fitter at the Comrie pit and was on the strike committee at Lochgelly; meanwhile, she worked full time as a lab technician at Auchterderran Junior High School and had two children aged six and eight. When the Easter holiday began, she went to help the cooks, who were smoking while they prepared the potatoes for stovies (a potato and onion stew) for two hundred miners. 'Where are the families?' she asked. Back came the reply, 'Ocht, lassie, this is a man's strike centre!'[13] She was stunned: 'We can't be feeding one half of the population and not the rest of their families.' With one of the cooks – who was a shop steward in the National Union of Public Employees (NUPE) – she decided to call a meeting of women and set up a support group to organise the feeding of whole families:

> There must have been a lot of women who didn't feel they had any support at all. I'm sure they had friends and acquaintances. But as it was, I think it was about forty-five women turned up, which was amazing. And I wasn't even at the meeting because by this time I was back at work. But I had sent a letter to them saying I was hoping that we could get a Women's Group together. And I said if we do get a group set up, we need to have constitution because we'll need to look at raising funds and stuff like that. So this was read out and the women agreed and when I came back home from my work that night, I found out that I'd been elected the Secretary in my absence because I had the sense or the fortitude or whatever to put the letter together and to get it organised.

This was the easy part. The idea of feeding whole families in the strike centre did not go down well with the miners. 'Because there were hundreds of bairns, it was really noisy,' Linda admitted. 'The men didn't like that. To placate them they organised a separate sitting for the women and the bairns.' Then there was the question of fundraising for the support group and its activities. They began to sell things that they had cooked and made – 'one girl made the most amazing rag dolls', which sold for £15, and soon they had a fund of £300 in a separate account. This brought them into conflict with the Dysart Central Strike Committee:

They came to us and said, 'You'll have to give us half your money.' 'What?' 'Yeah, aye, because you're part of the strike centre and all our income has to go to the Central Strike Committee.' I'm going, 'That's not happening. We're buying our own food.' We were getting great donations from the local butchers and bakers and stuff as well, right enough. And I said, 'The money's not going back there. If we're raising it here it's staying here and it's feeding the people in Lochgelly.' Willie Clarke wasn't happy with that because he wrote me a letter.

This standoff was especially galling because the women of Fife were an integral part of the strike effort, and the NUM leadership knew it. The support of miners' wives was demonstrated in mass rallies which demonstrated that the strike was not just about men's jobs, but was about defending communities and families. Linda Erskine reflected:

I think they began to realise the benefit of having the women onboard. And I kid you not, they'd say, 'You're going on a rally on Saturday.' 'Right, so where are we going?' 'Aberdeen this week.' And the next week it was Chester and then another week it was London. We were like lemmings, we just got on the bus and went wherever we were sent.[14]

Two or three miles away, in Lochore, there was a similar issue. The soup kitchen at the Miners' Institute was only for men. Margaret Mitchell – whose father had been killed in an explosion in the Lindsay pit, Kelty, in 1957, when she was six months old, and whose husband David was a fitter at Seafield – had worked in the Babygro factory in Cowdenbeath and for GEC in Glenrothes new town, but now had twins aged four. As in Lochgelly, she and a few women whose husbands were on the strike committee at the Miners' Institute went there to sort out the problem. 'The women in the kitchen weren't happy that they were feeding the wives – they should be cooking it themselves,' she said. 'So we took over the kitchen.'[15]

To run the soup kitchen and to raise funds for it, they set up a committee, and Margaret became its vice-president. The president they elected was Mary Coll, whose grandfather, Gustav Keicher, was a German Catholic who had come to Scotland to work as a barber and had been interned during the First World War. Her father was a miner at Glencraig. She herself had worked in domestic service and in 'hundreds of factories' and had left an abusive first marriage, before marrying Owen, a miner at Castlehill. The reason she had become president, she admitted, was because she was 'more vocal then and more fiery'. They had a decent relationship with the strike committee, although its treasurer, George Bauld, was rather tight with money. They raised a great deal of their own through raffle tickets, jumble sales and bingo. Mary worked for Bayne's, the local baker, who 'was really good. He used to send us our rolls and bread and everything for the soup.' They also worked with the miners, who went in vans 'up to Kinross to the farmers where there were plenty tatties and turnips and things like that. They used to come back with bags of tatties and turnips and everything so we could get fed.'[16]

Cath Cunningham, whose husband Harry was the picket organiser at Cowdenbeath and a delegate to the Dysart committee, did not mince her words about how difficult it was to shift the thinking of the union men:

We made sure at the beginning that we got our women's committee set up. We had a hell of a week, shouting and swearing at each other, men and women. But we had to get ourselves established, we had to make the men see.[17]

Cath became the spokesperson of the Fife women on the Dysart committee, going head to head with Willie Clarke. The chair of the Cowdenbeath Women's Action Committee was Carol Ross, who had seen one of her sisters die in foster care; she had two children, aged four and eight, both diagnosed with cystic fibrosis, but she did not hesitate to throw herself into the fight. Her husband Robert (or Rosco) was branch secretary of SCEBTA at the Cowdenbeath Workshops and was on its strike committee; but this did not necessarily help. The women had little trouble opening the soup kitchen to families, as well as to striking miners. The main issue arose as autumn set in and they worried about how they were going to heat their houses, now that their coal allowances had been stopped by the Coal Board. Carol's third child, Cameron, had been born in August and was in hospital with viral pneumonia. The only way to get the coal allowance was for a GP to sign a note to the effect that a child was ill; but the GPs refused to sign and the strike committee – despite Rosco's presence – refused to prioritise the issue. As Carol recalled,

'Ah well,' said them, 'we'll bring it up at the next committee meeting.' And I said, 'And when's the next committee meeting, then?' 'Oh, I think it's not due 'til Friday. It'll not be 'til Friday.' I said, 'No, that's not good enough.' So after we had fed everybody that day, I said to all the women, 'Right' – the clinic was right next door to the strike committee – I said to them, 'Right, girls, come on, let's go, the men aren't going to do anything, we'll do it.' So we marched out of the strike committee, up to the clinic, up to the doctor's surgery, and we had a sit-in. And the men were absolutely livid. Livid with rage, that we'd had the audacity not only to defy them, because they hadn't given us permission, but the very fact that we had a sit-in, and we were taking everything away from them.[18]

The emergence of women in the public sphere posed a challenge to many a miner's sense of traditional masculinity. During the strike, they were no longer earning money or enjoying the camaraderie of work. They had fought on the picket lines, but had been defeated at the battles of Hunterston, Ravenscraig and Orgreave, where Carol's husband had beaten a retreat. Now they seemed to be losing control of their womenfolk, who were becoming active in their own right. Cath Cunningham drew an interesting distinction between the men's attitude to the role of women in general and to the role of their own wives:

The men liked the women to be involved. It's alright for other men's wives to be involved, but not for their own particular wife. Not my husband, but there were men like that. When you think about it, they had never been in the house with the children before, and doing the domestic role. It was a step up for us. All the things we were getting involved in were new and exciting, whereas they had taken a backward step, because they didn't have their workplace involvement, and maybe they had to take second place to some things we wanted to do.[19]

She admitted that the change of gender roles was also a challenge for her husband Harry. He was at home with the baby and unable to process his feelings, while she was out in the world. It made her feel guilty, but at the same time she personally felt transformed:

My husband would get depressed at times. I'd say, 'What is it?' 'Nothing, I'm alright, there is nothing wrong with me.' But it was getting him down. I was at work and he was watching the baby. I felt guilty being back at work and should have been at home with the baby. I was coming to Dysart. I was attending meetings. I felt as if I was bionic. A lot of women felt like that during the strike.[20]

In South Wales, the relationship between union men and miners' wives was a good deal more cooperative – partly because the union realised that the women were more experienced in the supply and distribution of food, and partly because the threat of government sequestration of union funds in late summer forced a formal separation between the union and the support group, for fear that its funds would be sequestrated, too. What also became clear was that women were coming out of their shells as a consequence of assuming organisational or speaking responsibilities in the public sphere.

The key figure was Hywel Francis, lecturer at Swansea's external studies department and founder of the South Wales Miners' Library, who lived in

Crynant. He observed that strikes stood a greater chance of success if they were supported by local communities. He convened a meeting of the chairs of the Blaenant and Treforgan lodges and Phil Bowen, the Blaenant chair, became chair of the support group. Miner's wife, ex-postmistress and community activist Hefina Headon was asked to become secretary. Hywel himself volunteered to be treasurer and used his address book to solicit donations. He was especially proud that then 'my sister's sister-in-law, Sally Head, who was a successful BBC producer, did a whip-round inside the BBC and that raised £700'. The domination of the union men did not last long, and women were brought in to look after the organisation. As Hywel explained,

The union then around about the same time said that there would be food centres to be set up and they voted £1,000 to each centre, and there would be about ten of them or whatever. The lodge started to use that money that they'd been given very foolishly. They sent a miner to go to the local shops to buy what they considered to be essentials, like bags of sugar, lots of tea. So we had to sack, get rid of those people and we took a decision early on that all the food centres had to be led by women who knew what common sense dictated. The women knew what food to buy and so on.[21]

Leadership of the food centres was provided by Kay Bowen, Phil's wife. Kay suffered at school from undiagnosed dyslexia and had worked for a couple of engineering companies, before getting married at twenty and having four children. She developed a large-scale enterprise, organising the supply of food from Tesco's in Neath, but also keeping local shopkeepers in business. Onllwyn Welfare Hall was used as a warehouse, where weekly provisions were made up for each of the ten food centres in the villages of the Neath, Dulais and Swansea Valleys, where in turn food parcels were made up for striking miners' families. There was a powerful egalitarianism at work. As she said:

Every parcel was to get the same amount, whether it was a family or a single miner, because to me, you couldn't really do it any other way. We were actually supporting the *miner*, or the person who worked in the colliery, to make sure if there were children in it that they would have more fruit maybe, but that was all. Every parcel was the same.[22]

Structures had to be modified in late July and early August, when the news came through that the government was seeking to hit the NUM hard by sequestrating its funds. It was felt best that Phil Bowen should hand over the chairmanship of the support groups to Hywel Francis, who was not a miner. Hywel handed the treasurership over to Christine Powell, who gave maths tuition to his children, Hannah and Dafydd, and who, he was convinced, was a maths teacher (although she insisted that she taught physics). Hywel then recruited the services of Phil Thomas, a Cardiff law lecturer friend, to go to the bank to withdraw the support groups' funds. The bank manager, said Hywel,

> didn't know what the bloody hell had hit him. He'd just come back from holiday. I think he'd had a bereavement as well and there was a delegation of about six of us, plus Phil, and Phil threw the law at him. He was in a panic and we said, 'We'll hold you personally responsible. We want this money released now' . . . So within the hour we had the whole bloody lot, but then, I don't know what it was, £5,000, £6,000, but we didn't know what to do with it. So we gave a lump of it to the local baker, another lump to the food store and I still had about £3,000 or £4,000 left at home.[23]

Christine Powell, as the new treasurer, was entrusted with the money temporarily. She thinks there was a good deal more of it, and she found the experience rather scary:

> We dealt in cash and at one point I think I had about £35,000 worth of cash under the spare bed in the house. At the time Stuart was working

three nights a week, safety shifts on the pumps. So I was in the house on my own with about £35,000 in cash and the dog sleeping on the spare bed.[24]

In the Afan Valley, which runs down to Port Talbot, and the Llynfi Valley, which runs down to Bridgend, there was similar cooperation between the union men who set up the support group and the women who ended up running it. After the strike began, a meeting was called by Phil White of St John's colliery, the right-hand man of the lodge secretary, Ian Isaac, at the Miners' Institute in Nantyffyllon, just outside Maesteg:

> Idwal Isaac, Ian's father, became the chair. Donna Jones was the secretary. Shirley Wells, who was the deputy headmistress of the local secondary, became the treasurer. So we constituted ourselves as the Llynfi-Afan Valley Miners' Support Group. But I was heading up there. I was overseeing it. Very close, that relationship that was there between the support group and the lodge. Because it had to be.[25]

Donna Jones, from Blaengwynfi, where the Afan pit had closed in 1969, was extremely well equipped to be secretary. Her own family had been devastated by mining hardship, and she had turned down a place at Bristol University to bring in an extra salary working for the National Insurance Office.[26] As her daughter Jude recalled:

> On a Sunday, she would have the cheque book out and she'd be looking at all the stubs. My brother and I were, 'Don't go in the kitchen. Mum has got a cheque-book face on.' Now I realise she was balancing the books for the family. She was making sure we had enough money.[27]

Through her work, which involved ensuring that miners obtained the compensation due to them for mining injuries and illnesses, Donna was well connected with the GPs who worked in the Valleys (and with their wives). These included Brian Gibbons, the left-wing doctor in Blaengwynfi, and Julian Tudor Hart, who combined his general practice in Glyncorrwg with research on pneumoconiosis and with standing as a Communist Party candidate in elections. Tudor Hart's wife Mary, of Welsh farming stock, had studied in Vienna and been arrested in London on a peace march in 1963, before becoming his research assistant. Donna Jones saw Julian as 'quite a revolutionary doctor then. A man of the people really', and fondly remembered the parties given by Mary in Glyncorrwg or in their cottage on the Gower Peninsula to sustain the support group workers.[28]

Donna Jones was not accustomed to public speaking, but had to do it in order to prise money out of Afan Council in Port Talbot, so that miners' children could be provided with shoes and warm clothing for the coming winter. She went to the council meeting with Idwal Isaac, the support group chair, who told her blithely, 'You won't have to say anything at all. I'll say it all for you.' It did not work out like that, as Idwal was banned from speaking; instead, it was Donna's passion, indeed her tears, that secured funds for the children:

Idwal got up, opened his mouth, said something political and they said, 'Mr Isaacs, this is not a political issue. Will you please sit down? Is there anyone else here that can speak?' Oh my God. I'm going to have to get up now and speak. So they said, 'Mr Isaac do not prompt.' So I'm standing there thinking, 'What am I going to say?' So I just said what I felt. Tried not to say anything political. You know, it was the winter. It had been months. The children were going back to school. We had two hundred children. I thought that, you know, the majority of the wealth for the people in Port Talbot had come from the mines in the beginning. That they were glad enough to take our money when our kids would go down to the beach. Why couldn't we have some-thing back and how are we managing? I said, 'Well we're actually managing because we're trying to be resourceful and we've had to cash in all our insurance policies, all our endowments and everything just to keep yourself going. So the majority of us are without house insurance and life insurance and things like this.' And I could feel myself starting to cry and I thought, 'Oh God, I'm crying now.' It said in the paper afterwards, 'Miner's wife cries and gets £5,000.' And I came out and I said to Idwal, 'Well if crying will get us £5,000, I don't mind that.'[29]

The most difficult situation for support groups was in Nottinghamshire. Here the striking miners were in a minority and were not backed by the union. Miners' wives set up action committees to feed the families of striking miners, but were opposed by most people in the community. The pressure also told on families, which were divided, and on relations even between husbands and wives, where roles were being renegotiated.

Elsie Potts, who had gone to rescue her husband Bill at Orgreave, lived in Warsop Vale, a mining village technically in the Derbyshire coalfield that had been built in the 1890s by the Staveley Coal and Iron Company to serve Warsop Main colliery, where Bill worked.[30] Their daughter Lisa explained that 'Around here the striking miners were in the majority. But in the collieries nearby, like Clipstone, Ollerton and Welbeck, which were all Nottinghamshire, and Forsby, the strikers were in the minority.' During the strike, Elsie, a dinner lady, became involved in the Warsop Main Women's Action Group, which ran a soup kitchen and food parcel service in the Church Warsop Memorial Club. It was not the easiest place to work, continued Lisa, because the legacy of the General Strike weighed heavily in the area:

Church Warsop is a satellite village of Warsop Vale. It was built during 1926, at the time of the General Strike, and it was actually built to house the miners who went back to work and their families. In actual fact it is still to this day called 'the alley', short for 'scab alley', that goes back to 1926. You know the General Strike. Then you know it's locally referred to as 'the alley'.[31]

Just up the road from Church Warsop was Meden Vale, known as Welbeck Colliery Village until the 1960s. That is where Anne Heaton (later Hubbell) lived when she worked as a cleaner at Welbeck colliery. Her husband Harry was the training officer at the colliery and voted to strike; though she initially voted not to strike, she soon came round to the cause. She became involved in the Welbeck Women's Action Group where, she said at the time, 'we've all found a common cause. We've found something we believe in and we're pulling the same way.'[32]

At Welbeck, as Lisa Potts observed, most of the miners were not on strike, following the line of the Nottinghamshire NUM. The Welbeck Women's Action Group occupied the village hall to set up a soup kitchen, but it was ejected by the NUM, which wanted the hall for itself. The women protested outside the hall, but a working miner came up, tore up a fistful of grass and threw it at them, saying, 'Eat that!' In September, they organised an occupation of the village for five days and barricaded themselves in. Their occupation became a *cause célèbre*, with supporters visiting from other pit villages and even a film company taking an interest. The occupation ended when the local council gave them full use of the school facilities for their soup kitchen. This celebrity led to calls to spread the word about women's action during the strike. Anne was invited to London, and spoke in public for the first time. It was frightening, but gave her a new confidence in her abilities:

All our lives all we've ever done is looked after our families, washed the dishes, cooked the meals, cleaned the house. We've been kitchen-sink women all our lives. We've never had to do anything like this. So when you have to stand up and speak it's terrifying. Your knees shake, your bottom lip shakes. I think we've got more confidence in ourselves. We do things we'd never thought of doing.[33]

Anne felt that their action was good not only for the women, but also for the men. 'It boosts the men's morale, to get together with the wives and the children, and laugh and joke,' she said. 'If you just stand on the picket line you get depressed.' Their action, however, was also a challenge to traditional husband and wife roles and put her marriage under pressure. 'Harry doesn't mind me doing,' she began, referring to her new life as an activist, but then she thought again:

Now, if he says anything to me, I just give him one back. Occasionally we'll have a bit of a grumble. A couple of weeks ago we really had a blow up. I think all the street could hear us. The pressure builds up and sometimes you have to let fly.

Her final line was, 'I won't be happy to go back the way I was.'[34]

Under the slogan of 'Close a Pit, Kill a Community', the strike broadened out to mobilise threatened mining communities and the womenfolk who were defending those communities – and their own families, too. Generally, men and women worked together over this campaign, and the support of the women encouraged the men to keep fighting. But there were also issues. Women often came up against the traditional sexist attitudes of the union men, who thought that, while the support of the women was appreciated, they should stick to a subordinate role. Some husbands had similar thoughts about their wives spending more time outside the home. And yet, it was through their support for the strike that women gained in confidence and developed a sense of their own identity. Lastly, support in the community was far from universal, even in Areas where the strikers were in a majority. But where they were in a minority, as in Nottinghamshire, both the union and the community opposed them, making their campaign extremely difficult.

6

'WE ARE WOMEN, WE ARE STRONG'

On Saturday 12 May 1984, a national women's rally was held in Barnsley for women's support groups from all over the country. Although only two thousand women were expected to attend, in fact around ten thousand poured into the town from Kent, Staffordshire, Yorkshire, Lancashire, County Durham and Wales. Jean McCrindle, a lecturer at Northern College in Barnsley and one of the organisers of the event, wrote in her diary that there was

> A marvellous, exciting, exhilarating, jubilant crowd of about 10,000 from all over the British coalfield. Only Scotland was absent. Beautiful sunny day. Banners made by women and children with small slogans, colliery banners and men at the back. Drum majorettes interspersed at beginning, middle and end . . . We all had our shirts printed with Women Against Pit Closures and we marched at the front with Jack [Taylor] and Arthur, 'the most kissed man in Barnsley' the TV called Arthur who loved every minute of it. Signed a hundred autographs on bras, bared backs and T-shirts and quite amazed at the sight of it all. Women sang and shouted themselves hoarse (me included) and couldn't stop dancing.[1]

The women marched to a meeting in the Civic Centre, where they were addressed by the Yorkshire miners' leader, Jack Taylor, and NUM leader

Arthur Scargill, who for the first time recognised the part that women could play and urged them to join the picket lines on which so many men had been arrested. Among the women who spoke were Maureen Douglass (wife of Dave Douglass, miner at Hatfield Main and picketing supremo in the Doncaster Area) and Lorraine Bowler (a miner's wife, student at Northern College and one of the Barnsley Women Against Pit Closures). Lorraine declared that:

> Men and women should work together. We ought to be one voice as a working-class movement shouting at the government and MacGregor ... We as women have not often been encouraged to be involved actively in trade unions and organising. It has always been seen as belonging to men. We were seen to be the domesticated element in the family. This for many has been the role expected of us. If this government thinks that its fight is just with the miners they are sadly mistaken. They are now fighting men, women and their families. I have only one message now and that is for Mrs Thatcher and her government. Men, women and families are together and now you've got a bloody hell of a fight on your hands.[2]

For Lorraine Bowler, the most important thing about the Barnsley rally was women leaving domesticity and adopting a public, organised role, alongside their menfolk in the NUM. Henceforth they would not simply be wives and mothers, but would fight against the Thatcher state, 'men, women and families'.

Jean McCrindle, who chaired the meeting in the Civic Hall, had a slightly different take, which was explained by her background as a communist and a feminist. 'I came from a political family,' she said in a 2012 interview. Her parents were both Scottish communists, inspired by the anti-fascist struggles against Oswald Mosley in Britain and the Spanish Civil War. Aged seventeen in 1954, she joined the Young Communist League and was briefly engaged to Marxist intellectual Raphael Samuel. Her father stayed loyal to the party after the Soviet invasion of Hungary in 1956, but she broke with it and joined the New Left, falling in love with another Marxist intellectual, E.P. Thompson. While a student at St Andrews, she was introduced by Thompson to Lawrence Daly, a miners' leader of Irish Catholic origins who also broke with the Communist Party in 1956. She remembers tracking him down to Lochgelly Miners' Club, where he was singing Irish folksongs and she joined in with Scottish ones. Converted to feminism by Simone de Beauvoir's *The Second Sex*, she tried to spread the feminist gospel to a group of miners' wives in Ballingry, and then to miners' wives in Lanarkshire, when she became an organiser for the Workers' Educational Association in Glasgow in the early 1960s. The huge challenge for Jean and other socialist feminists was precisely to combine socialism and feminism: 'to spread our ideas to working-class women, whether more nurseries or abortion on demand'.[3]

After 1979, as a lecturer at Northern College – an adult education college for working-class people, sponsored by the trade unions – Jean taught political thought and women's studies. She herself became involved in the Miners' Strike because, as she told Sheila Rowbotham in 1986, 'there were groups of women up at Northern College as students who were miners' wives or married to men who were students of ours, who wanted to set up a women's group in the Barnsley area, and they did that in the first week of the strike'.[4] This group was the Barnsley Women Against Pit Closures (BWAPC), with Jean McCrindle elected as treasurer, and as secretary Marsha Marshall – a miner's wife from Wombwell. For McCrindle,

This was the opening we'd always wanted to have. Not just groups of middle-class people like ourselves but a big section of the working class. This was our achievement, to help the working class to organise and to articulate their lives.[5]

There were, nevertheless, tensions within the Barnsley group between university-educated socialist feminists, like Jean McCrindle, and miners' wives, who lacked that education but were gaining in experience and confidence, and who came to challenge the women who had initially trained and organised them. 'We were always anxious about people calling us a bunch of privileged, middle-class women,' admitted McCrindle.[6] This was not surprising, as she had a rather top-down way of doing things: 'I probably had all those skills to do all that organising,' she said of the 12 May 1984 rally; but she did not fully understand why some of the working-class women in the Barnsley Women Against Pit Closures movement resented her leadership. As she confided to her diary,

> Tonight WAPC try to sort out all our hostilities to do with Anne H[unter]'s aggression. She tries to defend herself, then defuse it, then throw it back on me, then when most of us have had our say she lashes out and sulks. Lorraine [Bowler] has a go at me too. Both say I'm patronising and maybe I am but I'm not sure what they mean.[7]

One of the disputed questions was whether feminism was initiated by educated, middle-class women in the women's liberation movement, or whether it emerged organically from women in the labour movement. After the strike, Jean told fellow socialist feminist Sheila Rowbotham:

> I get told off by some miners' wives – articulate miners' wives who've been at Northern College – for claiming that it was somehow or other feminism that thought up all these ideas. They like to think that it has been created by the miners' wives as a working-class feminism which owes very little to the women's liberation movement. And they are quite fierce with me about it. But I can't really accept that there were none of these ideas floating around because I know that there were. I was teaching them myself for six years.[8]

Miners' wives indeed developed their own brand of feminism and were very possessive of it. Unlike the women's liberation movement, it incorporated a dimension of class, so that they saw themselves as women fighting alongside their men to defend their class. As Marsha Marshall said,

> This is a women's fight as well as a men's. Thank God there are women like us who intend to fight and protect their class in the same way that MacGregor and Co. are fighting to protect the interests of theirs.[9]

Betty Cook, the miner's wife who was also a shop steward in the Union of Shop, Distributive and Allied Workers (USDAW), argued that 'working-class feminism' was explicitly a pushback against middle-class feminism, which emerged from their own experience of struggle:

> The middle-class women in the movement already knew about feminism through reading, campaigning and the camaraderie that had developed from being together as women with ideas. They saw the Miners' Strike as a great opportunity to spread the message. The clash came when some of the miners' wives brought their own brand of working-class feminism to it.[10]

Her friend Anne Scargill put it more pungently, referring to 'these middle-class intellectuals like those women's libbers I first met'. She continued: 'I don't mean that in a nasty way. They have a lot of things going for them which we haven't had and it was only confidence that we were lacking. But our confidence goes a long way.'[11]

This conflict came to the surface when a National Women Against Pit Closures (NWAPC) organisation was set up at a founding conference at Northern College over the weekend of 21/22 July 1984. It brought together over fifty women from coalfields in Wales, Leicestershire, Nottinghamshire, Derbyshire, Yorkshire, Lancashire, County Durham and Scotland, with a weighting of fourteen from Yorkshire. At the first meeting, Anne Scargill read out a letter from the NUM leadership, which expressed the view that 'the officials of this movement should be in the main miners' wives. This would prevent any problems with the media re control or infiltration of the women's groups by any political faction.'[12]

This communication provoked protest from some of the politically active non-miners' wives who were very involved in the Miners' Strike. Kath Mackie was chair of the Sheffield Women Against Pit Closures (SWAPC) and a member of the Communist Party; but she was the wife of a steelworker, not a miner. She complained that 'she and other non miners' wives had worked hard from Day One of the strike to raise money and support, and felt that they should be represented on the committee'. A vote was taken on a show of hands that all NWAPC officials should be miners' wives, which ruled out Kath Mackie, although the NUM had never wanted such an explicit decision. After the meeting, and in private, a few non-miners' wives were co-opted, including Jean McCrindle as treasurer. A fudge was also worked out, whereby 75 per cent of the delegates to the next meeting should be miners' wives.[13]

Because Sheffield was not a mining centre, but a steel city and a university city, the SWAPC was not dominated by miners' wives. These, if they came, took the bus into the city from their mining villages. However, because, under Scargill's presidency, Sheffield became the new national headquarters of the NUM, it was possible to find female NUM employees to bridge the divide. One of these was Barbara Jackson, who was not a miner's wife, but had working-class origins and was a shop steward in the Colliery Officials and Staffs Area (COSA) – the white collar branch of the NUM. She had been brought up in Pitsmoor, a deprived district of Sheffield, the daughter of a labourer and a mother who had been in service. She failed the 11-plus and left school at fifteen for a job in a department store. At twenty-one she became involved with a hippy and had a daughter. But when her partner swanned off to the Isle of Wight Festival, she thought, 'I don't want a life like my mother had, where my father had got no power in the outside world but acted like a bloody king in his own home.' She threw her boyfriend out and reinvented herself, accessing social security for her daughter, finding her own flat, joining the tenants' association and the Labour Party, marrying again – this time to a hard-working car mechanic – and embarking on a new career in the pensions and insurance office of the National Coal Board in Sheffield. Her feminism was burgeoning, but ill-defined: 'I was obviously aware of Germaine Greer's book *The Female Eunuch*, burning your bra, all of that. And some of it meant something to me. And some of it meant nothing to me.'

Barbara had some experience of picketing during an overtime ban in the winter of 1983–84. Because overtime meant Saturday mornings, the picket was quite successful and Arthur Scargill joined them a couple of times. However, when the strike broke out in March, she was one of only six in the pensions office who went on strike and joined the picket line. Feeling isolated, she joined the SWAPC. Since she was already in a union and a member of the Labour Party, she was not fazed by the fact that it had been set up by a couple of communist women. She did, nevertheless, observe that the group was 'quite Sheffield dominated, people who mainly worked for the Council, or people that you knew were involved in feminism or the SWP [Socialist Workers Party] or Labour Party or Socialist Party'.

Alongside these women who took easily to public speaking there was, said Barbara, 'a fair sprinkling of women who came in from the pits – Carol, whose husband worked at Brookhouse pit, Margaret from Thurcroft, she was a canteen worker . . . and they were different to us'. The question arose of whether they could be mentored without being patronised:

There ended up being tensions because some people felt that the miners' wives or women should be coming forward and chairing the meeting. In theory that was a good idea but a lot of the mining women didn't recognise themselves as wanting to do that or feel capable of doing it. There was this element of feeling that – I don't really know how to word this properly – that people ought to be brought on, ought to be given confidence, because a lot of them were being confident, speaking at big meetings, but to develop it so that everyone has the potential to be more of a leader. And that was difficult at times.[14]

Despite these tensions, the SWAPC stayed together during and after the strike, and in 1987 brought out a book entitled *We are Women, We are Strong*.[15]

Tension in the mining villages between those miners' wives with an education and a history of political activism and the more conventional miners' wives was experienced from a different angle by Maureen Douglass. She and Dave had come to Dunscroft, seven miles north-east of Doncaster, and she studied at Hull Art College while he worked at Hatfield Main. She played a part in the Hatfield Main Women's Support Group, but was not really involved in the soup kitchen in nearby Stainforth, where they lived:

I think perhaps, perhaps there were a lot of women, miners' wives in the strike who felt that their most significant and useful role might be similar to what they did, and this is probably true of me, as well. What they normally did. They were housewives, they cooked, they cleaned, they sorted out clothes . . . They saw that as their most useful role and they did it absolutely brilliantly, you know. That wasn't my most useful role, that wasn't how I saw my thing in life at all. I don't think I would have been very happy in a soup kitchen, quite honestly. So I did the other thing, you know, making the speeches and going to rallies and organising pickets, filling vans with the wrong petrol.

Maureen felt estranged, both as an artist and as an activist. She had been involved in various Trotskyist groups with Dave and had tried to infiltrate the Labour Party at Goole. She also began to build herself a reputation as an actress, appearing in Cinema Action's 1983 *Rocking the Boat*, a film about strikes on Clydeside, and Doncaster Arts Cooperative's play *Bread and Roses*, about a miners' strike during the Second World War. This new departure alienated her from the women's support group, where she was seen as breaking solidarity with miners' wives, albeit for a left-wing cause:

> Towards the end of the strike, I don't know how close it was to the end of the strike, I stopped taking a very active role in the women's support group, because it got back to me and I can't remember how it got back to me, but I was told that people had been saying that I was only doing it because I wanted to be seen. Because I'd been in a play at the time, so I'd been, you know, doing some acting, and they said it was me just doing it for myself, to become famous. So, you know, and that hurt. Hurt an awful lot. So I just thought, no, I'll just stand back now, they can think what they like.[16]

Meanwhile, in the Barnsley Women Against Pit Closures, matters came to a head in the autumn of 1984. Over a period of six months, the miners' wives had gained confidence, organising soup kitchens and food parcels, speaking in public to raise money, even dealing with the media. The fact that Anne Scargill was of particular interest to the media caused a serious problem. This flared up when Anne was invited to speak in Ireland and was accused by the BWAPC of not having the prior authorisation of the collective. The more general issue was that miners' wives – who were increasingly considered the backbone of the strike – were more in demand for speaking engagements than were feminists. As Betty Cook said:

> Anne was, if you like, different to the rest of us. She was in the spotlight because of Arthur . . . I think there was a lot of jealousy because of Anne, who she was . . . It was a heated meeting. And we went with, broke up at the end of the meeting, and then, on the, on the evening it was quite a few phone calls going around, that we decided we'd got to do something. People wanted miners' wives to go and speak. They didn't want women who weren't involved in the mining communities.[17]

As a result of this heated meeting, the miners' wives broke away from the BWAPC to found their own organisation, which they called the Barnsley Miners' Wives Action Group (BMWAG). It held its first meeting on 26 November 1984 at Worsbrough Miners' Welfare, where Anne Scargill had set up a soup kitchen, and had representatives from Hoyland, Wombwell, Dodworth, Woolley, Hemsworth, Houghton, Denby and Park Mill. It brought together women who worked in the local soup kitchens and food parcel services, and prioritised funding and support for them. Marsha Marshall was elected secretary, Betty Cook minute secretary and Elicia Billingham treasurer.[18] Elicia had emerged from an almost Dickensian background in Barnsley: her mother, a barmaid of Gypsy origin, lost four children in ten years before Elicia was born in 1941, and her bricklayer father then died when she was ten. Talented and imaginative, she was moved by the fact that Anne Brontë was buried in Scarborough. Though she passed the 11-plus, there was no money to buy her the school uniform to send her to grammar school. She worked as a seamstress and ran off to London with a football player. Later she found Danny, a Dodworth miner who had picketed at Saltley Gate, but could neither read nor write. She met Betty Cook, who introduced her to the BWAPC and drove her to meetings in her car. Betty, Elicia, Marsha and Anne formed the core of the Barnsley Miners' Wives Action Group, which they nicknamed 'The Bumwaggers'.[19]

In County Durham, while there was a good deal of tension between miners' wives and men from the Durham Miners' Association in setting up support groups, there was relatively little friction between miners' wives and socialist feminists who got involved in supporting the strike. There were several reasons for this relative harmony. Socialist feminists in the Area had generally acquired a university education, but often they themselves came from mining stock. They did not live in ivory towers, and were frequently involved in the local community as teachers or social workers. And they belonged to the same political organisations, whether it was the Labour Party, or the radical ginger group Independent Labour Publications, which was very strong in the Durham Area, or Peace Action Durham, a branch of CND. They often congregated together both for fundraising gigs and for meetings of the Durham Area Miners' Support Group, held in the Crossgate Club.

Kath Mattheys (later Kath Connolly), who became secretary of the North Durham Constituency Labour Party Miners' Support Group, was a teacher at Roseberry Comprehensive School in the mining village of Pelton, outside Chester-le-Street. Her father's family were miners at South Pelaw, although her father (who spent the war in the navy) managed to keep out of the pit until after she was born in 1950, but then needed to earn a higher wage. Her mother's father was a miner who was killed at Crookhall in 1941. Kath passed the 11-plus and went to grammar school and then to teacher training at St Hild's College. Her then husband Bob was an engineer at Northern Engineering Industries, Gateshead.[20] Kath worked very closely with miner Bill Frostwick, who would spend the week picketing with the Dirty Thirty, before coming home on Friday, when:

> I had to go up to the local Labour Club to dish the parcels out for the striking miners. The club used to give miners parcels and a couple of pints, and things like that. Every Friday night there was always some-thing on in the Labour Club.[21]

Kath and John Savory lived in Chester-le-Street and John worked at Westhoe colliery on the coast. They also used to go to the Labour Club on a Friday night, and they both delivered and received: 'My husband used to deliver some of the food parcels,' said Kath Savory, 'but we used to get a food parcel off them anyway.'[22]

Anna Lawson, who helped set up a support group at Sacriston, was neither the daughter nor the wife of a miner, but she did nevertheless have a mining background. Her grandfather had been a miner at Craghead, but her father, Fenwick Lawson, had won a scholarship to the Royal College of Art in London to train as a sculptor. She was born on a houseboat in

Hampton Wick. Her father came back north to lecture in Newcastle. Anna was expelled from her Catholic school for organising a strike and interrupted her nursing training to hitch-hike round pop festivals, marrying a Hell's Angel and having two children before her husband died in a motorbike smash. In 1982, she returned to Sacriston, where she was regarded as middle class and a hippy.[23] Curiously, she was politicised by her babysitter Veronica, who was going out with a Black Panther and who campaigned around the IRA hunger strikes, Nicaragua and Peace Action Durham, going to Greenham Common. During the Miners' Strike, Anna threw herself in with a group of miners' wives and other local women to set up a support group for miners' families, and consulted Heather Wood in Easington about how best to go about it. She organised a picket around a striking miner's house to prevent the electricity being cut off, advised mining families on how to hang on to benefits for their children, and raised funds by setting up a second-hand clothes shop in a disused cobbler's shop.[24]

Pat McIntyre was at the centre of the Durham Area Miners' Support Group. Her Scottish grandfather had been sacked for setting up a gas stokers' union in 1903, and the death of her father near Dunkirk in 1940, when she was five, pushed the family deeper into poverty. She was disciplined by her Catholic school for 'preaching communism', went on the Aldermaston marches, joined CND and later founded Peace Action Durham. She went to Durham University as a mature student in 1976 to study sociology, and in 1979 began a PhD on labour politics between the wars. Her husband Vin was head of the careers advisory department at Durham University, and they were both heavily involved in Independent Labour Publications (ILP) – the successor organisation to the Independent Labour Party which campaigned for democratic socialism within the Labour Party.

Early in the strike, Pat and Vin met Mary Stratford, who helped set up the support group at Great Lumley, and they cooperated to prevent the union taking control of the Durham Area Miners' Support Group. After that, Mary said, they 'became lifelong friends, who were real left-wing Labour people, fantastic people'.[25] Vin became the organiser of the food parcel enterprise of the Durham Area Miners' Support Group, based at Redhills, working alongside Johnny Dent, a long-distance lorry driver with a Communist Party background, who was a recruiting sergeant for the ILP. Meanwhile, Pat proved herself a superb orator, singer and composer of political songs for weekly fundraising gigs, such as 'The Tory Version of Law and Order' to the tune of 'The Teddy Bear's Picnic'.[26]

Among the women who gravitated to the ILP and the Durham Area Miners' Support Group were Michaela Griffin and Lotte Shankland. Michaela described herself as 'working class', but then corrected this to 'lower middle class'. Her father was a Scotsman of Irish Catholic heritage who had worked for the Admiralty in Portsmouth and Hartlepool, where she was born. She was a rebel at grammar school, went to Greenham Common, studied sociology and social administration at Durham University, became a social worker in the Easington area and engaged in fundraising with former student friends during the strike.[27] Lotte Shankland came from an entirely different background, the daughter of a Copenhagen stockbroker who married a Durham University Italian scholar, Hugh Shankland. An accomplished artist, she specialised in making banners for the anti-apartheid movement, CND and the Save Consett steelworkers' campaign. She worked as a community artist with women prisoners in Durham gaol, with young offenders at Low Newton remand centre, and then with the Community Arts Association, doing outreach work in Easington. During the strike, she was recruited to the ILP by Johnny Dent, raised money through another second-hand clothes shop she set up with Pat McIntyre in Hallgarth Street, Durham, and toured with a miners' wives revue that included Dorothy Wray. She also collaborated with Heather Wood to produce a booklet called 'The Last Coals of Spring: Poems, Stories and Songs by the Women of Easington'.[28]

The balance of power between middle-class socialist feminists and working-class miners' wives was rather different in Leicestershire, where there were fewer than thirty striking miners' wives. They were not only isolated among the working miners' wives, but were also scattered geographically across a number of villages and towns, including Loughborough and Leicester. They did not form a substantial body, as in Barnsley, or a significant minority, as in Sheffield, and therefore almost-gratefully accepted the offer of external help when it came.

Key to that outside help was Jane Bruton. Her background was both middle and working class: her father was a local government engineer in Birmingham, but her mother's father was an electrician from Wolverhampton, and her mother was not easily accepted by her father's family because of her working-class origins. Jane was brought up in Croydon, attended grammar school and went to Leicester University in 1971 to study social sciences. There her political education began. She joined the International Socialists, occupied the university's administrative block and helped problem families on the Braunston estate. During the miners' strike of 1972, she picketed a power station, and later that year supported female Asian workers in a Mansfield hosiery strike. In 1974, she supported Asian workers in a strike at Imperial Typewriters (in which, although she did not know it at the time, future Dirty Thirty leader Malcolm Pinnegar was also involved). As a feminist, she also campaigned in 1975 against an anti-abortion bill.

After graduating, Jane thought about social work, but then trained to be a nurse in Sheffield. There she met Paul Mason, from the coal and cotton mill town of Leigh in Lancashire, who was studying music and politics. Although his grandfather had been a miner, his father combined driving a lorry with playing the trombone in dance bands, while his mother, brought up in Liverpool and the daughter of a Polish-Jewish musician, taught in a primary school. Paul picked up his Marxism from the Lamp bookshop in Leigh, was purged from the International Socialists, joined Workers' Power, and supported the steel strike in Sheffield in 1980.[29]

Jane and Paul returned to Leicester in time for the Miners' Strike and threw themselves into it through the Leicester Trades Council, which was dominated by public-sector workers. Jane was elected secretary of the

Leicester Trades Council Miners' Support Group on 23 March, and their first task was to find accommodation for Kent and South Wales miners who had come to picket the working Leicestershire miners.

Excluded from the Miners' Welfare in Coalville, and barred from most pubs (apart from The Barrel in Bagworth), the Dirty Thirty often met at the house of Phil and Kay Smith in Barlestone. Kay had been born in the mining village of Bagworth; but, she said, 'the houses were literally falling down' and they were moved to an estate at Osbaston when she was fifteen. 'I've got no roots after that. It was just awful, just a terrible wrench.' She went to work in a hosiery factory, where she earned a decent wage. Then she met Phil, who worked at Bagworth colliery. Mining was what gave meaning to her life: her grandfather had been involved in the 1926 strike, and her father – the pit delegate – had been in the strikes of the 1970s. She rejoiced when Phil decided to go on strike in 1984, but she was shy herself and welcomed the help of Jane Bruton when it came to setting up a women's support group:

I got introduced to this woman, a nurse, and I think her name were Jane Bruton. She came to the house, and a few of the other women got invited, well everybody, all the women got invited to come. And Jane said about getting a support group going, and she sort of pointed us in the right direction, what you need is this, that, and the other. So we set up a fund and everything else, what we needed to. And then they needed a speaker. So it were, 'Kay'll do it!' and it were like, 'What?' 'Cos nobody else wanted to do it.[30]

As a result of meeting and working with Jane Bruton, Kay became more confident. She was prepared to disagree with the Dirty Thirty on the subject of traditional gender roles, but she remained close to her family and, in particular, sought the approval of her father. In addition, unlike in Barnsley, there seems to have been little friction with feminist socialists such as Jane Bruton. Indeed, the framework of support provided by Jane and the Leicester Miners' Support Group was crucial to the success of the Dirty Thirty.

Kay told the historian of the Dirty Thirty David Bell that after the first meeting, when the husbands came to pick up their wives, Malcolm Pinnegar asked them what they had decided to do:

I said, 'Yes, we're going to picket.' He says, 'You ain't.' He looks at my husband and says, 'Tell her, Smithy. She's not going picketing.' He says, 'I can't do nowt. She'll do what she wants.'[31]

They set up a fund to finance food parcels for the Dirty Thirty, but also made sure that the money raised went towards essentials, including 'women's things'. Very soon, Phil was organising the collection and distribution of food from their garage, while Kay was going off on public speaking engagements, because Jane Bruton had told the miners' wives that 'You'll have a bigger impact if one of you does it.' Jane gave her some coaching in public speaking, and Jane's Leicester group ferried them to meetings in Leicester, Milton Keynes and Northampton. Kay and Margaret Pinnegar also served as Leicestershire representatives on the NWAPC. As Kay recalled:

The first time I stood up in public I'd written about six lines and I stood on a platform at some hall, I think there might have been forty people there . . . So I stood up and read what I'd written, because I just couldn't . . . I were shaking, I were absolutely petrified. And people clapped and at the end I said to me dad, 'What did you think?' And he looked at me and he said, 'You were very good, me duck,' he said, 'but you spoke too fast.' But I never stopped getting nervous. I always got nervous . . . I think I finished off saying like, you know, 'We are proud of the Dirty Thirty and we'll support our men.' Something along them lines.[32]

In Nottinghamshire, where striking miners and their wives were a small minority, the women were perhaps more concerned with surviving in a hostile environment, than with developing any form of feminism. There was great interest in the Nottinghamshire coalfield from socialist feminist activists from metropolitan areas, but how far this contact helped in developing the thinking about the role of women is difficult to say.

One of those socialist feminists was Helen Colley, born in Dagenham to a car-worker, who had been a ship's engineer during the war and then worked in Chatham dockyard until it closed. Class was an issue in her family life: Helen's Catholic mother felt that she had married beneath herself and was keen that Helen should receive a convent education. These contradictions followed Helen through her life, as her older brother, who had joined the Socialist Workers Party, 'talked to me about how to be a rebel at school and do it properly'; he also bought her Chairman Mao's *Little Red Book* and Karl Marx's *Selected Writings*. She ran off with an artist boyfriend for a couple of years to the bohemian scene in Bath; got into Oxford; through her new boyfriend, Andy Buchanan, joined the International Marxist Group (IMG); and picketed the Cowley car works during the 1980 steel strike. After Oxford, they went together to Hackney to implement the IMG's 'turn to industry'. Helen worked on the buses – which at that time, she said, employed 'loads of people with PhDs, loads of immigrants who couldn't get a job using their qualifications, and people like me who got an education but didn't want to get on the hamster wheel of professional work or whatever' – and became involved in strikes, protests and Rock Against Racism.

Helen's involvement in the Miners' Strike was another chapter in building links between socialist feminists and the tumultuous working class. She and Andy welcomed a group of Notts miners who were fundraising in London, and hosted one of them – Mark Hunter, a striker at Welbeck (though originally from Brighton) and a punk, 'a real outsider down the pit'. She and Andy were then sent by the IMG to Nottingham, where Helen again worked on the buses, getting a good sense of the mining villages. Her main contact was Mary Donnelly, a retired teacher who had been in the IMG and 'helped to found in Nottingham the first ever

Women's Movement Centre in Britain'. Mary was involved with Women Against Pit Closures in Nottingham, many of whom, said Helen, were 'students or just doing part-time work . . . we could live on being unemployed, so they would go picketing and things like that'. Mary was also involved with the women running soup kitchens, and she took Helen round them. Helen was appalled by the isolation of the strikers:

> Families had stopped speaking to them . . . members of their families were throwing bricks through their windows and daubing graffiti on their homes. Their husbands were getting into fights in the Miners' Welfares. It was like a war within those communities.

Feminism was not an issue, and Helen herself was more interested in connecting the Miners' Strike to the anti-apartheid movement through the fact that the strike was being undermined by the import of coal from South Africa:

> Mary said, 'We'll just go around the canteens on Sundays and we'll meet up with people.' So that I would go around with her on Sundays and we'd do Sunday lunches and then we'd sort of discuss politics, and then we'd suggest things that they might like to do, so we'd bring a speaker from the ANC [African National Congress] or somebody from Latin America solidarity, there was all that stuff that had been going on in Central America at the time. Lots and lots of different things. We'd do a talk about something that was about another – about anti-apartheid, struggles that would connect with them.[33]

The situation in Scotland and Wales was very different. The women's groups seem to have sprung up independently of middle-class socialist feminists and they did not have recourse to such women for leadership. Jean McCrindle's failed attempt to spread the feminist message to Scottish miners' wives dated to the late 1950s and early 1960s, and there seems to have been little progress in the intervening years. Carol Ross, chair of the Cowdenbeath Women's Action Committee, was the daughter of an Irish labourer, although in fact he was a trained chemist, had been compelled to leave Ireland because of his republican politics and made his children watch *University Challenge*.[34] Before she was married, Carol worked as a clerical officer in Edinburgh, and two of her sisters went on to have successful careers in public life with the Scottish National Party. Meanwhile Linda Erskine, secretary of the Women's Action Group in Lochgelly, came from mining stock, passed the 11-plus and by rights should have gone to Beath High School with her sister's best friend, the future crime writer Ian Rankin. Instead she was sent to the local Auchterderran Junior High School, where she later worked as a lab technician. She needed little help to impose herself as an organiser and to become politicised.[35]

In the Neath, Dulais and Swansea Valleys Miners' Support Group, key roles were held by women; but again, they were not openly feminist. Hefina Headon, secretary of the group, came back with the Welsh delegation from the women's rally in Barnsley with a message for the Yorkshire women: 'You're not going to simple us any more.' This indignation, however, was more about regional rivalry than women's rights.[36] Christine Powell, treasurer of the support group, described herself as 'not a sort of girlie girl myself'; she was dedicated above all to the financial viability of the operation. Kay Bowen, meanwhile, had her hands full collecting and distributing food on a weekly basis to ten centres across three valleys. The only feminist in the support group was Margaret Donovan, who set up a women's group that was separate from the support group. According to Hywel Francis:

> Margaret Donovan led a completely separate part of the support group, identifying the need for a totally autonomous voice for women politically. They had their own aspirations and their own views about things, not just about the strike. She began to articulate that she was the person

who drove it. The men thought that women shouldn't do this, but they gave up fighting it.[37]

One of those who came on board with Margaret Donovan was Siân James, whose husband Martin worked at Abernant colliery. She knew Margaret through CND and the ballet class their daughters both attended. Siân had not got involved in the strike until August, and confessed that originally 'as long as my lace curtains were the cleanest, my children immaculately dressed, their hand-knitted clothes made with love, I was happy'.[38] Then, at a public meeting in Neath that October, listening to a male speaker droning on, she told Hefina, 'I could do better with a paper bag over my head.'[39] She and Hefina became a double act, travelling as far as London to speak in support of the miners. At the same time, Siân became very involved in Margaret Donovan's group, which was invited to send delegates to the South Wales Women's Support Groups, or South Wales Women Against Pit Closures, which was set up in Cardiff in June. The original delegates from the three valleys were Hefina and Margaret, who drove a 'clapped-out Saab'. Then Hefina eased off and Siân took her place. Later she reflected on her transition from being a strong 'Welsh Mam' to a politically aware feminist:

I think it started off as being matriarchal. I would say that a lot of us – I can't speak for other people – but we were what I would call 'proto-feminists'. Because we'd grown up in communities where it was the women who made the decisions, the Welsh Mam. If a Welsh Mam said, 'You will hand over your pay now, you naughty boy,' 'You're not going to play rugby today because you came home drunk last night,' you'd do it! But we didn't really understand that it was political, that feminism was more than being independent or strong, it was about the way the women were treated and how men treated women . . . So I'd say we were very *strong* women, but the feminism – that recognition of what we were doing – was part of a *wider* thing, and we needed to give other women support and help.[40]

Through the women's group, Siân's main ally soon became Ann Jones, whom they picked up at Hirwaun on their way to meetings in Cardiff. Ann and her friend Barbara Edwards were lynchpins of the Hirwaun support group, feeding the families of miners who worked at the Tower colliery; but they were not interested in peeling potatoes. Ann had been contacted by militants from left-wing groups such as Socialist Action and the Socialist Workers Party, who were keen to find a genuine working-class base in the Valleys, and in return gave miners and miners' wives a public voice for building support. According to Ann:

> These people were coming and talking to us. Really in a way they were using us. Only we didn't realise that at the time. They could have a platform through us. So they started arranging meetings where they wanted you to speak and the first one I did was down in Swansea . . . It was done by Socialist Action, and it was a chap called Brendon who organised it. Well I must have had a little bit of a flair for it. Perhaps I talk too much, I don't know, but after that I was asked to speak in a lot of places. By now through a group in Cardiff we had met and Women Against Pit Closures Wales was formed. I was one of the members, the founder members of that.[41]

A little later, there was a clash between miners' wives Siân and Ann and the leader of the South Wales Women's Support Groups, Kath Jones, who was neither a miner's wife nor Welsh. Born in Poplar in the East End, she had been a telephonist during the war and had come to live and work in South Wales after marrying a Welsh commando. She became involved in the Union of Post Office Workers and was its delegate to the Trades Council in Cardiff. She was deemed well placed in trade union terms to become secretary of the South Wales Women's Support Groups, but conflict arose between Kath Jones and Ann Jones about both tactics and power. In time, Ann and Siân decided to challenge Kath Jones for the chairmanship of the South Wales Women's Support Groups. There was a feeling, as in Barnsley, that although not all miners' wives wanted responsibility, some did. Ann's opinion of Kath was:

> She wanted to rule. She wanted to be the secretary. She wanted to be the chair. She wanted to hold every position in Women Against. I just wouldn't have it . . . I think with Kath she was afraid I was going to take some of the power from her which, when I did become the chair, she nearly had a heart attack. I talked to her and then when I wasn't the chair you [Siân] became it straightaway after me which didn't suit her either.[42]

Through a network of women's support groups, action groups and Women Against Pit Closures, miners' wives gained experience, skills and confidence. They became active outside the home, travelling, speaking in public and making new relationships. The most important encounter was probably with feminists, who tended to be middle class, university educated and politicised. In some cases, this was not a problem. The wives of the Dirty Thirty were so isolated that they welcomed the advice given by Jane Bruton, nurse, feminist and socialist. In Nottinghamshire, the input of activists such as Helen Colley was appreciated, but it is not clear how deep was the relationship forged there with striking miners' wives. In County Durham, there does not seem to have been tension between miners' wives and feminist socialists. The former were highly intelligent women who already worked outside the home, while the latter, such as Kath Mattheys (now Connolly) and Pat Macintyre, were 'organic' intellectuals, who had themselves grown up in working-class and mining communities; and they all belonged to organisations like the Labour Party and the ILP. In South Wales and Fife, miners' wives seem to have formed their own women's groups without the help of outside feminists, and to have learned, as Siân James did, how to progress from 'Welsh Mam' to 'proto-feminist'. It was in South Yorkshire that the sharpest conflict arose between miners' wives and middle-class socialist feminists, many of whom had come from outside the area. The wives came to feel patronised and, as they developed their own working-class feminism, broke away to found their own Barnsley Miners' Wives Action Group. Significantly, they sustained the fight for longer. Whereas the planned 'First Barnsley WAPC book' never got beyond the draft stage, because of the discordant voices within it, the Barnsley Miners' Wives Action Group published its own compendium, *We Struggled to Laugh*.[43]

7

CONNECTIONS

'I think in early May I ended up doing the street collections in the front street in Chester-le-Street. About five or six of us. We took a fair amount of money. And this is how initially I got involved.' Shaking a tin was the original means of fundraising for the Miners' Strike, and for David Connolly it was the way in to supporting the miners. David's father was a community policeman at Trimdon, near Sedgefield, but he identified emotionally with his mother's father, Thomas William Kendal, who had died aged thirty-one in a pit accident at Bowburn colliery in 1939, going back in to fetch men who were still down the mine. David went to Warwick University in 1974, was elected secretary of the university Labour Club, became interested in workers' self-management and moved back to Pelton Fell, County Durham, in 1977, finding a job with the Industrial Common Ownership Movement in Sunderland. He met Pat and Vin McIntyre through Independent Labour Party Publications, and was put onto fundraising by Kath Mattheys:

In the July obviously there was the Miners' Gala which was an overcast day. By that time I was in the ILP, who were producing hundreds and hundreds of different miners' support badges. So I became a badge seller . . . I got pretty good at selling badges. In the August there was the women's march in London and at the last minute as I recall, I was asked if I wanted to go on the bus and I said, 'Yeah, I'll go.' We went overnight, and it was a red-hot day; we got into London at about five or six o'clock in the morning, it was red hot even then. There was this massive women's march, which was immensely powerful and emotive and everything; loads of kids.[1]

David's was a fairly typical story of an outsider who nevertheless had an emotional connection to the mining community, becoming involved in fundraising to sustain the strike. As the months passed, he became more engaged, and also travelled further afield: from Chester-le-Street on a Saturday morning to Durham on Gala Day and to London for the women's march on 11 August 1984, when a petition with 100,000 signatures asking the queen to help them defend their families and communities was delivered to Buckingham Palace.[2] David specialised in selling the enamel buttons that each identified a colliery on strike, and which were avidly collected by miners and supporters alike. What he did not say was that Kath Mattheys was also on the march and, brought together by shared activism, they later married.

A hundred miles south, Jean Crane, secretary of the Askern NUM Women's Support Group, was wondering how they could improve on shaking tins in pubs on a Friday night in Doncaster. 'We didn't do too badly,' she recalled, 'but we weren't doing well enough.' Then her husband Pete had a brilliant idea, which was to contact as many trade unions as they could:

Somebody, I don't know who it was, gave me a book and it was just full of unions like the National Union of Candle Makers, just every union you could think of, honestly. And I got that, I got the book and me, Gwen Goodwin, Sheila Gibbon, and I think, in fact, I know it was Yvonne Ellis, we sat round my kitchen table and we hand wrote a letter to every single union in that book . . . Hundreds. Honestly, I can't even, I can't even begin to write the things that they have unions for . . . And honestly, you wouldn't believe how many replies we got with cheques.[3]

Not all the replies, to be fair, came with cheques. Some responses were disappointing. The National Union of Railwaymen (NUR) said that it had already given the miners £65,000 in cash and kind to support travel to rallies; but it did make a 'special donation' of £50. The Union of Shop, Distributive and Allied Workers (USDAW) informed them that it was sending money direct to NUM headquarters. Terry's, the chocolate manufacturers in York, which was also approached, simply said no. Most upsetting, a request to Butlin's on 21 July about using their Filey Holiday Centre in North Yorkshire for a children's holiday was refused on the grounds that it was on the verge of closure and 'not fit for habitation'.[4]

Where connections were made and money sent in, the support group invited members of the union to come and visit their mining community, in order to thank them and to see how the money was being spent. In turn, unions invited miners or their wives to come and speak at their meetings, in order to strike a chord as real people with powerful stories of suffering and struggle.

Jean Crane and Dianne Hogg built a link to the Association of Clerical, Technical and Supervisory Staff (ACTSS), the white-collar section of the TGWU, at Euston. It sent a delegation to Askern in mid-October with twenty-five boxes of warm clothing, four boxes of non-perishable food for food parcels, and £500 in cash. As Dianne recalled,

everybody came to my house. I fed 'em. They were an odd bunch but nice. Dave [surname unknown] stopped at our house a few times, he was doing a run from London to Joan O'Groats to raise money. Pete took him picketing once.[5]

Thanking the Askern community, the ACTSS enclosed a card for Pete Richardson, who was in Durham gaol. In early December, it invited a group of Askern miners and their wives to London, and the proceedings finished with a benefit concert at the New Merlin's Cave pub at King's Cross.[6]

In a similar way, Graham Dean of the Southwark branch of the National and Local Government Officers' Association (NALGO) persuaded his branch to adopt Askern. He visited the community, staying with Jean and Phil Crane. In return, he invited a group of Askern women and miners to his union's AGM on 14 November. This turned out to be a baptism of fire for Jean, who for the first time stood up in public and was praised for her performance:

> There were probably five couples and we were supposed to meet for this meeting. Phil and I got there and nobody else turned up. And it turned out that all the other couples thought, they don't need ten of us there, we won't go. So it turned out there were only me and Phil there, and they wanted us to talk. I didn't even know what to say. So what I did say was, 'I think the best way to go about it would be, if you ask us questions, and we'll do the best we can to answer them.' And that's what we did. And it turned out it was really, really good. And when it finished, somebody said to me, 'You should definitely be the first Labour woman prime minister.'[7]

A third powerful contact was with Liz Sullivan, London organiser of the Civil Service Union, based in Paddington. Jean Crane remembered her as

> a lovely lady. She campaigned for us, she raised a lot, a lot of money for us. And she would come down at every opportunity. She'd bring donations, she'd bring other people with her and introduce them to us. And then they'd go away and raise money for us. Yeah, she was very active.[8]

After one of her visits, in December 1984, Liz sent a message of solidarity and encouragement, with hope of an ultimate victory:

Meeting you two weeks ago was a great pleasure to me and all the CSU people who were able to have the opportunity. You made a great many friends in London and we will stand by you . . . To be able to meet people with such courage and humour after nine or ten months of struggle and hardship is a privilege to all trade unionists. You are an example to us all, and you are making history. We look forward to getting plastered with you at the Victory celebrations.[9]

Two hundred and fifty miles from Askern, a communist GP and his activist partner were thinking about ways in which they could use their connections in the medical world. Julian Tudor Hart and Mary Hart at Glyncorrwg were pillars of the Llynfi-Afan Valley Miners' Support Group. They gave as much as they could from their own limited resources, but as Christmas approached they played upon the fact that their GP practice was also a two-person research centre, investigating miners' diseases, and had attracted medical people from all over the world to come to observe it. Their round robin of 5 November 1984 was on the back of Julian's pen-and-ink drawing of a Welsh village with the caption '*Pentre Diwaith*', 'Village Without Work'. It explained the historic predicament in which the village found itself and elicited a wide and generous response:

Since 1968 when we started our Visitor's Book at the Queens [sic], over 150 doctors, medical students and other health workers from 47 countries have come to Glencorrwg. We hope that you have happy memories of our friendly community . . . Since we came here 22 years ago, three collieries in the Afan Valley have closed with the loss of 2,100 jobs, all our railways have closed and the steelworks at Port Talbot has reduced its workforce from 15,000 to less than 5,000. The only colliery left in our Area is St John's Cwmdu, Maesteg, and that is on MacGregor's list for closure . . . We're now into the eighth month of the strike during which children have outgrown shoes and clothes. For the whole St John's district we have to raise £5,000 a week to feed and clothe the striking families. Despite all kinds of local fundraising activities (we even had a very successful gala concert in the local Conservative club) there's no way we can raise all this locally . . . So we're asking our friends to help . . . The miners and their families are holding out not only to defend their jobs and our community, they may be defending your future as well.[10]

The largest donation, of £1,000, came, remembered Mary,

from a friend called Rhys Vaughan. He was a son of a steelworker but a grandson of a miner and he was a solicitor in Manchester but was born near Maesteg and we received it, I think, on something like Christmas Eve.[11]

Each coalfield had its hinterland of places where they concentrated their fundraising activities – North Wales for South Wales, the North East for County Durham, Clydeside and the north-east Scottish coast for Fife, the M1 corridor for the Dirty Thirty, and Ireland for both the South Wales and the Yorkshire miners and their wives. For all coalfields, London was the Land of Cockaigne, where riches were assumed to concentrate, and so everyone made their way there in time, although the Kent miners tried to defend it as their patch.[12] Support also came from abroad, either in money or in kind (such as providing holidays for miners' children); a particular source of backing came from a group of women miners in the USA.

Among the ambassadors and fundraisers from South Wales, Ali Thomas of Blaenant was among the most successful, becoming known as the 'foreign minister' of the Neath, Dulais and Swansea Valleys Support Group. After picketing in North Wales failed, he and his mates went back to seek funds. In Anglesey, he tried to raise money from the aluminium works, but the 'right-wing trade unionists' told them to 'go back and have a ballot before you ask for our support'. They collected £370, but lest they pocket it were ordered to buy food supplies there and then, and were escorted to Lo-Cost. Ali found that they had a much better response outside the Welsh labour movement. They went to a meeting at Bangor University, chaired by a communist from Grimsby – 'an excellent young man' – and were delighted to be invited back for a meal by a large bearded Welsh nationalist, because they 'hadn't had dinner in weeks'. They had even more luck when they attended the national Eisteddfod in Lampeter during the first week of August and played on the Welsh dimension of the strike. They did not have to go round with a bucket, but shared a tent with NUPE and received donations from people from 'all walks of life'.[13]

Hywel Francis, the chair of the Neath, Dulais and Swansea Valleys Support Group, was also at the Eisteddfod, furiously networking among his friends in the Welsh Labour History Society and Welsh Language Society. News came through that weekend of the death of the actor Richard Burton, born the son of a miner in Pontrhydyfen in the Afan Valley, which deepened the sense of national loss. Welsh identity played a significant part in fundraising for the miners, Welsh slogans acted as rallying cries and the presence of Welsh-language broadcasting made possible reporting on the strike that was more sympathetic than that offered by the UK national media. Hywel Francis remembered that

we raised quite a lot of money on the Eisteddfod Field, and there were miners collecting money on the outside ... The Welsh Language Society developed a number of slogans: '*heb waith ni fydd iaith*' – 'without work there will be no language'; '*cau pwll byddwch yn lladd cymuned*' – 'if you close a pit you will kill a community'. And that had a powerful resonance. The Welsh Language Society in particular was very non-sectarian and would work with others or independently, everywhere. So we used the Welsh-language radio and television a lot who were invariably sympathetic and because it was a minority channel you tended to get away with things.[14]

Ireland was another important destination for fundraisers. This was partly because of the Irish origin of many mineworkers and partly because the Irish, too, had ongoing historic issues with the British state. Ali Thomas went to Dublin and spoke at Liberty Hall, which was the headquarters of the Irish Transport and General Workers' Union (ITGWU); there he received a promise of support. Phil Bowen, the chair of Blaenant lodge, went on several occasions, getting the boat from Pembroke to Rosslare. He was supported by the ITGWU in setting up a base in County Cork, where, his wife Kay teased him, Phil stayed with 'his Irish mum', Miss O'Marney, 'and she'd give him big pieces of lamb to bring back and jars of things!' The Waterford Glass factory, where the workers were in dispute with their employers, was a good source of funding, and Phil always asked for the money to be made out in cheques to the South Wales NUM. As a result, he confessed:

> We did get caught out one time, myself and Ali. We were in Waterford and we didn't have any money, did we? So we had to do something not quite right. We booked into a hotel, stayed there for bed and breakfast, said that we were businessmen in some part of Waterford and said that we were going back. Had our breakfast, put us up for the night, and we didn't pay, we didn't come back. Bit embarrassed about that.[15]

From Yorkshire, the Barnsley Women Against Pit Closures also sent delegates to Ireland, above all to Dublin. Anne Scargill demonstrated solidarity by joining a picket line of the Irish Distributive and Administrative Trade Union (IDATU) at Dunnes Stores, where a young shop assistant, Mary Manning, had been suspended for refusing to check out grapefruit imported from South Africa as a way of boycotting the apartheid regime.[16] Elicia Billingham followed in her stead that August, invited by the Dublin Council of Trade Unions in Tallaght. She combined fundraising with taking a group of twenty Barnsley schoolchildren on holiday. Fellow trade unionist John MacDonald organised trips to the races, the zoo and the beach for the kids, and in the evening Elicia went with him to meetings in pubs and clubs to stir up support. It later emerged that the generosity of the Dublin Council of Trade Unions was an unsung response to the British miners sending a shipload of food and clothing to 200,000 Dublin workers starving during the 1913–14 lockout.[17] Elicia's abiding memory, however, related to more recent events, when she was forced to turn down a bucket of money offered by the IRA:

So this couple shouted me over, and they says, 'Under that table is a bucketful of money' – and I mean a bucket full! And I were, 'Ooh, Jesus' . . . And John MacDonald kept shouting me over. So I picks the bucket up and takes it. He says, 'Licia, give them that money back.' And I went, 'What?' He says, 'It's IRA.' And I said, 'I don't care if it's KCD!' He says, 'I mean it, I'm telling you. What'll happen when you go back home, they, they'll want your address, and if they've owt, you know – like they were doing bombings then – they'll want a safe place and they'll want to stop with you.' And I went, 'Oh really.' Anyway, when I'd looked, they'd gone. They'd gone. So I says, 'Now what do I do?' He says, 'Ah well, we'll take it and we'll give it them back.'[18]

The miners' wives of County Durham hoped that they might have success raising awareness and funds from the students at the University of Durham. Mary Stratford of the Lumley Miners' Support Group and Elspeth Frostwick of the Chester-le-Street group went to speak to them, but to little effect. 'They didn't know County Durham outside that tight little college system,' Mary told Pat McIntyre after the strike. 'They were supposed to be the cream. If they are, God help us!'[19] In 2020, she elaborated:

I got what I would call an ill-informed response . . . one bloke's response was, 'Well, they closed down pits because there isn't any coal. What do you want them to dig, mud?' Didn't respond too well to that one . . . My view is if you get to a prestigious university, surely you open your

mind and you seek to know . . . surely to God you would open your
mind to what's going on beyond the four walls in which you live. So I
was a bit shocked. They just didn't have a clue. So it was more the level
of ignorance, I suppose, for want of a better word. I was quite shocked,
and I know Elspeth was as well.[20]

One exception to the ignorant students was Neil Griffin, a railway
signalman's son from Hartlepool, who had taken a BEd at Durham and
taught English and media studies to children at a Darlington comprehensive and then to young offenders at Low Newton remand centre. He was
also a musician and played at fundraising gigs in the pubs and clubs of
Durham city and County Durham, alongside Pat McIntyre. In addition,
he was involved in a recording studio for young people set up by a group
of unemployed steelworkers, the Consett Music Project. This organised a
fundraising evening at the Consett Empire Theatre with a bill including
Lindisfarne, the Newcastle-based folk-rock band, with lead singer Alan
Hull, that had made 'Fog on the Tyne' in 1971, and the Essex-born singer-
songwriter Billy Bragg, who released 'Between the Wars', which included
the old Kentucky miners' song 'Which Side Are You On?' Neil Griffin
remembered that:

> Lindisfarne were very big supporters of the strike. Billy Bragg . . . you
> know, Billy Bragg still is a very big supporter of socialism . . . I remember
> there being a concert, a gig in Consett that Billy Bragg played at, and I
> think we might have played that. In fact, we did play that as well,
> because I borrowed Allan Hull's amplifier and broke it.[21]

At the end of the night, a Durham Miners' Wives Support Group choir
sang 'They'll Never Beat the Miners', composed by local folksinger Ed
Pickford. After the concert, the artists were accommodated at the houses
of the miners' families. Billy Bragg stayed with David and Dorothy Wray
in Leadgate. The enthusiasm was passed on to the children of the strike:

their daughter Sam, then fifteen, was proud to say that 'Billy Bragg slept in my bed. Obviously I wasn't in it at the time.'[22]

In Fife, the striking miners could also draw on some local talent for fundraising. There do not seem to have been fundraising connections with England, but Scottish identity was played on through links in sport and entertainment. Former Clydeside shipbuilder and comedian Billy Connolly did benefit performances at Kelty Working Men's Club and the Lochgelly Centre Theatre. In August 1984, a charity football match was organised by the Cowdenbeath strike centre and *Newsnight* cameras were on hand at North End Park to capture the Dunfermline Athletic manager, Jim Leishman, score a 'cracking goal'.[23]

Meanwhile the young miners' wives of Lochgelly needed special support. 'At the time we had I think two girls, maybe three, but I definitely recall two were pregnant,' recalled Linda Erskine, secretary of the Women's Action Group in Lochgelly. 'And unlike most other folk where you're able to prepare, because their husbands were on strike, they were really struggling.' Fortunately, help was at hand thirty miles away, in the shape of the Dundee Trades Council: on the initiative of trade unionist Marie Vannet, it adopted Lochgelly for the purposes of providing help in cash and kind. There were strong links between Dundee and the mining communities of Fife: female workers in the engineering factories of Dundee regularly came for nights out in Lochgelly, becoming known as 'Dundee Fairies'. Some of them found partners there. When they adopted the Fife mining communities, they sent layettes for new-born babies, in return asking only for a photo of the baby.[24] One of the mothers to receive these precious supplies was Carol Ross, chair of the Women's Action Committee in Cowdenbeath, whose third child, Cameron, was born during the strike:

The layette I got from Dundee was just out of this world . . . There were nappies, somebody had actually crocheted the most beautiful christening shawl, you had stuff like that in it. You had creams, lotions, everything that a new-born kid could have. Everything, everything, that would last them for months. It must've cost an absolute fortune, they were just amazing.[25]

Much further south, in Leicestershire, the Dirty Thirty gave up on picketing early as a hopeless task and concentrated on fundraising, travelling far and wide as the poster boys of the strike. Darren Moore, only twenty-two when the strike began, was politically aware, drafting a motion for the Young Socialist conference in Scarborough at the end of March to the effect that 'The TUC must call a general strike.' His main focus of money-raising activity was Milton Keynes, where the Trades Council sponsored him and a trio of striking miners from Derbyshire and Staffordshire to stay for several weeks:

People who supported us had set up a rota of where you'd stay, where you go for a meal, and then in the day you'd either you do collecting or other stuff. We used to collect in the shopping centre there. Then if there were any meetings we'd go to the meetings and then probably at night we'd talk at meetings, Labour Party meetings, union meetings.

Milton Keynes held a Miners' Day on 30 September, and Darren ran in the half-marathon. Meetings were not always plain sailing: speaking at Aylesbury, at the invitation of NALGO, Darren was unable to persuade those present to vote a weekly levy, and was shocked when one trade unionist said, 'Don't worry about it, when the Welsh miners are evicted, we'll buy the homes up for holiday cottages.'[26] More successful, ironically, was his speech to HM Tax Inspectorate in Leicester, where a young shop steward, Simone Dawes, a member of the Socialist Workers Party, was hoping to push her boss, Clive, into setting up a support group:

My friend and colleague, Maxine, elbowed me in the side and said, 'You see who's on the stage? He is the best-looking miner I've ever seen.' So I looked up and there he was. I thought, 'Oh, he is quite nice.' Then

I focused on what I was going to say, and I gave Clive a right battering. And then Darren said to me later on, 'Oh I wondered who that gobby lady was.' So that was the first time I saw him, and then we went down the pub, as you did in them days, after the meeting and Darren came and Clive came, we all had a drink and then . . .'[27]

If Milton Keynes was the stamping ground of Darren Moore, that of the Scottish Girvan brothers in the Dirty Thirty was Northampton. Their main contact there was Alan Duxbury, a member of the Communist Party and a NALGO official. A first task was to overcome southerners' prejudices about who miners were. As Bob put it,

We were sort of aliens. A lot of these people when they first saw us – and I don't mean to be rude – expected us to have flat caps and a whippet. One night they organised a quiz night to raise funds for us. It was at the NALGO union club in Northampton – 'University Challenge'. We had a team, the university lecturers had a team, and there was a team of teachers. And we beat them hands down. They just couldn't believe it.[28]

Another high point was a packed-out meeting organised in Northampton Guildhall on 16 October. Tony Benn was the star speaker, with Malcolm Pinnegar and Kay Smith the voices of the Dirty Thirty. The Girvans also travelled distances, with one thing leading to another, and perfected their performance. A teacher at Countesthorpe Community College in Leicester, June Chenoweth, pointed them towards Marlborough, where her mother June and her Quaker friends had set up a support group and wanted striking miners to speak. Bob Girvan went that November with another pair from the Dirty Thirty. They had their own prejudices to overcome, too:

Me, Barry Draycott and Mick Poli went down and I told Mick they were Quakers and that. We get there and we're talking and the first thing Mick said was, 'You don't look like they do on the porridge oats packet, do you?' . . . We were like a travelling show by then. Barry was a union official so he knew all the facts and figures. My wife was heavily pregnant at the time so I was giving it from the family view, not having much money and that. And of course Mick, because he looked the part, he used to make up picketing stories. Which were true anyway. He'd be sitting with his feet on the desk and we'd say, 'Christ, tone it down a bit.'[29]

They need not have worried. June Chenoweth and her friend Rosy Berry set up a Marlborough and District Miners' Support Group that made regular contributions to the Dirty Thirty.[30]

The co-leaders of the Dirty Thirty, Malcolm 'Benny' Pinnegar and Mick 'Richo' Richmond, went much further afield. They spoke at Bold, in Lancashire, and were appalled by the hardship suffered by miners at Westhoe in County Durham.[31] Malcolm, according to his wife Margaret, was 'a natural speaker':

He'd never done public speaking, but he had spoken at the union meetings and all this sort of thing. And he could put it together, you know, he could put a sentence together, and put a speech . . . never had any notes. If questions were thrown at him he would answer them, you know, whether you agreed with him or not he would answer them.[32]

Benny and Richo went up to Scotland, exploiting the fact that Richo's wife Linda was the daughter of a steelworker from Ravenscraig. Margaret, who was working as a quality controller in a hosiery factory, seems to have coped with Malcolm's absences, although their daughter Claire, seventeen at the time, admitted, 'I lost my dad through the strike.' Richo's wife Linda also suffered from his absences, so he took her to South Wales – where they were put up by Christine and Stuart Powell – because he wanted her to understand the solidarity that was central to the strike. As she reported at the time to Ashby Labour Party,

> Mick tried to explain what was what but I was scared and didn't take much notice. It soon became obvious that Mick was serious because within three weeks the phone was ringing virtually non-stop. The pressure on me just got too much, and I had to go away to my mother's to escape from the life our daughter and I were leading. I needed to think. After ten days I decided I would return and try to understand this terrible strike. It was only when Mick was called to a meeting in South Wales that it hit home to me. He took me along because I was low. After meeting the brave people of the Valleys, my mind was absolutely made up. I realised what the fight was all about: jobs, communities, the very way of life. Mick and I still have arguments but I try to understand.[33]

Interviewed in 2020, Linda returned to the strain of Mick's absences and the fact that she was effectively managing the operations centre of the Dirty Thirty:

> Then, when the strike came, everything went to pot really. I never knew when Mick would be at home, so the dog had to go, because he would go over the country, him and Benny, or the phone would be constantly ringing, looking for him . . . Somebody had to be in the house near enough all the time because I couldn't have nobody to have [my daughter] . . . It was hard. And I'd really, really had never been in a position like it before. I met a lot of good friends through it, made a lot of enemies through it.[34]

To sustain the strike, often at great personal cost, fundraising had to go on. London, of course, was generally seen to be the most obvious and fruitful destination. The miners from the small Kent coalfield regarded it as their backyard, but were under pressure from miners from other Areas.

One Kent miner said that they tried to organise a meeting via the unions and Labour Party to share out between coalfields what was collected in London, but complained that 'the South Wales miners would not join in', and by Christmas there was 'a bloody Yorkshireman on every street corner in London'.[35]

The Welsh miners were indeed very active in London. Four months into the strike, in July, Ali Thomas went there with Dai Donovan. Ali had a contact at the *Daily Express*, while Dai's brother-in-law was in Brent NALGO. They stayed in a special-needs school in Haringey, where they were looked after by three supporters (Fay, Joe and Julian), who worked for the Greater London Council (GLC) and arranged their meetings. In front of an audience, their different styles complemented each other. Dai, said Ali, 'lived on nervous energy' and was 'very aggressive', pointing out that 'Mrs Thatcher calls us the enemy within', whereas 'I'd have them with their hankies out and cheques.'[36] For example, addressing the civil servants of Brent NALGO, Ali told them that he was one of eleven children, and that 'In the last war, I woke up one day with two new brothers, two evacuees from the West of London. We came to your need then, I want your help now.' They were introduced to key members of the GLC, then under Ken Livingstone, and Ali remarked that 'the powerful people in that building were all women'. One of them, Jenny Fletcher, chair of the women's committee, invited them back to her home on a Friday night for a meal. They paid their hosts back in kind by canvassing for three Labour councillors on Tottenham's estates. Ali concluded that the people on those estates – some of whom were later involved in the October 1985 Broadwater Farm riot – were worse off than Welsh miners. It was 'a real education', he reflected. 'It was hard to believe the conditions these people live in.'[37]

As Welshmen, the miners used the male voice choir to develop their emotional appeal in London and in other cities. The choirs of Onllwyn and Crynant, neighbouring villages in the Dulais Valley, were brought together as the South Wales Striking Miners' Choir and had their first outing at Lewisham's Albany Empire, which had recently been reopened by Princess Diana, on 18 September. The following week, they performed at the Liverpool Empire on the same bill as George Melly.[38] As Phil Bowen, who was a baritone in the choir, remembered:

> We actually did a concert – I think it was in Lewisham in London – with a band called the Test Department, and they were a sort of percussion, steel, heavy metal. And I recently found out now they had a record made.[39]

Called *Shoulder to Shoulder*, the album's tracks included 'Stout-Hearted Men', 'Comrades in Arms', 'Myfanwy' and 'Take Me Home'.

Miners' wives, too, were involved in long-distance fundraising. There was an increasing demand for them to speak, as they were regarded as the protectors of the family and the community. Sometimes they were reluctant to put themselves forward – and even more so, to be put forward. Kay Jones and her mother – known as 'Betty the union', because she was a shop steward at the Ystradgynlais watch factory where Kay worked part time – went to London at the request of Betty's brother, Tom Jones, who had previously been fundraising with Dai Donovan. According to Kay,

> Her brother used to say, 'You're going to London.' 'What do you mean I'm going to London?' 'Oh, you've got to go to London.' I remember going with my mother along with others. We got out at Elephant and Castle and I think it was the South Bank Polytechnic, this huge, huge place. We landed in this room and of course my mother thought that she was going to have to present a plate or a mug or whatever they'd had commissioned. But instead she had to make a speech. I remember the moment because I remember my mother saying, 'When I get home I'll kill him.'[40]

Like the Welsh, Durham miners and their wives made the long trip to London to raise funds. On one occasion, Mary Stratford went with Bill

Frostwick to make common cause with locals and activists protesting at the flattening of Silvertown in East London by the London Docklands Development Corporation. Mary, like other miners' wives and miners themselves, reflected on the cultural misunderstanding of southerners: 'Their perception of miners was that they lived in little two-by-two colliery houses and had fires. Trips to the pit in their boots. It was like sixty years out of date, you know.' That said, although she came from a struggling community in County Durham, she reflected that in Silvertown,

I'd never seen deprivation like it. There was deprivation in mining communities at that time, but they were communities and they support one another. They still had a sense of what community is and you're all in it together – joint sort of support networks and families.[41]

The common cause, nevertheless, was that miners and East Londoners were both facing the power of the state and global capitalism, and were having to mobilise their respective communities against them. A rally was held with the usual opposition MPs. Mary Stratford remembered that

Tony Benn was speaking. Dennis Skinner was there. They were just coming in and out. And I spoke and I think Bill [Frostwick] spoke. My bit was just about what it was like to be a member at the support groups. It was a huge fundraising and raised a lot of money. We collected on the streets in London around that time and met some lovely people and they came up.[42]

One veteran Durham miner who went down to London was Ernie Foster, who worked at Seaham, was on the Durham Miners' Association Executive and was a leading light of the Spennymoor and District Trades Council. He made use of a connection with Bernard Regan, a Stockport teacher of Irish Catholic origin who had done a master's degree in Marxism at Durham University in 1970 and had met Foster through their joint activism. In 1984, Regan was teaching at Quintin Kynaston comprehensive school in St John's Wood and had influence in the Inner London Education Authority through his membership of the International Marxist Group (IMG), the Socialist Teachers Alliance, the National Union of Teachers (NUT) and the Inner London Teachers Association, which was dominated by left-wing teachers. Foster explained that Regan

> told me if we could get down to London and get round the schools, speaking . . . he could arrange for meetings to take place to inform teachers in schools for us to go and speak to them. And we went round quite a number of schools in London and we raised quite a lot of money.[43]

Meanwhile Regan said that from County Durham

> two or three people would come down and almost every week . . . report on what was happening, explain the situation, why the action was taking place, what they were hoping to achieve, what their objectives were. And then they would hold a collection in the school. So every week we raised money and it would vary, but it was significant amounts of money. I mean, I think about in those days, maybe about a thousand pound a week or something like that.

One problem that Regan did point out was the pedantic bureaucracy of the Inner London Teachers Association, which on one occasion prevented the suspension of their procedures to allow Ernie to make a report. 'I was livid about that,' he said, 'because people's plight was desperate. I mean, Ernie told me about some of the travelling miners who lived far away from local communities and were living hand-to-mouth.'[44]

Alongside teachers and local government employees, among the most committed supporters of the Miners' Strike were the print workers. Like the miners, they were highly skilled, unionised and politicised, with a great sense of camaraderie created by hardship. They worked in Dickensian conditions, often suffering lung complaints from ink mist and paper dust thrown up by the whirling presses. One of them with links to Yorkshire was Paul King. The grandson of a 'petty thief and bare-knuckle fighter' from Bethnal Green and son of a self-educated insurance broker and milliner, he failed the 11-plus, but thrived in the 1960s South London club scene as part of the Mod subculture and as a Millwall supporter. He was artistic, and his life was transformed by a six-year apprenticeship as a print worker, becoming a member of the elite National Graphical Association (NGA), which had its own chapel in each newspaper works, as did other unions like SOGAT – the Society of Graphical and Allied Trades.

The attack on trade unions brought miners and print workers together. King supported the mainly Asian female workers striking for trade union recognition at the Grunwick film-processing laboratories in Willesden in 1976–78; later, in 1983, he turned out in support of strikers targeting the newspaper owned by Eddy Shah in Warrington, where he had his nose broken. For King, the government's plan to close the pits was a declaration of war on the miners' union. With support from the media, the hostilities would then extend to the printers:

> They had a full closure plan and you saw how the media was playing up to this because they recognised by supporting Thatcher they could take on the print unions at the same time. It was all part of the tale. And a lot of us who worked in Fleet Street saw this coming down the line. That was one of the main significant drivers of why we were more than happy to support the mining communities. Virtually every newspaper, irrespective of the way they were editorially driven, adopted a region or regions. I mean, the *Observer* effectively were down in Kent. I believe the *Mirror* was as well. The *Financial Times* were up around Stoke because I ended up visiting Hem Heath a couple of times. And they came down to us. The casual chapel, which I was chairman of the

casuals, we were heavily involved in the area around Armthorpe in South Yorkshire. We supported the Armthorpe colliery. You have Bentley just a few miles down the road as well. So you've quite close attachments to them. And we were up there an awful lot, taking money up primarily, in any way, shape or form we could.[45]

Progressively, over time, fundraising stretched not only across the country, but internationally. The Miners' Strike attracted support from miners' unions, other trade unions and left-wing parties across Europe and further afield.[46] It was provided mostly in the form of money and food, but also through visits and holidays.

Lisa Potts, the daughter of Billy and Elsie Potts in Warsop Vale, remembered being invited on holiday by Dutch miners with a group of children from striking communities in Nottinghamshire on what turned out to be a family holiday:

Through the local NUM they had a raffle for all the children of local miners and the prizes were . . . I think about thirty children in total got to go for a week's holiday to Holland, split into smaller groups of about six and sent to different parts of Holland. Adults were asked to volunteer to supervise the groups. So, we were in a group where there was myself, my younger brother, Paul Mosley and three other girls were, two boys and four girls in total. And we went to a place called Appelscha . . . My mum and dad were responsible for myself, my brother and the four other kids. So, it was effectively a family holiday, the first foreign holiday we had actually. 1984, yes. And we sailed from Harwich to Zeebrugge on a seven-hour ferry . . . We had a lovely week, cycling and you know because cycling is really easy in Holland, it's very flat. And canoeing in the canals.[47]

Countries across Europe were also generous with supplies of food. Tom Adams, NUM branch treasurer at Frances and an experienced picketer, remembered the supplies that came from the Soviet Union to the strike centre at Dysart for wider distribution:

> Some of the stuff that came from Russia food-wise was out of this world. Great what they did. And they get much maligned, the Russians. But they sent some really good stuff, food, sugar cubes which were twice the size of your own sugar cube. Tins of pilchards and fish and stuff. It wasn't perishable, it was stuff you could keep and use when you wanted to use it. We were picking it up in trucks. I don't know how it got here but we were getting it with trucks. It would come to Dysart and we'd just unload the truck, putting it in the strike centre.[48]

On occasion, the food from abroad was difficult to handle because of what communities were used to eating. In her round robin of 5 November 1984 to potential donors, Mary Hart of Glyncorrwg wrote:

> French miners have sent generous consignments of food but they're not very well informed about what we eat. The last delivery included large quantities of couscous which no one had ever heard of and the macaroni not much use if you can't afford cheese to go with it.[49]

When it came to money, enterprising fundraisers went directly to the continent, exploiting connections they already had and making new ones. Jean McCrindle flew with Arthur Scargill to Vienna to pick up huge funds collected in the Soviet Union, took him extravagantly to a performance of *Tosca* at the Vienna State Opera and returned on the boat train with carrier bags full of cash.[50] Not to be outdone, in December 1984 Anne Scargill and Marsha Marshall went on a fundraising trip to Italy, at the invitation of the Italian trade unions, and were invited to speak on Vatican Radio. 'Not many people get that honour,' said Marsha, 'but being miners' wives they thought we should. I thought, fancy me being heard all over the world and that how brave they thought miners and their families were.'[51]

Meanwhile Phil White, who complained that the NUM headquarters at Pontypridd was not giving as much money to their support group at Maesteg as, for example, to Maerdy, because of its alleged left-wing tendencies, went to Germany in October 1984, using links to the West German Social Democratic Party (SPD) and the IG Metall trade union. His three-week tour of West Germany went, he said, from 'Aachen to Cologne, through Remscheid, Lubeck, through the Ruhr valley, Hamburg, the East/West frontier then down to Stuttgart'. He returned to South Wales with a suitcase full of Deutschmarks.[52]

The strength and warmth of these international connections is best illustrated by the visit of Kipp Dawson, a woman miner from Bethlehem Steel's Somerset Mine in Pennsylvania who came to Britain for six weeks in October–November 1984 on a fact-finding tour for the United Mine Workers of America (UMWA) and the Socialist Workers Party, which sponsored her. Her trajectory captured both the long march of radical causes in twentieth-century America and the connections that one activist could make across the British coalfields during the strike.

Kipp's grandmother had emigrated in 1912 from Łódź in Russian Poland to the USA. Following the murder in 1922 of her first husband – a Polish-Jewish immigrant and a communist – in Erie, Pennsylvania, she had moved to Los Angeles, where she remarried. Kipp was brought up in a communist family and compared her own mother to both Rosie the Riveter and Ethel Rosenberg. Kipp herself was involved in the civil rights movement, dropped out of college to run the Student Mobilization Committee to End the War in Vietnam in New York, and then became involved in both the women's liberation and the gay liberation movements. In 1979, she followed the Socialist Workers Party's 'turn to industry' and became a miner (which had become possible for women in 1974), at the same time 'coming home' to her family's roots in Pennsylvania.[53]

The British equivalent of the US Socialist Workers Party was Socialist Action, which invited her to speak at an International Solidarity rally in Manchester on 20 October 1984. She said that militant workers in the

USA were looking to two places for inspiration: the struggle of the Nicaraguan people and the strike of the British miners. She met Ann Jones of Hirwaun through Socialist Action. Ann spoke in Manchester on behalf of the South Wales Women's Support Groups and invited Kipp to Wales.[54] On 22 October, Kipp was in London, where she 'Met Dirty 30 including Malcolm ("Benny") and Richo (Mick Richmond), who invited me to meeting on 10/30. Supper with Richo, Benny, a nice young CP miner and others.' On 25 October, at 6 a.m., she was on a picket line at Agecroft colliery near Pendlebury and at Mansfield in the afternoon. 'Evening at Miners Welfare Club in Warsop where I spoke to a meeting of thirteen miners and four wives and others.' She then stayed overnight with Mary Donnelly. She picketed at Sherwood colliery at 5.30 a.m. on 27 October and at Bentley pit on 31 October, before speaking to a Socialist Action meeting in Sheffield.[55]

On 1 November, Kipp went to South Wales, where Ann Jones remembered that

> Kipp spent a lot of time with us and because they could – they weren't working – they took her up to see the pit and took her to see the shaft [of Tower colliery] and down the drift. Brian [Jones] took her all over the mountain in the car and she loved it.[56]

She met the South Wales Women's Support Groups and gave a powerful speech to a meeting of 300 women in Cardiff. She wrote in her diary that she had told them they were doubly strong – as women and as working class – and that the world needed them:

> I took the mike, faced the audience and said, 'My name is Kipp Dawson and I'm an underground coalminer from the United States.' Suddenly 300 women were on their feet, shouting and stormily applauding. And as tears filled my eyes all I could do was to raise my union cap in the air and to give them a clenched fist greeting. After that welcome I could

not let them down so in five to seven minutes I gave them greetings to let them know how much the whole world needs them . . . I told them I felt we are strong because as in the song 'Sixteen Tons', we have one fist of iron, being women, and another fist of steel, being working class. And as we use both fists together nothing can stop us as they are showing. I ended by reciting very slowly the last verse of 'Solidarity for Ever'. It went down very well, so much so that for the next hour I was quite deluged by women wanting to shake or hold my hand, wanting to thank me, wanting my address. I was given the badges of so many South Wales support groups. I was proud to be among them, proud to have brought some cheer and pride into their lives. They have given me so much.[57]

Kipp Dawson spun and developed a network of important relationships from her visit to Britain. Among the strongest was with Richo Richmond of the Dirty Thirty, whom she converted to the importance of the struggle in Nicaragua. He wrote to her after her return to the USA:

There is a void in my heart since you left our country but that void will be bridged when Malcolm [Pinnegar] and I can somehow manage to raise the finance to come over and see you and your brothers and sisters hopefully next year and maybe we can address a few meetings of the UMWA. We would like to have a kind of working vacation, if you know what I mean. There will <u>always</u> be a place in my heart for you Kipp – a lady of the top and highest order . . . <u>All my love to you</u>, Kipp, my fraternal greetings to UMWA and keep up the fight – especially to stop the war in Nicaragua – Please keep in touch, comrade. Love and Peace. Solidarity with the UMWA.[58]

She replied to him, putting her finger on the political and the personal in her contact with the Dirty Thirty. On the one hand, she said, they were a model for the struggle of the working class worldwide. On the other, international solidarity was founded on the comradeship and affection between fighters dedicated to the same cause:

> Always, dear Richo, you and the 'Dirty 30' are on my mind. You are starting to become known in the U.S. among socialist workers to start with, and from there your fame begins to spread. But it is far from enough . . . It is SO important for people over here to learn about you. In my book, you are the future, including the future of our class over here . . .
>
> I think you know, at least somewhat, how very much your comradeship and friendship mean to me. Wouldn't it be fine to work in the pit together? Or just to work side by side in defence of our union, our class, our future . . . Please give my love to Benny. I will write to him soon as well. Here is a <u>big</u> hug for you, Richo. I can see your smile now, and hear your laugh, and both warm me. Please write again soon.
>
> LOVE TO YOU, RICHO! VICTORY TO THE MINERS! VENCEREMOS! – Kipp.[59]

Fundraising for the Miners' Strike thus expanded in ever increasing circles – from tin-rattling among pubgoers on a Friday night or shoppers on a Saturday morning, to gigs organised on a regional basis, national letter-writing campaigns and speaking tours, and culminating in trips to Europe to raise funds and the visits of women miners from the United States. It drew on solidarity with the miners' cause and, in turn, promoted it. There was a sense that this was a historic battle between the organised working class and the capitalist state. Other trade unionists anticipated that fire would soon be turned on them. Government propaganda was at work and popular sympathy was not always present, as South Wales miners found on Anglesey and Durham miners' wives found in the university of Durham. Miners had to overcome clichéd images of themselves, and also learned that other working-class communities were often less well off than they were and frequently lacked their sense of community. Outside activists were drawn into the struggle, inspired by the sense that socialism had now found the proletarian base for revolution. It is true that miners absent for long periods on speaking and fundraising tours placed their marriages under intense pressure – and one of the largely unspoken dimensions of the strike is how far this resulted in infidelities. But emotional connections did develop, as between Darren Moore and Simone Dawes or between Richo Richmond and Kipp Dawson. The Miners' Strike was never just about money: it was much more about sympathy and solidarity on a grand scale.

8

LESBIANS AND GAYS SUPPORT THE MINERS

The place: a Wimpy bar in Praed Street, Paddington. The date: Thursday 6 September 1984. Dai Donovan, representing the Neath, Dulais and Swansea Valleys Support Group, freshly off the train from South Wales, met four gay activists, in order to pick up a cheque for £500. This was the fruit of a couple of months' collecting from the gay community in the pubs and clubs of London. To make the donation official, the four activists took Dai to a small presentation in one of those pubs, The Bell, at King's Cross. In his thanks, Dai said that his mining community 'extended the hand of friendship and solidarity to lesbian and gay comrades and friends in London', and he invited them to visit the Dulais Valley at a future date.[1]

Dai later recalled that there had been some 'nervousness' around 'the sexual politics of gay and lesbian', but that they soon found common political ground as enemies of Mrs Thatcher's repressive state and the hostile media. Just as the miners faced the harassment of their communities by the police, so gays 'were as much prisoners in London', equally harassed by the police and exploited by non-gay club owners because they had nowhere else to go.[2] 'We were overjoyed,' said Mike Jackson, one of the gay activists present that day, after meeting Dai Donovan. 'He was completely open, he didn't have a prejudiced bone in his body.' On their side, the gays and lesbians now felt that they were seeing through the lies and 'hearing the truth' about the resilience of the South Wales coalfield and the hardship suffered by mining families. Mike Jackson gave his version of the public reception:

> The Bell was our favourite place. It was the first what you might call alternative gay venue. It was full of young people, students and unemployed people. A more radical lefty element and more avant-garde music I suppose you'd call it . . . The Bell was always consistently the most generous crowd as well. That's an old story. We'd already been collecting at The Bell and knew that they were supportive. Dai just went down a storm . . . This man has just made a speech and everybody has gone mad. You've got to harness that. That's why LGSM [Lesbians and Gays Support the Miners] just grew so exponentially.[3]

The most charismatic of the gay activists present that night was Mark Ashton. He was born in Lancashire, but was brought up in Portrush, near Londonderry in Northern Ireland. Later, his father's work as an engineer installing textile machinery took him to Bangladesh. Mark visited him there and had his eyes opened to global poverty and injustice. He joined the Young Communist League, of which he became general secretary while employed as a hospital porter. The most organised of the gay activists was Mike Jackson. He was also from Lancashire – the cotton town of Accrington. His father had been killed in a car crash in 1962, when Mike was eight, and he had been brought up by his mother and grandmother, who, unlike most of her generation, hated Winston Churchill, because 'he sent British soldiers in to shoot Welsh coalminers and she never forgave him for that'. Mike was sent to a boarding grammar school – 'I think part of the idea was to man me up a little bit. Well, that didn't work.' He left homophobic Accrington for London and trained in horticulture at Kew Gardens, coming out as gay at nineteen. He went to Keele University in 1976 as a mature student and founded the North Staffs Gay Switchboard. Moving back to London as head gardener at Bedford College, Regent's

Park, he met Mark Ashton as a volunteer for London Gay Switchboard and was delighted to find that they were both socialists, as well as both gay.

Things started to happen when they were collecting for the miners at the Pride March on 7 July 1984. After the march, they adjourned to the University of London students' union, where the Labour Campaign for Lesbian and Gay Rights had organised a meeting and invited a young Kent striking miner to speak. 'It was standing room only,' Mike remembered. 'Mark just said, "We're onto something here." '[4] Mark placed an advertisement in *Capital Gay*, calling an inaugural meeting in his Elephant and Castle flat of what became Lesbians and Gays Support the Miners (LGSM). Mark Ashton was elected press officer and Mike Jackson secretary. A constitution was approved, stating that its aim was

> to organise amongst lesbians and gay men in support of the National Union of Mineworkers and in defence of mining communities. To provide financial assistance for miners and their families during the national miners' strike.[5]

Putting together this solidarity between lesbians, gays and miners was not without difficulty. The labour movement was not progressive on these issues and could be homophobic. 'Previously we had felt quite hostile towards trade union, macho-type bully boys, the macho mentality that ran through the unions,' Mark Ashton told the left-wing Italian review *Il Manifesto* in January 1985. For this reason, they decided not to give their money directly to the NUM, but rather to a mining community; the Labour Campaign for Lesbian and Gay Rights had already sent £40 to the Dulais Valley. Equally, it was not clear that all lesbian and gay activists would be sympathetic to the cause of the striking miners. Ashton explained that not all gays backed the striking miners, and some supported Mrs Thatcher:

> Just before Christmas the Gay Conservative Group decided to support the miners, those that are working, the scabs, but they've only collected

£25. They're the extreme right of the gay movement. Between the two groups there are quite a lot of people who are neither for nor against the miners. Many of them support us but not the miners directly. They ask, 'Why are you collecting for the miners instead of the gay community?' We answer that the best way to defend the gay community is to defeat Thatcher. But sometimes it's hard to convince people.[6]

Much later, Mike Jackson argued that the Miners' Strike gave lesbian and gay activists an opportunity to campaign openly, to shape a working-class homosexuality against those who thought it was a 'bourgeois deviation' and to assume some leadership in their community. 'What was so thrilling for Mark and me and all the rest of us,' he said, 'was that a lot of us did come from working-class backgrounds. We suddenly felt like we could flex our muscles within the lesbian and gay community.'[7]

Nor was it obvious that a traditional Welsh mining community would take easily to an offer of support from gays and lesbians in London, many of whom had fled intolerant communities where they grew up, in order to find some anonymity and freedom in the great metropolis. Mike Jackson found the address of the Neath, Dulais and Swansea Valleys Miners' Support Group and wrote to its secretary, Hefina Headon, to ask whether they would like to be 'adopted' by LGSM for the purposes of continuous support. When his letter was read out at the weekly support group meeting at Onllwyn Welfare, Siân James recalled that some of the men especially were uncomfortable: 'It was just very, very macho and this is where the macho nature of the community came out.'[8] Homophobic jibes were uttered, and it took women like herself to insist that LGSM be treated like any other group that supported them:

There were sniggers, there were jokes. I didn't understand some of the jokes that were being made. I had to go home and ask Martin what they meant. I hadn't personally heard the term 'shirtlifters'. It was things like, 'Oh, we'll have to stand with our backs against the wall.'

And I thought, 'I've had enough, this is silly. They give us money – let's get on with it, let's take the money.' We were insistent that if we were taking the money, we were going to invite them, like any other group, to see where their money was being spent. And it was the women who were at the forefront. It was the women who said, 'Do you know what? We're not going to treat them any differently to any other group.'[9]

Once Mike Jackson heard back from Hefina Headon, preparations began for a visit to the Dulais Valley. LGSM was growing and could no longer meet at Mark's, or in any other private home. From mid-September, it met at the Gay's the Word bookshop at King's Cross. In time, this venue also became too small, and meetings moved to a room over The Fallen Angel pub in Islington. Over thirty people signed up for a weekend visit to the Dulais Valley, scheduled for 26–28 October 1984.

One of those keen to go was Jonathan Blake – not working class this time, but from a middle-class Birmingham Jewish background and educated at Oundle public school. When he had announced to his mother, 'I'm going to be an actor!' she turned round and said, 'Well, that's wonderful, darling. I hope not like John Gielgud', who had been arrested for cottaging. Jonathan went to drama school and made a reasonable living as an actor; but he was then arrested by a 'pretty policeman' for 'cruising' in Brompton cemetery, convicted and fined £25. Things got worse. In 1982, after a trip to San Francisco, he was diagnosed with HIV. He remembered that he was 'totally winded. I'm thirty-three years old; my life is over.' He felt suicidal, but could not go through with it. The alternative for him was to live what remained of his life to the full. He attended Gay Pride. He joined Gays for a Nuclear-Free Future, there met his boyfriend-to-be Nigel – with his 'ochre and crimson pantaloons and mop of black hair' – and went to Greenham Common. Nigel then introduced him to LGSM. Jonathan found Mark Ashton 'very charismatic, he had this energy' and saw Mike as the one who 'held it together'. On the visit to Wales, Jonathan recalled:

There were two Hackney Community transport vans. I was one of the drivers, and there was a clapped out Volkswagen. There must have been about thirty or thirty-five of us that went down. We got incredibly lost. We missed our introduction because it was at about one o'clock. We all slept on Dai Donovan's living room floor, crammed in like sardines.[10]

Apart from the confusion because of arriving late, nothing was left to chance. Siân James rehearsed the elaborate ritual that had been developed to greet visitors:

People would come on a Friday night, about eight, nine o'clock. You'd put them up on the Friday night. Then on the Saturday, they'd spend the day with you as a family and we'd arrange to do something like visit somewhere, show them the collieries and what they were supporting. And Sunday morning might be a day where you'd do a family thing, take them to visit your family. And then Sunday afternoon, they'd come to the support group meeting, participate in the support group meeting. But on the Saturday night we had the disco, the fundraising disco, and they'd come to that. And Sunday afternoon, about five o'clock we'd wave them off on their way. And then if it was London, they'd be back around eight, nine o'clock, similarly if they were going to Manchester or Birmingham. They would be back to start work on the Monday.[11]

On this Saturday, members of the support group and LGSM went on a joint rally to Swansea, where some of them spoke, and in the evening came the social at Onllwyn Welfare. Mike and Jonathan both spoke of this as a moment of truth, when the lesbian and gay activists were introduced to the mining community as a whole in their own temple. Mike remembered that, as the swing doors opened,

We had to walk in single file because it was so busy. Two or three hundred people. Different generations with kids running around.

Grandmas, granddads, and as we walked in the tenor of the conversation dropped and we knew that was a response to us. We were fairly conspicuous. We were young. I was one of the older ones at twenty-nine. Mark was twenty-four, twenty-five. Some people had zany haircuts. You know, charity-shop chic and stuff like that, and we knew that was a response to us and it's amazing just within a second how your world changes because someone stood up and started applauding us. And the whole concert room, people just started and gave us a standing ovation and my hair was standing up on my arms. Because we were in this crocodile, we were looking at each other going, 'Wow. This is amazing.' And history changed at that moment.[12]

Jonathan recalled the awkward moment gay men walked in, seeming to be greeted by silence and convinced that they had done the wrong thing, until the applause broke out:

I remember that there was this real sense of trepidation. So much that I don't actually remember walking in. But Mike [Jackson] says that there was this awful silence as the door opened and you just thought, 'Shit, we shouldn't be here.' But then somebody applauded and it was extraordinary. We were welcomed with such warmth and generosity, really welcomed. And from there it was bingo and dancing all the way.[13]

There were reasons for this hesitation on the part of their hosts. The arrival of men who, with their trimmed hair and bright shirts, were so radically different from the Welsh miners and were now dancing with their wives was a challenge to their traditional masculinity. Usually, Welsh men spent most of the evening at the bar, going onto the dance floor only for the 'smooch'. Siân James explained that 'the smooch was the last dance, so if you had a wife, you better dance that one dance or there'd be hell. And if you had your eye on somebody, this was your chance to walk her home.'[14] Philip James, the Treforgan miner, was even more confused to be asked to dance by one of the gay men: "'Let me tell you now," I said, "I don't dance with the wife and I certainly ain't dancing with you . . . Welshmen don't dance." '[15]

For the Welsh women, things were completely different. Jayne Headon was sixteen at the time. She had been brought up by Hefina as her daughter, though she was in fact her granddaughter. Sometimes she visited her mother Jennifer in Walthamstow and Streatham Hill, and was aware of ethnic diversity; but she had not encountered the gay community:

> For me living in South Wales in the middle of the Valleys we didn't see many people that were different. So, yeah, I was quite excited about them coming down and bringing a bit of a life into the community. I suppose because it was quite a sombre time when we were going through the strike.[16]

The first thing that struck Jayne was their appearance: 'I mean, pretty much everybody dressed the same in our mining villages – the same jeans, the same top, the same jacket. Everybody was very stereotypical; everybody looked the same.'[17] The colourful new arrivals disrupted the familiar pattern of couples and families:

> It was very traditional here: everybody expected a man to be with a woman, and that was the way things were. It was a very macho culture. If you looked at a group of miners they'd all be men, they'd all have wives and children, and that's how it had been for their mothers and fathers before them, and so on.[18]

Above all, however, a very shy and tongue-tied Jayne found that talking to the gay men brought her out of herself and enabled her to relax. 'Mark Ashton took me under his wing,' she said. 'He always had loads to say, so I didn't really get to say much. But I did want to ask about their lives as gay men, how they lived and what they did in London.'[19]

For Mike Jackson, going to Onllwyn was like a homecoming. As his grandmother hated Churchill for crushing the Welsh miners at Tonypandy, so he hated Thatcher for doing the same seventy-odd years later. Moreover,

Hefina reminded me of my grandma. Physically she was very similar. Short, quite rotund, quite fierce, and as is common with a lot of those old industrial communities the women were often fierce matriarchs . . . She had this thing where she'd fold her arms together and push her breasts up. My grandma did exactly the same thing. Always in stilettoes. She never wore flats and of course all the gay boys loved that. It was like, wow!

While they loved the Welsh women, the gay men of LGSM were intrigued to discover that there was one gay man in the village – Cliff Grist, a former miner and amateur photographer. Mike Jackson remembered that

on the way back to London in the minibus – I can't remember who stayed with Cliff – but they said, 'We've got gossip.' 'What's the gossip?' 'We found the gay one,' and we went, 'Oh.' People have said, 'Was Cliff out?' Well not in the way that we were. He didn't exactly go around wearing gay badges or working for Gay Switchboard because there weren't any gay badges and there was no Gay Switchboard. If his homosexuality was something he chose to hide then the prospect of twenty-seven out young LGBT activists descending on this community would have terrified the life out of him and he would have run for the hills. He did the opposite. He offered to accommodate us from the beginning and very, very quickly came out to us.[20]

Two of those who were accommodated were Jonathan Blake and his boyfriend Nigel. They returned after the strike, when they visited Craig-y

-Nos Castle, further up the Swansea Valley, which had been bought in the 1870s by an Italian opera singer and made into a miniature Bayreuth. Blake was explicit that

> actually the person that one most remembers was Cliff Grist. Nigel and I sort of stayed with Cliff, and then kept in contact with him. After the strike had ended, I remember we went down, because we were going to go to Adelina Patti's house, because there was an opera. So we went and stayed with Cliff.[21]

The visit of October 1984 was reported positively both by the Neath, Dulais and Swansea Valleys Miners' Support Group and by LGSM. The Support Group's weekly, *The Valleys' Star*, focused on what the miners and 'these kind, caring people from London' had in common in terms of facing police brutality, and how this had only redoubled their efforts to support the miners:

> A large group from London stayed in our area last weekend. This section of supporters have worked tremendously hard to provide us with £2,000. Our representatives have met these kind, caring people from London and have been amazed by their willingness to help our cause. All the violence which our miners have experienced at the hands of the police does not surprise this group of people. The 'boys in blue' have been handing out this treatment to them for a long time. Even though they are discriminated against for what they are they are still prepared to travel around London with NUM badges on their lapels, collecting here, there and everywhere.[22]

The minutes of LGSM underlined the friendship and solidarity of the two communities, the beauty of the gift offered by the miners and the wonderful experience they had enjoyed:

There was much merriment that evening and vast quantities of alcohol were consumed, much friendship extended between our group and those women and men of Dulais. Sunday morning we visited Treforgan colliery and witnessed the appalling underinvestment at the mine. In the afternoon we attended their support group meeting. Mike J. gave a short message of solidarity and thanked them for their generous and warm hospitality. Tom Jones (Dulais) then presented us with a gift in recognition of our support (this was a gleaming piece of anthracite and a miniature miner's lamp mounted together on a varnished wooden plinth). Dave Donovan addressed the meeting just before we left to return to London. He reported that our visit had been a success in the eyes of the people of Dulais. In addressing those from his own community he said that LGSM had been wearing NUM badges on our lapels for months now and that, as a mark of solidarity, they should wear our badges 'with respect and pride'. Mark Ashton reported that the visit was the best experience of his life. (Mine too! MJ)[23]

After their return, Mike Jackson sent a personal message to fellow secretary Hefina Headon which placed the miners and mining communities at the forefront of the struggle. 'The visit to Dulais was one of the happiest moments of my life,' he wrote. 'At the end of the day it is your brave and principled selves who will win this victory but we are on hand to offer whatever help we can.'[24]

Six weeks later, LGSM organised a return visit. Members of the Dulais community were invited to a benefit concert to raise money for the miners. The event, held at the Electric Ballroom, Camden, on Monday 10 December, adopted the title 'Pits and Perverts'. Top of the bill were Bronski Beat, whose lead singer, Jimmy Somerville, was a friend of Mark's. As Mike Jackson explained:

Mark had been hanging around with Jimmy Somerville as a close friend long before Jimmy's ascendance to fame. Jimmy is from Glasgow. From a really rough working-class background in Glasgow. Mark was from near Derry. So that was pretty grim where he was coming from. The two of them just got on like a house on fire and just went around terrorising London, from what I can gather. You know, kind of sexual cowboys.[25]

The occasion was a triumph, although the miners, miners' wives and daughters like Jayne Headon certainly experienced a clash of cultures. Before the concert, the support group was invited for a vegetarian meal at The Fallen Angel pub. Siân James recalled:

Well everybody panicked, absolute panic . . . And so, when we parked the van up in Islington we all went for fish and chips because we thought the vegetarian food would be horrible – stuff like mung beans and rice and that crap – and we'd end up starving. But when we got to The Fallen Angel there was all this lovely food. All lovingly prepared. It was really beautiful – it didn't look like any vegetarian food we'd ever imagined. And we looked at each other and said, 'Shit. Wish we hadn't eaten that fish and chips.'[26]

Now they were exposed to the lifestyle of the gay community in London, to the idea of alternative gender identities and sexualities. Siân James explained that they discovered a whole new world of relationships and being together:

In a sense, it is another world, because it was the first place I'd ever come across where men and women were equally using the same toilets . . . So suddenly, you're looking at things from other people's perspectives. You're talking about people having transgender alter-egos. I remember going to a party in somebody's flat and our host opening the door completely dressed up as a Spanish flamenco dancer. 'Nice dress, Steve,' like. 'Do you like it?' 'I think it's lovely, Steve.' Because of the flamboyancy of that person's character. And then talking to lesbian friends about how they'd felt growing up and having this exchange of experiences of what it's like to be a young woman and not under-standing that they didn't want to have relationships like their families and friends had.[27]

For Jayne Headon, who was much younger, things were more chal-lenging. She and her friend Bethan, it is true, were taken under Mark Ashton's wing; but they now had to act as if they were gay:

Two of us who were younger, Bethan nineteen, me sixteen. When we went up to London for the first time Mark Ashton decided he would have the young 'uns and so we went and stayed with him and his boyfriend, partner at the time, Johnny. He took us all over different parts of London that definitely opened my eyes. We met Jimmy Somerville because he was his friend and we went round the back entrance to the night club Heaven. He kept holding my hand and said, 'Pretend to be gay. If you feel uncomfortable just squeeze my hand,' because I was quite young and naïve.[28]

Jayne's encounter with gay men was one thing; her encounter with lesbians another. She was shocked to witness same-sex relations in public and was turned off by the politics of lesbianism, which she found humour-less and needlessly man-hating:

And then I went to the toilet and wow – there were women having sex in the toilet, very loudly with the cubicle doors open. So I ran out of there. I was really frightened. I was just a sixteen-year-old girl from the Welsh Valleys . . . I attended a women's day they had organised. That was the first time I'd met a whole load of lesbians all together and to be honest they struck me as the grumpiest people I'd ever come across. I didn't see one of them smile . . . it was all 'Women, women, women, and men shouldn't exist' kind of thing. I didn't understand at the time why they were so cross all the time.[29]

If she did not get on – at this stage – with lesbianism, Jayne was exposed to debates about women's liberation, which did not necessarily have to threaten traditional couples. Back in the Valleys, she joined the women's group that Margaret Donovan and Siân James had set up alongside the main support group:

We came back from London and decided to have these female work-shops in the Onllwyn Welfare. We started inviting lots of different speakers and had workshops to empower women. We got that idea from when we were up in London, from all the different groups we were with that weekend. We had the women's group. Siân, Margaret Donovan, Karen, David Williams' first wife. Myself, Bethan. I don't think Christine [Powell] was in that very much. She was part of it but not always there. A couple of older women, Nancy, Phyllis. We met at Coelbren because David Williams and his wife ran the club there. It was giving people really the means to fight for what they wanted.[30]

These encounters between the mining communities and the gay and lesbian communities undermined the traditional, stereotypical relation-ship between miners and miners' wives. The men were without work; and if they were not yet losing the strike, defeat on the battlefield was clearly a possibility. The women had already stepped forward to run soup kitchens, organise food parcels, stand on picket lines when their men faced arrest, and address public meetings. Now they encountered and began to under-stand same-sex relationships, because the gay men were prepared to talk about them. As Siân James recalled:

Sometimes they would confide in us about aspects of their sexuality, which were shocking. Pretty extreme things, especially in the height of the HIV scare. But the thing was they trusted us to see it. They were trusting us with a very important part of themselves. They didn't want to hide behind any falseness.[31]

Mike Jackson, speaking to an LGSM conference in London just after the end of the strike, underlined the point about trust. For him it was both personal and political. Two communities under attack from prejudice and persecution had initially been nervous about how they would be received by the other, but now formed an alliance to fight for 'what is right, just and moral in the face of isolation'. This involved

deepening our mutual trust and honesty. It's happened already for many of us on a personal level – mining families, lesbians and gay men laughing, dancing, singing and getting dead drunk together. Let's build from that strength and keep developing our political and community links between each other and extend it to all those fighting for a peaceful, democratic and socialist world![32]

Siân James did go on to be more political, and twenty years later was elected to fight for a fairer world as a Labour MP. But what she also learned from her contact with LGSM was a more open, emotional and demonstrative approach to relationships than was the custom in the Welsh Valleys. In a word, the women of the mining communities became happy with a form of intimacy that transcended the family and cemented friendships:

It was the first time we'd had a relationship with men where it was perfectly acceptable to be sitting in those situations with them, and to be very affectionate, and not think that there was anything wrong with it. You could see people showing affection very openly. I don't mean sexual affection, just hugging and kissing. And in the Valleys we just didn't do those sorts of things. Only with our family and behind closed doors. We were always very affectionate with our parents, for example, holding hands or hugging them. But not outside the family, not even with close friends. Why would you think about doing that? It just wasn't done in the communities we were raised in. Someone flinging their arms round you would have been seen as soppy. People would have said, 'Oh don't be so soppy, don't be so silly.' Suddenly we were seeing people who were very demonstrative and who had a different lifestyle and a different experience more than anything. It was very liberating.[33]

9

A STATE OF SIEGE

After the Battle of Orgreave, the miners were on the back foot. The tactic of a mass picket to stop coal supplies to a major coking plant, which was supposed to deliver victory to the miners, ended in failure and humiliation. At the end of the summer, the government and the Coal Board decided to launch a new back-to-work policy. The traditional self-policing of mining communities was ended, as small armies of police from London or Manchester were sent to 'occupy' them and get a few striking miners back to work. This would allow the government and the media to spin the story that soon the majority would be back. In those villages, any strike-breakers were ostracised, their windows smashed or their homes daubed with graffiti. The mining villages were effectively placed under a state of siege, in order to protect the strike-breakers and keep the pickets in check. The police became increasingly brutal with pickets, arresting them on charges of breach of the peace or worse, and sending them up before the courts in short order for sentencing. Very often a notice of dismissal arrived from the Coal Board days or even hours later, signalling that the police, courts and Coal Board were working together in a cruel offensive.

At Hatfield Main colliery, near Doncaster, the police arrived on 21 August 1984 to take three strike-breakers back to work. 'A scab at every colliery,' said NUM branch delegate Dave Douglass, 'would have the advantage of tying down the pickets to their own backyards and would give an excuse for outright occupation of the military heartlands by riot police.'[1] He drew parallels with Northern Ireland to explain the Metropolitan Police's colonialist and racist attitude towards an entire population to pacify the North and demonstrate the 'futility of resistance' to the Thatcherite state:

> The women, children and teenagers of the village have had the horrors of occupied Ulster explode on their streets, have felt the sharp edge of uncontrolled brutality and repression charging down their garden paths, smashing through their back doors into their kitchens . . . The Metropolitan Police have become infamous for their anti-Northern hostility, the abuse being directed at the miners' Northern accents, 'thick Geordie bastards' or 'ay-up, ay-up, ay-up' in mock imitation of the Yorkshire greeting. Black miners were especially singled out by the Met for the normal torrent of racial abuse, ape-like gestures and monkey-like cries . . . They didn't come to 'contain' us or 'match us in numbers' as the popular press would have you believe. They came to bury us, to show the futility of resistance . . . When stories started to drift out of the mining villages being under 'police occupation' we meant just that . . . The police went to war with the mining communities.[2]

Initially, Douglass and NUM Branch Secretary Peter Curran tried to defuse the situation at Hatfield. They asked to meet the management to get permission to talk to the three strike-breakers; but the management refused to speak to them. Curran called a meeting of striking miners at the Miners' Welfare to decide on the next step, while Douglass decided to raise support in the surrounding villages:

> It was obvious that the community had to be roused, and loudspeaker vans toured Dunscroft, Stainforth, Thorne and Moorends, urging every available person, men and women, every fit person to head to the pit gates to defend the strike against the police and the scabs. Within minutes they were streaming from every direction towards the pit,

women with their children, a team of young BMX riders from Thorne, the buses were full, and people hitherto uninvolved left the club and made for the pit.[3]

Returning to the incident in his 2010 *Ghost Dancers*, Douglass's account was more autobiographical: 'I launched a tour of the villages in a loudspeaker car, rousing all our members to come down, defend the picket lines and demonstrate our feeling to the scabs.' Talks were now arranged, as Curran was allowed through and one of the strike-breakers decided to come out and rejoin the strike. Douglass adopted the non-violent tactic of sitting in the road to await the return of the strike-breaker bus at the end of the day: 'I mass the ranks of pickets and urge them that we will sit down in front of the line of riot cops just as the scab bus comes down the lane with the workers.'[4] The sit-down was a tactic to focus protest on the strike-breakers, rather than on the police, forcing the police to lay down their arms in order to remove the people sitting in the road and exposing them to pickets throwing bricks and bottles. The police then began to target non-violent protesters on the road. Interviewed in 2020, Douglass elaborated:

It annoyed me that we always ended up fighting the police and the scabs got away, unmolested in the bus. When the purpose of the picket was to make it clear to the scabs on the bus that we didn't approve of them. So I had arranged a mass sit-down outside the pit gates. And I had instructed my likely lads that they were to wait until the bus nudged through the crowds as they were carrying us away, before they attacked the bus, and not to attack the police. So everybody, with great bravery, sat down. And there's a famous picture of us sitting down. As the bus comes forward, and the police had put down the riot shields and the clubs, in order to carry us away – which is what I had planned – then a whole volley of bricks and bottles came over. And the cops immediately ran in with the snatch squad and started braying [beating] everybody sitting on the floor. And people have retold that story saying I was doing this 'peace man, non-violence, they won't hurt you'. I wasn't doing that at all, that wasn't my notion. But people tell the tale differently. And they ran riot through the village then. Mounted charges and all the rest of it, and the lads retaliated. And there was pitched fighting on that day.[5]

A hundred miles further north, at Easington colliery, on the coast of County Durham, the police and Coal Board reckoned that if they could get even one man back to work – someone with mental health issues or a criminal record, who was more malleable – this would be enough to break the logjam of the strike. Meanwhile, an occupation of the village would provoke protest and enable a slew of arrests and convictions that would demonstrate that the balance of power had now shifted decisively from mining communities to the state.

Heather Wood, who organised the women behind Save Easington Area Mines, had moved to Easington Village, just above Easington Colliery Village. She described how provocation from the Tory MP for Newcastle Central led to a police invasion of Easington on 24 August in defence of a strike-breaker miner:

On the evening of 23 August Piers Merchant who was a Tory MP at the time came on the television news and he said, 'Why is it that the Durham Constabulary cannot get one man in at Easington pit?' The next morning – by then we lived in the Village, John and I and the boys, but I insisted that they still went to the colliery primary school – so I always drove them down. You turn a corner coming from our house and there's a great big green, common land in the centre of the village. And as I turned the youngest, Peter, said, 'Look at the green, it's black.' And it was. It was black because it was full of police. It was like a panic. It's anger, it's a panic, it's fear of what was going to happen. I turned the next corner and there was a police blockade.[6]

Paul Stratford, a Durham mechanic who came from Easington and worked there, but who lived inland at Great Lumley, heard the Tory MP speak and was one of hundreds of Durham miners who turned up to stop the strike-breakers getting into the colliery. They were told by a Mr Breck, the manager, that a miner called Wilkinson would come through the front gate. This happened again the next day and the pickets turned him back. On the third day, a new, younger manager was brought in, with whom the miners had no relationship, and smuggled Wilkinson in at the back. 'So the Coal Board had reneged on their agreement,' said Paul, 'and the next thing you knew, it just all went up. All went up, you know, the police has done this, done that, and there was cars got smashed inside, the manager's car, the engineer's car.'

Over three days of trouble, fifty pickets were arrested. Paul himself was set upon by a police snatch squad and clung to a bus stop to try to stop them dragging him away. Sent the same day before a magistrate in nearby Peterlee, he was banned from coming into Easington, where his parents lived. He replied defiantly:

Me father's got pneumo[coniosis], me mother has a bad heart. I tell you now, if owt goes wrong with them, you're gonna have to put us in prison, because I'll be just making my way through anyway.

In November, he was then sent before a court in Seaham on a trumped-up charge of stealing a police helmet. He was lucky to have superb defence from the NUM's barrister, Vera Baird, who later became Northumbria police and crime commissioner. She ridiculed the police evidence and had the case thrown out:

This Vera Baird said, 'Right, so you were on the picket line, and Mr Stratford came up to you and stole your helmet.' 'Yes.' 'Took it off your head.' 'Yes.' She says, 'Regulation single chin strap or double chin strap?' 'Double chin strap.' She said something else, 'Right, now I want you to look at Mr Stratford,' and I'm like looking, 'I'm going to put it to you, if Mr Stratford got hold of a helmet, and a double chin strap stopping it from coming off, I'm going to put to you that Mr Stratford would have snapped your neck.' And I went, 'Christ, I'm gonna get done for attempted murder here. Oh bloody hell.' So he said, 'Yes.' So she says, 'Are you sure it was him that stole your helmet?'[7]

Not all those arrested had the same good fortune. Some who were not picketing or involved in the protest were caught up in the trawl of arrests and convictions. The life of Heather Wood's cousin, who was not even in the fray, was ruined by arbitrary arrest:

My cousin had been dropping his girlfriend off not far from the pit. On his way back they plucked him off the street. He hadn't been part and parcel of what was going on. He was taken to court. His solicitor tried to explain. The judge said, 'I'm not listening to individual cases. You're all the same. You're going to prison.' He went to one of the local ones, it wasn't Durham. I remember, his mum and dad went away on holiday and the prison governor rang my mum and dad and said, 'You do know David shouldn't be in here.' He was studying engineering. His exams were due. 'I'm willing to let him come home to sit his exams if you are prepared to act as the responsible persons and make sure he comes back.' That's how dangerous these people were. Even the prison governor – 'We know he shouldn't be here.' And that no doubt changed his life. He didn't continue with his engineering and he's not in the best of health.[8]

Back in South Yorkshire, in early September the situation was becoming even more desperate. The Coal Board and police acted together to occupy villages, get strike-breakers back to work and arrest and sack angry picketers. Ringleaders were targeted and their mates were not always there to support them.

At Askern, the Coal Board management supposedly persuaded a miner called Gordon Cufflink and four or five of his mates to break the strike. As elsewhere, they did not go down the pit, as no work could be done by so few; they simply stayed for a shift drinking tea in the Coal Board offices. The striking miners decided to storm the offices where the strike-breakers were being held. Out in front was Pete Richardson, who had already been arrested on a picket at Bilsthorpe early in March, and had then seen action at the Sheffield rally on 19 April and in Mansfield on 14 May. He was convinced that the assistant manager, Buxton, had it in for him and was working with the Manchester police who had occupied the village:

> I was very active in the union during the strike. The guy [Buxton] didn't like me. We were all in the yard, and he made sure that I was one picked out . . . The Manchester chief constable arrested me. He got his orders from somewhere and I have no doubt that he got them off Buxton . . . Some of the guys said, 'If you arrest him we'll tear the place apart, rip the control apart.' I was arrested, me mates backed me but people drifted off. I got sacked that day.[9]

Richardson's sacking by the Coal Board changed his life. It was a major blow to his work prospects and affected the whole family. 'I got the sack on my eldest son's birthday, 9.9.84,' he wrote in his prison notebooks. 'A nice present for our Wayne.'[10]

Peter Robson, another Askern miner, observed the incident from a distance. He confirmed that Pete (whom he calls 'Richo'), was singled out not because he was the ringleader, but because he was a militant and a troublemaker and the Coal Board wanted rid of him. Meanwhile Robson was keen to protect his reputation as South Yorkshire's 'best-dressed picket' – and was anyway hurled out of the way by a huge policeman. He suggests that other troublemakers were either agents provocateurs or not the main target:

Richo got sacked because this one particular day, we knew they were sat in the offices, the scabs, and we stormed the offices. And my abiding memory is, I jumped over these quite low iron railings, to run towards, and I looked up and I swear to God, it was the biggest policeman in the entire world, stood in front to me. And he was Asian. I thought, 'Oh Christ.' And he was in full gear. I looked at him and, 'Oh, I'll go back.' I was always voted best-dressed picket guy. I had a really good pair of trousers on, me last ones. And all he did, he just picked me up and chucked me over these low railings and I landed on my knees and all me, yeah. But they stormed . . . and they had double glass doors and they got broken. Nobody could say, 'He did it, they did it,' but they blamed Richo. And that was their excuse for getting rid of him . . . But at the same time . . . one of the lads was pictured on the cameras going round with a big stick just smashing the windows. Never got sacked. They targeted Richo because he was quite militant. He was very aggressive, all his life. He'd fight a brick wall, Richo. It was just an excuse to get shot of him.[11]

Pete was arrested for 'criminal damage and incitement to riot'. He was sentenced to two months in prison and was sent to Durham gaol. He called it 'a real sickener. I had got time for something I did not do.' The best support he got was 'letters from my wife Sue and all my mates who wrote in'.[12]

In Nottinghamshire, the situation was entirely different. The working miners were in the vast majority and were amply protected by the Metropolitan Police, who were bussed in to pacify the striking minority. Ken Bonsall, whose grandfather had come from Maltby, south of Doncaster, to work at Welbeck colliery near Mansfield, and whose father and elder brother were striking miners, was sixteen when he left Meden Comprehensive in Warsop in June 1984 and immediately became involved in picketing. His prospects of becoming a miner himself at Welbeck were doomed, unless the strike was won. However, he reflected: 'Welbeck was a police state, you couldn't get in or out. It was occupied. A few times we'd try in the morning but it was blocked.' In the late summer, the local police were replaced by the Metropolitan Police, who, says Ken, were aggressive and abusive. They corralled pickets into what Bonsall suggests was like a concentration camp, humiliated them by making them turn away from the strike-breaker buses and provoked them, in order to arrest them:

We couldn't even picket Welbeck. So, me and my dad had walked down back lanes and especially when the Met come . . . Nothing compared to Met when they come up. They'd been told to be antagonistic. Even to where, you know, you got abuse and scorn from the police. Really, to wind the miners up . . . Once they moved the picket line away from the pit gates to the top of the hill where there was a cricket pitch. They put a really big spotlight, a really thick chain and moved them back away from the road. The picket line had to go away from the road, up the steep banking, behind this thick Panzer chain on these iron stakes. One day they were making all striking miners turn round while the people were going to work. They would drag people out who didn't turn round. They were kicking them in the back of the legs and if people turned round, then snatch squads would just go in. You're talking about three or four police deep constantly shoving you and making you turn round. It's your dignity and everything. They wanted flash points, they'd been told to wind it up.[13]

Meanwhile, a campaign was intensifying to support the working Nottinghamshire miners as the best way of breaking the strike. It was sanctioned by the prime minister herself. Andy Stewart, Conservative MP for the newly formed seat of Sherwood, asked Mrs Thatcher to make public her support for the Notts miners, and on 15 September she wrote them an open letter, saying:

Andy has been to see me today and let me know your views. May I say how greatly I and other people appreciate what you are doing. You are an example to us all. Margaret Thatcher.[14]

In parallel, David Hart, the flamboyant entrepreneur who was promoting the National Working Miners' Committee, had meetings with Margaret Thatcher on Monday 6 August, Wednesday 29 August and Thursday 11 September.[15] On 18 September, he wrote a note for her entitled 'Winning the war against Scargillism', which he presented as 'a coda to our recent conversations'. He reprised the concept of 'the enemy within', which she had used when speaking to the 1922 backbench committee on 19 July, flattered her and endeavoured (as if there was any need) to strengthen her resolve:

> The Street sees you as the embodiment of everything that Scargill is trying to attack. Even a minor victory for Scargill would be a major defeat for you . . . There is an enemy within. We are at war. At home. Prosecute it with the same degree of determination and control as you exercised in the Falklands . . . All strikes can be broken provided the management have the will and the nation has the stamina. I have absolutely no doubt about the latter.[16]

Hart did not mention that dirty tricks were also part of his portfolio. A frequent visitor to Nottinghamshire in his Mercedes, he made contact with Bob Taylor and Ken Foulstone, two strike-breaking miners at Manton colliery. He tutored them to apply – via a firm of Newark solicitors paid by Hart – for a High Court injunction against the NUM. This ruled in late September that, in the absence of a national ballot, the strike must not be characterised as official or national by NUM leaders. When Arthur Scargill continued to refer to it as such in public statements, he was served with a writ for contempt of court on 3 October, while he was attending the Labour Party Conference in Blackpool, and the NUM was hit by a massive fine of £200,000.[17]

This betrayal by two of their own comrades infuriated the striking miners of Manton, led by David Potts, the NUM branch secretary. A seasoned fighter, he had sustained a bloody head at Babbington, been arrested at Harworth colliery on his daughter's birthday, 2 May, and encountered police violence at Orgreave. A few days after the Blackpool incident, Potts and his mates decided to have words with Taylor. A car chase ensued along one of Worksop's main streets and Potts found himself accused of attempted murder:

> We'd always meet at Manton Colliery Athletics Club. And we were in there one afternoon, we'd been out picketing. That was our soup kitchen as well. We were discussing various things and somebody came in and said, Bob Taylor had said something about us and was up at the Maltings at the Railway Station. So we went up there. He wasn't there. Driving back we came down Eastgate, to a junction. One of the guys in the back of the car said, 'Hey, that's Bob Taylor.' I just pulled out and as he reached one of our pickets he swerved and tried to knock him off his bike with his car. Well this incensed everybody in the car. Me as the driver I went up by the side of him – this was one of the main streets in Worksop – and we were going alongside each other for quite a while, shouting obscenities. And one of the things I shouted at him was, 'I'll kill you.' We went side by side for quite a while, till we got up Kilton Hill, and he got away. But I'd said this, 'I'll kill you.' That evening I went to the Club again to talk to my members about what we were going to do the next day. Came out with me wife, went to the fish shop. Pulled in the street where we were living at the time. Police swooped, 'You're under arrest for the attempted murder of Bob Taylor.' 'What are you talking about?' They took me away and I never saw the light of day for another month.[18]

This incident found its way into Ian MacGregor's memoirs, where he stated:

> The thugs and the bullies kept up the pressure on the men who dared take the union to court. Two days after the writ was served at Blackpool

two striking miners were charged with threatening to kill Taylor and his family after an accident in which a car tried to run them off the road on the way home from a shopping trip.[19]

David was confined in Lincoln prison with his brother John, who had been in the back of the car, but who was let out because of his good conduct in the army. At Mansfield Court, David was generously stood bail by Graham Allen, a Notts-born Labour councillor of Tower Hamlets, who took him back to his house in Stepney, from where he had to report daily to police until 17 December.[20]

Meanwhile, the NUM suffered another massive blow, when the National Association of Colliery Overmen, Deputies and Shotfirers (NACODS) – which, in a ballot held in September, had finally voted by over 80 per cent to come out on strike on 25 October – suddenly changed its mind. Some sort of behind-the-scenes deal had been struck concerning an independent review of which pits would be closed and which left open, and the strike was called off two days before it was due. The impact on the striking miners was massive. In South Wales, Ann Jones was categorical: 'They betrayed us, because if Nottingham had come out and NACODS that strike would have been won.'[21] In Fife, the communist strike leader Willie Clarke saw it as a turning point. 'For him the fight was over on 23 October 1984, when the leadership of the pit deputies union refused to implement its members' 80 per cent strike vote,' said his son, Willie Clarke junior, a miner at Comrie during the strike. 'October 23. That was . . . for him, that was a point where we were actually fighting a battle we knew we couldn't win.'[22]

From this point on, the striking miners were more and more embattled, while the strike-breakers were encouraged both in their decision to return to work and in their aggression towards strike leaders. In Leicestershire, where the Dirty Thirty still held out, strike-breakers were actually supported by the NUM leadership at Coalville.

On the evening of Saturday 17 November 1984, sixteen-year-old Claire Pinnegar went to a party in Barwell with a few of her friends and then

walked back to their home village of Stoney Stanton. With them was Les
Turner, a couple of years older than she was and a working miner. On the
way, Les said, 'I just got to work, and me dad would go mad if I didn't
anyway, 'cause I got to pay my mum, I got to pay the board and I've gotta
work.' Claire, whose father Malcolm was the leader of the Dirty Thirty,
replied, 'No, it's not about the money, it's about the pits and trying to save
the pits. You won't have a job if you don't fight to save your jobs.' When
they got to Stoney Stanton, there was still time for a drink, so they went
into one of the pubs. At the bar was Les's father Johnny, very drunk, who
wanted to know why Les was with the daughter of the strike leader. He
started 'mouthing off' and saying, 'I'm going to come and kill him. I wanna
kill your dad.' When she got home, she told her dad and he sent her
upstairs for safety.

Very soon Johnny Turner came to their house, accompanied by his
sons Les and Melvin and a few other young working miners, and began
hammering at the back door. Malcolm's wife Margaret took up the
story:

> Malcolm said, 'Look, Johnny, it ain't the time, it ain't the place, the girls
> are in the house. You know, we'll do this some other time. Just leave.
> Get out of the house.' But then [Johnny] just went for Malcolm, we're
> still in the kitchen, he was still in the kitchen, and just dived through
> the back door on top of Malcolm. So they ended up on the floor, and
> Malcolm said to me, 'Call the police!', because if this were the other way
> round, the police would be here. So I rang the police, and I rang Richo
> [Richardson], actually. I said, 'You've got to get over here Richo, I need,
> you know, we need some help.' Said, 'Okay.' Bearing in mind how far
> apart we all were. And they were more or less grappling on the floor. I
> rang the police and told them and I said and let me just tell you, 'This
> is mining trouble, and it's a working miner has broken into a striking
> miner's house, not the other way round.' So, 'Okay, okay.' Well, it never
> . . . they didn't seem as though they were coming, to be honest.

Malcolm overpowered Johnny and decided to sit on top of him until the police came. Johnny threatened, 'I've got a knife you know, I'm gonna stab ya'; and Malcolm was worried that the lads outside might get involved. The police took an inordinate time to arrive, although the general feeling was that they would have been there in a flash if a striking miner had attacked a strike-breaker. Charges were brought against Johnny Turner, but the Pinnegar family felt let down four times over: by the police, the justice system, the Leicestershire NUM and their fellow miners. As Margaret said:

> He went to trial. And the NUM paid for everything. The NUM paid for his solicitor. The Leicester miners' union, Jack Jones. They paid everything. They paid his solicitor's fees, well, he were their solicitor, the Leicestershire NUM solicitor. And they paid his fine as well. They even had a collection at the pit for him, which didn't sit well.[23]

In Scotland, the strikers managed to get the courts on their side in so far as the legality of the strike was concerned, but this did not prevent something verging on a reign of terror being exercised against the miners. A Bilston Glen miner, Harry Fettes, who marshalled strike-breaking at his own pit, also used contacts in the Conservative Party to initiate legal action against the Scottish NUM in the High Court in Edinburgh to have the strike declared illegal. He did not get his way. Lord Jauncey found on 25 September that the strike in Scotland was legal, because all the appropriate procedures – from pithead meetings to a Scottish Delegate Conference and Scottish Executive meetings – had been followed the previous February.[24] This made no difference to Albert Wheeler, the Coal Board Area director in Scotland, who worked closely with the police and the courts to ensure that any arrest was likely to result in a conviction – and any conviction to job dismissal.[25] For every 1,000 striking miners in Scotland, 90 were arrested and 13.7 convicted. The corresponding rates for England and Wales were 45 arrested and 4.2 convicted. This meant that Scottish miners were twice as likely to be arrested and three times as likely to be convicted as their English and Welsh comrades.[26]

The initial skirmish was in July 1984 at Bilston Glen, where a significant return to work had been organised. Pickets came from all parts of Scotland – and even County Durham – to keep the strike-breakers out, and the confrontation with police was famously captured by journalist and photographer John Sturrock. Pat Egan, a young Frances miner who lived at Glenrothes and was close to Mick McGahey, was arrested by a snatch squad on the picket line at Bilston Glen. He thought that he was picked out because of his militancy and believed that a 'brutal' Albert Wheeler was behind it, because of the very short time it took from his conviction for breach of the peace in Edinburgh to the arrival of his dismissal letter:

I got fined £30. I came out the court and came back to Glenrothes and by the time I got in they had the dismissal letter sitting behind the door . . . Not even a stamp on it, it had been hand-delivered in a brown envelope with NCB on it. Just a handwritten letter saying, due to your conduct and being found guilty at Edinburgh Sheriff Court, you are now instantly dismissed.[27]

Ronnie Campbell, chair of the Lochore strike committee and known as 'Red Ronnie' because of his communist loyalties and militancy, was also targeted by the police. He had already been arrested for picketing at Ravenscraig steelworks and fined £80. In October, he was arrested again at the Frances pit, and this time was immediately sacked:

Went down to picket the Frances colliery at Dysart. We went to the picket lines on the buses, on the miners' buses that took the miners. And it so happened, when a miners' bus came round carrying working miners, of course, everybody started throwing stones, and that . . . We were there to stop them from going in. But they got in, through a lot of pushing, and arguing, and fighting with the police, and that. But it

218

was after the picket had finished, and the miners are going in, and we were on the way back to the buses, I got arrested . . . This police van drew up beside me, and this policeman ran out and grabbed me, and pushed me against the fence. He said, 'Right you wee b[astard], you're coming with me.' So, he took me, he arrested me, and he opened the van, and the van was full of policemen. And he didn't put me in, he threw me in. I landed on the floor of the van, and the policemen that were sitting, they started putting their feet on my back. I was taken to Kirkcaldy, and I was charged. Disturbance of the peace. And I can't remember, there was something else, but I can't remember what it was. I got fined £100 there. And then four days later, I got a letter through the door saying I'd been sacked for industrial misconduct.[28]

The mechanism for arresting and convicting miners' leaders was graphically described by Tom Adams, NUM treasurer at Frances, who narrowly escaped arrest that autumn when all his mates were rounded up. The Fife police turned up at Frances with photographs of those they wanted to arrest – above all, John Mitchell, a former Scottish amateur bantamweight champion, communist, NUM delegate at Frances and the pit's picketing coordinator:

They had tables out on the grass and they had photographs on them. Obviously never saw who was on the photographs. But you saw . . . the police were standing there and they were looking at a photograph and they were going, 'There he is, there.' They were pointing at everybody . . . John Mitchell who was the one guy they were after, definitely after him, and John Paige who was the branch secretary of SCEBTA at the time. They were the ones they were wanting. Those six definitely got arrested that day. They were going around saying, him, the Seafield committee and the Frances committee. And you saw them doing it. And I went to them and told the guys, these six, 'We're getting selected here, watch them, look at what they're doing. They've got the photos there.' 'They'll not touch us. We're the official six.' I says, 'Well I'm not getting arrested here today, lads.'

When the strike-breakers' bus came through and the pickets started to push, the police struck. Tom and another member of the committee had left the picket line and were watching the police, not the strike-breakers. As the police came, they made their getaway. Six were taken to Kirkcaldy Sheriff Court and their mates came along to the hearing: 'We were all shouting in the back going, "That's terrible, that never happened. That's a lot of lies"' – until the judge banged his hammer and threw them out. 'They all got fined, huge fines,' said Adams. 'They were getting fined £400 or £500 for a breach of the peace, which nobody ever got fined.' Immediately, the letters of dismissal arrived from the Scottish Coal Board. 'They were all delivered. It was an absolute set-up.'[29]

Not satisfied with arresting militant miners on picket lines, the police then began to arrest miners in their home villages, if they so much as insulted a working miner. In Lochore, there were a couple of strike-breakers in the village whose houses were protected by the police. They and others from the surrounding villages were taken by bus early each morning to inland pits, such as Comrie, or to the coastal pits of Frances and Seafield. During the evening of Thursday 15 November, a Comrie miner, Doddy McShane, a father of two, was accused of breaking windows in the house of one of the strike-breakers and was arrested. Early on 16 November, when it was still dark, another Comrie miner, Andrew 'Watty' Watson, just nineteen, was waiting in front of the Miners' Welfare for a picketing bus that would take him to Seafield when the strike-breaker van came through:

And then just coming up over the old railway bridge – I knew by the speed of the vehicles, the white lights coming towards me – that it was the convoy taking the working miners into Seafield colliery. So maybe because of the anger that had built up in the months from when we went on strike, I just felt, 'I'm going to show these guys how I feel about them.' Right. I stepped from the entrance of the strike centre through an opening in the wall with two big pillars. And I stood on the pavement and I gave the convoy the two fingers, aye, sticking the Vs up. Then the Transit van of working miners basically was right alongside me and just past me and no more. I can't remember shouting anything or raising my voice. It was just a gesture of two fingers towards the scabs in the minivan. And next thing I know . . . I just heard a car stopping. It was the last police car in the convoy. So I just stood because as far as I was concerned I hadn't done anything really bad. I'm only showing them how I felt about them, not verbally but with a hand gesture. And the policeman got out the passenger seat of the panda car or the police car and opened the back door and basically grabbed me and I offered no resistance. And he just flung me on the back seat of the police car. He jumped in the front seat of the passenger side and told the other policeman to drive off, keep following the convoy.

The police then left the convoy and took Watty to Cowdenbeath police station, where he was put in the cells. He saw Doddy McShane's shoes outside another cell door and realised that he had been arrested, too. They were taken in the same van to Dunfermline and hauled up before the sheriff that same morning. Watty was charged with making a 'throwing gesture' among other things and the court lawyer advised him to plead guilty. When Watty said that the charge sheet was 'three-quarters lies', the lawyer warned him that McShane, who had gone up to the dock before him, had pleaded not guilty and been remanded to Saughton prison in Edinburgh for three weeks. Watty therefore pleaded guilty, was fined £150 – which he knew the NUM would pay – went home and thought little more of it:

Then the proverbial shit hit the fan on the Tuesday morning. The P45, the letter of dismissal came through from the . . . I think it was the colliery manager or the head office of the Coal Board. The letter was addressed to me, so I had to pluck up the courage to show my mother and father the letter, which wasn't a very good experience. But I showed them it . . . The letter says you're basically . . . you're dismissed . . . It was a heart-wrenching moment.[30]

The stay in Saughton prison was traumatic for Doddy McShane and his family. His daughter Janet, who was twenty at the time and worked in a Dunfermline textile factory, recalled:

He was an ill man, I mean, he'd never been locked up before. He shared a cell with somebody who had robbed a bank and somebody who had attempted murder, and I believe he still wrote to one of those men after he'd come out . . . We got to visit. My mum had begged me not to go, begged me, because the state that he was in when she went. I think she took my sister, and my sister was really not well after that, she was only thirteen. In fact, she wasn't even thirteen, she was twelve.[31]

Doddy was brought to trial on 6 December and fined. Shortly after that, he received a notice of dismissal from the Coal Board. He appealed to an industrial tribunal, but his appeal was rejected.

In South Wales, where the strike remained solid for longer, fewer strike-breakers gave fewer opportunities to the police to drive a wedge between working and striking miners. Much of the media, especially the Welsh-language media, supported the strike. Police forces were brought into Wales, but in the Swansea Valley they were from Tameside, outside Manchester – not the regular Manchester force, and certainly not the Met. The NCB South Wales Area director, Phil Weekes, was very different from Albert Wheeler in Scotland and was keen not to brutalise mining communities. Few miners were sacked, and most of those were reinstated when the strike ended. A Wales Congress for the Defence of the Mining Communities was set up in October 1984 with broad political and church support, with a view to opening the way to a negotiated settlement.

In the Swansea Valley, at Ystalyfera, there was one single strike-breaker – a miner called Len Lock, who broke ranks and decided to go back to work at Abernant. David Williams, a Blaenant miner who lived in Coelbren, had been at Easington to help with the picketing and had witnessed the events surrounding Wilkinson, the strike-breaking miner there. David regarded the two cases in a very different light: whereas Wilkinson had isolated himself in the community and had been manipulated by the Coal Board, 'Len Lock didn't give a damn about anyone . . . He was a pig of a man.'[32]

The local community picketed Len Lock's house, but he managed to get onto the works bus that toured the region looking for strike-breaking miners to take back to work. However, when the bus got to Abernant colliery, there was a picket of men and women waiting to greet it, including Martin James who worked there, Siân James and Kay Jones' mother – 'Betty the union'.[33] It stopped in front of the pit gates and would not go in. As Siân James remembered:

All hell broke loose, because the police couldn't hold everybody back. Everybody surged forward. I don't think anybody could believe it. The police couldn't believe it. So he did, he jumped off the bus. He jumped off the bus and he started walking towards the gates. I don't think anybody was prepared for it. The police held everybody back and were arresting people. So they went potty didn't they? They went potty and there were bricks flying. I remember a brick hitting the top of a Black Maria.[34]

On Siân James's living-room wall is a wonderful primitivist picture of Betty Jones poking Len with an umbrella as he tried to get through the gates. Martin was one of six pickets arrested and taken to a cell under Pontardawe magistrates' court. The case was heard in February 1985, and Martin and the others were given a discharge conditional on not picketing anywhere else in the country. 'The police actually sent a senior officer to give evidence,' recalled Siân James, 'who said – what did he say, Martin? – that the situation had got, basically that there was overreaction on both sides.'[35]

Some of the women who had flexed their muscles picketing at Abernant then took this further at a weak link in the chain on the western fringe of the coalfield. Cynheidre was an isolated pit that recruited from rural Carmarthenshire. Its displaced lodge chair, Tony Holman, had run a subversive campaign against the strike, while the new chair, Tony Ciano, struggled to keep the men out on strike.[36] In the first week of November, the men began to creep back to work at Cynheidre, and at an emergency meeting of the Neath, Dulais and Swansea Valleys Miners' Support Group at Seven Sisters it was decided to send in a group of women to occupy the site and stop the pit working. The message was also one of gender inversion: the wives of striking miners were ritually humiliating the less-than-men who had gone back to work.

A first breach was made on Friday 9 November, when a group of women from the Dulais Valley and St John's, Maesteg, occupied the pithead baths. When sixteen of them – including Edwina Roberts, Margaret Donovan and Siân James – returned on Sunday 18 November, got through a window and barricaded themselves inside the manager's office, the manager despaired, 'It's not them bloody women again!'[37] Their first victory was a media one. The manager, said Margaret Donovan, was 'absolutely neurotic' about bad publicity and confessed, 'I'm not bringing the police in here. The publicity would kill us.'[38] For the women, it was the other way around:

We wanted the oxygen of publicity. We're very, very lucky in Wales, *very* lucky. In 1982, we'd had S4C, Channel for Wales . . . We had a homegrown media, and that media was based on the Welsh language. So we had things like Radio Cymru, Radio Wales. We had a local Welsh media and Welsh-based newspapers . . . And most of the people working for them, if you dug long enough, you'd find a miner at the bottom of their families. Even just one – their dads, their brothers, their cousins, even if you had to go back a little more, it would've been a grandfather or an uncle. So we had a very willing and open press that was looking for content. So we decided we'd give it to them.[39]

As well as a publicity coup – an antidote to scenes of violence that were always attributed to the pickets – the occupation was a subversive attack on the masculinity of the mining industry. '*We* could go in there as women, because they couldn't take the ultimate sanction against us: they couldn't sack us,' said Siân James. They invented their own forms of charivari, to further unman the men who had already demeaned themselves by going back to work. When they occupied the pithead baths, they greeted the men as 'scabby bastards' and prevented them from taking a shower.[40] Siân later admitted:

We did very naughty things, like save every bit of wee, and the first morning when the men walked in underneath us, we threw all the wee over them. After that, they took them in through the back door.

Finally, they pulled off a power inversion. They humiliated the manager and then they subverted the hierarchy of the Coal Board. They used the manager's private toilet and shower. They went through his desk, found a collection of pornography (which he later claimed he had confiscated from the men) and threw it out of the window. Then they used his private phone, exploiting the fact that, ever since the 1966 Aberfan disaster, by law there had to be two phone lines in each colliery. Siân again:

Oh, what's this? Internal telephone directory for British Coal. So we ring British Coal headquarters in London. 'Hello, hello. This is Miss Davies. I am the secretary for Mr Jones, who is the manager of Cynheidre colliery, South Wales division of British Coal. I'd like to speak to Mr Ian MacGregor's personal assistant, please.' 'Two minutes, Miss Davies.' The next minute we're through to Ian MacGregor's personal assistant! . . . 'Would it be possible for Mr Jones to have a word with Mr MacGregor, please?' 'Oh, I'm afraid he's not in at the moment. Shall I take a message?' 'Tell that fucking bastard . . .!' And we slammed the phone down. Ten minutes later, up the stairs, bang, bang, bang, on the door. 'Open this bloody door!' 'What's wrong now? What's the matter?' 'Who's been on the bloody phone to British Coal headquarters?!' 'Not us.' 'Somebody's been phoning British Coal headquarters! And I've just had a fucking earful off somebody up there!'[41]

Unfortunately, this inversion of power did not last for long. The solidarity of the Welsh coalfield was fracturing – not only on the extreme west, but in the powerhouse of 'American Wales' in the east. On the 'fateful day' of Monday 19 November, the first strike-breaker went back to Merthyr Vale. To prevent this, the striking miners set up a car barricade. The second day, in the pouring rain, the police got through. They then blocked the roads, so that pickets trying to get to the Mountain Ash colliery in the next valley had to go overland. A journalist took wonderful pictures of a snaking line of miners with lamps coming over the mountain.[42]

An even blacker day arrived on Friday 30 November 1984, when a taxi taking a strike-breaking miner along the M4 to Merthyr Vale was hit by a breeze-block thrown from a motorway flyover by two young miners from the Rhondda. The taxi driver, David Wilkie, was killed and the perpetrators, Dean Hancock and Russell Shankland, were arrested and charged with murder. This was a public relations disaster, used ruthlessly to discredit the strike. 'I felt as disturbed and sickened as did all from our mining communities,' wrote Rev. John Morgans, born in the Rhondda and moderator of the United Reformed Church.[43] The Welsh mining community tried to rally round. Blaenant miner Lyn Harper said in 1986 of the taxi driver:

I did not feel any sorrow for him then and I don't now. We were at war and they were doing everything possible to stop us. If you are not prepared to fight you may as well jack it in from the word go.[44]

226

Interviewed again in 2019, he still held the same opinion:

> You have to accept that when you go to war there's fatalities. It's part of it. It's regretful, but they weren't . . . we didn't make heroes out of them, but we didn't chastise them either.[45]

The case of Hancock and Shankland was a blot on the record of the South Wales miners, but it was an exception. Other miners were arrested for intimidating strike-breakers, but – unlike in Yorkshire or in Scotland – those cases were few and far between and were resolved at the end of the strike. Phil White, on the NUM Committee at Maesteg and one of the Broad Left, was accused of intimidating a miner who had gone back to work and their conversation was recorded at the taxi company where the latter also worked. White was one of four dismissed in February 1985, but the matter was resolved in secret talks at the end of the strike between Emlyn Williams, president of the South Wales Miners' Federation, who had fought in tanks in the Desert War, and NCB Area Director Phil Weekes, who had fought in the RAF.[46]

As the summer of 1984 ended and autumn drew in, striking miners felt an increasing sense of betrayal, humiliation and injustice. Betrayal, because small but significant numbers of miners had gone back to work, further fracturing the front that had never been fully united, even in March, and turning communities against each other. The decision of NACODS in October not to join the strike was a body blow. Humiliation, because the proud tradition of mining communities policing themselves had come to an end, as police forces from outside the area occupied their villages, protecting the strike-breakers and arresting the pickets. Injustice, because arrested miners were sent before courts where the police bore false witness, the magistrates and judges showed no mercy and the Coal Board was on hand to serve dismissal notices. These were devastating moments for those miners who were the most committed to the cause and would pay the highest price. But a long winter was coming and the war was not over yet.

10

CHRISTMAS

'Wilkinson wasn't the issue. A few scabs going back wasn't the issue,' said Alan Cummings, chair of Easington lodge, referring to their first strike-breaker. 'Christmas was the thing.'[1] Anna Lawson, secretary of the support group at Sacriston, fifteen miles away, recalled that 'one child got a Christmas card from, it turns out, we think, from the police. It was, "What are you gonna get for Christmas?" on the front, but then nothing on the inside.'[2] Linda Erskine, secretary of the Women's Action Group in Lochgelly, echoed the sentiment: 'From about October onwards these women – and dads, I suppose, as well – worried about how their kids were going to get anything at Christmas.'[3]

Christmas 1984 was indeed a milestone in the history of the Miners' Strike. It marked ten months of the strike, which had lasted through the spring, summer and autumn, when there was less demand for coal and the timing and legitimacy of the strike had been questioned. Now the strike was going to plunge into winter, when demand for coal would intensify and the miners might triumph by managing to 'switch the lights out' across the country. At the same time, however, many striking miners had had enough. They were running out of reserves, whether material or moral, and some were drifting back to work in order to recover the wage that would enable them to get through the icy season.

Christmas was also a challenge to mining families and mining communities. Families had mobilised to confront the hardship of living without a man's wage, without the deliveries of concessionary coal that they normally received from the Coal Board, improvising other sources of income and supply. Grandparents, parents, uncles, aunts and siblings came to the assistance of family members who were struggling. Communities had mobilised to set up soup kitchens and provide food parcels to striking families, and were raising funds to pay for these. But these same communities were under pressure as some men went back to work, setting strike-breakers against strikers, bringing in the police, who protected the strike-breakers and arrested pickets, threatening the cohesion of those communities and their ability to sustain the strike. The taunting of a child by the Durham police about getting nothing for Christmas was shorthand for the futility of the whole exercise and parents' inability to care for their children. At stake for striking families and communities would be whether they would be able to provide presents for the children and put a turkey on the table for Christmas dinner.

Hardship among striking families had begun with the strike, but it had intensified with every passing week. Miners had been well paid, compared to people with jobs in manufacturing and elsewhere, but that 'family wage' was now gone. Striking miners were paid a pound or two a day by the NUM for picketing, plus petrol money if they used their car; but in Leicestershire, where the Area NUM opposed the strike, they got nothing. Following the clampdown on picketing in the autumn, increasing arrests, court appearances and convictions, some miners – such as Pete Richardson in Askern or Ronnie Campbell, Doddy McShane and Watty Watson in Lochore – were dismissed by the Coal Board before Christmas arrived.

In a minority of mining families, the wife worked either full or part time; this cushioned the blow a little, although women's wages were usually set well below men's. Linda Erskine went back to her job as a lab technician at Auchterderran Junior High School after her second child was born in 1978 and could make up some of the wage of her husband George, an engineer at Comrie. Jean Crane of Askern was the manager of a newsagent's in Doncaster, while her friend Dianne Hogg worked part time at a newsagent's in the village, while Phil and Pete were picketing. In Coalville, Linda, the wife of Richo Richmond – who was up and down the country for the Dirty Thirty – had a part-time job in the Palitoy toy factory. In the Swansea Valley, Kay Jones worked part time in the Smiths watch factory; her husband did not picket, but made some money doing odd building jobs. In the nearby Dulais Valley, Christine Powell, treasurer of the support group, continued in her career as a physics teacher in Swansea. Meanwhile, Marilyn James recalled: 'I was lucky enough, a friend of mine gave me a job in a shop. At least we had food, didn't we?'[4]

Many wives were at home with small children and unable to work outside. They were dependent on child benefit, which was limited and not always easy to obtain. Marilyn James, who had two daughters, said, '£14 a week we were having, Phil, for the kids and I wasn't supposed to give you any of that. So you weren't supposed to eat.' Kath Savory, who had to give up work to bring up two sons and a daughter in Chester-le-Street, also remembers, 'We had to live on £14 a week. That was from the DHSS.'[5] Kay Riley, spokesperson for the Dirty Thirty Women's Support Group, took a seven-year break from the hosiery industry to raise two sons. She recalled that:

picketing money would be deducted from the benefit payment, your social security would arrive late or if you rang up they'd say, we forgot to post it, so you'd have to go and sit in the office and wait for them to give you your cheque or you won't get your milk token . . . You'd get it eventually, but they'd make you wait.[6]

Child benefit might cover weekly basics, but not bigger outlays, such as shoes or clothes for school. Here the support groups often had to intervene. Donna Jones, secretary of the Llynfi-Afan Valley Miners' Support Group, managed to prise £5,000 out of Afan Council in Port Talbot for these items.[7] Mary Stratford, secretary of the support group at Great Lumley, said that:

a lot of families by October had no money for shoes and kids grew out of shoes as you well know. We had no shoes left. So one or two of the families sent them [to school] in plimsolls, black plimsolls. And the kids were sent home and excluded, in a former mining community. Absolutely disgraceful. So that was when we realised there was a problem with that, and that's when one of the county councillors organised a shoe thing and we were eventually able to get shoes for kids.[8]

With so little coming in, families had to cut back on their expenditure. Most mining families lived in colliery houses or council houses, for which rent was not that high. Kenny McKitten, an electrician at Murton, and his wife Allyson lived in a council house in Great Lumley with their new-born, Jenna. Allyson rang Barclays Bank every month to inform them that they were still on strike and they 'Never bothered us at all, did they?'[9] The situation was often problematic for the minority of miners who were homeowners. Mary Stratford, who, with Paul, owned a house in Great Lumley, recalled that:

Some lucky individuals, the Sunderland and Shields Building Society said to them, 'Forget, don't give us it, keep that money and you can catch up at the end.' My building society threatened to repossess me if I didn't pay on time. So all of that [family allowance] went to the building society. I couldn't siphon off any, they wouldn't let me. They said if I fell behind at all, they would go straight in.[10]

Interestingly, Bagworth miner Nigel Jeffery and his wife Wendy, who worked for an insurance broker and had just won £4,000 on the pools, enabling them to buy a house, thought that their TSB manager was sympathetic, because he came from a mining background in the North East. As Nigel recalled:

I had to go down and say, 'Look, I've just you know, I've just gone on strike.' I says, 'My father's out, my two step-brothers are both out.'

And he was quite sympathetic, I think, obviously with the name of Mr Collier. I think he did explain at the time that he was from the North East himself or his family was. There had been strikes back in '72 and '74 that some of his family had been involved in. So he's quite sympathetic. And obviously, with Wendy still working, it was a case of he asked how much Wendy could afford to keep the mortgage, you just had to make a minimum payment. So we agreed a £50 minimum and then we'd obviously catch up. But it took years after it – didn't it? – to catch up; something like fifteen years, ten to fifteen years.[11]

Given that rent and mortgages – reduced or not – had to be paid, striking miners had to find other ways to cut costs. Andy Varley, a miner at Manton in Nottinghamshire with two small children, did not want his wife Sue to work, although she managed the family budget brilliantly. He picketed Manton pit and did not have a 'side job', as others did. He was forced to sell his car, but recalled that he was ripped off.[12] Bill Potts, a miner at Warsop Main, gave up smoking and stopped going out to the Memorial Club at Church Warsop, except on Wednesdays and Sundays to play dominoes, in order to keep their four children.[13]

Striking families found all sorts of ways of improvising and getting by. Given that pits were generally built outside towns, where the coal happened to be located, miners had allotments, found casual work in the fields or did other odd jobs. In Yorkshire, Harry Walker, a miner at Woolley who lived in semi-rural Kexborough, kept pigs and chickens on his allotment and was also an accomplished poacher. 'He were handy with shot gun,' said his son Steve. 'He'd go down fields and shoot some rabbits, pigeons, ducks. So there were always summat to eat. We never went without.'[14] In Great Lumley, Kenny McKitten, who was the son of a farmhand, went back to work on the farm for £10 a day and also did some rewiring work near Consett. 'I remember they paid you with a £50 note,' said his wife Allyson. 'It was like winning the pools.'[15]

1. The Scottish mining village of Ballingry set among the low hills of Fife. Mining families moved to new estates here after the Second World War when the old mining village of Glencraig down the hill was condemned, but there is still a bleakness about it.

2. Washing day in the South Yorkshire village of Askern, in the shadow of the Coalite plant. If the wind changed, families had to bring in their laundry to avoid contamination from the fumes.

3. A rally in support of the strike in Rotherham, spring 1984. Mining was passed on from father to son, but if the pits closed there would be no jobs for these boys to go to.

4. Miners' wives and supporters from Chester-le-Street at a rally in London, August 1984. Under the banner Kath Connolly is in red, Elspeth Frostwick in blue.

5. Elicia Billingham, treasurer of the Barnsley Miners' Wives Action Group. Involvement in the strike gave working-class women a new confidence and strength.

6. The second visit of Lesbians and Gays Support the Miners to Coelbren Miners' Welfare in the Dulais Valley, 2 March 1985. Jayne Headon is second from the left, Mark Ashton fifth from the left and Siân James on the right.

7. Orgreave, near Rotherham, 18 June 1984: the pitched battle between striking miners and the police. Mounted police with batons charge young men who run and climb for their lives.

8. Hatfield colliery, South Yorkshire, 21 August 1984. Striking miners organise a sit-down to prevent a bus of strike-breakers from getting through. Violence was to follow.

9. Mass pickets confront police at Bilston Glen colliery, Midlothian, July 1984, to prevent miners returning to work. Arrested picketers were likely to be taken to court and dismissed by the Coal Board.

10. In the winter of 1984–85 angry striking miners observe strike-breakers board a bus to work in Leadgate, County Durham. Dave Wray is standing in the doorway; Peter Byrne is walking to his right.

11. Drawing of a Welsh mining village sent as a fundraising Christmas card by Dr Julian Tudor Hart and Mary Hart of Glyncorrwg in the Afan Valley, 15 November 1984. '*Pentre Diwaith*' means 'Village Without Work'.

12. Children at a Christmas party at Frickley Miners' Welfare, South Yorkshire. Christmas 1984 came nine months into the strike and hardship did not prevent celebration.

13. Miners salvaging coal from a slag heap at Bentley colliery, South Yorkshire, 4 January 1985. Their perk of free coal was stopped during the strike and cold and tiredness show on their faces.

14. The return to work at Maerdy colliery in the Rhondda, 5 March 1985. Defeated after a year-long strike, the miners tried to keep their heads high, but this show was not always managed.

15. Mining communities and their banners pass speakers on the balcony of the County Hotel, Durham, during the Miners' Gala of July 2019. Pit closures led paradoxically to a resurgence of the pride of mining communities in some parts of Britain.

16. A woman and her child in the South Yorkshire mining village of Grimethorpe after the strike. Pit closures left a legacy of unemployment, poverty and ill health.

In Fife, there were plenty of opportunities in farming and fishing. 'In October you used to pick the tatties, tattie picking for the farmers,' said Mary Coll, president of the Lochore Women's Support Group, who earned £25 a week from working at Bayne's bakery. 'The miners went and picked tatties for a fortnight and they got paid for that. But after that all the tatties were picked. In November, December and January, February – oh, it was hard.'[16] Ronnie Campbell's younger daughter, Margaret, who was fifteen during the strike, said that to relieve her mother's anxiety,

> I asked my mum and dad for permission to go and pick tatties and berries for a living. I went to that tattie field. And I did pick tatties for £12 a day. And what did I do with that money at the end of the week? I put clothes on my back. I didn't drink, I didn't smoke, I didn't take drugs. I gave my mum some.[17]

Margaret's older sister, Anna, worked at a local supermarket and gave the £25 a week she earned to her mother. More adventurously, Willie Clarke junior, a Comrie miner living in Ballingry, decided to catch a nice salmon in rural Perthshire, about twenty miles away, to grace the Christmas dinner:

> I'm a great fisherman, fly fisherman. The week before Christmas '84, a few of us decided to go up to Gleneagles, you know, a salmon river up there. Unfortunately things didn't work out too great. We got a couple of salmon but our driver ended up getting arrested by the police, which meant we were miles from anywhere with waders and all sorts of stuff. There were four of us altogether. We ended up getting arrested and locked up in Crieff cells for poaching salmon from Gleneagles Hotel.[18]

Especially devastating for mining families was the loss during the strike of the concessionary coal they received from the Coal Board, and which they used to heat their homes and provide hot water. Said Mary Coll:

We were frozen, we couldn't get coal. We had no coal in the winter. Oh my God, we were all freezing. We used to sit in the kitchen and put the oven on just for us to get a heat.[19]

A common response to the interruption of coal deliveries was coal picking or scavenging. This was strictly illegal, but miners felt that they had a moral right to this necessity and were happy to take the risk. First prize went to John McClelland, a miner at Seafield. With a few mates he made his own opencast 'coal hole' near his home in Cardenden. Seemingly tolerated by the local police, it provided for both the family and (at a small price) the local community. Lea, his daughter, who at the time was at Auchterderran Junior High School, where Linda Erskine was the lab technician, remembered:

They went to an area where nobody else went, it wasn't an area where people would walk, they had to go over a farmer's field, and they would dig out coal. And then they actually made a team. They had riddles where they had to shake the coal, and they had the pile of what they called dross, which was the stuff that fell out of the bottom, and then they had the coal. And they would bag it up. Now that's what they used to heat their homes. But they also sold it to local people who weren't getting coal . . . And what was sold was what kept the rest of the bills paid and kept food in our belly . . . The coalhole was what got us through the strike.[20]

Terry Ratcliffe, brought up in Ballingry and a miner at Solsgirth, went coal-picking in the opencast mine of Westfield, and did not seem to have been stopped by the police either:

There was a railway track, an open railway track run along at the bottom of these houses here, right along to Westfield and they used to be on motorbikes with their bags of coal in it going up and down the line. A lot of boys used to go and get it and used to sell it. But a lot of miners used to go just to get some for their fire. Nobody ever bothered you.

There was tons and tons and tons of coal was stolen from there and they didn't bother.[21]

Further south, the police were not so tolerant and people had to be more secretive. Near Barnsley, Steve Walker and his brother knew of a 'secret stash' in the village of High Hoyland, where there was an abandoned pit. 'We used to shovel it out and riddle it and get all stone out of it and fill bags of coal up. And me dad's mate came up with his Land Rover then and we'd bag it up and take it home.'[22] In Manton, Josie Potts was less fortunate in her attempt to get some coal from the nearby tip and she was afraid that her actions would threaten her husband's job:

We'd got a fire that was a hopper filler, fed it through top. And we had no hot water and four girls. So I went on to pit top and I saw one of those blokes and I said to him, 'Can I get a bag of slack?' And I'd got kids with me. And he said, 'Yes.' So I got a bag, brought it back so I could have some hot water and that. Anyway, police come this time, riot shield the lot. They said, 'Drop what you've got. You're under arrest.' Sent for police at Worksop police station, they come in van, and anyway they talked and everything and they let me go. And I thought I'd get Billy sacked, you know, but I didn't.[23]

An alternative to coal-picking was logging. Pete Richardson, who was dismissed from his job at Askern in September, helped Dianne and Pete Hogg make up and deliver food parcels. But he also went cutting wood in local woods with a chainsaw.[24] In the Afan Valley, things were more organised, and a concession for logging was agreed with the Forestry Commission, which looked sympathetically on the support group's request. Donna Jones explained how this supported the local population:

We wrote to the Forestry Commission and asked them was there any way that they would give us an area of land. Obviously they had loads of forestation. You're not allowed to cut trees or whatever and they said, 'Yes.' So we sent a party of men in from here. We raised money to buy a chainsaw. Gave the men something to do when they weren't actually picketing in the day. They went down and cut the area in the forestry. The farmer in Gelli Farm lent them equipment to put the logs onto. They sold the firewood to people who wanted firewood. Gave it to the old aged. Gave it to the men obviously because they were all reliant on coal.[25]

Clearly, when striking families were under so much pressure, help from the wider family became hugely important for those who could access it. Parents might help with some bills or with Sunday dinner, although they might have more than one son who was a miner. Siblings could also help if they were not in the mining industry, but were sympathetic to the cause. Friends in the support group who were not miners might also lend a hand.

In Askern, Dianne Hogg was earning £38 a week part time, and her daughter Lesley contributed the £10 per week she got from her Youth Training Scheme. Dianne's mother had abandoned them when she was sixteen, and her father had died at the beginning of the strike, but her in-laws stepped in: 'Pete's mum did his dinner on a Sunday. We went there.'[26] Later she continued:

Pete's mum and dad always paid his phone bill. But that's all the money we had coming in. Oh, and Pete got £1 a day picketing and always put it in pot; always. Never been a gambler, Pete. Never been a really big drinker.[27]

The families of Bill and Elspeth Frostwick in Chester-le-Street were also a great support. Bill's father had left the mine with a lung condition to work on the roads and had very little money, and Bill was away all week picketing in Leicestershire. But he had three brothers, while Elspeth had two sisters, and thanks to the support group, both were close to Kath Mattheys. As Elspeth recalled:

Bill's family [three brothers] was brilliant. And we know there was a lot of hardship and people we know. It broke marriages. They lost their homes. We were really, really fortunate. My dad would give us money to pay the electric bill, your brothers did the same, my [two] sisters would say, 'Don't worry, this weekend I'll make dinner.' and Kath would say the same. You know, 'Come to us for dinner, I'll make that.' Christmas, she came with a Christmas tray for us, can you remember?

'I was maybe thirty before my mother kissed me on the cheek in terms of hello goodbye,' said Mary Stratford in County Durham. But intimacy was not everything. Her mother was a great support during the strike, paying the bill for the phone that Mary needed to run the support group:

I was getting the red letters and then in July they were going to come and shut it off. And she said, 'You can't be without a phone, Mary, I'm paying your bill.' And I'm saying, 'Mam!', because my mam had three sons and a son-in-law on strike, you know. I said, 'You can't.' She said, 'That's my contribution. That's my contribution to the cause. I'll pay your phone bill.' And I was able to keep me phone until Christmas and then I got cut off.[28]

The community played a role in encouraging those miners and their families who were struggling and persuading them not to go back to work. If the support group or union branch could help the miners, they were more likely to stay out. In Great Lumley, Kenny and Allyson McKitten and their new baby were really struggling. But they both contributed to, and benefited from, the support group of which Mary Stratford was secretary, and they heeded the advice of the union. Mary, who understood how to work the welfare system, advised Allyson that she may be able to claim for Kenny, who was not working, on her maternity allowance. Allyson recalled that Mary 'took us to somewhere, Easington Lane, I think. She came, she picked us up; I didn't drive then. Took us over there and . . . fought my corner and I got it backdated, so I had a bit of money coming in.' Even then, they were losing heart and were thinking that Kenny would have to go back to work. But they talked to the union, which impressed on them the importance of solidarity:

> It was hard. And to tell you the truth, near the end of it we were about to give in and say, 'Gonna have to gan back to work.' Went and saw Dennis, the union man, and he said, 'Don't. It's the worst you can do. We'll not be long, we'll not be long a being back.' And if we hadn't talked to him . . . and now when you look back you think, 'Thank God you didn't go back,' because they'd still hate them.[29]

Mary Stratford herself had some sympathy with those who went back, not least because of the cases of terrible hardship she saw through the support group. In this sense, she said, her attitude was different from that of the Durham miners' leader, Davey Hopper. She drew a distinction between those who went back relatively early and those who went back late:

> You know, I differ from some of my comrades because Davey would probably never forgive a scab, ever. My view is if they went back before Christmas, I would never have anything to do with them ever again in my life. But those people who were pushed back February, March, who were on their knees, whose families were breaking up, who were just in a dreadful state. How can you say that they're the same as people who've broken a strike quite deliberately? . . . You know, there's a point at which people break.[30]

Further south, in Nottinghamshire, things were still more difficult, because the striking miners were such a small minority. Not only were communities divided, but so were families. It is sometimes argued that where the wife was committed to the strike, the husband would stay out; but this was not always the case. Karen Bonsall, who became secretary of the Warsop Main Women's Action Group and worked on the food parcels, and whose then husband worked at Warsop Main, explained how they used to shout at the strike-breakers. But her husband felt more and more isolated and eventually decided to go back for the sake of his job and the children. She did not agree with him and suffered to see him become a strike-breaker like the others:

> Feelings were really bad in the village. It was only a small village. And people started to go back to work, which it was so difficult, because I mean, it was a year, and it's a long time to have no money coming in. Some families really struggled, some did go back to work. The animosity, really bad. Every day, they'd be stood at the bottom of the street. We went every day with children and shout at the men as they got off of the bus. They had been working. Real horrible time, really. Weren't very nice at all. It split a lot of families up. It split a lot of friends up, it was a really, really difficult time . . . My ex went back at Christmas. I didn't want him to go back. I cried when he said he was going back. But there'd been a lot of propaganda saying that, oh, you know, 'Most of the people have drifted back now. So, there's only few. So, they're not going to have jobs.' And then we'd got our house and we got two children, and he was just worried that, you know, if he lost his job, what would he do? I didn't want him to go back but he did. He said that if he went back he wouldn't go on the bus. He walked through all his mates, shouting at him. Awful.[31]

At Manton, where a majority of miners were solid, things became more difficult after Taylor and Foulstone tried to break the strike. David Hopkins was one of those who wobbled as the weather grew colder. He did not live in Manton pit village, but on the Prospect estate in Worksop, which distanced him from his comrades. He had never been enthusiastic about the strike and had not been involved in picketing. When others began to return to work at Manton, he decided to follow them. The fight seemed to have been lost. The timing was decided by the suffering of his baby daughter. He felt guilty about going back and hated the jeering he now attracted, but felt that he had to look reality in the face:

The vast majority of Manton men drifted back in November 1984. My daughter was coming up to her first birthday, November 16th, and her birthday was on the 18th. And she came up to me and she was shivering and I thought, we don't have a fire, a coal fire. I thought, this is ridiculous. And I stood up and said, 'Right, I'm going back to work tomorrow.'

It was a foggy morning, a really thick fog. I can remember looking out of the front door, looking both ways, locking the door – it was like being at war. I can remember running down about half a mile to where the bus was picking people up and really nervous. The bus had all steel meshing so that the windows didn't get broke. I can remember seeing one of the pickets at the bottom of the pit lane. Some of the people on the bus were cheering and jeering at them. I can remember looking at one chap, how disappointed he looked. It was a cold morning. They were still stuck out there and we were going to earn some money and he was on strike not earning money. I felt guilty but I thought, no, I've made my decision and it was the right decision. We'd lost. All you can do is lose more money.[32]

Interviewed again in 2021, Hopkins recalled the same fear of being found out and accused of betrayal by his comrades. On the other hand, he reassured himself with the thought that they had done their best for ten months, that most men were now going back to work and even those on the picket line would very soon change their minds and face reality:

Most of Manton went back. There were only 120 who stayed out on strike, out of 1,200 people. I can remember that morning, not putting the light on. I got up in the dark, got my food ready. Got to the end of the street, looked both ways, went the back ways to this place called The Innings, expected somebody to jump out on me. When I got down to the pub there were just loads of people, I couldn't believe it. They had about four busloads.

I can remember feeling sad when I went past the pickets. I felt sad but I thought, we've done our best. We can't do any more. Some of the people who threatened me were back at work a few days later. So they soon changed their minds. I was playing football and some guy tried to break me legs in a training session. The chap was back at work three days later. How fickle can you be?[33]

In other coalfields, the battle continued anxiously, but with determination. Fundraising was becoming more difficult, as enthusiasm waned among the public as well. But as Christmas approached there was another push – not only nationwide, but also internationally – to ensure that money, supplies and gifts arrived in time for Christmas.

In Yorkshire, as we have seen, miners' wives were active. Jean Crane addressed the AGM of Southwark NALGO on 14 November.[34] It was in December that Anne Scargill and Marsha Marshall flew to Italy to solicit support for the Barnsley Miners' Wives Action Group from the Italian trade unions and were interviewed on Vatican Radio.[35] Although they had formally broken with Barnsley Women Against Pit Closures, they kept their relationship with Jean McCrindle, who took Anne and Betty Cook to London to collect donations that had been received:

Jean McCrindle took us down to London, and it was a little mews. This little house they took us in. And I couldn't believe it, there were stacks and stacks of big mail sacks all in this house, all in this room we're in. Loads and loads of letters with cheques in for people that had sent in donations towards Christmas for us. It's unbelievable. And you'd get letters with a cheque to say, 'I'm a lone parent, we can have beans on toast for our dinner, use this to buy a chicken.'[36]

In County Durham, the situation was becoming particularly desperate. David Connolly remarked that 'in October we started seeing the serious fall in the amount of money that was coming in' to the Chester-le-Street support group from different sources. Street collections were drying up quite badly:

People who were previously giving us, they were just passing us on the street; and I think that was a kind of recognition that they were telling you, 'The strike is lost; why don't you give up?'[37]

At the end of November, Kath Mattheys, secretary of the North Durham Support Group in Chester-le-Street, adopted a broad strategy. She wrote to local churches to ask for funds for the food parcels, which cost £3 per week and went to ninety families in difficulty, underlining that 'Whatever our political beliefs we believe that we have a commitment to our community which transcends political issues.' She also wrote to Social Democratic and trade union comrades in Kamp-Lintfort in the Ruhr, with which Chester-le-Street was twinned, saying, 'We hope that when you hear of our struggle you will be able to help us.'[38] Another idea was to organise a twelve-mile sponsored walk on 22 December between two threatened pits, Sacriston and Herrington. Local Labour MP Giles Radice and MEP Stephen Hughes were persuaded to take part, in order to raise the profile and, with it, the funds.[39]

Most ambitious, however, was the 'Toy and Turkey' project conceived by Anne Suddick, secretary of the Durham Area Miners' Support Group. Every miner's child would receive a Christmas present and every miner's family a Christmas turkey, in order to demonstrate that thanks to the solidarity of the coalfield, the sacrifices made for the strike would not leave people to go without. Dave Wray was given the task in November of going to Dewhurst's the butchers, only to be told that every turkey in its vast warehouse had been sold:

> Somebody had the idea we go foreign, we go abroad. I am lying in bed one night and I got a phone call, 'You have to get down to Redhills.' And I asked, 'What's the matter?' It was Dave Hopper: 'Get down to Redhills.' And I go and there is this huge bloody van; it was driven across Europe and across the United Kingdom and he came to Redhills to give the turkeys in the middle of the bloody night.[40]

At Redhills, the tireless Johnny Dent was in charge of the food parcel operation and had experience of mysterious tins arriving from the Soviet Union; but this was something special. Matt Smith, one of his assistants, a sociology student with some French, was roused from bed at five o'clock in the morning on 21 December to talk to the French lorry driver who had brought the lorry-load of frozen turkeys, but who was also delivering to Scotland and had to be back by Christmas Day.[41] It was agreed that the turkeys would be stored at Murton colliery, which had a huge, unheated Miners' Welfare, from where they would be distributed to support groups across the county. The assignment for Chester-le-Street was collected by David Connolly and Billy Frostwick, who did complain about the size of the birds. 'I've seen bigger wood pigeons,' he jested.[42]

One Christmas mission bypassed County Durham on the way to the mining community of Blyth, in Northumberland. Paul King, a Fleet Street print worker, took the train with some mates from King's Cross to Newcastle. They got to Blyth Welfare, avoiding the police, and put a stash of money behind the bar to provide drink and food for the miners and their wives, before distributing presents to the children:

> We got off the train and we had hundreds and hundreds of presents, literally trolleys. Those big trolleys full of presents and a lot of cash.

And we were met by some guys from Blyth colliery in the yellow NCB vans. We managed to get all the presents in and we were literally playing cops and robbers all around Newcastle with the police, all up to Blyth. I kid you not. We were racing around everywhere. And we got up to Blyth colliery and we're getting to the Welfare, the community centre, and 'We're just about to pull the screen down on the bar,' as we walked in. It was about half a dozen miners in there and the shop steward, or whatever they call them, so I remember him saying, 'Hang on, these guys have come up from London, you can't shut the bar.' Because obviously we would get an awful lot of hassle from the police. And Bobby Green had put down the biggest wad of notes you've ever seen . . . These men and women hadn't had a drink; they didn't have much to eat for an awful long time. And so within a couple of hours it was rammed, absolutely rammed with people. Within the parameters of what was going on, they're really enjoying themselves. And then obviously we distributed the presents to the children, principally to the children.[43]

Over the border in Scotland at Christmas time there was a cocktail of experiences, as might be expected. Margaret Mitchell and Mary Coll, the vice-president and president of the Lochore Women's Support Group, had held a raffle in October or November and had gone with Margaret's husband David, a pit electrician at Seafield, and George Bauld, the treasurer of both the Lochore Miners' Welfare and its strike committee, to buy children's presents from warehouses in Glasgow. 'We got a list of all the miners' bairns that was needing a toy for Christmas,' said Margaret, 'and we had a wee Christmas party, and every bairn got two toys.'[44] Less successful was the trip to Glasgow by Tom Adams, branch treasurer at Frances colliery. The striking miners from the Dysart centre were told that the Glasgow steelworkers had three lorryloads of chicken for them and that they should send trucks to pick them up. There was a mix-up and they arrived to discover that the chickens were already on their way to Dysart. A steelworkers' Christmas party was in full swing, and one of the guests was Scottish comedian Gregor Fisher, who persuaded the steelworkers to be more generous than they might otherwise have been:

> We were walking out the place, there were still bottles – bearing in mind we had nothing for Christmas and New Year – there were bottles of spirits and everything lying. There was a litre bottle of Grouse sitting. And I just picked it up. I was walking out and I can't remember the guy's name, he was one of the leaders of the steelworkers there at the time, 'Oh you can't take that, son. That has to all go back.' And Gregor Fisher never lost his head at him, but he says, 'For fuck's sake, man, they've got nothing. Let him take the bottle of whisky.' 'Aye, okay.' I drunk the lot before we hit the Forth Bridge getting back.[45]

Meanwhile, the support group at Cowdenbeath took a delivery of frozen chickens from the printers' union SOGAT. The story became tied up with that of the strike-breaking by one of the Cowdenbeath Workshops' employees. His house, guarded by police, was approached by a drunken striker, and Iain Chalmers, of the Cowdenbeath and Dysart strike commit-tees, living nearby, saw the danger:

> I was out the house like a rocket. I got him, I said, 'What are you doing?' He says, 'I am going to give him this fucking chicken right through his fucking living room fucking window.' I says, 'No you're not, come on.' And got into an argument with him. He was wanting to throw this and the policeman's looking at the two of us as if to say, 'I'm not really wanting to be involved here, you know.' I managed to get the chicken off him and take him round to where he lived and it was the next day he says, 'I appreciate what you did.' Thought, 'Oh God, don't get me wrong, I was all in favour . . . but I was protecting the striker, not the scab.'[46]

Christmas in the South Wales mining communities seems to have been less edgy and better provided for by national and international donations.

Christine Powell, treasurer of the Neath, Dulais and Swansea Valleys Miners' Support Group and a physics teacher in Swansea, said that 'obviously Christmas was going to be a pinch-point', but

> I recall I was coming home every night to the hallway [which was] full of parcels because a Swedish journalist had written an article about the strike and he was on an economics newspaper and they were sending things for the kids' Christmas.[47]

On behalf of the Llynfi-Afan Valley Miners' Support Group, as we have seen, Phil White, lodge official at St John's, Maesteg, went on a tour in October to raise funds from West German steelworkers and Social Democrats. Meanwhile, as we saw above, Mary and Julian Tudor Hart, who wrote to all their contacts from their Glyncorrwg GP practice, received their largest donation from one Rhys Vaughan, a local man who had become a solicitor in Manchester: 'We received it on Christmas Eve,' recalled Mary. 'It was in the post, this £1,000. I can't tell you how excited we were because that really meant turkeys for lots of people.'[48]

For Ann Jones of Hirwaun, the main providers were SOGAT and a benefactor in Norfolk. Her only misgiving was that her three teenage children did less well than the younger ones:

> The Christmas of the strike – now the ironic thing about that is that I told you I was very involved with SOGAT and SOGAT came down with busloads of stuff – some of those kids had stuff on that Christmas they wouldn't have had if their fathers were working. I remember one woman said, 'Oh look,' she said, 'tins of biscuits, chocolates.' And of course Tower children also had a present because the Social Club still had money in it. It wasn't for everybody the same because if you were a teenager, like mine, the games and books and things just didn't apply, but luckily enough my kids never moaned. They didn't moan, but the little ones had quite a good Christmas and we actually did have a

turkey. Somebody up in Norfolk donated a turkey to every miner in South Wales.[49]

The Christmas parties held in the Miners' Welfares up and down the country were showpieces of the solidarity and resilience of the mining welfares after ten and a half months of being out on strike. At Askern, the women's support group was going to make a splash. Dianne Hogg, the treasurer, approached a local cake factory for misshapen cream cakes they would never sell and crammed them into her empty freezer, ready for the party. They invited

all the kids; not just Askern kids. They got a list of all miners that lived in Knottingley, Featherstone, Upton, all over where miners come to Askern pit. And Sheila [Gibbon] and somebody else went to all the houses and asked how many children they'd got, and would they be coming to this Christmas party. And we made sure every child had a present, and we made sure every child had a really, really good day.[50]

Jean Crane, the secretary, reiterated that

we provided a present for every single one of them kids. And Sheila was Father Christmas, and I was a clown and Dianne was a clown. And it was just an absolutely brilliant day, with food, it was absolutely packed. And the people that couldn't come or didn't want to come, we still made sure that the kids got the presents.[51]

The enduring memory of Dianne's oldest daughter, Lesley, then seventeen, who worked in the soup kitchen, was that in accordance with the leading role that women were now taking in the village, 'There was a Mother Christmas. There wasn't a Father Christmas, there was Mother Christmas.'[52]

For the children of mining families, the Christmas of 1984 was, of course, not extravagant, but it created enduring memories because of the happiness that was experienced in the midst of hardship. It was also some-times strange because of the presents sent from trade union and commu-nist organisations in countries such as East Germany and the USSR, which supported the strike. Dafydd Francis, whose father Hywel was chair of the Neath, Dulais and Swansea Valleys Miners' Support Group and who was ten years old at the time, knew that the message was

> Christmas is not going to be ostentatious. You're going to be sensible because we're going to have to think of others and we'll donate money to the local Support Group, knowing this is the right thing to do. I'm not going to have two Action Men this year. It'll be one.[53]

Jude, the daughter of Donna Jones, said,

> I remember my brother getting a plastic tank and I remember I got some sort of game. We got some chocolate and I think it was just the glamour of a present from East Germany. It was blimey . . . My mum said to me that the presents have been donated by people supporting the strike in East Germany.[54]

In Leadgate, County Durham, fifteen-year-old Sam, the only daughter of Dave and Dorothy Wray, was used to being spoiled. In 1984

> I remember I got a cream-coloured plastic bangle watch that probably was very cheap and I got a coat that my auntie had made and a package that I think it was from Russia, with little bits of sweets in. I had gone from being a quite spoiled child who did very well at Christmas to have pretty much nothing, but I really didn't care. It was just such a fantastic Christmas.[55]

Fifteen miles away, in Spennymoor, Lynn Gibson, the nine-year-old daughter of a shift charge engineer at Easington, vividly recalled the present she received that year, courtesy of the French miners and Save Easington Area Mines:

It was like a miniature suitcase, it was about this big, with a little handle on it; a little black hard case. You opened it and it was black with red and silver stripes on it. Very eighties in design and I used to use that to carry my chalk and beam shoes and hand grips for gymnastics. I used that box until I retired from gymnastics when I was about seventeen, eighteen. So a good ten years I got out of it and I found out later that that was actually a present from the French miners, and it was organised by a lady called Heather Wood.[56]

If Christmas was a high point, the New Year was a low one: things were looking increasingly desperate. Striking miners and their families who had made it to Christmas lost hope in the New Year when no end seemed in sight. Ray Maslin, a forty-seven-year-old miner from Manton, recalled that, shortly after Christmas, Pete, 'a big pal of mine came round and he said, "Ray, I'm going to work." I said, "Pete, if you want to go to work, you go back to work."' 'I would never have gone back,' insisted Ray, and indeed he had a badge awarded to the 137 Manton miners who stayed true; but he was not angry with his friend and understood his family situation. 'My wife never said get off back to work, but there were a hell of a lot of the wives who did. My wife supported me, bless her.'[57]

Gary Fisher, a cousin of both David and Billy Potts, confessed:

I went back a week before it finished, a week before strike was over, if I'd known it were going to be over I would have stopped out. Hardest thing in my life, crossing the picket line.[58]

Josie Potts was the strongest of women, but even her strength could not prevent her husband going back, however much she and his brother tried to dissuade him:

One day my husband said to me, 'I've had enough Josie, I've had enough. We can't keep going without food.' And he went back towards the very end. And his brother came to see him and he said, 'Bill, don't fall out with me.' And he says, 'Brian, I'm not falling out with nobody. There's only so much you can take. She [Mrs Thatcher] starved us back to work.'[59]

As the trickle of miners going back became a stream, so the anger of those who were staying out until the bitter end grew sharper. Pete Richardson, who had been dismissed from his job in September and had done time in Durham gaol, threw a brick at the window of a strike-breakers' bus in Askern on 6 February 1985. Arrested for criminal damage, he claimed in his journal that it was a response to the strike-breakers 'putting two fingers up' at the pickets. Interviewed in 2020, he elaborated: 'I threw a brick at the thing . . . The people inside, the scabs, used to get up, laughing and joking, so when I threw this [whoosh] they got down like. It were to shut 'em up.'[60] For Pete, the return to work had already opened up a rift in his extended family. Alan, the husband of his wife Sue's sister Maureen, had quietly returned to work, and when this was discovered it broke apart not only Sue and Maureen, but also Pete, Sue and her father, who – years before – had confiscated Sue's first baby, born out of wedlock, and now wanted the family divisions hushed up:

In strike her husband started working again. He were a miner. And me dad told me that he was working and I told Pete: 'Alan's working.' And I don't know how it got back to our Maureen. But I saw me dad when we were picketing, I saw him in Welfare, and I gave him some money to get a drink and he said, 'I don't want your money.' He threw it back at me. 'You have to tell him everything, telling Pete about Alan working. You have to run to him and tell him stuff.' I said, 'He's my husband.' And me dad never spoke to me since that day. He still didn't speak to me before he died. So me and me sister fell out.[61]

To stop the flow back to work, Betty Cook took part in a massive picket on Woolley Edge, reinforced by the Barnsley Trades Council, women's groups and the Socialist Workers Party. 'We had a caravan doing hot food,' she said. Then things went wrong. She was serving an old miner a cup of hot soup when he was set upon by the police and arrested. When she ran to remonstrate, she was told that she would be next. She captured the moment of hopelessness:

There was blood all over the grass. The bobby dragged the miner away and I just stood there in the cold, trembling with anger. I watched the blood mixing with the rainwater and running down the lane. It was as if that blood was running out of all of us.[62]

In County Durham, David Wray witnessed the beginning return to work at Leadgate, where he, his wife and Norman Henderson had battled to sustain the soup kitchen in the Methodist chapel that kept striking miners fed. The tension between striking and strike-breaking workers getting onto a bus at Leadgate was captured one wintry morning by Martin Herron, the son of a Consett steelworker and community photographer for the Consett Photo Archive. He regretted not having caught on camera the moment of family violence that followed:

One day, me and my friend Norman were standing outside the chapel and a few of them were standing, and one of them was sitting by. Then Norman said, 'Them bastards are going back to work.' This was a Friday; so, on the Monday we found out that they were going to be picked up in Leadgate opposite the working men's club. So, a few of us went up and stood across the road and there they were on the other side of the road and then a sort of armoured bus came along. One of the main instigators of the call back to work [was there]. His sister came along the street and as he was getting on the bus, she hit him. She nearly took his head off. In front of everyone . . . whoosh. But he got on the bus; and that was the start.[63]

In the first weeks of the New Year, the support groups were engaged in a final campaign of fundraising for the beleaguered mining communities. The net was cast ever wider, with a flurry of missions to continental Europe that were facilitated either by the trade union movement or by moderate or radical socialist parties. David Connolly and Bill Frostwick of the Chester-le-Street support group flew from Manchester to Copenhagen to receive funding collected by the trade union of Carlsberg brewery workers:

After a couple of days we went to Nakskov which was twinned with Chester-le-Street which was a train journey away. There we got treated extremely well, got interviewed by the radio, got interviewed by the daily local paper which was a social democratic paper, woke up the next morning, and there we were the lead story with a photograph on the front page and the paper launched an appeal for Chester-le-Street miners, which eventually sent over I think about £1,100. So we were probably about £2,000 up on that trip.[64]

From Yorkshire, two of the Barnsley Miners' Wives Action Group went abroad in February. Interestingly, they encountered challenges from male trade unionists, but forged ahead on women's issues. Betty Cook, who had been injured on the picket at Woolley Edge, went fundraising in Switzerland, joking that most people on crutches were coming back from Switzerland, not going out there. They concluded with a conference in Geneva, which was joined by delegates from a bakers' union meeting there at the same time. Betty was incensed that a colleague there from her own union, USDAW, which was trying to promote the role of women, preferred to prop up the bar, rather than listen to her speak for the mining communities. I said to him, 'We're in the middle of this big campaign . . . you've got two women speaking at a great international meeting. And you can't be bothered to come and support us!?'[65]

Elicia Billingham, for her part, flew to Italy as a guest of the Italian General Confederation of Labour. She spoke at a benefit concert in

Bologna for a thousand people, each of whom had paid £5 for a ticket; but she had difficulty getting the miners' cut from the organisers, who seemed to her to be Mafia types. She confronted them about paying up, insisting, 'Because if you don't, it'll be all over the papers.' As a result, she came home with 'about two grand, might have been more'. Elicia took her chutzpah to a meeting of the women's movement in Italy:

These women, in these factories were fighting for summat, like we were fighting for pits. And one of them says to me, 'I wish we'd got the same courage as you've got.' She could talk English, her actually, she were lovely. She says, 'Could you tell me, give me a bit of an idea what we've to do?' And I said, 'Just stand up for yourselves and just go forward. Don't let them walk all over yer.'[66]

Fundraising for the strike went on right up to the bitter end – and indeed beyond. Darren Moore, the youngest of the Dirty Thirty and Malcolm (Benny) Pinnegar's right-hand man, was recruited by Jane Bruton to her left-wing Workers' Power group. Through it came an invitation from an Italian revolutionary group to speak about the Miners' Strike and to rally support. On 17 February, he headed out for two weeks with a Yorkshire miner from Rossington and a South Wales miner. He found himself at the sharp end of feminist criticisms of left-wing movements, but his abiding memory was of seeing his efforts at international solidarity cut brutally short:

We spoke at Rome University, we spoke all over. We went from Turin to Naples which were nine hundred miles, overnight, so we spoke in Turin and then we spoke in Naples the next day . . . We spoke at a rock concert somewhere, we went on the radio a couple of times . . . All the time we had a translator. We used to get some interesting comments. One woman got up and she were like ranting about the Communist Party. I said, 'What's she saying?' She says, 'All the Communist Party wants to do is fuck young women' . . . And I remember on the last day, there was this guy, in this rail workers' club and he was a Communist Party guy, and he saw me speaking and he says, 'I want you to come back for another week. We'll pay for you to do another set of meetings.' And I flew back into Luton, Benny picked me up, and I says, 'They've asked me to go back and do another week of meetings.' And he says, 'The strike's over tomorrow.'[67]

Also caught out by the end of the strike was Ann Jones, who went to Sweden to raise money with her friend from the Hirwaun Women's Action Group, Barbara Edwards. The trip was organised on a shoestring by Socialist Action, in which she was an activist:

We had no money, right. We went to Sweden on a one-way ferry ticket because they were going to raise money for us to come back, and Mars bars because we had to buy Mars bars to get half-price tickets to go to London to catch the ferry in the first place. And we didn't have money to buy a meal when we got there . . . I'd never been on anything like that in my life. I'd never been abroad . . . We done meetings as soon as we came off the ferry at different places. The news had broken that the strike was over, and of course I was crying. There's a photo actually in a Swedish newspaper, 'The little Welsh woman cries as the miners return to work.'[68]

As the twelve months of the strike drew to a close, the hardship in mining families and mining communities increased. It was not just the loss of the wage; it was also the loss of concessionary coal for heating, the demands from utility companies, landlords and mortgage lenders, and the battle to retain benefits that the state wanted to pare down or remove. Strike endurance was enabled by many women in mining families working full time, and vital help came from the wider family – so long as it was not divided by the strike. There was plenty of improvisation – from logging to coal-picking and poaching. Christmas stood out as a moment when the resilience of the mining families and communities was celebrated by those families and communities. But the hardship took its toll, and some miners and their families could not sustain it. The drift to work that began in late summer and autumn accelerated after the New Year. Miners, miners' wives and their supporters had to look internationally, as well as nationally, for support. Ironically, some were still abroad fundraising when the news came through that the strike was over.

11

THE RETURN TO WORK

As support for the strike began to falter, the NUM was put in a very difficult position. It became divided between those who argued that the union should aim at a negotiated settlement with the Coal Board and the government, and an orderly return to work that protected the unity of the union and the cause, and those who believed that the fight must go on, that after a whole year out victory was around the corner, and anything else would be surrender. This was partly a division between coalfields, with South Wales and County Durham being more in favour of an orderly return to work, and Yorkshire, Scotland and Kent more in favour of continuing the struggle. But even in South Wales and County Durham, there were many rank-and-file miners and their wives who wanted to fight on.

The orderly return to work option was advocated by the Wales Congress for the Defence of the Mining Communities, which had its inaugural meeting in Cardiff City Hall on 21 October 1984. It was the brainchild of Hywel Francis, the chair of the Neath, Dulais and Swansea Valleys Miners' Support Group and a bridge between the South Wales NUM (of which his father Dai had been general secretary between 1963 and 1976) and other communities in South Wales – from the Labour Party to Plaid Cymru, from the women's movement to the farmers, and from the trade unions to the churches.[1] A key figure he won over was Rev. John Morgans, the moderator of the United Reformed Church in Wales, whose grandfathers had both been miners and chapel deacons. 'Two aspects of Welshness press me in the same direction,' he wrote in his diary, when the Lewis Merthyr miners went on strike early in 1983: 'Welsh Nonconformity with its radical Puritan commitment and the Rhondda political and working-class tradition.'[2] Morgans was thrown into the political arena, wrote to the church leaders in Wales to secure their support for the strike, and acted as an intermediary between the NUM and NCB in a search for a negotiated settlement. On 19 November, along with three other church leaders, he spent the morning in Pontypridd with Emlyn Williams (president of the South Wales Miners' Federation) and George Rees (Dai Francis's successor) and the afternoon at the NCB in Cardiff with Philip Weekes (NCB South Wales Area director) and his deputy, Arthur Shambrook. Between the two meetings, he stopped for a pub lunch in the Caerphilly Mountains.[3]

The urgent concern of Hywel Francis was that while the strike was 98 per cent solid in South Wales, it was collapsing in other Areas, putting at risk the unity of the movement and the survival of the union, and threatening defeat. As he remembered:

The strike was collapsing in Scotland and we were uncertain about what was happening even in Yorkshire. So we sent, under cover, without even telling the union, the NUM, two vanloads of food up to South Yorkshire to ascertain what was going on . . . Phil Bowen reported back to us in support group. 'You wouldn't believe. The pit villages are split, those who are scabs are scabs for ever now, they made no attempt to bring them back out. They're not allowed in the miners' clubs or if they are they sit alone. It was visceral.' Well, we weren't going to allow that to happen.[4]

Lyn Harper, the craftsmen's rep on Blaenant lodge, reported that the Yorkshire miners 'spent all their time on mass picketing' and that women were being sent to London to walk the streets, collecting money. 'I honestly believe,' he concluded after the strike, 'that we were so successful because we weren't next to starving.'[5] Meanwhile fellow Blaenant miner and 'foreign minister' Ali Thomas took funds up to Midlothian on Christmas Eve; they concluded that in Scotland 'the strike had clearly broken before Christmas'.[6] He was right, in that half of the miners had gone back at Bilston Glen and a quarter at Monktonhall; but Fife remained solid until February.

In the light of these assessments, the Wales Congress for the Defence of the Mining Communities held an emergency meeting at the NUM headquarters in Pontypridd on 3 January 1985. The meeting approved a letter from the Council of Churches for Wales and the Catholic archbishop of Wales to Prime Minister Margaret Thatcher, making the case for an independent review of the mining industry and, as a step towards it, a negotiated settlement of the strike. John Morgans was one of a Welsh church delegation invited to meet Peter Walker, secretary of state for energy, on Wednesday 23 January. The meeting did not go well. 'All our proposals were totally rejected,' he wrote. 'We were greeted by a half-hour lecture on the future of the coal industry and then, after we had deigned to present our case, it was swiftly and ruthlessly demolished.'[7] A week later, on 30 January, they met Coal Board Chairman Ian MacGregor, but things went no better. 'The Board, the Government, did not wish any of those suggestions to be pursued,' concluded Morgans. 'They were instead in quite a different struggle which demanded the defeat of the NUM and the creation of quite a different coal industry.'[8] On 4 February, his diary entry was even bleaker: 'Mrs Thatcher's extremism will not allow her to mellow or move. She will budge only if her political safety depends on it.'[9]

Three weeks later, on 26 February, a Yorkshire Area NUM Delegate Council was told by delegates from moderate North Yorkshire that pits like Selby were now demanding an organised return to work, arguing that men were increasingly voting with their feet. However, Dave Douglass, delegate for Hatfield and a strike militant, was concerned about three miners from his pit who had been sacked and for whom he felt responsible: 'The bottom line for us was we didn't go back without an amnesty for all the people who were sacked.' At an emergency meeting of the Yorkshire Area Council on Saturday 2 March, a show of hands was taken and the motion for an unconditional return to work was won by thirty-nine votes to thirty-one. Douglass fought to reverse this decision:

> We lost the vote in Yorkshire on a show of hands. The majority voted that we go back. And we called for a card vote, so the big pits, like mine – I had thirty-four votes – outvoted whole ranks of little pits, to vote that our position was we stayed out until we got an amnesty, which was Scotland's position as well.

On the card vote, which gave greater weight to the bigger pits, a narrow majority of 561-557 voted to hold out for an amnesty and the Yorkshire delegation took this to the special NUM Delegate Conference in London the next day.[10]

County Durham was much more like South Wales in its solidarity and moderation, unwilling to push the fight beyond the limit of what was possible. A special Area Conference called by the Executive Committee on Friday 1 March agreed that it was unreasonable – on humanitarian grounds – to call on the membership to endure still further personal pain and sacrifice to themselves and their families, and supported 'a national policy decision of an orderly return to work'.[11]

The decision was not an easy one. Families like the Stratfords had thrown everything into the strike, and Paul took the view that nothing had changed for the strikers, while the government, which had spent millions of pounds funding the police operation, must soon run out of cash. As he said in 2020:

> I couldn't see why we should go back then. Got nowt to lose. Been out that long, and I was looking at the costing of the strike . . . I thought, the government is spending a hell of a lot of money.[12]

His brother-in-law, Michael Hunt, secretary of the Easington Mechanics' Union, was also against a return. His sister, Mary Stratford, had driven forward the support group at Great Lumley, but was keenly aware in 2012 that the longer the strike went on, the greater the danger to her family and her marriage:

> The only time I've disagreed with my brother and my husband through the strike, because my argument was – when the conference was on at the end – that the vote had to be to go back. Because the only other option was to decimate the whole thing. My family would have split because nobody could go on any longer. Families did split – ours didn't. We all stayed out. But I have to say if it had gone on any longer and Paul would have gone back but you know. We then would have seen a split, you know, without a shadow of a doubt.[13]

In her 2020 interview, Mary added the argument that she had a boy, Peter, who was not yet three years old, and was expecting another baby, Helen, a true child of the strike. She made a connection between the drain of pregnancy and the loss of will to stay out:

> I was pregnant, in the early stages of pregnancy. And, you know, that was draining enough and all you were seeing day in and day out, was the slow drip, drip going back . . . I remember the conference where they made the decision . . . We were at Paul's mam's with the bairn for the day. It was on and I had to go out, I had to go out for a walk. We were waiting for the news to come whether they decided to go back or not. And Paul and I, it was probably the only thing we were really split about. He didn't think they should go back. I said, 'You've got no option but to go back. If you don't go back, this will destroy the union and destroy everything we've worked towards. It will lead to all sorts of divisions' . . . So it was a huge relief for me that they voted to go back. Paul was not happy, but the decision was made. And you go with the democratic vote.[14]

On Sunday 3 March, the NUM National Executive Committee met at the TUC headquarters in London. It split 11-11 on the South Wales resolution, tabled by Emlyn Williams, on a return to work on Tuesday 5 March. NUM President Arthur Scargill, for so long the voice of radicalism and resistance during the strike, declined to use his casting vote, reluctant to bear alone the responsibility for continuing or ending the strike. To break the impasse, the question went to an NUM Delegate Conference, which voted 98-91 for the South Wales resolution on an unconditional return. The Durham miners voted with the Welsh, but were opposed by the Yorkshire, Scottish and Kent miners. A Yorkshire motion calling for an amnesty for sacked miners was defeated 91-98.[15] There was a huge amount of anger about what was seen as an acceptance of defeat. One of the Welsh delegates was Phil Bowen. 'And as he was coming out Emlyn Williams was set upon by people,' remembered Hywel Francis. 'Phil Bowen is a big fellow and had to put his arm round Emlyn and pushed people away.' He went on, rather disparagingly, 'Kim [Howells] used to call them Clapham colliers. I called them London miners, the ultra-left who wanted the strike to go on for ever.'[16]

Among those protesting about the decision to return to work were the Dirty Thirty. They had been determined all the way through, and indeed had acted as ambassadors for the strike in meetings across the country and abroad. Darren Moore flew back from his fundraising campaign in Italy, having been in Naples on 1 March, and was met at Luton airport by Malcolm Pinnegar and Richo Richmond.[17] They went straight to the delegates' meeting in London. There is a photo of them outside the TUC building when news of the decision to return came out, shouting, 'We're not going back.'[18] Dave Douglass recalled that Arthur Scargill himself was jostled and called a traitor, while '"We're not going back" was the united chant of the crowds.'[19]

In Fife, Sean Lee, the fiery Seafield miner, and his mates vented their feelings by getting drunk at the Miners' Institute in Lochore and then making their way to Ballingry police station – which, surprisingly on that day, had been left unlocked and unstaffed:

Last day of the Miners' Strike, feelings were running very high. Scargill came on the telly and said, right, that's it, lads, it's finished, which was pretty hard to take. Probably first point of call was the Miners' Institute, two or three pints, and a lot of lads arrived. Everybody's in the same mood. We took the law into our own hands, I suppose. Several, who shall be unnamed, went to the police station up the road, took out all the files from all the drawers . . . I found my one. It's got a stamp on it, red letters, 'ANARCHIST'.

Interestingly, although he had been arrested at Ravenscraig and Cartmore, Sean had not at this point been dismissed. Nor was he dismissed for the events at Ballingry police station, but rather for an incident that occurred later that evening, when he and a few of his mates began lobbing bricks at a strike-breaker's house:

. . . suddenly this policeman appeared out of a car. There was a wrestling match and he hit me with his truncheon. I took it off him and I hit him with the truncheon and then the dogs came, and the reinforcements and the dogs came, and I got arrested.

His dismissal came after the return to work, shortly after his court appearance.[20]

The stories of how the miners went back were divided. One version was that they went back with honour, heads held high, retiring from the field of battle after a year's strike, having done their best for their jobs, their families and their communities. The other version was that nothing could disguise the defeat, the humiliation, which was painful to bear. Convicted and sacked miners were abandoned, as the majority now went back to work. Those who returned now had to work alongside the strike-breakers, who were protected by a Coal Board management that was determined to show who was boss. Verbal or physical violence by former strikers against strike-breakers risked instant dismissal. Former strikers were often segregated, put on the night shift or given painful and dirty jobs out of the way. This did not prevent the war continuing, silently, underground. Meanwhile mining families and communities closed ranks against the strike-breakers. If they did not move away, they faced ongoing isolation and abuse.

In the Rhondda, the return to work at Maerdy was broadcast over the media as the embodiment of pride in defeat. Rev. John Morgans was up early on Tuesday 5 March to witness the event, which took place a few miles from Tylerstown, where he had been brought up:

> It was like a pilgrimage to drive through Tylerstown to arrive in Maerdy by 6.30. We joined the procession as it wound its way up to the pit, led by the Tylerstown band and the advancing dawn. Remarkable experience as the miners stopped to line the road and applaud the supporters, and then for the supporters to do the same for the miners of this pit, where not one has returned to work.[21]

A different view was held by Ann Jones of Hirwaun, whose husband Dai John worked at Tower colliery. She argued that the spectacle of bands and banners sent out a false message that the miners were glad to return to work. For her, the militant trade unionists in what she called the 'red pits' were conscious only of defeat after the fight had been called off by their leaders:

> Some of the pits went back with the banners, with the bands. Not in Tower colliery. Not here. We had nothing to blow a trumpet at. We were defeated. That was it . . . It was on the television, wasn't it, and you've got all these people now chanting and shouting and banners waving, 'Oh, you see the miners wanted to go back anyway. It was Scargill who kept them out. Now they're celebrating going back.' We weren't celebrating going back. So Tower didn't do it. [Penrhiw]ceiber didn't do it. Really what you would call red pits didn't do it. Where the union was the strongest and the most militant.[22]

Hywel Francis blamed the 'ultra-left' who wanted the strike to go on for ever; but in fact there was a sizeable rank and file of miners and miners' wives in the Neath, Dulais and Swansea Valleys who did not want to go back to work. Christine Powell, wife of Blaenant miner Stuart and treasurer of the support group, admitted that they were 'very, very weary', but that 'if they could have held on a little longer they might have won'.[23] 'I thought we were within a couple of months of achieving what we wanted,' said Abernant miner Martin James. His wife Siân agreed, underlining the need to stand by the convicted and sacked miners:

> You see for us as women it was, we had come so far, what did we have to lose to stick it out a bit longer, and when we were being told about cohesion and when we were being told about an orderly return to work is the way forward now. Our next question was, okay, what about the sacked and jailed men? You're not giving us anything about the sacked and jailed men. Right. What's the plan?[24]

There was even talk in this rank and file that the return to work had been a stitch-up – even a plot – organised by the South Wales NUM leadership. David Williams, another Blaenant miner and friend of Martin James, reflected that the possibility of a return had been aired for some time:

> On the turn of the year perhaps, Emlyn Williams, the leader of the Welsh NUM, was starting to say things like, 'We need to save face.' Obviously, meetings had been taking place. It left a bad taste in your mouth, mind, that we'd been out for twelve months and had nothing to show for it, nothing at all.[25]

Ann Jones of Hirwaun became convinced that plans for a return to work had been laid in secret by the South Wales NUM and its allies weeks before the end of the strike:

Before the Porthcawl meetings were being held and they were being held in secret and miners were not being invited to them. Now a lot of this I can't go into details because I've got to prove it, but we all know that the meetings took place out of the way in a pub on the mountain . . . There was uproar in the Valleys, when found out about this because somebody else had been drinking in the bar and had overheard and seen things. They denied it and they'll deny if you ask them outright today, but it isn't deniable. It is true and one very, very, Welsh important person who thinks he's important had instigated that meeting.[26]

One reason why the return to work in South Wales was relatively easy was that there were few sacked miners and their cases were dealt with by negotiation between the NUM and the NCB. There was, of course, the exceptional case of Dean Hancock and Russell Shankland, the young miners who had dropped a block of concrete on a taxi carrying a strike-breaker to work on 30 November, killing the driver, David Wilkie. Hancock and Shankland were immediately arrested and there was no chance that they would ever be reinstated. They were indeed sentenced to life imprisonment for murder on 16 May 1985.

Less intractable was the case of Phil White, lodge official at St John's, Maesteg, who was dismissed in February for the alleged intimidation of a miner who had returned to work. He had gone to the miner's other place of work, a taxi office, and had been recorded confronting him. South Wales NCB Area Director Philip Weekes was under pressure from MacGregor to get more strikers back to work and to deal harshly with their intimidation, but according to White, Weekes 'knew that the fallout of this get-back-to-work stuff was going to rip communities, families and friends apart'.[27] Interviewed by Hywel Francis in 1986, Weekes said that the Welsh should be able to sort out their own disputes. 'Down here,' he suggested, 'we could protect ourselves against the verbal battles going on in London and Sheffield.'[28] A fortnight after the strike ended, therefore, White was given his job back at St John's.

Things were very different in Scotland, where Area Director Albert Wheeler had waged a ruthless campaign to have militant miners arrested, convicted and sacked. Under his regime, 206 miners – or 1.5 per cent of striking miners in Scotland – had been sacked, as against 0.6 per cent in England and Wales.[29] Twenty of those sacked miners were from the Dysart area, including Ronnie Campbell, Pat Egan, Doddy McShane, John Mitchell and Watty Watson.[30] After the contentious national vote on Sunday 3 March, however, the miners at Seafield and Frances and the Cowdenbeath Workshops voted to return to work on 5 March; they were followed on 7 March by Polkemmet, Bilston Glen and Monktonhall, with Longannet and Comrie following on Monday 11 March.[31] Tom Adams, NUM branch president at Frances pit, was impressed by the band piping them back to work, but shocked by the number of miners who took immediate redundancy:

We took a decision to march into the pit at the back of a pipe band with a banner and stuff like that. So when we got into the pit, we came down the pit road, marched in . . . And when you're walking into the Frances, you walk to the left and that was the pithead baths. And walked to the right was all the offices and stuff like that. And this is where I got probably the biggest shock of my life. Three-quarters of the men on that march walked to the right and signed and left the industry. Took their £1,000 and never went back in the pit. That to me was a shock. I never went on strike to lose my job. I went on strike to save my job. I just couldn't believe it.[32]

Pat Egan, the branch secretary at Frances, who had been sacked in July 1984 after a picketing incident at Bilston Glen, drew a powerful comparison between Scottish and Welsh pits. 'There was nobody sacked in Wales, or nobody stayed sacked in Wales. Everybody in Wales got their job back,' he said. By contrast, 'In Scotland, we tried, we'd made an amendment that if victimised miners got their job back then we'll look at a return to work.

But it got beat.'[33] Returning miners would be confronted by the painful spectacle of some of their mates being turned away.

Two of those who were dismissed at Comrie pit were Doddy McShane and young Watty Watson. Watty's account of the return to work high-lighted the refusal of the pit manager, Davie Seath, to let them march back to work in style, the violence that then broke out and what happened to Doddy. According to Watty, Seath had told them: 'You can march back to your work, but you'll be through that wee side gate.' Watty continued:

> So we had to take the banner down and that. You had to [walk in] single file to go in . . . All of a sudden somebody threw their pit piece and it hit [Seath] square in the shooter, from the back of the crowd. He just sort of brushed it off. He was a big hefty man. And Doddy McShane piped up, 'That's all you deserve.' Doddy was standing next to me. I'm trying to hide from him . . . And Davie Seath said, 'Oi, McShane, have you something to say because you don't even work here anymore.' Right. And I could see Doddy's face just . . . he was ready to just . . . because of that . . . it wasn't a shout or wasn't anything, you don't work here anymore, McShane. Big Davie Seath. And I was, sort of, cowering more down behind Doddy. And Doddy was a wee fellow. I can see the disappointment in Doddy's face. That was the day that we started the fight for the six, the Benarty Six and the other two hundred men in Scotland.[34]

In spite of this management brutality, the Scottish miners retained their militancy and the union remained strong enough to stand up for them. When Robert (Rosco) Ross, Cowdenbeath Workshops branch secretary for SCEBTA and on its strike committee, went back to work and one of the strike-breakers asked him for a hand, Rosco told him to fuck off. He was immediately summoned to the manager's office and knew it was serious, but he counted on NUM solidarity:

I said, if you want to speak to me, I'll get my union rep. You are not entitled to pull me in on my own, and there's two of yous sitting there threatening me. I said, if you've got any issue, or that guy on the shop floor has got any issue, I said, we'll convene a meeting with my shop steward here. And I walked out. And everybody in the four sections have come down, and they were fucking clapping their hands. And I knew, this was what it was going to be like from day one.[35]

More than this, Peter McCutcheon, a miner who returned to work at Seafield and who came across as mild-mannered, explained how strike-breakers could be surreptitiously ostracised and punished. This would be underground, out of sight of the officials, or in front of men who subsequently claimed not to have seen anything. The most notorious case concerned strike-breaker Geoff Bowman, the attack on whose house had led to the arrest, trial and sacking of Doddy McShane. Revenge came from McCutcheon's old school friend Eck Watson:

Eck was walking in the road, Geoff Bowman coming towards him. He uttered something to Eck. I never heard what it was and the next thing Eck skelped him a beauty, a right-hander, square in the face. And Bowman went down. And he told him, he said, 'Get up and I'll finish you.' Bowman reported it. None of us seen a thing. But I think Bowman had goaded him, had said something to him. So Eck just hit him . . . He hit him underground. Aye, hit him about three and a half, four thousand feet under the Forth, just ladled him, it was a beauty. Just the one, but he told him.[36]

In County Durham, where the NUM leadership had only narrowly opted for the strike a year earlier and in March 1985 backed the Welsh initiative of a return to work, there was nevertheless a sense of sadness, rather than of triumph. Kath Savory of Chester-le-Street, whose husband John worked at Westhoe, near South Shields, sensed that this was the beginning of the end:

That was a real sad day. That was horrible. I couldn't watch the news. I couldn't watch the news on the telly. I was so tearful just seeing all these miners walking back to work. And that was really sad, yet at the same time they'd proved a point. But the thing is that they knew that the mines were going to go anyway.[37]

There were cases in Durham of miners going back with banners waving, but this was rarely in front of cheering crowds. Instead, the striking miners were seen to be troublemakers, about to confront the strike-breakers and having to be corralled by the police. Peter Byrne, who lived at Blackhill, outside Consett, travelled back to work at Wearmouth, which he described as 'scab city'. He described a confrontation between his 'marra', Greg Fellows, and the police over the colliery banner:

I went back to Wearmouth, and we would march in behind the banner, from The Duck, which is where they all used to meet. And the police made us walk through all the little narrow back streets. They wouldn't let us walk with pride down the main roads. And then when we got to the colliery gates there was police cordon and vans across the gate . . . You could see, in the colliery yard, men who were working, scurrying here there and everywhere, you know, all the scabs, all scurrying about . . . Perhaps they felt they were protecting them, but one of these young coppers, and I'll never forget it, grabbed a hold of the colliery banner . . . You know that were your colours. And I can still remember Greg just went for him and knocked him out the way and ripped the banner away from him . . . And that young copper got the fright of his life mind, you know, because I thought to myself, 'What the hell were you thinking of, to do that; to try and take that from us?'[38]

In County Durham, the management tried to separate striking and working miners, to prevent trouble breaking out. Paul Stratford said that when they returned to work at Easington, the manager put us, put me, another lad, and another lad – you work it out – waiting to go in the cage to go down, kept all the naughty boys back till the night shift. We're all the troublemakers I think he was saying.

The former strikers stuck together and tried to have nothing to do with the working miners: 'you just blanked them. They didn't exist, them.' The issue nevertheless arose about whether camaraderie would kick back in if a strike-breaker got injured:

I mean, the code of the pit is that if you get injured, then you go help them, you know. And that was one of the questions, that was asked in the pit, if Davie, who was a scab, if he got injured, what would you do? Would you go help him? So you think, 'Well, he's a pitman,' you know . . . And one of the lads says, 'Yes, I think that and all. I think, if you hear that somebody's hurt and you're in the area, you would go to see what you could do.' At first you wouldn't think 'scab', but by the time you were walking there, you would think 'scab', and you'd sit down, have a rest, it's a long walk, get up, have another sit down. But you would go, yes, very slowly.[39]

As in Scotland, the Durham management enjoyed its moment of triumph and took the side of the working miners against troublemakers. When Bill Frostwick returned to Herrington, he recalled,

I was in the minority because having been an official in the mine, most of my colleagues went back to work. There was only a handful of us that stayed out. We were labelled really as militants and left-wing and Scargill lovers.

Herrington closed in December 1985 and Frostwick moved to Vane Tempest, where the management gave their trusted men a name and a status, while the former strikers cultivated their own solidarity:

We had a group called the Royal Family who were the bosses' hand-picked men. And it was strange that every one of them had gone back to work, every one of these Royal Families. We were outsiders really and some of my immediate bosses y'know, they didn't like us at all because I've been out on strike for a year. And that I had left-leaning attitudes and thoughts. But as I said I brought some good lads down with us, and we all stuck together, and it lasted and closed in 1993.

Bill Frostwick never forgot who the strike-breakers were:

I've got a list of everybody who went back to work and everybody who didn't. And I still got it now. Because someone said, 'You remember so and so, but I can't remember, did they get back to work?' And I said, 'I cannot tell you now, but I can tell you once I have a look on my sheet, see if his name is on the sheet.'[40]

Miners' wives like Dorothy Wray in Leadgate had the same opinion of strike-breakers who remained in the community, even years later. She regarded them as traitors and would still not speak to them:

The majority of people stuck it out until March. But it was like being stabbed in the back I think. Life went back to normal. I passed one of them the other day when I walked the dog, and he looks at us and I think, 'You can keep looking, mate, that's never gonna happen.' And another one would smile and I was thinking that 'This smile is never gonna go anywhere, mate, because no way – if you were on fire in the street I wouldn't spit to put it out.'[41]

In Askern, accounts differed as to whether the return to work was a triumph or a tragedy. Councillor Mike Porter, in many ways the father of the village, highlighted the sadness of the community, but above all its unity and its pride:

We met outside the Welfare Club, we marched through the entire village. And there were old Welsh miners in their eighties, sat on walls, crying, married women crying, and I was crying when I kissed the kids that morning. The children asked their mothers why I was crying. I said down the speakers, 'You hold your heads up high.' And they did.[42]

Miner's wife Dianne Hogg picked up on the same combination of sadness and pride. But she underscored the conflict and the fact that the Kent miners, who were young men and as committed to the strike now as they had been a year earlier, had come up to picket the pit and prevent the return to work:

> It were like watching a movie where the heroine dies and all you want to do is sit and cry. It were fantastic, and sad as well. To see the men of this village, and women and children, march round this village, heads held high. It were a great feeling. You just wanted to cry. You had old men, standing on the doorstep, crying. And when they got to the pit, there was a picket line. The Kent miners. They didn't go back until the end of the day.[43]

At the heart of the conflict was the fate of miners like Pete Richardson, who had been convicted and sacked and hoped that his mates would stand by him and not return to work until he was given his job back. He took heart from the arrival of the Kent miners, who continued to picket, much to the annoyance of the Askern branch secretary, Pat Hewitt. Pete now felt abandoned by his own union and in hostile territory:

> When I got there I saw two Kent lads, introduced myself and stood with them as the march came to the top of Pit Lane. I was really sick about it. The Kent lads asked Pat [Hewitt] to turn back and not cross the picket line. Pat asked us to move our picket line. One or two people started to shout, 'Let's get back!' The Kent lad, only about twenty-two,

had his say and the crowd jeered him. At this point I had my say. I swore, and for this I am really sorry, for there were wives and children in the crowd, but I was maddened at all the stick this lad was taking for men like me. I was getting the impression that I was back picketing in Notts; but happening here.[44]

The union at Askern had indeed passed a mandate several times to the effect that 'This pit will not work until Pete Richardson's got his job back.' Just before the return, however, Richardson and three other sacked miners were asked by the union committee to release them from that position:

> I was asked not to push for the mandate, but to let the men go back, and then the older element of the workforce could then get their redundancy. They would then take industrial action if I was not reinstated. I was expecting them to keep their word and fight for my job. I would not have left anyone else behind and I had not expected them to leave me behind.[45]

One of his mates, the best-dressed picket Peter Robson, said that the night shift delayed its return that one night because Pete had been sacked, but then gave in and went back. 'Pete's very bitter about most of us,' he admitted, 'but the spirit wasn't there.'[46]

At Manton, formally part of the Yorkshire coalfield, but in Nottinghamshire, where 137 miners stayed out to the bitter end, the issue of victimised miners also arose. Here, however, they showed more solidarity than was on offer at Askern.

David Potts, Manton NUM branch secretary, who had been arrested for threatening to kill super-strike-breaker Bob Taylor, was let out on bail just before Christmas. On Wednesday 6 March, he led the return behind their banner of the 137 miners, although he knew that he would not be given his job back:

We met up at Manton Club, we got the banner with us, the branch banner, we walked down Retford Road, up the pit lane, I led them up there. I went to the time office where we normally draw my cheques, I went to the window, said 404, which was my number, 404, and they just said to me, 'You don't work here anymore.' That's it. And they said that to thirteen other people as well. People who had been arrested or done some damage to property. I knew I'd lost my job. I just did it as a token gesture. Out of the thirteen there were four of us who never went back.[47]

Not only did the management refuse to take back the victimised miners, but it also locked out the whole column of striking miners. Andy Varley, one of the 137, took up the story:

We marched back. We shut Retford Road off. They got the banner out but we never had a band so we just walked up. [The official] who worked in personnel, was on top taking photos. I shouted up, 'You couldn't buy us out, could you?' When we got round corner they'd locked all the doors. Canteen and all. All locked down. We just turned round.[48]

Interestingly, the striking miners were then joined by 200 of their colleagues who had already gone back to work, but came out again in solidarity with the sacked and locked-out miners until the branch meeting on the following Saturday.[49]

There seems to have been less antagonism at Manton between those who had remained on strike and those who had gone back, because so many had drifted back just before the end. Besides, they could all agree that the real villains were Ken Foulstone and Bob Taylor, the super-strike-breakers who had instigated the return to work in September and served a writ on Arthur Scargill. Andy Varley drew a distinction between Manton and Creswell, just over the border in Derbyshire:

Creswell, when they went back they said, 'Any word of scab, anyone who took a dislike to you and reported you, you were sacked.' Manton weren't like that. The only bad feeling was for Foulstone and Taylor and them that went back early, like them five.[50]

David Hopkins, who went back to work at Manton in November 1984, was also keen to argue that most of the strikers' hostility was directed at Taylor and Foulstone, who had instigated the return to work, and was happy to tell the story of how Taylor was driven from the pit:

Most of Manton was back. To be honest Manton was not a bad place to work after the strike. Those who had stayed out were a minority and they had to adapt. I think most people got on well afterwards. There was very little animosity between most people, at least not openly. The only animosity was towards those who first went back. Those first few who went back did end up moving. Bob Taylor and Ken Foulstone, they had to move away. They were seen as the instigators . . . When we went back to work, he was still at the pit, Bob Taylor, and we used to have these material shuttles like little flatbed carriers of girders, you used to tie it to a rope. Rope haulage going up and down the mine, and he was studying the rope and someone switched it on. He was stood in front, nearly knocked him over. We all looked and thought, someone's done this on purpose. And we never saw him again after that. He'd gone, he disappeared.[51]

Things were not so easy in Annesley, where Steve Williamson had remained branch secretary and campaigned for the National Working Miners' Committee. He provided the perspective of what it was like for a working miner – and one with union authority – when the minority of strikers came back to work, baying for blood. Unlike his colleague John, he tried to calm local difficulties, not inflame them. He was careful to segregate the striking miners on the night shift and to spy on them. He retained his constitutional position as secretary, but was always under attack:

You can imagine when they came back, they'd be very vocal. My partner in crime I used to work with, he was so vocal. Saying terrible things to people. After meetings I used to take him for a pint and say to him, 'John, be careful. It's alright when you've got forty or fifty people behind you, shouting and bawling, but when you go back to work and you're on your own remember, people have got memories.' He finished up going to another pit, because he'd had several good hidings . . . The majority of our strikers were all on nights. It suited me and the manager, we kept them all together. We had several disputes at our pit, it started on the night shift, they used to fire people up. We'd got spies in their camp, they came back to work to disrupt and get rid of all the union officials. When I used to go down the pit on visits, some of the things they'd written up on the bunkers, the chutes, 'Williamson out'. We knew who were doing it. But every time it came to a vote I got 90 per cent. But they were chipping away at me to be honest. For years I was never opposed. In the last few years I was opposed but I was opposed by bloody idiots.[52]

The situation at Welbeck colliery, which had been heavily protected by the police and where the strikers had been a small minority, the return to work was similarly fraught. Ken Bonsall of Warsop, aged seventeen at the time, qualified as a miner two weeks before the end of the strike. He did not want to begin work at Welbeck before the strike ended, but was persuaded by his father, who said, 'these are the jobs we are fighting for'. After the strike finished, the management at Welbeck operated a reign of terror against the striking miners, categorising them as communists, downgrading them to menial jobs and putting them at constant risk of dismissal:

What they had to do was go back to work with their tail between legs, and then be told in the canteen, 'You've got to see the manager before you go down the pit.' Hillsley was the manager then. They all went for a dressing down. One by one into the office to see the colliery manager to be told, 'They've got their eyes on you, step out of line and you'll be sacked. We've got your card marked, you're commies, you're all communists' . . . They didn't go back to their old jobs, all their jobs had gone, they'd been given to scabs. So like my father, a chargeman on a coal face, his job had gone to someone else. They sent them on menial tasks, just shovelling coal dust that accumulates on roadways miles from anywhere, and they all had to do that work together. Kept separate. For a time. You had to work your way back in, let that be a lesson to you.[53]

Things were made worse in Nottinghamshire by the secession from the NUM of the Union of Democratic Mineworkers (UDM). Working miners were elected to branch and Area posts on the Nottinghamshire NUM and campaigned for autonomy, so that they would not be subject to control by the NUM Executive under Arthur Scargill. The crisis point was reached on 9 May 1985, when the NUM Executive decided to dismiss Roy Lynk and David Prendergast from the Nottinghamshire NUM for gross misconduct. In response, the Nottinghamshire NUM held a ballot on 14 May on opposing rule changes that gave the national NUM greater powers over the different Areas, which (it was feared) would result in Nottinghamshire being further disciplined. The motion was carried by 73 per cent of the membership – 15,157 votes to 5,631. Roy Lynk announced:

The Notts membership has shown overwhelmingly that they will not be dictated to by an unrepresentative clique in Sheffield who wants to impose sinister rule changes on them. Nor are we prepared to put up with these people trying to get rid of the Nottinghamshire leadership.[54]

Two months later, in July 1985, the NUM Annual Conference approved the NEC proposal for rule changes by 174-58, and the Executive, in private session, expelled Lynk and Prendergast for gross misconduct and insubordination.[55] The secession of the UDM went ahead, with a campaign fought against 'the true face of Scargillism', and in a ballot on 23 October, 72 per cent voted to form a breakaway union (17,750 votes to 6,792).[56]

This impacted straightaway on Ken Bonsall, who wished to remain in the NUM at Welbeck but was subjected to systematic harassment to make him give up his membership. As he explained:

> You automatically got put in the UDM and if you wanted to stay true to the NUM you had to go to the office of the HR manager and sign to say you wanted your money diverted back to the NUM. Completely illegal . . . You did it, you thought that was it. And the week after you'd go to time and wages and say, 'Could you just tell me, you know my union subs, are they paid to the NUM or the UDM?' 'Just one minute, Ken. Yeah, UDM.' 'Okay, thank you.' Then you'd have to go across the yard to the manager's block again to the HR manager and say, 'I signed last week for my money to go to the NUM and it's gone to the UDM.' 'Sorry Ken, I don't know what's happened there. Just sign there' . . . So three times I went over. It deters people, unless you definitely wanted your money to stay in the NUM. That is how it was set up at Welbeck colliery. Three times I had to sign and check that my money was being paid to the NUM. [We] were the diehards who wanted their money paid to the NUM and not to a breakaway union.[57]

An even grimmer account was given by Helen Colley, the IMG activist who had moved from Hackney to Nottingham in February 1985 and who worked as a bus driver while supporting the strike. She recalled that at Welbeck, NUM supporters were victimised, set upon and sacked in a concerted campaign by managers and breakaway unionists to ensure the triumph of the UDM:

> It's like the strike didn't come to an end in Notts. Everyone had to go back to work but there was still a huge struggle. Because you can imagine how the NUM guys were treated. They were victimised by

management, brutalised. There were instances of rape, man on man rape. There was a huge amount of violence down the pit . . . They were particularly trying to pick off the leading activists, the guys who took up their roles as shop stewards for the NUM. The big struggle was to try to get the management to recognise the NUM alongside the UDM. My friend Mark was sacked for putting up a notice on the noticeboard at the pithead advertising an NUM meeting. He was sacked for that. That was at Welbeck.

She added that Mark later took his own life.[58]

In Leicestershire, the Dirty Thirty were totally exposed when they went back to work at Bagworth colliery. Not only did they number only 30 among 1,500 miners, but they were not supported by the Leicestershire NUM, led by Jack Jones, who had opposed the strike. Curiously, they were given greater protection by the manager, Mr Bond – a Geordie who sympathised with their cause.

Malcolm Pinnegar, the leader of the Dirty Thirty, who had himself been physically attacked by a strike-breaker in his home the previous November, described the return to work as 'walking the gauntlet'.[59] Nigel Jeffery said that there had been no bands and banners, just abuse from working miners and the threat of unemployment:

For us there was nothing. Just the threat of losing a job, really. We didn't know what to expect. We didn't know whether we were going to turn up and be sacked for what we did. I mean, we'd had abuse during the strike from people in our villages. We'd even been called scabs by scabs. We were being called the scabs because we're on strike.[60]

Bobby Girvan explained to one of his Quaker supporters in Marlborough that when he and two others from the Dirty Thirty were lowered back into the pit in the cage on Thursday 7 March, they were confronted by a posse of working miners who mocked them, but whom they saw off:

We were let out and we walked towards the safety gates some forty yards on, only to be confronted by a herd of scabs blocking our way, singing mockingly, 'Here we go, Here we go, Here we go!' As the three of us stood face to face with these continuous offspring of Spencerism, one of them said to us, 'You'll have to walk round the back road, you're not coming through here.' On hearing this we just walked forward slowly staring at them. As we did the scabs fell silent and parted a narrow patch for us to walk through, which we did with pride and dignity.[61]

His brother Sam complained that another group of the Dirty Thirty was treated badly:

They sent us over to Nailstone Wood, out of the way. Me, Mick Barnes, Richo and Phil Smith, probably the best face workers there. They sent us to Nailstone Wood, to clean out the drift belt in freezing cold, wet and windy conditions, on good money though. Kept us away because they didn't want us to start anything, did they?[62]

The Dirty Thirty were given some support by the Bagworth manager, Mr Bond. He allowed them to work together underground, enjoying safety in numbers. According to Nigel Jeffery,

Mr Bond was there, and he was from the North East. His heritage was from the North East and what have you, and he actually congratulated us for what we'd done. He says, 'I have every sympathy on what you've done.' He says, 'Make no mistake, you know, you won't be losing your job. Your job is still here if you want it.' He says, 'I know it's going to be hard for you to go back to work with these people.' He says, 'What we'll try and do is we will keep you together as a group.' I previously worked with two brothers down the heads. I then went back to work with Benny, Malcolm Pinnegar and with Darren Moore. So they kept the three of us, and all we had to do was keep us heads down, just working in the head, that drove the roadways, and we'd be alright. Yes, the manager was so sympathetic. it was unreal, actually, it was good.[63]

On the other hand, ironically, the Dirty Thirty was confronted by the downright hostility of their own union, the Leicestershire NUM under Jack Jones. He held the view that they had taken unofficial strike action, and by not paying their subs for a year had forfeited their membership of the union. Darren Moore recounted the confrontation that occurred in the pit canteen:

And then the Leicestershire NUM came in. There were two of them come in and said, 'We can't represent them underground.' Because we hadn't paid us subs for the year. Now we said, 'Well, they've been waived by the NUM. Anybody who's on strike, has had the union subs waived by the NUM.' They said, 'No, this is Leicestershire Area, got their own rules. So, if you go underground you are not represented, so if you have an accident, you can't use the Union solicitor. I think one of them said 'you need to go away and sort it out' . . . Basically, as far as they were concerned we were being unconstitutional, we'd been in an unofficial strike, that's how they saw it.[64]

They phoned NUM headquarters and soon had the subs situation resolved. But that was not the end of the matter. The Dirty Thirty were then told that they were not allowed to speak and vote at NUM branch meetings. They had to appeal to the High Court against the Leicestershire NUM to have this reversed. They succeeded in this on 13 September 1985.[65]

The only advantage the Dirty Thirty had over the striking miners of Nottinghamshire was that they did not have to face a challenge from the breakaway UDM. There was a campaign led by Terry Hughes of the Ellistown pit to swing Leicestershire behind the UDM. He was given the backing of the Coal Board and was offered a job as recruitment officer at the new 'superpit' of Ashfordby, which was dangled before the Leicestershire miners as their secure future, and was designed to be a UDM closed shop. But Jack Jones, who had failed to support the Dirty Thirty, ended up campaigning for Leicestershire to stay in the NUM – something that Pinnegar said he should have done all the way through – and in the ballot of October 1985 Leicestershire miners voted by 65 per cent to stay in the NUM.[66] According to Darren Moore, 'Bagworth was solid. We were at Bagworth, so I'd like to think that we had a bit of an input into that.'

The return to work in March 1985 was thus anything but a straightforward process. It exposed divisions between moderates, who looked for a negotiated settlement and an orderly return to work, and militants, who believed that victory was within their grasp. At some pits, the miners returned behind banners and a brass band, 'their heads held high'; at others, they slunk back with heads bowed in defeat. The issue of whether to stand by miners who had been victimised and sacked deepened antagonisms, and inevitably they were abandoned by mates who wanted their jobs and wages back. In the pits, war continued between striking and working miners, and this time the strikers were the embattled minority, at constant risk of intimidation and dismissal by a management that was relishing being back in the saddle. In Nottinghamshire, the situation was complicated by a war between the breakaway UDM and the stalwarts of the NUM; meanwhile in Leicestershire, the Dirty Thirty found themselves persecuted by the Area NUM, which had never supported the strike. If the camaraderie of miners had once existed, there was little sign of it now.

12

THE FIGHT GOES ON

Three months after the end of the strike, Mick 'Richo' Richmond wrote to Kipp Dawson of the United Mine Workers of America, with whom he had struck up a friendship during her visit to the striking coalfields, to say, 'A play has been written about us, "The Dirty Thirty". It is excellent and I wish you could see it. Here is a leaflet for it.' The flyer advertised the summer tour of *With the Sun on Our Backs*, a play by Tony Stevens, performed by the Utility Theatre Company.[1]

Very quickly after the defeat, the Miners' Strike became the stuff of legend. The highs and lows of the strike were transformed into dramatic art and international celebration. *With the Sun on Our Backs* was written by an English lecturer at Nottingham Poly and based on video footage recorded during the last months of the strike. The central character was based on miner's wife and secretary of the support group Kay Smith, who remembered that

> the group that did the play, they'd come to the house because they
> wanted to study me, to get the accent and our work, for them to do
> their acting bit and you know, portray me, or what I were like and
> everything else.[2]

Kay was invited to contribute to the programme notes of the play, and wrote:

For the first time women and men were united as one. Women from all coalfields broke the shackles of being housewives and mothers. We stood and fought, we gave everything we had, we will always be able to look our children in the eye.[3]

The music for the play was written by Paul Mason, the partner of Jane Bruton of the Leicester Trades Council Miners' Support Group, a talented trombonist, teacher and activist in the Workers' Power group. Mason said that the video recordist Kate Ford burst into tears while filming Kay Smith giving a speech. He also recalled that 'the actors were radical students, mainly from the Poly. They had a theatre comp called Utility, very much designed around the communist Utility Theatre of the '30s. It was overtly agitprop, very Brechtian, funny.' The opening night was at the University of Leicester in June 1985. It was then performed at a Workers' Power summer school in Sheffield, at the Edinburgh Fringe and in a string of Miners' Institutes. 'This was weeks afterwards,' said Mason. 'They saw their own strike mythologised. It went down a storm, it filled entire halls.'[4]

The role of Kay Smith was played by an actor; but in another theatrical production, miner's wife Maureen Douglass went on stage herself. Maureen had spoken at the women's rally in Barnsley on 12 May and was involved in the women's support group at Hatfield Main, but she was also an art student and pro-Palestinian activist. During the strike, she was asked by playwright Ron Rose of Doncaster Arts Coop to play a miner's wife in *Bread and Roses*, set in the midst of a miners' strike in the Second World War. This toured Miners' Welfares, but she attracted criticism from other miners' wives for 'putting a feather in my cap or making myself more famous', for setting herself apart from the community. Then, echoing *With the Sun on Our Backs*, Ron Rose and his team

decided to do a verbatim thing about the strike. This was while the strike was still on, and they interviewed a lot of people, got a lot of verbatim material and put together a production called *Never the Same*

Again, which was about the women's support groups . . . Ron asked me to be part of that, and there were a lot of professional actors in it as well. It was directed by Stephen Daldry.[5]

The play came out in the spring of 1985, toured locally and was then revamped for the Young Vic as *The Enemies Within*, directed by David Thacker. Maureen's acting career took off. In 1987, she left her husband Dave and their house in Dunscroft and moved to London.

The mining families of County Durham projected their community solidarity into the bright lights of London. The Consett Music Project of musician and teacher Neil Griffin and the Durham Miners' Support Group had organised fundraising gigs during the strike, and had brought in performers such as Billy Bragg and Lindisfarne.[6] After the strike, they continued to raise funds for sacked miners, making an LP and enlisting the support of GLC leader Ken Livingstone for a Concert for Heroes in the Albert Hall on 2 March 1986. As Griffin remembered:

> Ewan MacColl and Peggy Seeger were on the bill. I never got to meet them, but I ventured out of the dressing room and went into the main hall to listen to them and it was absolutely spellbinding. Because, you know, he wrote 'Dirty Old Town', 'First Time I Ever Saw Your Face'. He's the real deal. But then there were all these people backstage milling about like Andy Kershaw, who's still on the telly I think, and Ralph McTell, a significant hero of mine musically.[7]

Also on the bill were Lindisfarne, Tom Robinson and Paul Weller of The Style Council who, as the Council Collective, had produced 'Soul Deep' in the winter of 1984–85, with proceeds going to the families of striking miners.[8] The evening concluded with the Durham Miners' Wives Support Group singing their signature song, 'They'll Never Beat the Miners'.

The Miners' Strike was a vortex into which many other political and trade union movements – local, national and international – had been sucked and, in many cases, transformed. These included the women's movement, the gay and lesbian movement, the peace movement, the anti-apartheid movement and 'Third World' (as it was then called) revolutionary movements. The miners themselves were transformed and radicalised by exposure to these movements. After the strike, miners and miners' wives were widely regarded as heroes in many quarters, having battled with the Thatcher state for a full year to defend their jobs, families and communities. They were invited to campaigning events nationwide and worldwide, and were proud to be integrated into global protest movements, which included the workers' movement in East Germany, of the revolutionary Sandinista regime against the US-backed Contras in Nicaragua, and of the African National Congress against apartheid in South Africa and its imperialist backers. The miners' activism fed into other struggles against the Thatcher state, such as the gay liberation movement and the printers' strike at Wapping in defence of their own industry. The danger of involvement in these wider struggles was that the activism of miners and miners' wives became somewhat marginalised; but it also fed back into a second wave of activism around 1992, when a new tranche of pit closures was announced. And this time it was the miners' wives who were on the front line.

On Saturday 9 March 1985, a mere six days after the National Executive of the NUM voted in favour of a return to work – six days during which the majority of miners trooped back to work – a national rally of Women Against Pit Closures was held in Chesterfield. This was a celebration of the year-long struggle. Ann Lilburn, a miner's wife from Northumberland and member of the national committee, said that it was a 'marvellous event'. The minutes of the WAPC meeting on 16 March recorded that 'Although the strike is over WAPC is now firmly established. The rally was a splendid end to the strike.' However, the rally also highlighted the fact that the national and international support elicited by WAPC had had the effect of marginalising the inner core of miners' wives. The list of speakers included Arthur Scargill, Chesterfield MP Tony Benn, Brenda Dean, general secretary of SOGAT, Joan Ruddock, chair of CND, Greenham Common activist Christine Drake, Ellen Musialela of the South West Africa People's Organisation (SWAPO) and speakers from Chile and Iran.[9] The minutes subsequently noted that:

> Several delegates felt that there had been too few miners' wives on the platform . . . They had decided to drop some miners' wives from the speakers list rather than other speakers. The problem was to balance WAPC speakers and women representing the wider labour movement and international groups. The Committee agreed that in future we must insist on our right to be heard. Betty Heathfield had not originally been asked to speak at the rally and was only eventually asked following the intervention of Ella [Egan] and Anne [Scargill]. Betty herself said that she felt very badly let down by people she thought would have supported her. Delegates were shocked to hear that Betty had been badly treated. A vote of confidence in Betty was passed.[10]

Four months later, in July 1985, a group of Women Against Pit Closures was invited by the East German miners' union to Erfurt. East Germans had provided a good deal of support for the strike of the miners against what they regarded as a capitalist and imperialist state, and now wished to welcome the battling wives in person. Scottish miner Pat Egan recalled that 'my wife Margaret, she went to East Germany. Because they invited the miners' wives over to East Germany at the time, and I think they drew the names out a hat, and she was picked to go. She went and I was left watching the baby.'[11] Barbara Jeffery, wife of Cliff Jeffery of the Dirty Thirty, was also invited and went with her two children, Lynn and Dean. They were taken to a hotel in the Thuringian forest and on a series of visits, including to a winter sports centre and Buchenwald (the children going that day to a toy museum instead). They came home with gifts of coats and clothing and propaganda cassettes and projector slides exalting the trade unions, new technologies, youth, women and peace under East German socialism.[12]

The reputation of the Women Against Pit Closures also spread to the USA. In June 1986, Kipp Dawson of the United Mine Workers of America, who had previously campaigned for civil rights, women's liberation and gay rights, invited Anne Scargill and Betty Cook of the Barnsley Miners' Wives Action Group, together with Betty Heathfield of WAPC, to attend a conference of the Coal Employment Project. This had been started in 1977 and helped women to secure and keep jobs in American mines, to obtain maternity and medical leave, and to combat sexual harassment and discrimination. The following November, Kipp returned to the UK for a conference of the International Miners' Organisation, together with her friend Libby Lindsay, who in 1976, at the age of eighteen, had followed her step-father into the West Virginia mines. Libby was struck by the combativeness and suffering of the British miners, and especially the Women Against Pit Closures:

A lot of sacked miners, and so many people made redundant. And, just hearing their stories, oh, my gosh. Orgreave. I mean, I'm thinking, you know, I maybe kind of got self-prideful in thinking I'm tough enough. You know, kinda battle-worn. I had no idea. Meeting the women against pit closures was so humbling and inspiring. My Lord, what amazing women . . . So organised, so strong and brave and resolute. God, they're amazing.[13]

Meanwhile, in South Wales the involvement of women in the strike fed into an interest in the struggles of women through history and in the importance of education to further their ambitions. On 25 May 1985, Onllwyn Miners' Welfare Hall, which had been the food parcel centre of the Neath, Dulais and Swansea Miners' Support Group, was given over to a day school on the subject of 'Welsh Women Make History'. This included a showing of a film by Deirdre Beddoe and Sheila Owen Jones about Welsh women's protest, entitled *I'll Be Here for All Time*; a film called *Smiling and Splendid Women*, about the activities of the women of the support group, including picketing the Port Talbot steelworks and the Cynheidre colliery occupation; and a discussion led by Margaret Donovan.[14]

A more permanent outcome of the strike in the Valleys was the creation of a women's adult education cooperative, which had its first meeting in Onllwyn Miners' Welfare Hall on 5 June 1986, and which in early 1987 found permanent premises in offices abandoned by the Coal Board in nearby Banwen. The driving force behind it was Mair Francis, whose involvement in the strike had been limited by looking after her third child, Sam, who had Down's syndrome, but who was now keen to help women develop the skills they had learned during the strike and afford them the new working opportunities they must seize as the pits closed. As she put it:

People like Kay [Bowen] and Hefina Headon and Siân James were expected to speak in big rallies. They'd got a lot of confidence. I don't think they wanted to lose those skills. So the next step was what about us? The mining industry was changing because there were some miners who were on strike, whose wives were teachers, like Christine [Powell] or nurses. So it wasn't like it was in the previous generation where the women were at home and the men came home from work – well before the pithead baths – the bath was there. This was in the '80s. Women's expectations were different from previous generations and I think they wanted to do something for themselves which would benefit the family and the community.

The cooperative was called the Dulais Opportunities for Voluntary Enterprises (DOVE) workshop. It used what Mair called 'Tory language' to secure funding from the Welsh Office and 'apparently our bid went right to the top'. But it also took the image of Picasso's dove of peace, which reflected Mair's role in CND. The workshop began by offering traditional skills, such as hand and machine knitting and spinning and weaving, but it also offered courses in computer skills, domestic electricals, beauty and health.[15]

Kay Bowen, who had been held back at school by undiagnosed dyslexia but had come into her own organising food distribution across three valleys during the strike, was one of those to benefit from DOVE, getting three GCSEs and going on to get an A-level in psychology at Neath College. After the strike, she said:

> We wanted to get more involved in life in general, and that's where DOVE came from, up in Banwen. Yes, there was a lot of people afterwards who got jobs, who were housewives before, or had perhaps only a part-time job and wanted a full-time job afterwards. It did open women's eyes to a lot.[16]

The Miners' Strike helped to develop a working-class feminism, which then took off into its own orbit. It had also produced a link between miners and gay rights activists, which initially provided funds for mining families and later to sustain the gay rights movement itself. Ironically, the second visit of the Lesbians and Gays Support the Miners (LGSM) took place on the weekend of 1–3 March 1985, just as the Delegate Conference back in London was voting on a return to work. An LGSM conference was held at the London Lesbian and Gay Centre's premises in Cowcross Street, Farringdon, on 30 March. Dai Donovan of the Neath, Dulais and Swansea Valleys Miners' Support Group was invited to discuss the gains of the strike, and nine women from the Dulais Valley were presented with a Ford Transit van for their campaigning, painted with the motto: 'Provided by the Lesbians and Gays Support the Miners, London'.

The agenda of the LGSM, however, was no longer only about the miners. There were speakers from the Rhodesia Women's Action Group, the National Abortion Campaign and the Terence Higgins Trust, which addressed the threat of AIDS and the social panic surrounding it. In his speech to the conference, LGSM Secretary Mike Jackson admitted that the gay community had not all supported the miners: 'some were fearful, some were cynical, some were ignorant while some did not give a damn anyway'.

He drew strength from 'mining families, lesbians and gay men laughing, dancing, singing and getting dead drunk together'. But then he suggested that they broaden the agenda:

> Let's build from that strength and keep developing our political and community links between each other and extend it to all those fighting for a peaceful, democratic and socialist world.[17]

On the occasion of the Gay Pride March, Saturday 29 June 1985, it was LGSM that now invited the miners to join their parade. Mike Jackson remembers that now the LGSM banner, its band and its following was out in front, while the miners' banner was some way behind:

> We got to the head of the march. Jonathan [Blake] was holding one banner pole, I was holding the other one and there was a bank of about thirty photographers all taking photographs of us. It was an amazing feeling and we'd embellished the banner as well for the day. We put ribbons of suffragette colours, green, purple and white. We'd got red balloons stuck to the corners of it. We'd blown up a hundred red balloons and tied them on . . . We'd got a London-based socialist band called the Big Red Band to come and march with us, and very cleverly our banner – which Mark [Ashton] made – he'd written on the back of it the first verse of 'Solidarity Forever' which is such a simple idea but such a bloody good idea . . . There are photographs of that day that have been unearthed recently and you'll see our LGSM banner and the next banner is the Blaenant lodge banner that the miners brought. It's way in the distance. There is such a crowd behind us.[18]

The support of the miners helped to push forward the gay rights agenda. For Mike Jackson, 'politically the high point happened a few months later still at the TUC and the Labour Party conferences when the

NUM backed the LGBT motions'. In September 1985, the TUC passed a motion to protect homosexual men and women from discrimination in employment and the workplace; and that October, the Labour Party conference voted for the repeal of all legislation discriminating against lesbians and gays, including lowering the age of consent from twenty-one to sixteen, preventing police harassment and enjoining local authorities to increase awareness of these issues.[19]

Personally, however, Jackson confessed:

> I'm afraid it defeated me, the Miners' Strike. I kind of lost all interest. I was just left angry. It didn't make me change my politics. If anything it set them solid, but as far as activism I'd worked my butt off that year and I just wasn't interested.

Mark Ashton's death from AIDS in February 1987 was also a huge blow to Mike: 'I did love Mark and I never managed to have a sexual relationship with him, but I did love him and it was really hard for me to deal with.' The lesbian and gay movement went on and worked with the labour movement through Trade Unions against Section 28, which fought the part of the Local Government Act 1988 that banned local authorities from 'promoting' homosexuality, but Mike Jackson had no part in it.[20]

Radicalised by their own strike, miners became involved in campaigning politics more widely. A key issue, especially for Welsh and Scottish miners and their supporters, was the way in which the full power of the English state was mobilised to attack their jobs and their communities. There was a direct line between the Miners' Strike and the rise of Welsh and Scottish nationalism. Hywel Francis, who had chaired the Neath, Dulais and Swansea Valleys Miners' Support Group, recalled that

> when I discussed it with people subsequently, Dafydd Elis-Thomas, for example, who became the first speaker in the Welsh Assembly, said, it

all started then. The whole eventual momentum towards devolution, having been defeated in '79. The actual bringing of Wales together in support of the miners.[21]

Iain Chalmers, who had been 'foreign minister' of the Dysart Area strike committee, said:

I was heavily involved in devolution. Again, the Scottish Parliament set up, I've still got my membership card somewhere. What really set me apart from a lot of my colleagues in the Labour side was we got devolution, we got Holyrood, the Welsh got their Assembly and . . . well Northern Ireland [the Good Friday Agreement].[22]

Other miners and former miners became involved in international political movements, often inspired by the anti-apartheid movement or by revolutionary movements in Latin America. Darren Moore, the youngest member of the Dirty Thirty, continued to pursue left-wing politics. He joined the National Rank and File Miners Movement, which aimed to continue the struggle that the NUM leadership had called off in March 1985. It was based at the Camden NALGO office that had supported the strike and was linked to Workers' Power. Launched in Sheffield on 1 June 1985, it held its first conference on 12 October 1985, bringing together rank-and-file miners, building workers, teachers and local government workers. 'It involved a lot of the sacked miners as well, so we were trying to raise money for the sacked miners by selling badges and various things,' said Darren. 'I agreed to edit the paper.' After his trip to Italy, he also continued to develop international solidarity, soliciting donations from the Barcelona dockers and the Spanish anarcho-syndicalist Confederación Nacional del Trabajo (CNT). Meanwhile, six months or a year after the strike, he bumped into Simone Dawes, whom he had met at a NALGO meeting during the strike, 'out selling the *Socialist Worker*'. They went to see a play at the Highfield workshop in Leicester about a strike by South

African gold miners, featuring their gumboot dance. 'We sort of got together after that,' he said. 'So that was one positive thing to come out this strike.'[23]

Support for the anti-apartheid movement caught up others in the Dirty Thirty. In August 1985, Mick 'Richo' Richmond, Cliff and Nigel Jeffery and Kay Smith's husband Phil were invited by the United Mine Workers of America to attend a conference at Oberlin College, Ohio. Richo had been educated in the politics of Nicaragua by Kipp Dawson; and now he was amazed to find himself on a platform next to Oliver Tambo. As he marvelled:

Here's a miner from Ibstock and here's Nelson Mandela's right-hand man. I looked round and thought, 'What am I doing here?' We were all supporting each other, the anti-apartheid people, the striking miners, the Sandinistas from Nicaragua.[24]

After their return home, Richo wrote to Kipp:

The trip to America was everything and more to us. What can I say, Kipp? We were treated like heroes. The comrades were fantastic, the classes brilliant and the whole thing <u>has</u> changed all of us. I was very pleased with <u>our</u> panel. I was proud to address the Final Rally and I owe all this to you.[25]

Engagement with South African issues was often promoted by outside activists, but it certainly resonated with striking miners. Jane Bruton, the activist and nurse who ran the Leicester Trades Council Miners' Support Group, went on in 1986 to promote the boycott of South African goods in Leicester Royal Infirmary.[26] Helen Colley, the IMG activist who was sent to support the Miners' Strike in Nottinghamshire, resumed her involvement with anti-apartheid activism, which involved both miners and railwaymen. As she explained:

One of the things in terms of their international outlook was the whole thing around South Africa, because Thatcher was importing coal from South Africa. There was a connection with the RMT, the rail workers, because they were expected to transport the coal . . . The RMT were also very involved in supporting their counterpart union in South Africa, there was a whole left-wing leadership under Geoff Revell. So there was a kind of triad thing which meant that the anti-apartheid stuff that I'd got involved in more centrally when I was living in London – going on pickets and demonstrations, the South Africa Embassy – but then I got really involved in it when I went to Nottingham. There was a really close relationship between the NUM, the RMT and the anti-apartheid movement. We did a lot of things together. We did joint conferences. I've got some photos. There's me, Geoff Revell and a guy called Panduleni Itula who was a member of SWAPO and Betty Heathfield. And there's a picture taken from the fundraising social at the end of the evening and there's me, one of my friends from the anti-apartheid movement and Itula, and we look hot and sweaty and happy and exhausted.[27]

The energy of the Miners' Strike fed not only into the anti-apartheid movement, but also into the Wapping dispute of the print workers. The print workers had been among the most supportive of the miners, and their turn soon came when their industry was threatened by news magnates backed by the Thatcher government. In January 1986, they went on strike against the plan of Rupert Murdoch's News International group to shift production from Fleet Street to a computerised plant in Wapping, sacking 6,000 printers and attempting to break their unions.[28] Paul King, the National Graphical Association printer who had supported the miners in Nottinghamshire, Yorkshire and Northumberland, observed

the collusion that went on between employers and the government, literally hand in hand. For Thatcher, it was Murdoch's *Sun*, *Times*,

Sunday Times and *News of the World* supporting the Conservatives. So the payback was allowing the police force to be used as thugs against the workforce. This was violent. It was violence on a completely different scale.[29]

He himself was arrested on the picket line and taken to court, accused of threatening behaviour.

The Welsh miner's wife Ann Jones, who was involved in Socialist Action and Women Against Pit Closures, felt that her advice to the SOGAT printers who backed them during their strike was now justified. She had urged them not to give money to the miners, but to stop printing Tory lies which blamed the miners for all the violence:

When SOGAT went on strike themselves a man came up to me and he said, 'Do you know I've got to apologise to you.' I said, 'Why is that?' He said, 'Because I didn't believe that the law of this country and the police forces could treat people the way that you miners were saying they were doing. My God,' he said, 'have we learned the hard way, because for everything they practised on the miners' . . . Wapping was horrendous. Horrendous, Wapping was.

Ann went to picket Wapping with her friend Siân James and her husband Martin. They were shocked that despite the presence of families, the police were exceptionally brutal:

Siân: I was up on top of a barricade in Wapping. Martin shouted to me, 'Move. Move. Move you stupid cow.' I turned around and I looked behind me and they were coming down on horseback.

Ann: Well that was the night because there was women and kids there. Pushchairs, everything. And when we were walking it was starting to look strange. They started putting these barriers along the pavement further than they'd ever been before. So you couldn't move out and all of a sudden you could see. Linford Christie had nothing on me that night, and I can't move fast. I'm over those barriers and I'm not ashamed to say, we were hiding. We were hiding behind a bus because they were looking for anybody.

The account of Paul Mason, the partner of Jane Bruton, a member of Workers' Power and composer of the music for *With the Sun on Our Backs*, highlighted what had been learned during the Miners' Strike – whether by miners, print workers or left-wing activists – about violence, the power of the state and how to tackle it. Now the gloves were off:

We went down on the first mass picket of Wapping . . . That was a mass picket with more of the ferocity of anything except Orgreave. Because by then all the respectability, the law-abidingness, the deference to authority had gone out of the left of the labour movement. So on that demonstration the print workers got a lorry, drove it to the front, crashed it into the gates, threw fireworks at the police and the next minute we were in a pitched battle . . . Why Wapping on 1st May sticks in my mind was that the balance of politics had changed. There were miners all around on that picket and the general gist was, 'Enough messing around, there's no more messing around with the state. We're not going to wait till they attack us.' So they came all tooled up. Without worrying what people might think they were picking up bricks, forming barricades. And the left were as well and the printers had already drawn that lesson.[30]

Five years later, the miners still had a fight on their hand. Since the year-long strike had ended, 125 pits had been closed, with the loss of 100,000 jobs. Now the remaining mines were threatened by the rising importation of coal from international markets and the coming on stream of North Sea gas.[31] In October 1992, following another Conservative election victory, Michael Heseltine, president of the Board of

Trade, announced the closure of thirty-one of the remaining fifty pits, with the loss of 30,000 jobs.

What Dave Douglass called 'the last stand of the miners' took the form of a massive demonstration which converged on Hyde Park on Sunday 25 October 1992. Four chartered trains and seventy coaches left Doncaster, six trains and forty coaches left Durham. Scottish miners marched in overalls and helmets from Glasgow to London. The common view was that Arthur Scargill had been right all along about secret plans for pit closures.[32]

Women Against Pit Closures also went into action. Anne Scargill and Aggie Curry were part of a group of women who occupied Markham Main colliery, Armthorpe, on 11 December 1992 and remained underground for two days.[33] Pit camps on the model of Greenham Camp were set up outside half a dozen pits scheduled for closure. One of those was Grimethorpe colliery, where Anne Scargill and Aggie Curry set up in a four-berth caravan, along with Betty Cook. They made a failed attempt to occupy the pit and were then tipped off by two Lancashire miners' wives, Dot Kelly and Lesley Lomas, about the vulnerability of Parkside, the last working pit in Lancashire, which had stopped production and was organising visits. Anne Scargill dyed her blonde hair as a disguise and, with Elaine Evans from Grimethorpe and Dot and Lesley, joined a visitor party at Parkside at Easter 1993. Once at the bottom, they announced that they were occupying the mine.[34] Anne Scargill recalled that they kept themselves going with banter and jokes:

Next morning, we couldn't go to sleep because it were cold, it were cold. And I says to Lesley, 'Lesley, can I cuddle you? I'm not a lesbian, but can I cuddle you? I'm freezing!' Anyway, next morning, half past ten, he's coming down, manager. 'You've spoilt my holiday.' And Elaine says, 'Aye, and you've spoilt our lives, you shutting these pits.'[35]

The working miners of Nottinghamshire who had refused to join the strike in 1984 now found that, after 1992, their own pits were scheduled for closure. The Annesley–Bentinck pit was abandoned by British Coal in 1994, taken over by Midland Mining Ltd and finally closed in 2000. Trevor Taylor, a working miner and UDM branch delegate at Annesley, discovered that the private owners would not recognise the UDM. The best that could be achieved by a strike in the late 1990s was the recognition of an informal works committee. Ironically, the strike was called by Notts miners who then found themselves – much to the surprise of the management, which was counting on divide and rule – supported by their old enemies, the Yorkshire miners. Perhaps, in the final chapter, solidarity prevailed:

> In late '90s there was a problem and Annesley colliery came out on strike for the best part of a week. The manager in charge at the time was a Yorkshire manager and we'd got a lot of private contractors from the Yorkshire area. He mistakenly thought that the Yorkshire miners would never back the Notts miners because of '84. He was wrong. They backed us to the hilt. There was a group of Yorkshire miners and the manager says, 'The Yorkshire miners won't strike.' And this particular guy says, 'Come off it, gaffer, you know that if the cat walked on the wrong side of the canteen Yorkshire would strike.' They backed us.[36]

Mick Marriott was another working miner, but he always remained a union man. He continued working at Annesley under Midland Mining and reflected that 'It didn't recognise the union, but I was still a union man and I were paying my dues. I could still use the union solicitors and he knew I was a union man as well.' When the manager tried to get round a forty-eight-hour working directive by arguing that their work did not begin until they were at the coal face, he replied: 'No, you're wrong. We start work when we clock on. It takes an hour, an hour and a half, to get to the face.' From the moment they picked up their lamps and were observing mine safety, they considered themselves at work. Mick left when the pit finally closed in 2000:

And the personnel officer came to me and he said, 'I'm going to tell you something, mate.' I said, 'What's that?' He said, 'He [the manager] told me to get rid of you a couple of years ago. He said, "Get rid of him. I don't want him at this pit."'

Mick's mate Terry Stringfellow decided to take redundancy in 1994 and got a job with Wickes DIY in Sutton-in-Ashby, driving forklift trucks. There was no union recognition there either, but he still had his union reflexes. Asked by the manager after seven years in the job to work an extra fifteen minutes after closing time to prepare the shelves for the next day, he said, 'I'm fifty-nine. I said I've never worked for nothing. I said I've worked all my life but I never worked for nothing. And I said, I'm not starting now.' And he walked out.[37]

It is a truism that May 1968 did not finish in 1968, but continued into the early 1970s. '*La lutte continue*' was the slogan in France; '*Lotta Continua*' in Italy. The Miners' Strike came to a brutal end in March 1984, but it, too, had its afterlives. The strike continued in dramatic form in a multitude of plays and concerts. Heroes and heroines of the strike were invited to Europe and the United States and were lionised. The strike had drawn on the energy of other movements – from the women's movement to gay rights, from the peace movement to anti-apartheid and liberation movements; and in turn it contributed to them, losing its own distinctiveness as it did so. It became a model for other struggles against global capitalism and the Thatcher state; and when it came to the turn of the print workers at Wapping, the message was 'Enough messing around'. A final stand of the miners against closures in 1992 was, in fact, led by miners' wives using the methods of the Greenham Common women, and a brief union of striking and working miners was achieved at the turn of the millennium in pits that had been privatised.

13

RUIN

The defeat of the strike and the closure of the pits had a devastating effect on miners, miners' families and mining communities. The minority of miners who were sacked, often on trivial or trumped-up charges, found themselves blacklisted. Some never worked again, others did not find work for many years. The miners who fought so gallantly lost their skilled, well-paid and well-respected jobs. The loss of work was felt as a bereavement and related in their minds to other losses and deaths. The NUM lost its power and was often unable or unwilling to defend them. Remaining pits were privatised and did not recognise trade unions. Former miners spent long periods unemployed and languished on sofas in front of the TV, while their womenfolk often went back into education and found better-paid jobs. Threats to traditional masculinity put marriages at risk. When the men did eventually find work, they were at the mercy of the globalised economy, forced to accept low-skilled, low-paid, short-term jobs, often in competition with migrant workers.

At Askern, Pete Richardson was not only sacked and blacklisted by the Coal Board and imprisoned twice, but also felt badly treated by the union itself. In August 1987, the management decided to bring in thirty contractors to do some specialist work at the Askern pit. At a branch meeting, Pete managed to have an amendment passed that 'no contractor was to be allowed in until Pete Richardson got his job back'. This, however, was ruled out of order by the lodge officials and Pete appealed – without success – to Jack Taylor, the Yorkshire NUM president, to 'rule in my favour'.[1]

In order to assuage its guilt, the union paid Pete a small weekly stipend, but it did not last. It was terminated with a lump sum and the NUM effectively abandoned him:

> I didn't get my job back. I couldn't get dole but the union paid me some money on the side. It was enough for me, it was the average of people going back. Then Arthur [Scargill] come to see me in pit baths. He gave me this money, it was £2,000 odd, and he said, 'Look, that's it, we can't pay you no more' . . . That would have been about September time . . . He said, 'That's it, you're on your own now.'[2]

Pete Richardson did not give up hope that he might get back his job at the pit. In 1986, he drafted a letter to a number of influential people who, he hoped, might be able to help him. This expressed his pride at giving his all for the strike (only his dead heroes Joe Green and David Jones gave more), his anger at being betrayed by the union and a sense of frustration at his powerlessness:

> Dear Sir,
>
> Would someone like to help me? I am a sacked miner. I have no mucle [sic] to fight for my job. So I am relying on others to do my fighting.
>
> I gave my all for the strike and the cause, but now I feel that I am an embarrassment to the union.
>
> It is nearly two years since I worked down the mine. What is happening? Are the union just waiting for me to give up and get another job?
>
> Well it won't work. The NCB could not defeat me, and the NUM won't see me fade away. I have a right to expect my job and it is a right I wish to see fulfilled.

But what hope have I got, if the workforce is forgotten, as it seems the heroes JOE GREEN and DAVID JONES, who gave their lives for the fight [are], what chance have I got? I only lost my job. My problem is I want it back, but need help.

I am a proud man, and it took me quite a while to ask for the help I need. So to use an old pit saying, 'Someone pull their finger out.'

Yours FRUSTRATED

P.T. Richardson, sacked miner,

Ex Askern Colliery,

Askern, Doncaster, South Yorkshire.[3]

In answer to his call, he secured a reference from a local JP and Askern councillor, who praised his skills as a worker and his contribution to the community, while deploring the combativeness for which he had paid so dearly:

When Peter was at work his workmates all had a good word for him in regard for his competence as a workman. Unfortunately, however, Peter was very easily led and had to be at the forefront in a dispute, or for raising money for sport or charities. He has a very good record of working for the community in Askern. I am well aware of Peter's involvement in the strike, but as the years and months go by reasonable-minded people are beginning to wonder whether people such as Peter and Harry [Werrett] have to serve a life sentence for being one of the many at the pit gates during the strike. I feel that both these men and their families have suffered enough and a lot of miners in Askern must look at them and say, it could have been me.[4]

Pete applied for other jobs, but his record meant that he had no luck. ICI was recruiting and

they gave me a form to fill out and I'm filling this form out, telling them about my welding and this, that and the other. And then why

I had left the pit, that I was sacked for a year. Seeing that they just ripped it up and put it in the bin. So I didn't apply for no jobs. I took an allotment out and carried on from there.[5]

In 1988, he sent off for the prospectus of the Open College, which promised that 'Whatever your age, or education or occupation you can join the Open College and learn a new skill.'[6] Nothing seems to have come of this. Then ill health took over:

> I was already on sickness with bad legs, because I've got really bad legs. I was seeing a specialist at Doncaster, they sent me to Sheffield. I wasn't getting sickness pay, I was getting dole. I haven't worked since the strike.[7]

Forty miles away, at Manton colliery, the lodge secretary David Potts had been arrested with his older brother, John, after threatening strike-breaking leader Bob Taylor, sent to Lincoln prison, sacked and blacklisted. He was refused work repeatedly for ten years, whether by Sheffield Council, the English aristocracy or South African mines, until one person who trusted him gave him a helping hand:

> Our John retired. Ill health, he died of the lung disease. I tried various ways to get jobs but Thatcher wouldn't let me work. Blacklisted, it was blatant. I went to North Notts College and trained as a joiner, carpentry and joinery . . . Welbeck Abbey wanted a joiner to do the maintenance on the buildings. I went along, talked with the site foreman, who loved me because I was married and stable. 'Tell you what, there's a house goes with the job. Here's the key, take your missus and show her around.' But the land at Welbeck Abbey . . . belonged to Lady Anne Bentinck, the queen's cousin. This letter came from Lady Anne Bentinck, 'Sorry we don't want you.' Then I applied for another job, industrial relations officer at Sheffield City Council. It was coming

up to Christmas. I got a letter saying, 'You're on the shortlist of six, we're carrying out the interviews after Christmas, we'll be in touch.' Christmas came, Christmas went, January, nowt. What's going on? 'Oh sorry, Mr Potts, the job's been taken.' This was a Labour council. Mining officer in South Africa. They sent me an application form a month later, after the deadline date. Crazy. Couldn't get anywhere . . . Eight years. I tried setting up as self-employed but I hated it. Charging people, I wasn't very good at it. Tried it for a couple of years. I applied at North Notts College for student support. Unbeknownst to me there was a woman at the college, a fantastic woman. She knew me, knew about me as well. And she persuaded the principal to give me an interview. I hadn't had an interview for eight years. She stuck her neck out and they gave me a job and I worked there for fifteen years.

In 2010, moreover, David Potts's political commitment paid off and he was elected a local councillor. He won Worksop North for Labour and held it until 2019, declaring, 'I've always supported the underdog . . . I felt it was up to me and people like me to pick up the baton for them.'[8]

In Leicestershire, some members of the Dirty Thirty found themselves blacklisted and unable to find legitimate work. Bob Girvan, the elder of the Scottish Girvan brothers, was forced into the black economy. His strategy was to approach workers in local clothing factories who felt that they were underpaid and to pay in cash for designer products that he then sold in markets:

I found I couldn't get a job, that's when I started ducking and diving if you like. Which I enjoyed, really, because I found that I'm going to a factory, knock the door, nobody had done that before, it was all wholesalers. 'Hello, mate.' And as soon as you showed them that cash because you'd still got some of the old English factories, you've got a lot of Asians, and I even found some of the old Jewish community. And some of them, when they got to know you, they say, 'Go and help yourself.'

They trusted me. So, because they trusted in me, I wouldn't do them. I'd buy knitwear because that was what was in Leicestershire. So, I'm going buy it, and then sell it in the market. I cut out the middleman.[9]

Mick 'Richo' Richmond, the 'heart and flowers' of the Dirty Thirty, also found himself blacklisted. In addition, his marriage to his second wife, Linda Burton, broke up under the pressure of his debts and absences. Writing in 1986 to American woman miner Kipp Dawson, he described the toll that the strike had taken:

The aftereffects of the Strike have been a hell of a lot harder than I ever imagined. Creditors have tried to take my house and my Building Society have tried also. They all want the arrears that built up in '86. But we are holding them at bay. I have been summoned to court 3 times and each time the judge has accepted my offer to pay. So like I said, we are holding off the vultures and gradually we will get through . . . Unfortunately, Kipp, my life has for the last few months not included 'Socialist Action'. Linda, my wife, unfortunately gave me an ultimatum, either I ease up on 'outside' activities or we would separate. Obviously Kipp, there was no choice and my meetings etc. were virtually halted. I fully understand Linda's viewpoint. She was fantastic during the strike and very, very strong and supportive – but after the strike she wanted to revert back to near normality, something I found very difficult to do.[10]

After the pit closed, he was offered a job building the Channel Tunnel, for which, as a miner, he was amply qualified. But his past militancy caught up with him, and after he returned from Folkestone he received a letter saying that the offer had been withdrawn. He drew on the legal connections he had made during the strike and found that he had been 'blacklisted as a left-wing communist activist'. He eventually found a job in a cardboard factory, but said, 'I hated it. Full of scabs.'[11]

Meanwhile, Linda, the steelworker's daughter from Ravenscraig, barmaid and factory worker, had become a different woman through the strike:

> I think if I hadn't met the women on strike to give me the self-confidence that I am a person in my own right, I think Mick and I would have still been together, because if Mick said 'Jump', I would have jumped. I'd do anything for him. And I was always led to believe when you marry somebody, you marry them for life; no matter what. My dad used to say, 'You made your bed, you lie on it.' And so I met all these people that 'Oh Linda, you've got your own opinion, you have your own voice; don't take no shit off anybody. Stand up for yourself.'

Now the 'ultimatum' she imposed on his 'outside' activities was activated. 'He went out with other women, one, two, three. The third one I couldn't do it no more.' She and their two children left. Mick met a local widow, Marisa Cortes, at a harvest festival auction at The Black Horse, Whitwick, in 1994 and it was she who nursed him through his declining health, including a quadruple heart bypass in 2012. Linda remained in touch with him because of the children. As she confessed, 'Still love him, bit of my past but hate the way he is at the minute, because that's not the Richo that I know. Not Jack the lad. Definitely not the Richo I know. God love him.'[12]

In Fife, the impact of the strike was severe, and there were several painful cases of blacklisted miners who found it very difficult to get work. 'Red Ronnie' Campbell, chair of the Lochore strike committee, a miner from the age of sixteen and aged forty when he was sacked for picketing offences, recalled:

> I went for two or three interviews, and the minute they said to me, 'What was your last job?' 'Miner.' 'Why did you leave?' and I said, 'Dismissed during the strike.' And when I said that I knew, by the reaction, that I wasn't going to get a job, and I never got a job.

'I think what made it harder for you, too, Dad, mining was all you knew,' chipped in his elder daughter, Anna. Powerfully, his daughters rallied round. Twelve years after he was sacked, Anna, who worked in Asda, persuaded her boss to give him a job there as an in-store cleaner, which he did for ten years until he retired.[13]

Doddy McShane, forty-two when he was sacked, resorted to picking potatoes. He found a job briefly at Bilston Glen before it closed in 1988, and then at the private mine of Kellingley in North Yorkshire; but he became homesick working away from his family and gave it up after a year or two. He died just short of his sixty-sixth birthday in 2008, much missed by his family and a hero to the community. His son James said that his funeral was 'mobbed, absolutely mobbed. It's one of the biggest funerals I've ever seen.'[14]

Sean Lee endured blacklisting, addiction and meaningless jobs before he found fulfilment caring for people as badly (or worse) off as himself:

> I was blacklisted, see. I couldn't get a job for a while, so I had to work on the black. I worked in the fields which I loved after being thirteen years underground. To be able to sit and to be able to work in the sunshine was like heaven to me. It was black labour. We were on the dole, but we were working out in the fields to supplement our income.

He confessed that he descended into an 'abyss' of drink and drugs, before recovering and finding a job on the North Sea oil rigs: 'The money was fantastic, but I absolutely hated it.' And he gave it up after a year. He worked on building sites for a bit, but that did not work out either. Then he turned to helping the homeless in Dunfermline. 'I was working with guys with drink, drug problems, and I was there for ten years, and I loved it.' After that he worked with people with dementia in a care home near Kirkcaldy.[15]

Loss of work was often felt as a bereavement, and was linked in the accounts of former miners or their wives with ill health or the deaths of loved ones around the same time or later. Jean Crane and Dianne Hogg, who had organised the Women's Support Group at Askern, lost their miner husbands after the strike and had to pull out all the stops to keep their families together. Jean Crane lost her husband Phil two years after the pit closed:

> It was six o'clock, and he nudged me, and he said he just said, 'Jean, my head, something's gone wrong.' And he died. Just like that. Forty-three years old. And he had four grown-up daughters, he had five grandchildren.

After the funeral, she said, 'I was in this great big black hole.' She worked for Tunstall Telecom until she was sixty, sold her house and felt 'like the girls looked after me as well', as she lived with each of them in turn.[16]

Dianne Hogg's Pete survived longer, dying in 2015, after nearly fifty years of marriage. They had four daughters, twelve grandchildren and fourteen great-grandchildren. Dianne was a powerful matriarch, who made sure that the family was never in debt, paying all the bills on time. But there was also a shadow of violence overhanging it. Her second daughter, Susan, a hairdresser, left her builder husband and moved to Spain, only to be threatened by him with a gun when she returned for her father's funeral:

> She'd taped all his messages and he said, 'I'm gonna kill you; and I'm gonna kill your effin mother.' And I've never done a thing to him. And after he said to police, 'I don't know why I said that about Dianne.' He went to prison for twelve months. And she got a divorce just like that . . . Pete would have killed him if he'd been alive.[17]

Andy Varley, a Manton miner, was only thirty-nine when the pit closed in 1994. He had genuinely enjoyed minework and was one of the 137 Manton miners who stayed out on strike to the end. The sadness of leaving the pit was tinged with the sadness of losing his father, a veteran of the pit, who died of miners' diseases a few months later. Appealing to his wife Sue as a witness, he confessed:

> I've got tears in my eyes, I've never been the same since the pit shut. She'll tell you. The pit shut in February and my dad died in the June . . . My dad lived t' pit, he were all pit . . . He died then and I've got pit shutting. He died of dust and lung cancer. He had about six strokes in twenty-four hours, he couldn't breathe. It was hard. That was a big chunk. I was taken to Ireland fishing in the September. I've been fishing once since. I can't go. The pit shutting was a big thing to me. It's hard. I'd done about eighteen years. I loved working hard and being paid well. I lived and breathed it.

After that Andy was reduced to ill-paid, unskilled, insecure work for the council, and was the victim of an industrial accident. Subsequently he found work as a school cleaning supervisor, which enabled him to recover some of his dignity:

> I got a job straightaway, I went grass cutting for the council . . . Because it come to nearly two years, they had to lay me off . . . Then I took my HGV and went onto dustbins, private dustbin wagons. Then I had a car crash, somebody ran into the back of me. It did bugger me up. I had a long time off work. Then Josie [Potts] said, 'They want a cleaning supervisor up at the schools.' I went up in a suit and tie. I got that job. I got a lot of respect out of them lasses. Just before I finished they put out a pro forma, asking what have you learned in the last year. And you know what they put? Teamwork. Led from front.[18]

Ray Maslin, another Manton miner, was fifty-two when he retired from the colliery, after thirty-six years, having gone down at the age of sixteen. He related his loss to the death ten years later of his wife of forty-two years:

I finished in '89. They made me redundant. I got a payout, £34,000 I think. Banked it. It didn't last long. Our Josie died in '99. She were fifty-eight. We'd been away, we'd come back from Kefalonia, no, Cyprus. She was complaining about her leg, 'I've got this pain in my leg.' That was on the Thursday. We used to go down the club on a Tuesday. She was sat there, and said to her – because I used to go down at about seven o'clock and our Josie used to come down about eight o'clock – 'I'll see you down there, duck.' And when I got down one of my old mates said, 'Ray, you'd better get off home, mate. Your Josie's not feeling very well.' One of the lads nipped me home in the car. And when I got home she was sat where you are, and she were dead. She'd died. She had this blood clot. What do they call it? Pulmonary embolism. She were a good lass.

A year after his wife's death, Ray returned to the loss of the pit and of friendships and familiarity. He wrote an elegiac poem which was inscribed on a monument at the entrance to Pit Lane that incorporated the colliery's pithead winding wheel. Two of its four verses ran:

No lamphouse room, no pithead baths
No sound of boots, no belly laughs
No winding house, no winding gear
No creaking roof, no morbid fear

No pit canteen, no working hard
No offices, no timber yard
Just piles of bricks and grass and trees
There's nothing left 'cept memories

At nearby Hatfield colliery, Dave Douglass suffered a double blow. First, his artist wife, Maureen, left him in 1987 to pursue her acting career, and in 1990 married actor/director Vivian Munn. Dave looked after their daughter Emma, now a teenager, and even took a part-time job in a nursery. Second, although he remained NUM secretary at Hatfield, the colliery was privatised and bought out by the management in 1994. They 'made the conditions on who they would have coming back. So I was in exile then. On top of the Pit Lane.' He took the opportunity to do a master's in industrial relations and law at Keele that year and hoped to be made a fellow of Ruskin College, to write a book with Raphael Samuel on 'the last days of coal'. Unfortunately, Raphael died in 1996, putting paid to dreams of an academic break. In 2001, the management buy-out failed and the colliery was bought out by the entrepreneur Richard Budge, who was no more willing to accept the union at the pit and brought in miners from Nottinghamshire and Poland to scupper any militancy:

> He wouldn't recognise unions . . . and also, fifty per cent of the men he recruited at the pit came from Nottingham. Took me twelvemonth to get a successful union ballot at the pit. Now, these guys from Nottingham voted in favour of having a union. They didn't join themselves but voted that other people could join, which was something. He was also bringing in – we had a whole heading just of Polish miners recruited from Poland, not from Doncaster. So the overman, the deputies were all Poles and the intention was to try and break me, not have the union at the pit. So then they went bust. And then it looked like it was gone for good. That was when I left. But then after I left, it got bought by somebody else. And it stayed. It was the second last pit in Britain to close.

Douglass finally left Hatfield in 2006 and got a job with the Transport and General Workers' Union, seeking to unionise overworked, underpaid labour – mainly female and often foreign – in food factories in Yorkshire and the North East. He found that he was fighting a losing battle with the globalised giants and the reluctance of the workforce to embrace unionism:

I remember I tried to organise a bloody poultry, chicken factory in Thorne, which was my neck of the woods and absolutely de-human work. The best paid were the women in the kill centre, called it the kill centre. And they used to come out splattered in blood, covered in blood, killing these chickens. And I couldn't get them in the union. And in the end, I wrote a parody on Johnny Cash's 'San Quentin' called 'Thorne Poultry', 'I hate every inch of you, I see you from the chicken's point of view.' The only people who had any fight was the bloody chickens.[19]

Other miners from Yorkshire and Nottinghamshire also continued to work in the pits that were privatised, having to deal with the absence of trade union recognition and protection. Steve Walker, a miner at Woolley colliery, was only twenty-two when it closed in 1987. He transferred to Kellingley, which was under the Coal Board until 1994, but had to suffer the presence of 'a lot of scabs' and the alleged brutality of a manager. 'Fucking hell,' he exploded. 'There were two thousand men there, and inside twelve months, he'd got that figure down to nearly seven hundred. They couldn't wait to fucking go. They were fucking queuing up to take their redundancy.' At that point the pit was taken over by Richard Budge, under whose ownership there were a fair few casualties. One of those was Ian Cameron, who was killed in 2009 by faulty machinery:

They were fetching a face back with old equipment they'd kitted it out, with substandard fucking, substandard stuff, and it failed, basically. It fucking failed. Chock failed, the rope support failed, hydraulics on it failed, and it come down and fucking crushed him. Killed him. Simply because they bought cheap fucking tackle . . . Why spend a thousand pound on a valve, when we can get one from fuckin China for two hundred quid. It'll do, it'll be right. It won't, were it? Fucking killed him.[20]

Other redundant miners were also attracted to Kellingley as one of the last working pits. Ken Bonsall, a young Welbeck miner, married Karen, who had been secretary of the Warsop Main Women's Action Group and left her husband, a miner at Warsop Main who had gone back to work during the strike. At Welbeck, Ken was victimised by the management, but he refused to leave the NUM and join the UDM. He was unable to get a transfer to Thoresby, and was eventually told to 'Fuck off up north, you communist bugger'. When he went to Kellingley, it was assumed that, as a Nottinghamshire miner, he was a strike-breaker, until he persuaded them that he had been 'solid'. Ken expressed a great deal of the passion and anger he felt about the Miners' Strike and other injustices through a band he founded around 1988, inspired by the Pogues and Billy Bragg. Lee, his son with Karen, gave it the name Ferocious Dog, and Dan, Karen's son by her previous marriage, played the violin in the band.[21]

The working miners of Annesley colliery continued for a little longer than most in Nottinghamshire, in the pit that was now privately owned and did not even recognise the UDM. But even this pit closed in 2000, leaving them, too, now in their fifties, with the prospect of insecure, low-status, less well-paid jobs.

Trevor Taylor, the UDM secretary at Annesley, also continued until 2000 and then found a job as a part-time handyman on a BP forecourt down the road from where he lived, 'cleaning the pumps, helping when a petrol tanker come'.[22] Terry Stringfellow, as we saw, took redundancy in 1994 and found a job working on fork-lift trucks for Wickes DIY store. Mick Marriott stayed until 2000 and then went to work on railway track maintenance, doing nights and weekends, and was proud to say that the employer favoured ex-miners, because they did not waste time or make excuses: 'they're tooled up and they get straight on with the job'. Movingly, Terry and Mick confided that, although they had not gone on strike in 1984 because they had not been offered a ballot, they felt some guilt about their choice:

Terry: I must say, at the time and I've said it ever since, I did feel guilty at
         the time about going to work.

Mick: Oh, yes.

Terry: But it was the principle of the thing, not being given the chance to
         vote whether you want to work or not that made my mind up.
         Because I'd been told I got to go on strike without a ballot, that didn't
         sit with me.[23]

Steve Williamson, who had been secretary of the NUM at Annesley,
became secretary of the UDM. But the victory he won after a year fighting
the strike lasted no more than two years. He was driven out by the
continuing civil war in the pits and by the loss of his friends. He paid a
heavy price, as leaving the industry coincided with the breakup of his
second marriage:

Steve: I left in '87, August '87. We'd had a series of strikes. I'd lost interest
         in the union because every day was a battle. There was backbiting,
         bitterness, and when suddenly all your best friends have become
         your worst enemies, it's not nice. And I was going through romantic
         entanglement. I met my wife through drinking where Roy Lynk
         went, she worked behind the bar. There was an instant attraction. It
         took me several months to get a date because she was untouchable.
         But I worked on her, I tried.

Q: What about your wife back home, had you broken up with her?

Steve: I was playing the field, to be honest with you. I admit I was a poor
         husband, a poor father, I never had time for them.

With his third wife, Tracey, he left the pit and the local area and went into
the pub business. They were constantly on the move, as if pursued, buying,
running and selling pubs in Derby, Melton Mowbray and Wymeswold, near
Loughborough. When his dear sister, Pat, died, he decided to retire to
Derbyshire. Tortured by his past, he told people there that he had left the

mining industry before the strike. On occasion, too, the trauma of the strike and its bitterness returned to haunt him and tipped him into paranoia:

> When I was sixty I had an acute stroke, I had a two-inch blood clot. I was lucky to survive it . . . I've lost all my confidence. I'm doing all to speak to you, I went through patch of depression where I wouldn't speak to anybody . . . Then I went to see a psychiatrist who said I was not crazy, and then this lady come to see me for five months, and she regressed me back, and built all the confidence back in me. She was a wonderful lady . . . And I used to play golf every day of the week when I retired. And after my stroke, I couldn't play it. I couldn't go back, I couldn't face the people. I couldn't go shop – I went shopping, I used to run out. I went to this fish shop one night because I said, 'Oh, I'm going to have some fish and chips.' I ran home. I didn't go to a fish and chip shop. And I didn't know what was happening to me.[24]

Even if they were not blacklisted and found work outside the mining industry, former miners were reduced to lower-skilled, lower-status and low-paid jobs. The work was irregular and they had run-ins with job centres and benefit offices, which did nothing for the miners' sense of pride.

In Leicestershire, things were perhaps easier for Cliff Jeffery, who reached the age of fifty in 1985 and decided to take redundancy. 'I thought, well Cliffy, you've had some rough times down the bloody pit, you've had some narrow escapes, now's the time to bloody go.' He bought a bungalow on Anglesey, nearly two hundred miles away, and with his wife Barbara enjoyed 'a full view of the mountains. It were beautiful.' He had previously visited the island with a mate to fish, and now made a scant living catching and selling mackerel and bait, and enjoyed the freedom afforded by his camper van.[25]

Cliff's son Nigel also took redundancy at the end of the strike, aged only twenty-three, 'a kid really'. He took advantage of a retraining scheme offered by the Coal Board to become an HGV driver, working first for

Christian Salvesen – though he was never asked to do runs to Italy or Spain, just shunting vehicles in the yard. He moved to DPD, which opened a huge parcel delivery hub at Hinckley, but soon discovered that it did not recognise the union and eroded workers' rights. Wendy left her insurance firm to have two children and did not want to go back. She did a Higher National Certificate (HNC) at Stephenson College, Coalville, so that she could manage Nigel's business if he set up on his own, but he never did. She found some reward in running the playgroup attended by her children, and then in working with children with special educational needs. But eventually she found it all too physical and got a job through Barbara Jeffery's youngest son and his wife:

> I think I was getting a little bit too old for being spat at, my ribs broken, bitten, you know what I mean. I came out of it. And now, I do a nice gentle job of cleaning at my sister-in-law's firm, a valve company in Coalville.[26]

The haulage industry, which was central to the economy of the East Midlands, provided jobs for a number of ex-miners. Malcolm Pinnegar, leader of the Dirty Thirty, stayed at Bagworth until it closed in 1991, then moved briefly to Coventry pit, which closed very soon afterwards. He found a job with Leicester City Football Club when they ran their own lottery, but left on account of some ethical reservations. He was thrown back on driving 7.5-tonne trucks, 'working for this lad up the road', until he had a heart attack aged sixty-two in 2006, the year his wife Margaret retired from the hosiery business. Clouding their retirement plans. Malcolm's health was not good, and he succumbed to cancer in 2012. Colleen, his older daughter and a trained nurse, wrote a poem for his funeral that recalled his principles: 'If you see somebody that's in trouble, always help. If you see a hole, don't just walk round it, fill it.'

In South Wales, the pits closed soon after the defeat of the strike. Treforgan in the Dulais Valley and St John's in the Llynfi Valley closed at the end of 1985; Abernant colliery in the Swansea Valley closed in 1988; and it was followed by Blaenant in 1990. Some former miners managed to reinvent themselves and got decent jobs, but many did not.

Phil Bowen, the Blaenant lodge chair, was offered a job at Tower colliery, but turned it down: possibly because, as a moderate, he did not like its politics, but possibly because he had had enough of mining. He claims that his new direction was a matter of chance:

> A phone call came through, one of the boys who was a spark [electrician] had gone to British Steel working with a contractor and was looking for sparks to go in with this contractor to get this job underway.

Phil finished the job for the contractor and was subsequently offered a permanent contract with British Steel at Port Talbot, where he worked for twenty years.

Meanwhile, Martin James worked nights at Abernant colliery until its closure coincided with Siân getting her degree. He might then have taken a job at Tower, but, he said, 'no chance. No way . . . The last face I worked at it was a horrible bloody place. It was soaking wet. The conditions were terrible.' He stayed at home for six months as a house husband, then took a demolition job, but discovered that he couldn't stand heights. He then moved back to the Tick Tock factory, where he had worked before he became a miner, although it had been taken over and transformed by Lucas. What he really enjoyed doing was looking after the sheep on the family farm.[27]

Martin's schoolfriend and former Blaenant miner David Williams became an itinerant worker, hired by international companies, paid less than existing workers and repeatedly made redundant, before he found work with the local council:

> I went to work for an insurance company, I went to work for a double-glazing company, then I went to work with Sony Bridgend. I stayed there for about eight or nine years . . . Making the fronts of televisions

. . . I went to work then for a company called Visteon, in the old Ford factory on Fabian Way. And they went into a form of liquidation, and sold out to a company called Linamar . . . We were making axles for the E-Type Jaguar and the Baby Jaguar and, of course, the old Ford work with discs and drums, that was still going. So in fact you had two sets of workers on different pay: you had the old Ford workers, who were still employed by Ford on a rate of pay, and you had the likes of me who were on a different rate of pay. Less . . . They made me redundant. Well, the whole factory closed . . . Went to work for the local authority, as a recycling, refuse operator. On the bins.[28]

Philip James, who was made redundant from both Treforgan and Blaenant when they closed, was another itinerant worker who flitted not only from job to job, but from contract to contract almost daily. His wife Marilyn confirmed that it was no fun at all:

Philip: I went contracting in the collieries then with different contracting firms . . . Fitting. Underground fitting. I done that for a couple of years. I went to the steelworks. I haven't had regular employment – have I? – since 1990. The longest I've been in one place was four years . . . I've been in the steelworks, oil refineries, and paper mills. I worked in BorgWarner transmission factory in, was it Margam?

Marilyn: You were miserable when you worked there. He was miserable.

Philip: The thing is honestly I can't tell you how many jobs I've had because what you're looking at when I was out of work I phoned around. Perhaps on the Tuesday I'd be working up in Abervale. Wednesday I'd be down in Port Talbot. Thursday in Trostre. Right. I'd have three different employers in three different places. I just worked a day here and there, but we survived, didn't we?

After he took his pension, which was not enough to live on, Philip felt discriminated against when it came to being advised about what benefits he could claim. As a proud Welshman, he felt that he was being less well treated than those who had recently come to the country:

> My miner's pension had kicked in. So you're talking, that was about £100 or something. It wasn't a huge amount of money. You couldn't live on £100 a week can you or £120 whatever it was. So I goes down to sign on. The young girl tells me, 'Look if you're having this you're not entitled to Jobseeker's Allowance.' She said, 'Oh perhaps you'd be enti-tled to Pension Credit.' Well it's not that I'm racist but what I can see of it, to be honest with you, I think I'm wrong religion, wrong-coloured skin. If you've just come into the country they'll tell you everything you can claim for and they give you advice. You go down and you've worked all your life they won't tell you nothing. You've got to find out. So I see that system very unfair. They should treat everyone the same.

A miner – and the son of a miner – who earned good money in the mines and talked of the high-quality anthracite they brought to the surface as 'clinking like china', he was angry that a young woman would offer him low-paid, degrading jobs that undermined what was left of his sense of masculinity. 'A job centre is just a humiliating place to go and they're good for nothing,' he complained. 'They've got jobs there which don't exist, they're unliveable wages.' He went on:

> She asked me, 'What kind of a job are you looking for?' I said, 'I don't mind a shit job with tidy money but not a tidy job with shit money. I've got to live. I'm not working to come cap in hand anywhere' . . . I goes over there, chap said, 'I've got a job as a toilet cleaner.' They're hopeless. I told 'em, 'Until I get desperate you carry on looking for work that I want, not that sort of work.' They're absolutely hopeless.[29]

In County Durham, as elsewhere, former miners found it difficult to find stable, well-paid jobs when their pits closed. The choice was often between jobs with multinational companies that bought and sold factories with great rapidity, or working for the council. After Vane Tempest closed in 1993, Bill Frostwick retrained for the North Sea oil rigs, but then worked for ten years in a television factory and another ten as a warehouse manager. His wife Elspeth worked in a jewellery shop before becoming a receptionist at Grey College in Durham University, looking after a generation of students that were perhaps more amenable than those who had failed to support the strike.[30]

Kenny McKitten was only thirty-one when Murton colliery closed in 1991. He found work with a water treatment plant and plastic bottle factory, neither of which he enjoyed. As Allyson said to him,

> it took a lot of settling, didn't it, after being at the pit from leaving school and then having to go out in the big wide world, when you had your own community down the pit. That was hard for you, wasn't it?

Then Kenny found better jobs, first with the council, maintaining the street lighting, and then with the National Grid. Meanwhile, Allyson specialised in housing services, first with a private firm, then doing an HNC and becoming a housing officer for the council, then returning to work for a housing association, Riverside.[31]

Paul Stratford found himself unemployed when Easington colliery closed in 1993. He found part-time work for the probation service, doing community service work in public gardens with young offenders. He also became closely involved with the Woodcraft Folk, not least for his son Peter. In 2000, however, he had a nervous breakdown, which he traced back to an incident before the strike, when he had been trapped in a cage on the way to the pit bottom. 'To cut a long story short,' he confided, 'I've been on venlafaxine ever since.'[32]

In Fife, pit closures closely followed the end of the strike. Bogside and Comrie closed in 1986; Frances and Seafield in 1988; the Cowdenbeath

Workshops in 1989; Solsgirth and Castlehill in 1990; and Castlebridge in 1999. Mining activity then centred on Longannet – until major flooding closed it in 2002.

Rosco Ross, who had been at Cowdenbeath Workshops and on its strike committee, left in 1986, three years before they closed. Thereafter, he was constantly on the move looking for work. He moved from Bell's Whisky at Dunfermline to Sellafield in Cumbria; from North Sea oil rigs to Costain Mining in Jordan (where his main memory was of seeing Harrison Ford make *Indiana Jones*); and then full circle to the Rosyth shipyard, where he had started work in the 1970s.[33]

Andrew 'Watty' Watson, sacked at the age of nineteen for holding two fingers up at a strike-breakers' minibus, threw himself into fundraising for sacked miners and was amazed by the generosity of miners back at work and of mining communities:

> We set up stalls at our highland games. The donations were coming in thick and fast. Donations from the local Miners' Institute, collections from all the pitheads. Seafield and Frances were our main source of income for Dysart strike centre. Fishcross [strike centre for West Fife], the Longannet complex, Castlehill, Comrie, Solsgirth. It turned out a wee bit embarrassing because I felt I was coming out with more than a miner that was back in his work. That was the level of support. I got my driving test out of that money. I said, this is an embarrassment.

Just before Christmas 1985, good luck shone on Watty. He was given his job at Comrie back and went to work in the Longannet complex. In 2002, he found himself unemployed for the second time in fifteen years. He paid tribute to his wife Maureen, a miner's daughter, who had been an 'absolute rock. She's taken me on when I never had a job and then when we finished our family, I lost my job again.' Watty made a slow but steady comeback, securing a job as a part-time ticket inspector at Kirkcaldy, then as a train guard, and finally qualifying as a train driver for Scotrail.[34]

The defeat of the strike and the closure of the pits had a massive impact on the employment status of former miners – working miners, in the end, as well as strikers. Some were blacklisted and took years to find another job. Pete Richardson never did. Redundancy came as a relief for some; but for most it was felt as a massive loss. Many former miners moved from industry to industry and from job to job with no stability. They were regularly condemned to doing ill-paid, largely unskilled jobs as caretakers, cleaners, refuse collectors, delivery men, taxi drivers, warehouse or call centre staff, or petrol pump attendants. But even these miners and their wives found the resources and inspiration to give something back to their blighted former mining communities, which never completely died.

14

REDEMPTION

When I met Hywel Francis at the South Wales Miners' Library in March 2018, he warned me against an unduly downbeat verdict on the outcome of the Miners' Strike. To my initial thoughts about job losses, pit closures and the hollowing out of mining communities, he suggested that there might be more positive stories. Eighteen months later, when I returned to interview him for the project, he invited me to Banwen, the home of the Dulais Opportunities for Voluntary Enterprise (DOVE) workshop. He made a case for the specificity of the strike in Wales, the broad-based relationships that had sustained it and the new initiatives that had come out of it:

> It didn't feel like a defeat because there wasn't a defeat here. People had not been defeated. They'd held the strike together and they'd been sustained together and they'd learned so much and made new friendships and new alliances. It was very special to them, and it changed people's lives for ever.[1]

It is true that, after the strike and the pit closures, unemployment and low-paid, insecure jobs were rampant. Families were put under pressure and marriages broke up. Communities had the guts wrenched out of them, as shops and services closed; many people fell prey to alcoholism and drug addiction. On the other hand, many who had been involved in the strike went back into education and forged new careers, often in community-oriented professions such as social work, the probation service, legal advice and the care sector. Miners' wives, in particular, were transformed by the strike, took advantage of educational opportunities and began new careers. Enormous effort and imagination went into initiatives to save communities from decline and to regenerate them, whether professionally, through election as local councillors and even as MPs, or simply as loyal members of those communities.

The DOVE workshop, which opened in former NCB offices in Banwen in 1987, was the brainchild of Hywel Francis's wife Mair.[2] Mair was elected secretary of the Neath and District Adult Training and Education Committee, and as such coordinated the training at DOVE with further training at the Workers' Educational Association (WEA), Neath College and the adult education department of Swansea University, where Hywel taught. As attendance increased from 30 in 1986 to 120 in 1988 and 200 in 1995, new staff were taken on, paid for by the Manpower Services Commission. One of these was Julie Bibby, who began doing the payroll and driving students in the minibus, and finished as a course tutor. Money was also sourced from the European Social Fund, which was investing in 'Women in the Workplace' in former industrialised areas. This led to visits to Europe by Mair and her team – first to Sardinia, then to Belgium and Spain. Meanwhile Mair herself completed a master's thesis at Swansea on 'Women and the Aftermath of the 1984–5 Miners' Strike: a South Wales analysis'. She then became development officer of the South West Wales Open College and Access Consortium and, with Hywel, launched the Community University of the Valleys in 1993.[3]

One of the most dramatic regeneration initiatives in South Wales took place ten miles east of Banwen, at Tower colliery in Hirwaun. Phil White had been sacked from St John's, Maesteg, in February 1985 for intimidating a strike-breaker, but got his job back two weeks after the strike ended. When St John's closed in December 1985, he moved to Abernant colliery, until that too closed, and then went to Tower colliery. He became lodge chairman, alongside lodge secretary Tyrone O'Sullivan, and when Tower was itself threatened with closure in 1992, he headed up a miners' buy out of the pit which, with his Irish roots, he saw as a gesture of radical resistance:

> Anyway, what happened by the time that I got to Tower, was that so many other pits had closed in the area, and those that wanted to transfer – always remember this – were those loyal boys, those boys who remained in the industry, those boys who played their part in the strike. So what they did in the end was something like what happened back in the 1916 Easter Uprising. They all sent them over to this pit, which just became this big embroiling pit of everybody – best in the industry, from anyone's perspective. A lot of the best of the industry: good, loyal NUM members; really proud. Best of the best.[4]

A Tower Employee Buy Out (TEBO) team was set up with Phil White as secretary and Tyrone O'Sullivan as chair. Over 170 miners put in £8,000 of their redundancy money and sought private finance high and low as O'Sullivan spun a 'David and Goliath' story, garnering messages of support from Princess Diana, Pope John Paul II and Nelson Mandela.[5] Rather than fight the Tory government, said White, they played along with their popular capitalism discourse, and were told by government officials and Coal Board officials of the success of their bid at Rothschild bank. 'You can smell wealth,' said Phil White:

> There was this oak, the fittings that they had around them. On the one hand, disgusting, but on the other hand, Oh my God. An 'OMG' moment, sitting there, thinking, 'Who the hell in their lifetime is going to be sitting in the boardroom of Rothschild's?'[6]

The miners, hailed as 'working-class heroes' by the *Sunday Times*, marched back to work at New Year 1995.[7] The only problem was that some pigs were more equal than others. Ann Jones said of her husband Dai John: 'The day it opened John was the only TEBO member that went back in orange overalls. They all went suited and booted, but he doesn't toe the line, you see.' Dai John was one of the directors, but complained that 'they were all in offices. Well of course those poor buggers were down the mine, weren't they? I was still doing the same job.' The good news was that Tower lasted for another ten years.[8]

Ann Jones, veteran of the South Wales Women's Support Groups, was singled out for praise by Tyrone O'Sullivan. He recalled that 'the Cynon Valley women were a particularly strong force at this time and many became accustomed to public speaking. Among them was Ann Jones of Hirwaun.'[9] Ann regretted that 'when the strike ended I didn't go on to do anything. I wish I had.' She was also a 'Welsh Mam', who prioritised the education and careers of her children:

> The thing now when you think 'Oh how stupid it was' but my daughter wanted to go back to work for three months and she was doing an Open University course as well. And the three months turned into thirteen years.

She was ambivalent about that decision. 'Not that I regret that, but yes there are times I really do regret it.'[10] Her main consideration, though, was that 'I was so strong on my children having a good education and I've been lucky because they all have. My grandchildren have all got degrees. Only one hasn't been at university yet.'[11]

By contrast, Siân James, Ann's friend and ally in the South Wales Women's Support Groups, seized the opportunity for education for herself. She was nine years younger than Ann, only twenty-five when the strike ended, but realised how much leaving education at sixteen had limited her opportunities in terms of income, but also influence:

The bitterness at the end of the strike, really, was about the strike not ending in the way that I wanted or needed it to end. The realisation that all those things that I talked about, like gaining power, growing as a person, could quite easily disappear again, could just as easily be subsumed, you know, melt away . . . And realising that people who'd spent all of their time telling us what to think, do, act, and orchestrated everything around the strike, there was a difference between me and them, and the difference between me and them was that I'd left school at sixteen and hadn't progressed beyond O-levels. So what's that telling us? It's telling us that further education is good – it gives you a set of skills that can be used across a range of different things in your life. But Roy summed it up really, one of our gay friends, he said, 'What does a degree do for you?' 'I don't know, Roy,' I said, 'what does a degree do for you?' He said, 'You work shorter hours for more money.'

Siân went to the University of Swansea in 1986 to study Welsh language and history. She did not want to become a teacher of Welsh, despite the growing demand, but took a job as Welsh field officer with the National Federation of Young Farmers' Clubs. 'I'm the only person in Wales who can say that I personally serviced nine-and-a-half-thousand young farmers,' she joked.[12]

Other former miners and miners' wives also took the route back to college and university. Often they had to be persuaded to overcome their low opinion of their intellectual ability, because they had left education so early; but they now combined innate ability and an understanding of social hardship, in order to equip themselves to give back to their communities.

In County Durham, Dave Wray had no idea what to do when Sacriston pit closed at the end of 1985. But through the strike's support networks he knew a professor of sociology at Durham, Richard Brown:

Yes. I met him. I don't remember how but I met him. He said, 'What are you doing now?' And I said, 'Richard, I haven't the faintest, foggiest idea.' And he said, 'Why don't you go to university?' I said, 'Richard man . . .' He said something to me I will never forget; he said, 'You are clever.' Nobody ever said that to me in my life. 'You are clever; go to university.' So I went home, and I told the missus. And she said, 'Well, why don't you?' Because I mean, there were grants then. And if you were old like I was they paid you more. So I went to Durham.[13]

He graduated with a degree in sociology and politics in 1989, completed a master's and was recruited to teach industrial relations, rising to become a senior lecturer in social sciences.

Meanwhile, Dorothy Wray decided that she could not go back to life as it was before. 'Some people, like Mary Clark down the street, went back to being Mary Clark. And that was fine, that was absolutely fine,' she said. But it was not for her. She took A-levels in psychology and sociology, and did a sociology and social work degree at Newcastle Polytechnic. 'If the strike hadn't happened, I would never have done that. I would never ever have gone back to education or did what I did,' she said. 'I have worked twenty-three or four years in social work and I finished my career as a manager of child protection team', based in Stanley.[14]

Interestingly, one of her colleagues in Durham social services was Dave's 'marra' Peter Byrne. Peter had gone into the car insurance business after Wearmouth colliery closed in 1993, but then decided that it had no future and settled on becoming a social worker. He took a diploma in social work at Northumbria University – which Newcastle Polytechnic became in 1992 – and found a job 'working with Looked After Children, foster and adoption. And I loved it; absolutely loved it.'[15]

At Great Lumley, Mary Stratford, who had been secretary of the local support group, struggled with Peter (aged three) and Helen (born six months after the strike ended). She earned what she could filling supermarket shelves and delivering the Yellow Pages. Then everything changed:

I just saw a little advert in the *Northern Echo*, and it was about that big, five sentences: 'Are you involved in the community? Do you like helping people? Are you interested in helping people in your community? If so, contact this number. There's a job.' So I rang up and it was the probation service.

She became an unqualified probation service assistant and then took 'a leap into the unknown'. She did a degree at Northumbria University in 1993–95, qualified as a probation officer and became a manager, defending the service in the face of privatisation and as 'a local thing responding to the need in local areas. Now it's a sort of semi-community police force that's obsessed with risk.'[16]

Down the road in Chester-le-Street, Kath Savory had to put her own life together again, while dealing with wider issues in the community. After the closure of Westoe colliery, her husband John found a job in a private mine. He suffered a heart attack in 1998 and decided to leave Kath for a new life with someone else. Since the strike, Kath had run a self-help group 'for people that suffered from anxiety and depression . . . because I suffered from anxiety and depression myself'. When John left, she worked at a crisis centre every evening until midnight and then got a full-time job in social services, working with the mental health teams. Much of the time she was working in places like Easington, dealing with the fallout of the strike and the pit closures. 'People lost their houses, people lost their homes, people lost their friends; and that's maybe when their mental health problem had started.'[17]

Anna Lawson, who had advised mining families on benefits while at the Sacriston support group, now turned this into a career. She found a job teaching welfare benefits at Derwentside College, then dealt with benefits for George Mills solicitors, paid to do an LLB at Newcastle University, and briefly set up her own company advising on welfare rights. At this point, her ex-husband persuaded her to go to Taunton, where, she said,

I got a job in a solicitor's there, Broomhead and Saul, and I set up a welfare rights department there. There I stayed until 1992. And I was the vice chair of the women's refuge. I did all of the injunctions and domestic violence injunctions. I went out into the community, worked with social services and their clients and the CPNs [Community Protection Notices].

After some time, however, Anna felt the inspiration of her sculptor father pulling her back. She did a degree in art and art history at Bristol University and was offered a job teaching in the education department of Durham University.[18]

In Yorkshire, best-dressed Askern picket Peter Robson decided to take voluntary redundancy a year before the pit closed: 'By this time I was forty-six and I thought, "I've got to jump gun here, I'll never get another job." The thought of not working absolutely petrified me.' He went contracting to North Selby pit for a period, then found a job as a fitter with Rockware Glass in Doncaster, which makes glass containers, later switching to quality control. This, however, did not fulfil the debt to society he thought he owed. He and his wife Pauline adopted a Filipino boy and, at sixty-five, he said, 'I just felt I had more to offer workwise. And I bumped into an old pit mate who was working for [Mencap] and he said, "They want some more. You apply." And that was it.' It was perhaps a way of repaying the debt Peter owed his father, who had endured poor mental health and had died while Peter was a young man in the army.[19]

Even more pronounced was the transformation of Peter's fellow Askern miner Frank Holmes. Frank had pulled back from his life of drinking and infidelity and took little part in the picketing during the strike, because he feared his susceptibility to violent outburst. He became a youth worker at St Peter's Church in Askern, and then decided to train for the Church. He attended a Methodist Bible College in 1989–90, but fell out with a female minister, because he took a fundamentalist position that only men could be clergy:

I'm not a misogynist in any way. But if I, if I want to follow something, the Bible is the word of God, then to me, it's the word of God. It's not half and half. It either is or it isn't. I spent a year there and I got the prize for the most improved student of the year. And when I went up on the stage to receive this book, what they gave me, the woman in ministry, who were my tutor throughout the year, turned her back on me.

He acquired a vacant builder's yard in Askern, converted it and, in 1994, opened the Rock of Ages Evangelical Church. He was proud of its charity work, attempting to deal with the fallout from the pit closure and repairing problems in the community:

Over these last years while we've been here, we've done a lot of good work. We've helped people, babies who wanted operations abroad, we've given them money to go for these operations. We've helped local causes, abused women in Doncaster, drug rehabilitation. We've sent a couple of lads to a drug rehabilitation place and paid for them. And we've actually built quite a nice reputation up in the village.[20]

In Barnsley, Betty Cook was a shining example of a miner's wife whose early life had been crushed by unwanted pregnancy and heavy toil. She had come alive during the strike and was now desperate to embrace the opportunities that it had opened up, even if that meant leaving her husband. She had seen a good deal of Northern College, which was the base of Barnsley Women Against Pit Closures, and told the principal, Bob Fryer, 'When this strike is over I'm going to come to your college.' While her husband Don took redundancy and set up a business selling Whitby fish to pubs and restaurants, she started at the college. 'I started to feel equal to others, or nearly equal,' she said. She also met male students who, in terms of their curiosity, were 'a million miles away and a different species to Don'. She decided to leave him 'one night when he came home from the pub and demanded "bed work". I realised for the first time in my life I could say no.' This provoked a massive row with her mother, who 'told me I wasn't fit to be a mother or a wife. She used to ring me up and cry and say, "Go back to him, he's crying."' Betty would reply, 'Can't cry as many tears as he's made me cry, Mum.' She went on to Sheffield University in 1989 as a mature student, aged fifty-one. In her new world she met a former trade unionist, Bill, and formed a new relationship. The death of her mother in 1994 and of her epileptic son, Michael, were releases, but the shadow of the pit did not leave her. Her second son, Donny, who had gone to work at Kellingley, was killed in a rock fall there in 2008. Having proved herself by getting a degree, Betty gave back to the community. She worked at a call centre, phoning parents whose children had failed to turn up to school, until she was eighty-one in 2019. She also volunteered at a Salvation Army lunch club. 'I keep saying I love working with the elderlies, you know, eighty-two, I love working with the elderlies.'[21]

Betty's close friend Anne Scargill did not go on to further study, but emerged from the strike a different woman. She had been at the forefront of the struggle, but in a different way from Arthur, the national leader, who came home less and less:

> One day, he asked me to sit down with him and he made me a cup of tea, which was a bit of a rarity. He said, 'I think we have come to the end of the road' . . . When I got over the shock, I started to feel stupid and naïve and think to myself, 'Have I bloody wasted all these years?'[22]

Her parents both died after falls; but it was the death of her sister Joan that showed her a vocation:

> My sister died in the hospice. She had motor neurone disease. And it broke my heart, because she were a lot younger than me. So, I thought, 'Right, I'm going to work with the hospice.' So I went, and I asked them if I could be a, a volunteer. And they said yes.[23]

Meanwhile, after nearby Dodworth colliery closed in 1985, Paul Winter moved to Grimethorpe, until that in turn closed in 1993, when he was twenty-nine. He decided to take his redundancy payment of £17,000 and get out of mining. Applying for work as a caretaker at St Thomas à Becket Catholic Secondary School in Wakefield, he was asked in an interview what equipped him for the post:

> 'Well, to be fair,' I says, 'it's because I'm not a caretaker. I'm a miner,' I said. 'So if you send me somewhere and it's dark, I've worked in darker. If you send me somewhere cold, I've worked in colder. If you find me something that is hard graft like stacking chairs or moving tables or whatever, I've shoved trams around underground. If you're saying to me, I've got to work in the middle of the night, I've worked on three shifts when I was eighteen.' I says, 'It's precisely that I'm not a caretaker that will make me a good caretaker.'[24]

Unfortunately, his wife did not want to move from Barnsley's Kendray estate to the school, and 'that started downhill spiral really because I settled there and she never did'. Then the headmaster told him that he was

> '. . . one of the biggest underachievers I've ever come across in my working life.' He says, 'Why don't you do summat else? Why do you need to be a caretaker?' He says, 'We'll pay for it.' He says, 'Go out, get an education, do summat.'

In the event, Paul had to leave the school anyway, because he began a relationship with one of the teachers. He acquired further training and, in 2004, became site manager at Northern College, which he described as 'the Ruskin of the North', and representative there of the Unite union. After our interview in 2021, he sent me a poem, the last stanzas of which read:

We brought them down in 74,
When we had the power,
Even ten years later,
We weren't prepared to cower.

Thatcher couldn't beat me,
I wouldn't hear it said,
She feared the unions' power,
So shut the pits instead.

She had me on the ropes a while,
Both me and my lad,
But we both came back fighting,
And life is not so bad.

So if they're speaking lies of us,
We really weren't the foe,
I'm proud I was a miner,
And proud I had a go!!

Over the border in Nottinghamshire, David Hopkins recalled that: 'I think most Manton men wanted the pit to shut. They were sick of the rumours, sick of the Tory government, sick of how they were being treated.' His marriage had broken up in 1992 and he was looking for a new start. 'I think it was 14 February [1994] when we worked the last shift. And I can remember us all cheering.'[25] He was always a sportsman and took three weeks off 'training and running and doing the decorating' before finding a job as a trainee sports leader, working in former mining communities in Nottinghamshire. This led to a job in 2000 as a sports development officer at North Notts College in Worksop, where he met his second wife, Liz, who taught travel and tourism at the college. He also secured a £15,000 grant for a millennium project, interviewing former miners and collecting old photographs to write a history of Manton colliery.[26]

David Amos, a working miner at Annesley pit and UDM branch secretary there until the mine was privatised in 1994, clashed with his pit's new management, which refused to recognise any unions, and left in 1997. He had studied industrial relations at night school, while still at the pit, and decided to return to education after his 'gap twenty-four years'. Although he had left school without A-levels, he was taken on to do a BA in history and politics at the University of Derby in 2000, graduating with a 2:1 in 2002. At the same time, he secured a City and Guilds qualification as a tutor and taught for the WEA at Sutton College. He decided to write the history of the Nottinghamshire miners during the strike, and was awarded £10,000 by the UDM to do a master's at the University of Nottingham. This was upgraded to a PhD, awarded in 2012 and published in 2013 as *The Miners of Nottinghamshire: A history of the Nottinghamshire miners' trade unions*, vol. 4: *1980–85*. This achievement, which told the story from the working miners' point of view, says Amos, went down 'like a brick chicken-house with left-wingers', and on Facebook 'within the space of forty-eight hours my parentage was questioned two hundred times'. He nevertheless stuck to the view that working miners were not responsible for the defeat of the strike. On the contrary, he argued, 'the strike caused the end of the industry, in effect it speeded it up'.[27]

In Leicestershire, Darren Moore, the youngest of the Dirty Thirty, was only thirty when Bagworth closed. He thought about going to Coventry pit with Malcolm Pinnegar, but concluded that 'the coal industry was basically being eradicated'. Then, 'Benny [Malcolm] says, "What about driving instructor?" I says, "Okay, I'll try that." So, yeah, I retrained to being a driving instructor.' By then he had married Simone Dawes, had a small child and felt that he was not earning enough. She, however, was still working at the Inland Revenue and she suggested he do voluntary work. This changed his direction, so that now he was contributing back to a community eroded by the disappearance of the pits and the contraction of job opportunities for young people:

> I went to volunteer for the probation service, over in Leicester . . . there was a local project with what they call 'twockers', which are people who nick cars basically, who are into fast cars and taking without the owner's consent, that's what they called 'twockers'. So the idea was to get them interested in cars in a more positive way by building, you know, building up like an old banger, you know. And then, you know, once we've built it up, we used to take it over to Birmingham and take them around the track and things and try and get them interested in that rather than just nicking cars.[28]

He moved on to a job with the probation service in Nuneaton, trying to keep young people off remand, and then with a lottery-funded Warwickshire Welfare Rights scheme, helping people to access the benefits to which they were entitled. He ended up working in welfare rights for Leicester City Council, going to court to contest decisions by the Department of Work and Pensions to deny people benefits. Meanwhile, Simone herself moved from the Inland Revenue to community work, volunteering for Women's Aid in Hinckley, which dealt with domestic violence, and for Leicester Rape Crisis. After that she worked for Atherstone Council, abandoning her SWP militancy to help regenerate former mining communities:

> I went on to work on an estate called Camp Hill estate in Nuneaton, that had been built for opencast miners but had since gone down the swanny, and had become a sink estate. But because I'd got a foot in the community, it shifted it from political to community activism. I wouldn't employ people for example unless they lived on the estate.[29]

In Fife, there were also a significant number of former miners who opted for the caring professions. They were committed to giving back to mining communities that had been devastated by pit closures and that suffered from unemployment and problems related to alcohol, drugs, physical and mental health.

In Lochgelly, George Erskine had been an engineer at the Comrie pit, but was made redundant in 1985. He was very well read and wanted to become a journalist, but was told, according to his wife Linda, '"You haven't got the experience, you're too old." So at thirty-six, he was washed up.' He found bits of work at Rosyth dockyard and was then asked to do Christmas cover in a children's home. This was a turning point. He qualified as a social worker at Moray House Institute of Education in Edinburgh and then became a mental health officer.[30]

Terry Ratcliffe, who worked at Solsgirth and then Castlebridge, left in 1985 when his mate Andy was killed at the coal face and left hanging there. He became a builder's labourer for nine years, working as far as London and getting paid in cash. He then followed his wife to work in care homes, which were booming to cope with a sick and ageing population:

> Now she's doing nursing in the Western General in Edinburgh. The two of us have worked in care homes for the last twenty years. My whole family worked in care. My two daughters and my son and Margaret, my wife and that, we all worked in the same care home at one time. Levenglen in Scotlandwell. There's a new one opened up in Ballingry just up the road here, and we all applied for a job in there and we all got a job in that one. There was no travelling then, you could walk to your work. And I was there for eleven years.

He was particularly proud to have cared in Levenglen for Evelyn Bayne, who owned the bakery in Lochore that employed many local people and contributed significantly to the strike. Mrs Bayne insisted that he alone bath her and he was proud that 'I was the only person in the home who was invited to her funeral when she died.'[31]

The experience of Peter McCutcheon was similar. He was made redundant when Seafield closed in 1988, and then again when British Gas's Westfield research station closed in 1992. He worked on and off as a bricklayer, until a woman at the dole office suggested that he work with people who needed him. He did an HNC in social care at Lauder College in Dunfermline, and in 2002 found a job working in Rachel House children's hospice in Kinross. A nurse told him that the watchword was, 'Send the children to heaven happy', and he had a vivid memory of taking a dying child on a wonderful day out:

> We took him for a day's horse racing where he got his photo taken with all the jockeys, all the horses. Some of the Rangers team were there, so we got his photo taken with them. That was a bit of a gag on his dad, because his dad is a Celtic supporter. But his dad thought it was hilarious and brilliant and thanked us for it. So yes, they do come to die eventually, some of the children, but generally they come to live, to live their life, to have fun. And that's the rewarding side of it. And yes, it is sad when children die, but you can kind of take a wee bit to yourself saying, 'Well we helped them a bit. We did what we could. We helped them a bit.'[32]

Alongside the former miners and miners' wives who gave back to their communities through their professional lives were those who contributed through community activism, the trade union movement or elected office. Here women made just as much of a contribution as men, if not more.

At Lochgelly, Linda Erskine continued as a lab technician at Auchterderran Junior High School, became shop steward for NUPE, branch secretary for NUPE Fife and Fife secretary for Unison in 1993, when it merged with NALGO. In 1996, she became secretary of the joint trade unions in Fife and, after she retired in 2011, was elected a Labour councillor for Lochgelly, Cardenden and Benarty: 'I've always from when I became a councillor,' she declared, 'spent a proportion of my wages back into the community. Whether it be scouts or a church thing or whatever's going on.' Unemployment and poverty were serious in Fife and made worse by the Covid epidemic of 2020–22. She set up Lochgelly Lunches as the new soup kitchen, and helped develop the Cardenden drop-in centre. Among the poverty-stricken,

the poorest I saw was a woman that waited in December when it was snowing, because we always have queues. We don't open 'til eleven but the queue'll start forming about eight o'clock because that's the way folk are . . . She'd been standing in the queue, she didn't have any shoes, she had plastic bags on her feet, her clothes were thin, she was frozen. How she didn't have hypothermia was beyond me. But a lot of people had handed in clothes, so she went out with three pairs of shoes. I've seen poverty like I've never seen before. People struggled during the Miners' Strike but this level is different altogether.[33]

Carol Ross, who had chaired the Women's Action Committee at Cowdenbeath during the strike, became the court officer at Dunfermline Sheriff Court.[34] Her sisters also had stellar careers – Alice McGarry became the SNP councillor for Inverkeithing on Fife Council, while Tricia Marwick was elected for the SNP to the Holyrood Parliament and later became its presiding officer. 'She was there at Thatcher's funeral,' said her brother Sean, a onetime blacklisted miner, 'and I texted her and said, "Mind and give her a good stamping down when you're there, you know." Aye, because it still hurts. I mean, Thatcher, you know, what she did.'[35]

Pat Egan, who had been dismissed from Seafield for strike activity, but who got his job back at Frances, then went on to Longannet. He suffered a series of professional and personal crises which led him towards welfare rights:

My wife died in October 2001, 6th of October. My mum died on 27th, and the pit shut in April the following year . . . After Longannet closed [in 2002] I was going through the bereavement process at the time and as well, and my first job, I started working on a Saturday night with Kingdom Bakers delivering rolls at the weekend, Saturday, Sunday. And then I got a job on a building site in Kirkcaldy, labouring. They were building flats. And then I started with HMRC, the tax credits.[36]

Although it sounded boring, said Pat, it introduced him to how the system failed to pay people their due, something that he carried over to working for an Edinburgh organisation called FAIR, which secured welfare rights for people with learning disabilities and their carers. Both at the HMRC and FAIR he became involved in union politics and then found a full-time job with the Unite union, organising learning in the workplace, funded by the Scottish government. For the Labour Party he even ran for the Westminster Parliament in 2019, but did not manage to displace the SNP politician.

Former Frances miner Tom Adams also worked at Longannet until it closed. Because he needed a pension, he found a job as a prison officer and then drove HGVs, especially bin lorries. He also became a local councillor, continuing the work he had done as branch treasurer of the NUM at Frances, helping former miners to secure compensation for deafness and lung conditions. He took great pride as a local councillor at West Wemyss, fighting for justice for ordinary people:

I actually loved it for the fact that when you did win a case, see what, you got a card from somebody saying thank you for everything you've done for me, see the immense pride that comes on you when you've done that, just to help somebody in your community.[37]

In Easington, Heather Wood, who had been the driving force behind the women of Save Easington Area Mines (SEAM), was elected a Labour councillor in 1985 and 1989. She threw herself into saving the local comprehensive school, maternity hospital and banks, and dealing with social problems that affected both old and young people – problems that either followed the pit closures or had been imported into the town:

> A lot of the properties are in a disgraceful state. What local authorities throughout the country have done is any people, individual or families who have problems, they've pushed them towards Easington. They've been ghettoised in those properties . . . There's been a drugs problem for years, since the pits shut, a drink problem. I don't know what the teenage pregnancy rate is now but a few years ago it was massive. Everything seemed to go downhill. I think it's coming together now. It's mainly because old stagers as I call them, people who have lived in Easington all their lives are coming together and organising things to happen in the colliery now.[38]

Further south, in Leicestershire, Kay Smith, who had served with Margaret Pinnegar as Leicestershire delegates to the WAPC and who saw her character star in *With the Sun on Our Backs*, was persuaded after the strike to stand as Labour candidate in the local elections for Barlestone. There was no chance that she would oust the Tory candidate, but she overtook the Liberal and made a stand at the count, ignoring the advice of her campaign manager. It was her last political act:

> I went in a skirt I'd made, a top I'd made, and a cardigan I'd got for Christmas, and she says to me, 'When you get up on stage, you shake hands, you've got to shake hands with the other men,' and I said, 'What, Conservative? I'm not shaking hands with anybody!' Because she said to me, 'You won't win.' She says, 'Labour won't get in, but if you push the Liberals back, that'll be good, that's what we want!' So, obviously I didn't get in, I came second, but I didn't shake hands. They were there, the women, the Conservative people were there, the women had got fur coats on, they'd all had their hair done and everything, and

of course it had all come out of their funding, hadn't it? I've never voted, I've never voted since.[39]

More successful was Ros Jones, a miner's daughter and classmate of Jean Crane in Askern. She did well at school, trained as an accountant at Leeds Business School, worked for Sheffield City Council, married and had one daughter: 'I entered local politics simply to improve the lives of the village that I was born in.' She became a Labour councillor for Askern and then mayor of Doncaster in 2013, re-elected in 2017:

> We are pushing for levelling up the north with the south. And it's been starved of funding . . . Levelling up will mean that people have the same job opportunities, people having the same funding put into things like transport, which doesn't happen at the moment . . . We also want people to be trained so creating what we call the 'education city' so that our education comes together to deliver . . . We had to step up and ensure that people were not without food. So we created a Fightback Fund, where it could be applied for.[40]

Moreover, in honour of the mining communities, she organised the crowd-funding of a sculpture by Laurence Edwards of the heads of forty former miners and miners' wives, embedded in two blocks of York stone and unveiled in Doncaster in 2021.

One of her Labour colleagues on Doncaster Council was Charlie Hogarth, who had taken redundancy from Bentley colliery a year before it closed in 1993. He upgraded his skills as an electrician and found work with Doncaster Council, upgrading street lighting. He then did electrical maintenance on power stations and privatised mines like Selby, before returning to the council as an electrician on public buildings. He became involved in the local library, when austerity cuts after 2010 meant that it became a community library run by volunteers; and in 2014 he was elected a Labour councillor for Bentley. He saw the community library as a great enabler of hidden talent among those – perhaps like his former self – who had not received recognition or support:

> We had another person, lass, probably twenty-four. She'd got learning difficulties and she were very quiet and then eventually you couldn't keep her quiet . . . we had a little computer course, she was running it on her own. We had WEA classes, maths and English; she started going to them classes. She started going to college. She's now got a job; she's never gonna get Brain of Britain, but with self-esteem, given the confidence she's got in herself now.[41]

More severe were the social problems in Worksop that confronted miner's wife Josie Potts. The scourge of drugs swept through a community in which there were no jobs – and also devastated her own family; but this only served to strengthen her courage. Her nephew Stephen was found dead from drugs in a car park. Her own daughter J became an addict and Josie brought up J's son Matthew as her own. Shortly after John Mann was elected MP for Bassetlaw in 2001, she accosted him, asking, 'What are you going to do about heroin in Bassetlaw? It's rife.'

> Three weeks later John Mann contacted me and said to me, 'I want you to come on a panel if you will.' And I said, 'Right.' So we arranged it for the town hall and there was five hundred people turned up that day. And it were a couple of days it went on. He provided all tea, coffee, biscuits, sugar, milk. And there were lads coming in that were addicts, the parents. It were heartbreaking to listen to some of the parents . . . He'd got the deputy editor from the *Worksop Guardian*, Tracy Powell, he'd got a vicar on it, he'd got town centre manager. Anyway, he did this inquiry when parents were able to speak.

As a result of this involvement, Josie Potts was elected councillor for Worksop South East in 2007 and devoted herself to sorting out local issues, whether people's housing issues or 'delivering a play park to kids in Manton Villas. I could write a best seller, because I've never felt disappointed in helping somebody. You work with them, and they'll work with you.'[42]

The South Wales Valleys were even more blessed with men and women who emerged from the strike to become involved in local politics and community work. The Dulais Valley produced a brace of councillors and two MPs. John Morgans, the Welsh minister who had been closely involved with Hywel Francis in the Wales Congress for the Defence of the Mining Communities, went back to work on a deprived estate in the Rhondda. And Donna Jones, pillar of the Llynfi–Afan support group, continued to work for and to defend her local community.

Lyn Harper, who had been the craftsmen's representative at Blaenant lodge, decided on leaving the pit that he wanted to put something back into the community, but found that he did not earn enough:

> For the first time in my life I had this urge I wanted to do something which I hadn't done before, but if you ask me what it was I didn't know, I was restless. So as a result of it I went to work with adults with learning difficulties for two years and I absolutely thoroughly enjoyed it, but unfortunately I wouldn't earn enough money on it. I was just gradually taking money out of my redundancy money, and I told the wife one day, I said, 'Look, the redundancy money is there to tide us over until I find a job, but,' I said, 'I don't like this. I'm taking money out of it all the time to live.'

He took a job with the private mining company Ryan at Resolven, but conditions were so poor – with not even hot showers – that he exposed them to the local press. This awoke the politician in him alongside the union official, and in 1991 he became a local councillor for Crynant:

> Because of our involvement on the union you always had this feeling you wanted to try and make things better for people. So it seemed to me the natural progression because I didn't want to have a proper job anymore.

Horizons widened when Neath Port Talbot became a unitary authority in 1996. He became deputy leader of the council, meeting other ex-miner councillors around the country in the Coalfields Community Campaign, 'getting monies in from Europe to ex-mining communities'.[43]

Meanwhile, Ali Thomas, who had been effectively the 'foreign minister' of the Neath, Dulais and Swansea Valleys Support Group, became a local councillor in 1993 and later leader of Neath Port Talbot Council:

> I had an advantage where I worked with a lot of good people. I had an advantage where I knew what discipline was. I had an advantage knowing what people's upbringing is and what is needed and now their children are getting on and now wanting the children to have the best education and everything that goes with it.

As someone who had left school at fifteen to go down the mines that existed no more, his twin priorities were bringing jobs to the area and developing education – not least the University of Swansea, which gave him an honorary degree in 2015.[44]

Hywel Francis, who had been chair of the Neath, Dulais and Swansea Valleys Miners' Support Group and believed that the Miners' Strike would have been settled in South Wales, had they been left to settle it on their own, campaigned for Welsh devolution in 1997 and was elected Labour MP for Aberavon in 2001. He entered politics after the death of his son Sam, who had Down's syndrome and for whom he and Mair had cared for sixteen years, and introduced a Carers (Equal Opportunities) Bill in 2004. He used the expertise he had built up during the strike to improve the situation of long-term unpaid carers. As he reflected:

> What was also familiar to us was the way you'd achieve change and that the strategies that we developed in building alliances and partnerships that we'd witnessed over time, notably in the Miners' Strike, stood us in good stead.[45]

Soon afterwards, Siân James was selected to run as Labour candidate for Swansea East in the 2005 general election. When she was chosen, all her ex-miner husband Martin said was, 'Ah, right. Well I'm not leaving the sheep.' 'The thing that shocked me about Westminster,' said Siân, despite pushing through a bill regulating the sun bed industry to reduce cancer, 'was that I thought that Westminster would be about changing things. And I was frustrated by the pace of change.' She did learn, however, 'a new set of skills': 'but what I like doing the best is supporting local initiatives, fighting for local communities, giving advice to groups'. She had translated the momentum of the strike into securing the family income, acquiring more influence and improving Welsh affairs.[46]

It was not, however, necessary to be a local councillor, mayor or MP to improve local communities devastated by the closures. Moderator of the United Reformed Church in Wales John Morgans, who had been active with Hywel Francis in the Wales Congress for the Defence of the Mining Communities, had been brought up in the Rhondda pit village of Tylerstown. After the strike, in 1989, he resigned as moderator, left his house in leafy Cardiff and moved with his wife Nora to become the minister of Penrhys, a housing estate – built on the ridge between the two streams of the Rhondda, above Tylerstown – that had degenerated into a sink of deprivation, despondency and drugs. They were faced with the challenge of finding a role for the church in 'a collection of houses perched on top of a mountain in which lives a community [that] struggles to live':[47]

What kind of church does a secularised community want? They set the agenda. Things like, we need silence and stillness. A place where it is safe, a sanctuary. A place where we can celebrate births. A place where death is remembered with dignity. There had never been a funeral on that housing estate, never. No undertaker would go there. There was no launderette up here, nowhere for the kids to go in the evenings, no education programme for the young people to pull themselves out or youth leisure. Some of them were the grandchildren of the unemployed, third generation unemployed. They had no idea what work was, totally into the dependency culture, receiving whatever the state offers them.

While Nora worked with local groups to produce a community magazine, *Penrhys Voice*, John used his contacts to prise money out of the Conservative government (ironically from Peter Walker, the Welsh secretary, with whom he had locked horns over the strike in 1985), charities and churches, in order to build a church with a café, launderette, a 'nearly new' shop and four flats for incomers, and to fund a full-time education worker, a musician from Jamaica and an art worker. A hundred people were taken on holiday every year, paying only £10 each. 'It became a village instead of a housing estate' and 'a new generation emerged'. In 1995, he remembered, 'I buried eight young men. Four of them had taken their own lives and all had been involved in drugs.' On the other hand, in 1999 two young women became the first from the estate to go to university.[48]

In the Afan Valley, at Blaengwynfi, Donna Jones, who had been secretary of the local support group, threw herself – along with her husband Gary and others who had been active in the strike – into saving the local community. She became a director of the Co-op to prevent it closing, and pleaded with the bank to help out. The post office was now integrated into the Co-op and the library and cinema were run in the former Miners' Welfare by community volunteers. In a bid to keep the Afan Valley swimming pool open at Cymmer, Gary joined a team led by Dr Brian Gibbons, who would become a Welsh Assembly minister after devolution. Donna was also active in the Sunday Night Syndicate Club, raising money for charity. Their children Judith and Duncan, born in the 1970s, became, respectively, a teacher and a Welsh rugby international. Of course there were problems with unemployment, alcoholism and youth discipline, but community services were developed to meet these challenges. 'I've always had very strong views, but I've never been very vocal,' said Donna. But she refused to accept criticism of their mining community from an outsider who had no understanding either of the circumstances they found themselves in, or of the solidarity and pride at the core of their existence. When a newcomer to the community, a former headmaster of Australian origin – what she called a 'God squadder' – criticised the village in the church magazine, she hit back:

I felt that the article in last month's *Link* by Mr and Mrs D. was most inappropriate. True, valley communities do have a culture of going to pubs and clubs and this culture stems from our historical past when the village was a true industrial community. This culture can only be understood by those who understand and appreciate our past and live in close communities. Yes, we can read. Yes, we do drink. Yes, we do work and look for it wherever it is available. Yes, we do have some children and young people that are out of hand and for the most part people understand that it is social circumstances that cause these problems. Isn't it true that many towns and cities and other villages share these problems, not just our little village? More than this the community does stand by and help its own. This village has survived the General Strike, the recent Miners' Strike and seen many collieries closed. A population cut from 6,000 at the height of mining activities to around 2,000, from thirty-two shops to five, but we are still here. We still have societies within the village that use the pubs and clubs as their base and every year give back to the community thousands of pounds as well as funding worthwhile charities. This village has produced and is still producing individuals who have excelled in a wide range of activities and professions – teachers, doctors, dentists, surveyors, professors, headmasters, bankers, nurses, social workers, craftsmen, sportsmen and women, people working in and running local businesses, young people in apprenticeships and universities and further education, holding down jobs however boring and working long hours in factories trying to keep their families and their homes together in these difficult times.

This is our village, our home, our lives. It may not seem much to Mr and Mrs D., but we like it.[49]

Donna Jones put her finger on the trials and tribulations of mining communities, on hardships visited upon them rather than of their own making. In those circumstances, it was natural that there should be some drink problems and some delinquency; but her point was that the community had fought back against its own disintegration, through education, occupational expertise, charity work and commitment. Blaengwynfi was only one former mining community, but it spoke for many.

15

SHARED STORIES

Each person's story of unhappiness or the search for happiness after the strike was individual in its own way. And yet there were patterns. They both drew on and contributed to wider stories in the family and community of defeat and pain, survival and redemption. These stories were shared in general terms across coalfields from South Wales to Scotland, highlighting the brutal defeat of the strike, the victimisation of miners by the state and the Coal Board, the rapid closure of the pits and the devastation of mining communities. That said, the distinct profile and history of each coalfield meant that these stories were differently modulated. In South Yorkshire and Fife, there was an emphasis on the brutality and injustice suffered by miners, although the women of South Yorkshire developed their own story of mining women's struggle in liaison with mining women in the USA. In Leicestershire and Nottinghamshire, stories were shaped by memories of division and conflict between striking and working miners. In County Durham and South Wales, by contrast, stories emphasised the unified defence of mining communities and the preservation of their identity and legacy.

In South Yorkshire – in many ways in the vanguard of the strike – from where flying pickets had fanned out to ensure that other coalfields came out, the dominant story was that of the strike's heroes and martyrs. An annual memorial meeting was held in March each year, outside the NUM headquarters in Barnsley, to pay homage to the two Yorkshire miners,

David Jones and Joe Green, who had died on picket lines during the strike. This was given wider recognition after 1993, when a statue by the Barnsley-born 'People's Sculptor' Graham Ibbeson, representing a miner and his wife in mourning with a daughter and a baby, was unveiled by Arthur Scargill. It was dedicated to 'those who have lost their lives in supporting their union in this struggle'. Pete Richardson, the victimised miner of Askern, was a regular attender at these meetings, proud of his contribution to the strike, but regretting rhetorically that his sacrifice had not been on the same scale as that of Jones and Green.

Meanwhile, the Barnsley Women Against Pit Closures developed a more upbeat and international story. Anne Scargill, who separated from her husband in 1998, and Betty Cook, who had separated from hers ten years earlier, were invited by American woman miner Kipp Dawson to attend a reunion of the Coal Employment Project (a women miners' organisation) in Jonesborough, Tennessee, in 2013. They decided to strengthen their ties across the Atlantic under the auspices of the so-called Daughters of Mother Jones – named after a woman who was born in Cork in 1837, emigrated to Canada and then the USA, campaigned to unionise workers and was several times sent to jail. Links forged by Kipp's support of the Miners' Strike in 1984–85 were strengthened soon afterwards by an American miners' strike. As Kipp explained:

> During a very bitter strike in the United States, in South West Virginia, against the Pittston coal company in 1989, miners' wives organised in ways that evoke a lot of memories from the British miners' wives, from Women Against Pit Closures ... And they called themselves the Daughters of Mother Jones.[1]

Kipp's friend, West Virginia miner Libby Lindsay, said that Mother Jones

> was known as the miners' angel, but also known as 'the most dangerous woman in America'. Certainly a labour hero and certainly a hero to women, union women and to women miners for sure.[2]

Betty Cook added:

> She not only fought for the miners, but she fought for the children. The mill children, the children were in the coal mines. She was a ferocious woman. She called the miners 'my boys', and that's why she got Mother Jones. We decided that we, we would become – with the women miners – the Daughters of Mother Jones and it sort of strengthened us knowing Mother Jones' story.[3]

Anne, Betty, Kipp Dawson and Libby Lindsay met up again in Cork in 2014 for the Spirit of Mother Jones Festival, inaugurated by the unveiling of a plaque in the cathedral to Mother Jones on the 175th anniversary of her baptism. Anne and Betty also commissioned a banner from the Durham banner-maker Emma Shankland which portrayed Anne and Betty, Kipp Dawson and fellow American miner Marat Moore, and two suffragette predecessors – Emily Davison and former cotton mill worker Annie Kenney – under the immortal words of Mother Jones, 'Pray for the Dead and Fight like Hell for the Living'.[4]

The most powerful and intense shared story in South Yorkshire was, nevertheless, that of Orgreave. It retold the unequal battle of 18 June 1984, when police cavalry charged into T-shirted miners, scattering and humiliating them. It also highlighted the injustice and travesty of the 800 arrests, 206 dismissals and the trial of 55 miners charged with rioting. The trial collapsed on 17 July 1985, leaving an enduring sense that the resistance of the Yorkshire miners had been demonised as 'the enemy within' and ruthlessly broken by the Thatcherite state.[5] The first version of the story was captured by Jeremy Deller's 2001 filmed re-enactment of *The Battle of Orgreave*, co-commissioned by Channel 4, using a cast of a thousand ex-miners and members of re-enactment societies, with the aim of making Orgreave 'part of the lineage of decisive battles in English history'.[6] A second version of the story was developed by the Orgreave Truth and Justice Campaign (OTJC), set up in 2012 to agitate for a full public inquiry into the events of 18 June and, above all, into the question of police falsification of evidence at the trial.

The trigger for the OTJC was the September 2012 report of the Independent Panel that had been set up to look into the Hillsborough stadium disaster in Sheffield on 15 April 1989, in which ninety-seven football fans had died. The report detailed the falsification of 116 police statements, the spreading of unproven allegations and the efforts to blame the fatalities on the fans themselves. On 12 October, the Independent Police Complaints Commission (IPCC) announced a public inquiry into Hillsborough, and ten days later a young journalist, Dan Johnson, revealed on BBC Yorkshire's *Inside Out* parallels with Orgreave, with similar doctoring of evidence by South Yorkshire Police and wrongful accusations of riot.[7]

Barbara Jackson had spent the year 1984–85 picketing the Coal Board offices in Sheffield and with the Sheffield Women Against Pit Closures. After the strike she lost her job and went to Sheffield Polytechnic to study social sciences, going on to work in Sheffield City Housing Department. She had distanced herself from campaigning, but felt guilty in 2004 when she met Anne Scargill and Betty Cook running a Barnsley Women Against Pit Closures stall at a Chesterfield May Day. Then, after the Hillsborough decision, she felt that she had to get involved:

It was like everybody was going round going, 'Wow. They've won through. They've done something. They're getting somewhere.' And people started saying when I met them in the street, people who were involved, 'Orgreave will be next, won't it, Barbara?' 'Yeah, Orgreave would be next, you know.' 'I agree, Orgreave should be next, Orgreave is gonna be next.' And I thought, 'All the shit's gonna make Orgreave next thing then.' 'Are you telling me that Orgreave should be next? What are you going to do about it?' You're telling me and I'm thinking, 'What are *you* gonna do about it?' And I'm thinking, 'I don't want to do anything about it. I want *you* to do something about it. And then I [will] be able to join in and support you. I don't want to lead on this fucking thing. I've led during the year of the strike. I don't want to lead on it.' But I just thought, this window of opportunity, it'll go very quickly, if somebody doesn't take it.[8]

Barbara phoned up her friend Lesley Boulton, who had been captured in John Harris's famous picture of her being beaten by a mounted policeman at Orgreave, and they called an exploratory meeting. Only a handful of people turned up. One was the young miner Paul Winter, who had been at Orgreave and had a scar on his head to show for it. Another was Joe Rollin, who had been at primary school in Worsbrough during the strike. He had done an apprenticeship at the *Barnsley Chronicle* before working at West Ferry Printers on the Isle of Dogs, which was very hostile to unions, but had returned to Barnsley in 2010 to join the community arm of the Unite union. Barbara became secretary of OTJC and recalled that 'everybody ran the campaign from their home using their own printers, computers, phones. Nobody got paid any money at all.'[9] Joe Rollin became chair, setting up an email account and a Facebook page, and later being 'instrumental in designing and helping promote all the logos and T-shirts and actions throughout the eight years'.[10] Every 18 June, they held a rally called With Banners Held High; it effectively replaced the Yorkshire Miners' Gala that had died in 1995.[11]

The OTJC procured legal help and made a legal submission to the government in December 2015. Eventually its representatives were granted an interview with the home secretary, Amber Rudd, on 16 September 2016. Then, on 31 October 2016, Rudd rejected the possibility of an inquiry on the grounds that it was too long ago and nobody had died. This was a hammer blow and Barbara Jackson resigned as secretary in 2018. 'All energy's consumed by Brexit and Covid. There's no energy left for anything else,' she later argued, while former miners and mining families were 'depressed, deflated'.[12]

The flame was nevertheless taken up by a younger generation of South Yorkshire activists. They concentrated on finding ways of reaching out to young people who were born after the strike and were not necessarily from mining families. Joe Rollin organised a Death of Justice rally at Halloween 2017, exactly a year after Amber Rudd's refusal:

> We made these brilliant Dayglo posters and stickers with like Margaret Thatcher on, but with Halloween sort of twists. And there were hundreds of people showed up for it. Everyone came in fancy dress and we had a coffin at the front of the march. So, yeah, when we do things in Orgreave campaign, we try and use our imagination and make them fun as well as keeping it relevant for younger people to get involved in as well.[13]

Meanwhile, the post of secretary of OTJC was taken over by Kate Flannery, who came from a highly politicised Sheffield family, her father having been Labour MP for Hillsborough between 1974 and 1992 and her mother president of the Sheffield Trades Council. She herself had supported the Miners' Strike through NALGO and Sheffield Women Against Pit Closures. As secretary, she re-emphasised the targeting of young people, internationally as well as nationally, and linked Orgreave to other activist causes and campaigns, such as the Shrewsbury 24 Campaign to exonerate trade unionists prosecuted for involvement in the building workers' strike of 1972 and the campaign for justice and compensation for the families of the seventy-two victims of the Grenfell Tower fire in 2017:

> We've captured the imagination of lots of young people as well who won't necessarily come along to meetings. Why would you? You know, who wants to sit in a meeting with a load of old folk? But they'll come along to our events and activities and, of course, our relationship with the guys from Lesbians and Gays Support the Miners. You know, we do joint stalls together at Durham . . . We've done meetings in other countries as well. We've got a Swedish connection, a Danish connection, a French connection, and we've got friends who live in other countries

now, who wear the T-shirts and take photographs and send them to us and we post them on the Internet. So we do lots of things like that about making connections with other organisations. Because, you know, the Orgreave Truth and Justice Campaign isn't just about Orgreave. It symbolises what happened during the strike. But it also has connections with lots of other justice campaigns like Hillsborough, Grenfell, Shrewsbury, you know, so we continue to maintain all these connections and do a lot of work together, meetings together.[14]

· In Fife, the shared story was that of the campaign for justice by and for the 200 miners who were arrested, tried and sacked by the Scottish police, courts and Coal Board for exercising their right to picket during the strike. At a deeper level, it was also a campaign to protest against the effects of pit closures on mining communities, which became sinks of unemployment, sickness and drugs, and to recover the honour of those once proud pit villages.

After the closure of the Mary and Glencraig pits in 1966, Fife Council decided to remove the 'bings' or slagheaps that polluted the area over four square miles and to create a country park in what was called 'Britain's biggest facelift'.[15] Complete with boating lake, golf course, fitness trail and picnic areas, the Lochore Meadows, known locally as 'the Meedies', opened in 1978. This was an obliteration rather than conservation of the memory of mining, with only the headgear of the Mary kept as a reminder. In 1996, however, Fife Council popularised the name 'Benarty' – drawing together the four villages of Lochore, Ballingry, Crosshill and Glencraig – in order to access UK and European money. A Benarty Heritage Preservation Group was set up to curate the heritage of the mining communities and other local history. A central role was played by former miner and strike leader Willie Clarke, Communist councillor for Ballingry on Fife Council from 1973 and, from 1996, councillor for Benarty. He fought for and secured the promise of a mining heritage centre in the Meadows, but political opposition meant that this never materialised. The community centre that opened in the Meadows in 2018 was named after Willie Clarke, but he criticised the absence of the mining museum that had been promised twenty-five years earlier but for which funding had never been granted.[16]

The funeral of Willie Clarke in Lochore Miners' Welfare Centre in November 2019 served to bring together once again former miners, their families and the mining community more generally. 'There is no man more worthy than Willie Clarke to be described as a legend of our times,' said Colin Fox of the Scottish Socialist Party and former member of the Scottish Parliament, in his tribute. 'To serve a community with such dedication and personal sacrifice for so many years is in my book real testament of a legend, whose name will be etched for ever in local history.'[17]

The pride of Benarty, whether or not it had a mining museum, provided an identity for the 'Benarty Six', those miners in Glencraig, Lochore and Ballingry who had been arrested during the strike, sacked and blacklisted and for whom a campaign to pardon them was mounted. Andrew 'Watty' Watson, the youngest, who was lucky to get his job back and who worked as a miner until 2002, argued that for him the campaign began in March 1985, when Doddy McShane, who had been arrested the same November 1984 night as he, was not allowed back into the pit:

> I can see the disappointment in Doddy's face. And that was the day that we started the fight for the six. The Benarty Six and the other two hundred men in Scotland . . . I call them the Benarty Six, right. I always wanted to get a plaque made up of the names of the Benarty Six. Unfortunately two of them have passed away. There's the Benarty Four left but one of my goals – I'll not say it's a dream – one of my goals is to get a nice plaque and stick it on the Mary pithead gear down at Lochore Meadows Country Park, just the sacrifice that those five men made. George McShane who was Doddy, right. Then you've got Ronnie Campbell. Then you've got Ian Walker, then you've got Sean Lee, then you've got Tam Brown. And if that's five you just add A. Watson at the bottom. And that's the Benarty Six.[18]

There had indeed been calls since 1985 for an inquiry into the arbitrary and inconsistent arrests that targeted Scottish miners more than English or Welsh ones. Increasingly, the finger was pointed at brutal policing in Scotland, pressed for by the Scottish Coal Board, supported by the Scottish judiciary and ultimately authorised by the Thatcher government. The devolution of powers to a Scottish Parliament and government in 1999 opened the way for an inquiry into policing during the strike, which was demanded by Neil Findlay, Labour member of the Scottish Parliament for Lothian. University of Glasgow historian Jim Phillips demonstrated that Scotland had been treated particularly harshly, with 206 miners (1.5 per cent of miners in Scotland) dismissed in 1984–85, compared with 800–900 (or 0.6 per cent) in England and Wales. For every thousand miners, 13.7 were sacked in Scotland, three times more than the 4.2 per thousand in England and Wales.[19] There were anomalies of dismissed miners who had been arrested but never convicted, and 'strong circumstantial evidence that many of the sacked men were subsequently blacklisted by non-coal employers, notably in the construction industry'.[20] An independent review was commissioned by the Scottish government in 2018, led by John Scott QC. His report – *Impact on Communities of the Policing of the Miners' Strike 1984–85* – which was based on evidence gathered from the archives, from submissions and from testimonies given by those affected at public meetings held across the former coalmining Areas, was published in 2019. It highlighted the scars inflicted on mining communities by the defeat of the strike and the economic devastation that followed, and recommended that in almost all cases the victimised miners should receive a pardon from the Scottish government.[21] A Miners' Strike Pardon Bill for convictions of breach of the peace, breach of bail and obstructing the police was introduced into the Scottish Parliament in October 2021, was passed on 16 June 2022 and became law on 26 July 2022.[22] Ronnie Campbell, the late Doddy McShane and Watty Watson were thus pardoned, as was Sean Lee – except for the incident at Ballingry police station.[23] Thus, with its different constitution and nationalist government, the Scottish Parliament was able to achieve what had been rejected by the Conservative UK government in 2016 – something that is still a painful wound.

In County Durham, the story of miners' victimisation was less pronounced than in Fife, and the regeneration of declining mining communities was not isolated from the mining heritage, but drew power-fully on it. The history and solidarity of these communities had been enacted through the Durham Miners' Gala or Big Meeting, held annually every second Saturday in July since 1871. On that day, miners and miners' families from every pit, each with its own banner, would descend on the city to celebrate their struggles and sacrifices, to have new banners blessed in the cathedral, to listen to speeches from labour leaders and then to have fun. Local people would be joined by activists and well-wishers from far and wide. In 1952, the year after the Easington pit disaster, 300,000 people attended, but then a steady decline set in. Attendance fell in 1972 to 140,000, and in 1993, the year Easington closed, to 10,000. The closure of the pits and the loss of coalmining jobs seemed to be followed inexo-rably by the decline of the Gala. The Durham Miners' Association almost sold its headquarters at Redhills to the university and almost let the Gala fizzle out, as the Yorkshire Miners' Gala did at that time.

And yet a revival happened. From the mid-1990s, the Gala celebration became more and more popular. Despite the crisis, explained Jim Coxon, a former shift charge engineer at Herrington, who later worked for local government in town planning and economic regeneration, 'the two Union leaders [Durham Miners and Durham Mechanics] David Hopper and David Guy decided [that] the Gala shouldn't die; it should be kept alive'.[24] They found a sponsor in Michael Watts, a New Zealand busi-nessman who had links to the area and who made a huge donation to the Gala. George Robson, former finance secretary of the Durham Miners' Association, became the main organiser of the Gala and learned how 'the community needs to mention the magic word "education"' in order to access funding from sources such as the National Lottery, conveniently launched in 1994.[25]

Finding funding, however, was only one explanation for the revival of the Gala. The other was that mining communities had lost their pits, but not their pride. It was almost because coalmining had come to an end, and because the NUM had been defeated, that communities stepped forward to commemorate the miners who had shown such fighting spirit and had laid their bones in the Durham soil. Those communities desired to hand this legacy on to their children and their children's children. In 2016, the Gala was attended by 200,000 people.[26] According to former Sacriston miner Dave Wray:

> The Gala, it's almost like an icon for people who are looking for something. They've been shat on by the Tories, things are not good, the unions have no sway much now and people are looking for something. The Gala's there. It's the only one left and it's getting bigger every year. I don't want to sound too romantic but it's something you can go there and like charge your batteries. You see people, I see people there I see them once a year, right? Trade unionists, people on the left, people who want a good piss up, a shag in the bushes, whatever. It's there, all life is there.[27]

A colourful sign of this revival has been the vogue for mining communities to make new banners or to refurbish old ones. These banners – rallying points and victory trophies of those communities, and glorious examples of vernacular art going back decades – were often in a very poor state of repair or had disintegrated.[28] In 1986, the pit at New Herrington closed and, as if in sympathy, the banner was torn apart by the wind at that year's Gala. A Miners' Banner Partnership was set up at Herrington in 1999, chaired by former lodge secretary Bob Heron, with his wife Pat, a former shop steward in the clothing industry, as treasurer. According to Bob:

Part of what we are doing is about letting Thatcher and her like know that we are still here. They closed the pits and took the jobs, but every time we take the banner out we are saying to them, 'We're still here and we're still fighting for our communities.'[29]

This testimony was collected by David Wray and Carol Stephenson, colleagues at the University of Northumbria. It formed the basis of a case study arguing that the banner partnership had taken over from the lodge and the support group in order to 'emotionally regenerate' its community by drawing on a past 'community of memory'.[30]

Making new banners fired up a new cottage industry, in which a leading role was played by artists Lotte Shankland, the anti-apartheid, Greenham Common and Independent Labour Party activist, and her husband Hugh, lecturer in Italian at the University of Durham and activist in Peace Action Durham, together with their daughter Emma. Their business took on the domination of the market by Tutills in London, which had been making trade union banners since the 1940s. Emma, who made a banner for the Daughters of Mother Jones, also made one for the Durham Women's Banner Group, which included miners' daughters Heather Wood from Easington and Lynn Gibson from Spennymoor and which took as its motto, 'Feminism is the radical notion that women are human beings.' In this new phase, the most important development was to take their banner work into schools, to engage the schoolchildren and to make stories of struggle more inclusive. To mark the Commonwealth Games in 1998, they showed the various Commonwealth countries with which the schools had links in innovative ways. For Shincliffe, where two Bangladeshi boys were being bullied, they designed a banner featuring a Bengal tiger. 'There's nothing more cool than a tiger,' said Lotte, 'so these two boys became the heroes of the school.' At New Brancepeth, where the headteacher was keen to minimise controversy by choosing the 'white' Commonwealth country of Canada, Emma (who knew the country) taught the children how to highlight the importance of the Inuits and Native Americans.[31]

Going into schools and engaging schoolchildren in the shared stories of the Gala and the banners extended into teaching them about the mining industry in general. In 2015, Dave Wray and Jim Coxon returned from a conference at Ruskin College frustrated that so little of the work being done there was being seen or heard outside the walls of academe. They made contact with Dave Hopper of the Durham Miners' Association, which was refurbishing its headquarters at Redhills. They joined forces with Kath Connolly of the WEA, David Connolly of the North East Labour History Society, Carol Stephenson, miner's wife Mary Stratford, Heather Wood and Lynn Gibson of the Women's Banner Group and all former members of support groups, to set up Education 4 Action in order to develop children's activities during the week leading up to the Gala. In 2015, children dressed up as miners, were shown artefacts and heard folk songs from Bill Elliott and Judith Murphy. In 2016, Jim Coxon added a film on coalmining in the 1950s; and in 2017, the children were introduced to the work of the checkweighman, who decided how much coal the miners had mined and how much they would be paid, often leading to fraud and unrest.[32]

These proud and unifying messages were unfortunately not echoed in Leicestershire and Nottinghamshire, which had been the front line in the battle between miners for and against the strike. The stories handed down were stories of breakup, bullying and betrayal. That said, there were differences between them. The minority that went on strike in Leicestershire were abused locally; but nationally and internationally, the Dirty Thirty – like Shakespeare's Henry V's tribute to the Happy Few before Agincourt – became symbols of the resilience of the striking miners, while the working miners had no story. In Nottinghamshire, by contrast, where the striking miners formed a larger minority and the majority working miners refused to climb down, a divided memory of the strike shaped antagonistic stories that tolerated no middle ground.

The Dirty Thirty were attacked in Leicestershire as a bunch of militants who rocked the consensus; but they turned the discredit and attempts to marginalise them into a bond of comradeship and a badge of honour. They had travelled across the country, stirring up support for the strike. They spun webs of solidarity by hosting striking miners from other coalfields who came down to Leicestershire to picket – and by paying return visits. Bill Frostwick from Herrington stayed with Nigel and Wendy Jeffery on a regular basis, often cooking meals, and he hosted many of the Dirty Thirty when they attended the Durham Gala that July. After the strike, in 1987, he was best man at their wedding.[33] Two years later, Bill and Elspeth went on holiday to Greece with Malcolm and Margaret Pinnegar, and they discovered how many people had rooted for them all during the strike. 'It was the best holiday ever,' said Elspeth. 'It was just amazing to think that those people who live on the other side of the world were supportive, supported us during the strike. It was just fabulous.'[34] That fame, however, could also lead to practical jokes, as Margaret recalled:

> We went to Rhodes and then we went to Symi, a little island, and when we pulled up in this boat, this ferry from Rhodes, there was a picket line with placards up because somebody Billy knew was already on this island. And they were holding up these placards when we got there. Malcolm went, 'Oh, don't tell me. Don't tell me there's a picket line here!' It was 1989, and he says, 'Don't tell me there's a picket line, we can't get off the boat.' Of course, we were stuck on that boat, but it was Billy's friend that had organised it. So it was a joke.[35]

In their way, the Dirty Thirty acquired something of a cult status, acclaimed in print, film and song. David Bell, a schoolteacher from Ashby-de-la-Zouch – a Labour activist and local historian who had shaken tins and collected cans of food for the strikers outside an Ashby supermarket – interviewed a good number of the comrades for his book *The Dirty Thirty: Heroes of the miners' strike*, published in 2009. He concluded with a story of a visit by several of the Dirty Thirty and their wives, with their banner, to the Durham Gala in 2008. They were approached by a bandsman from Sunderland who said, 'We'd be honoured to have you walk in front of our band with your banner. We'll be playing for you.' 'We got in,' said one of the Thirty, 'and we marched with our banner held high and a band behind us, playing for the Dirty Thirty.'[36]

In 2012, Malcolm Pinnegar died, aged sixty-eight, of cancer. At his funeral, said Margaret, 'Nuneaton crematorium was full. Standing and standing outside.' 'All his favourite people all in one place from all walks of life,' said his daughter Claire, 'including the strike, because it was a big part, but all the other factions as well.' Added Margaret: 'Family factions, friends factions, strike factions. They were all, all there.'[37] In September of that year, a film, *The Story of the Dirty Thirty*, inspired by David Bell's book and made by Brian Langtry and Len Holden, premiered at the Phoenix cinema, Leicester. 'It's a story of heroism,' said Holden. 'The Thirty ended up being a *cause célèbre* for the striking NUM members.'[38] At the same time, Liverpool-born folksinger and songwriter Alun Parry wrote a song about the Dirty Thirty. This returned to the notion that they turned ostracism into pride, for once included their wives and families, and paid fulsome tribute to their heroism:

They were called the Dirty Thirty
So they wore their name with pride
As the only striking miners
They stood against the tide
Now if you call them heroes
They would surely disagree
But the Dirty Thirty and their kin
Are all heroes to me.[39]

In Nottinghamshire, which had been profoundly and painfully divided by the strike, there were two competing stories. One was of the striking miners and their union, the National Union of Mineworkers; the other of the working miners and their breakaway union, the Union of Democratic Mineworkers. These tribes, for tribes they were, did not speak to each other and often insulted one another. The striking miners felt betrayed by the working miners, who, in their eyes, had besmirched the good name of Nottinghamshire and meant that the county was removed from the collective memories of British miners.[40] The working miners felt victimised by the striking miners, who had refused them the democratic right to a ballot and had then, with their friends from Yorkshire and other coalfields, resorted to bullying them into striking. The Nottinghamshire Miners' Gala, which took place in Mansfield's Berry Hill Park, was held for the last time in 1983. In the spring of 1984, the park became a war zone in the battle for the ballot. Much later, there were attempts to build bridges between the two camps in the name of the history of the Nottinghamshire coalfield, but these struggled to span the divide.

In 2005, a group of striking miners decided that they were fed up with meeting only for the funerals of their old comrades, and set up the Nottinghamshire NUM Ex- and Retired Miners Association. Its driving force was Eric Eaton, former NUM chair at Newstead and Thoresby collieries and chair of the Nottinghamshire Area NUM. Located in a solicitors' office in Mansfield, the association began by offering cheap legal advice and advice on health services. After a request from Eastwood, they began to give talks in schools, showing artefacts from the mining industry. Plans were made to open a Nottinghamshire Mining Museum in Mansfield, and an appeal to raise £250,000 was launched, though money was very slow to come in. In 2022, its website announced:

> Our current home is in the East Unit of Mansfield Railway Station, opposite the Midland Hotel. We open for pop-up exhibitions, which are advertised via our Facebook and social media pages. We aim to open on a more regular basis. We are looking to gain larger, permanent premises, to display and house our extremely large and growing collection of artefacts.[41]

Its professed aim was 'to inspire pride in Nottinghamshire's coalmining heritage and the traditions of community, fellowship and solidarity that thrived in mining communities'. In order to achieve this goal, it made no mention of the Miners' Strike and made no reference to the fact that, as an NUM museum, it was a strike-breaker-free project of bona fide striking miners.[42]

The stance of the association nevertheless came across clearly in an interview conducted by Eric Eaton in 2015 with a group of former Bilsthorpe miners, a miner's wife and a member of their support group in Cambridge. This articulated an enduring sense of betrayal and anger towards those who had 'scabbed'. It was pointed out that men who had broken the strike in 1984–85 often belonged to families whose members had broken the strike in 1926, suggesting that 'Spencerism' was in their blood. This was not something that could be forgotten or forgiven:

Geoff: You can walk around Mansfield and there's still an atmosphere. It'll never go.

Yvonne: I was talking to a senior social worker the other week at Notts County Council. And after we'd done the business he said, 'Yvonne, I was to ask you something. You're from the mining community, aren't you?' He said, 'How far back does it go?' I said, 'Grandfather, great-grandfather. Father, brothers, husbands.' He said, 'Can I ask you, which side were you on in the strike?' I said, 'We were on strike. That's all we did.' He said, 'So, has this been resolved now, thirty years on?' I said, 'Has what been resolved?' I said, 'Do you want me to forgive [expletive deleted on the recording]?' 'Forget it,' I said, 'not even when I'm dead will that happen. That'll go to the grave with us' . . . Who was that bloke who came from Ashfield to our strike centre? An old man, in his eighties. He came with two of his family. I remember, it was a Tuesday, because that was dinner day. He was telling us who was

Malcolm: related to the scabs in 1926 and who were working today. And he named people in our village. I wish I had his memory.

Malcolm: I can always remember. I must have been twelve, thirteen. My father got killed in Glapwell colliery and he left my mother with four kids. My mother was looking through the window and she said, 'Come here, come here quick. Stand there. You see that bloke there, that little bloke walking up there. Your dad chased him up Cryony [as heard] pit. He were a scab in '26. So you see how it carried on.

Yvonne: It's not going to go away.

John: And we're not going to forgive, either.[43]

There were sporadic attempts to build bridges between the two communities by telling shared stories. David Hopkins of Manton colliery secured funding for a millennium project, interviewing former Manton miners.[44] He had lived in Worksop (rather than Manton pit village) and, as a miner, had gone back to work in November 1984. Thus, he personally straddled the divide between striking and working miners. But one of the strikers he interviewed later said to him, 'If I'd have known you'd gone back to work, I wouldn't have let you in my house.'[45] Drawing on the interviews and the old photographs he had collected, Hopkins published *Pit Talk: Memories of Manton colliery*. This adopted a century-long perspective, from the opening of the mine by the Wigan Coal and Iron Company in 1898 and the arrival of clog-wearing Wigan workers in open wagons, to the closure of the pit in 1994. In this narrative arc the strike of 1984–85 was only one episode.[46]

Thirty miles away, in Eastwood, former Annesley miner David Amos began his academic life as the historian of the Union of Democratic Mineworkers.[47] Subsequently he learned that the curating of heritage can be a powerful way of attracting external funding for community education projects. At the same time, it can facilitate dialogue between previously warring parties, enabling them to find stories that they might all cherish.

In 2015, he established Mine 2 Minds with Paul Fillingham, the son of a pit deputy at Blidworth and now a digital producer. Their website announced that 'Mine 2 Minds is dedicated to Mining Heritage, Culture and Education. We offer workshops, lectures, digital archives and public events to provide information, training and community engagement related to mining heritage in the East Midlands region.'[48]

Amos also established a working relationship with Natalie Braber, a lecturer at Nottingham Trent University and an expert on local dialect. She coordinated the East Midlands Coalmining Heritage Forum, which brought together heritage groups and local history societies, and spoke to striking and working miners alike.[49] One of their successes was to display the NUM and UDM banners of Bilsthorpe colliery in Bilsthorpe Heritage Museum, opened in 2014.[50] In 2021, they published an anthology of stories and poems from the East Midlands coalfield, in order to ensure that 'lives are not forgotten and that memories of "life in coal" are passed on to younger generations'. The chapter on strikes – 'Unity is Strength' – observed that 'The 1984–85 strike's domination of the subject means that earlier strikes are either forgotten or dismissed. Major coal strikes and lock-outs occurred in 1893, 1912, 1921, 1926, 1972 and 1974.' The collection also included an account by a policeman, Barry Harper, who concluded that 'There were no winners in this dispute, only losers.'[51] These bridge-building initiatives, however, did not command full approval in the striking and working mining communities. An interview for this study with a founder member of the Nottinghamshire NUM Ex- and Retired Miners Association was flatly turned down with this reflection: 'Just to give you heads up, there's someone you name who was a super scab, unfortunately this lets me out of your project.'[52]

The division of former mining communities in Nottinghamshire was dramatised in the 2022 BBC series *Sherwood*, written by James Graham. It focused on a double murder in Annesley in 2004, the first – with a crossbow – being that of NUM striker and activist Keith Frogson. His real-life murderer was a working miner, Robert Boyer – although it is unclear to what extent their workplace history provided a motive for the killing. *Sherwood* nevertheless highlighted the antagonism – bordering on violence – between those on the different sides of the dispute, even long after the strike. *Sherwood* portrayed Frogson in a favourable light, and its dedication was 'In Loving Memory of Keith "Froggy" Frogson, 5th July 1942–19th July 2004'. This interpretation was contested by David Amos, who said that he was personally bullied by Frogson and saw him as a skiver and the incarnation of Scargillism:

> James Graham, the playwright who you've probably heard of, who lived locally, he were talking to me last week, he's doing a six-part serial for BBC based on this double . . . there were two murders that went off in 2004 and one was this Annesley miner. He's now portrayed as an activist and all this, but he wasn't, he was a bully. Well, he made a beeline for me for the rest of strike and for the next ten years. He was an Annesley miner, his name were Keith Frogson. And I think of him, all the threats that he had, and in the end, the great irony of this thing was he was never at work before, which I was telling James Graham last week. Because they portrayed him as this great hero and that. I said, no, no, no, no, no.[53]

At the end of the drama, Detective Chief Superintendent Ian St Clair, played by David Morrissey, persuades Daphne Sparrow, played by Lorraine Ashbourne, not to take her own life, as she was on the point of being revealed as a police informer who had lived in the community since the strike. 'We need to stop being trapped in the past,' he says. 'What matters is the here and now.' Achieving that in Nottinghamshire, however, remains a tall order.[54]

In South Wales, in sharp contrast to Nottinghamshire – and much more like County Durham – there was a dominant story of the strike that was positive and unifying. The coalfield had held firm to the end, with 98 per cent of miners remaining out; and it then returned to work in good order. There was only one regrettable episode: the death of taxi driver David

Wilkie, who was carrying a strike-breaker to work on 30 November 1984. What the Neath, Dulais and Swansea Valleys Support Group newspaper *The Valleys' Star* called 'Welsh resistance' to the English Thatcherite state fed, within a decade or so, into enthusiasm for Welsh devolution. John Morgans, the nonconformist moderator who had played a key role in the Wales Congress for the Defence of Mining Communities, reflected that

after the Miners' Strike the awareness began to spread that if there had been a Welsh solution the pits would have died with dignity and the communities might have found a new way of life. So the next time there was a vote on devolution the mining valleys all voted in favour of devolution.[55]

Hywel Francis, who had chaired the congress and became an influential supporter of devolution, gave the example of Philip James, the Treforgan miner who was wrongfully prosecuted for unlawful assembly and riot at Orgreave and who, in 1997, became 'one of the speakers at the launch of the Yes for Wales Devolution Campaign at Cardiff Castle'.[56]

The story that came to characterise the strike in the Neath, Dulais and Swansea Valleys was that of the extensive connections forged by its support group in order to sustain striking miners' families. A particular focus was on the link between the traditional mining community and the avant-garde group Lesbians and Gays Support the Miners. Originally aired in the 1986 video film *All Out! Dancing in Dulais*, this came to the attention of playwright Stephen Beresford, who had been at RADA when the second wave of pit closures took place in 1992. Many years later, he made contact with Mike Jackson, the secretary of LGSM. Mike was initially not impressed, because no media approach had ever come to fruition; but this was different:

For several years after the strike I was approached by various writers, radio, television, plays, authors or whatever who'd heard about LGSM and were thinking about doing something . . . every single one of them came to nothing and then that was it. Radio silence for eleven years. Then in 2011 I get a telephone call from Stephen Beresford . . . Never heard of him, I was by now fairly lackadaisical. I said, 'Yeah, yeah come around. I live in King's Cross. I'll tell you my story.' It was really, here we go again, it'll probably amount to nothing. However, when he told me that it was – I can't remember which of the big Hollywood studios – it was either Paramount or Universal, I just sat there. I tried not to flinch but I just thought, fucking hell, Hollywood. Jesus . . . He's a bright man is Stephen and he realised that if he was going to make this project work he had to get our trust completely . . . We worked with Stephen for three and a half years on the whole project.[57]

Some time later, Siân James, by now Labour MP for Swansea East, also received a phone call from Beresford, who came to see her in the House of Commons. She was also initially sceptical, but very soon saw the possibility of having their story told to a much wider public:

About a fortnight after I'd met with him, he got back in touch and said that he had pitched the idea, that he'd been commissioned to write the dialogue, the actual story. And a fortnight after that he gets back and says, 'They like it, they're buying it. They're going to do it for the BBC, and they're talking about appointing, getting the actors in.' So a fortnight after that, I get another message to say that Bill Nighy and Imelda Staunton had signed up . . . The next thing they tell us is that they want to pay us £1 each, Martin and I, for the rights to use our names. So this is the point where you start to think, what's this about? Why am I doing this? Why am I getting involved in this? It's not about promoting me; it's not about promoting my story or anybody else's story. But it's a story that my friends would love to have told. They deserve to have the recognition of this story. So I said to Martin, 'Should we just go with the flow?' And he said, 'Yeah. If it helps in any way. And we know how special things were and we want others to understand how special things were.'

Siân was also won over by the director of the film, Matthew Warchus, who had directed the stage version of *Lord of the Rings* and Alan Ayckbourn's trilogy *The Norman Conquests*. 'Matthew describes *Pride* as a rom-com,' she said, 'but it's not a rom-com between two individuals – it's between two communities that fell in love. Isn't that lovely? It's about two communities that fell in love.'[58]

Beresford and Warchus were keen to meet the miners, miners' wives and other LGSM activists who would be part of the story. Jonathan Blake, who had been living in Brixton with HIV since 1982, was contacted by Beresford, who then wanted to introduce him to Warchus and the actor who would play him:

Doorbell goes. I go to the front door. There's Stephen Beresford standing there. 'Where are the others?' 'Oh, there's a costume fitting – they'll be along.' So I said, 'You can come in, have tea but no cake until the others come.' We sit there chatting. Doorbell rings. This man thrusts his hand out, introduces himself as Matthew Warchus. And over his shoulder I see McNulty from *The Wire*. So they come in, and Matthew was brilliant. He just took over the proceedings and was asking us about our backgrounds and our histories and how we got involved. And after about an hour, Stephen says, 'Why don't you take Dominic [West] out and show him the garden?'[59]

Beresford was also keen to go down to the Dulais Valley, in order to meet the cast and explore the surroundings that would feature in the film. Mike Jackson recalled:

Eventually I took Stephen down. We hired a car in Swansea and I took him around the Valleys and he met Margaret Donovan. He'd met Siân already in London anyway and I also introduced him to Dai Williams who was a kind of grassroots man who wasn't a kind of leader in the same sense that Dai Donovan was, but he was a good stalwart miner, who was brilliant to LGSM. So Stephen did actually meet as many people as we could.[60]

One person they did not manage to meet was Hefina Headon. As her daughter Jayne remembered:

At that point she was in a sheltered home and that's when her dementia had properly kicked in. So she didn't know who I was then either and I just said to them probably best not to because she won't know and they never did. So they never interviewed her in the end and they never went to see her.[61]

Hefina died in 2013. In the film, she was portrayed as a larger-than-life character by Imelda Staunton.

In May 2014, the film was taken to Cannes, where it won the Queer Palm award, and was shown for the first time in London that September. 'When the film finished it was silence, there was just dead silence,' recalled Siân James. 'And Matthew Warchus said, "What's wrong?" And we all said, "Nothing. We're just stunned. We're just stunned how you've captured us all, everything and everybody, how we felt about things." '[62] The film was a huge success. Mike Jackson was delighted that it appealed to a new generation of young people and an LGBT community that was less embattled than it had been thirty years before, in part because of their struggle:

Then there's a whole new generation of people who don't know anything about it and particularly when you look at the LGBT community, the change partly effected because of exactly what we did. The change of the LGBT community has been phenomenal. There are a lot more out LGBT people than there were ever before, but a huge swathe of those will be too young to know anything about it. You know, one of the most heartening things about *Pride* the movie is the biggest cohort of fans that's taken everybody by surprise has been and consistently remains people under twenty-one.[63]

The film had an effect not only on the LGBT community, but also on the mining community – the other partner in the rom-com. The Neath, Dulais and Swansea Valleys Miners' Support Group was revived and began to meet again. Hywel Francis, its former chair, brought out a new edition of *History on Our Side* in 2015, the front cover juxtaposing a black-and-white photo of the return to work at Maerdy in March 1985 and a colour photo of Mark Ashton at the Pride festival the following March. The caption read: 'Including the inside story of the film *Pride*'. New forewords were written by Mike Jackson and Siân James MP, by-lined as 'Secretary of the re-formed Neath, Dulais and Swansea Valleys Support Group'. The love affair continued with a plaque that was unveiled in Onllwyn Miners' Welfare in honour of both Hefina Headon and Mark Ashton, while Siân led a delegation from the Dulais Valley to Jonathan Blake's seventieth birthday, in his beautiful garden, in July 2019.

It would be wrong to think that the story of *Pride* was the story of the Miners' Strike in South Wales. The experience of the Neath, Dulais and Swansea Valleys, with their organised support group, was very different, for example, from the experience of Hirwaun in the Cynon Valley, let alone the Rhondda. Nor is it true that this was the only story in the Neath, Dulais and Swansea Valleys. Hywel Francis suggested privately that Siân James saw the strike through the lens of *Pride*. True, her profile had been greatly increased by the film, thanks to the lively character based on her (and rather at the expense of Hywel's). But Siân and her husband Martin had another story, too – different from Hywel's story of an orderly return to work: theirs told that of rank-and-file miners who wanted to continue the strike beyond March 1985.[64] This conflict resurfaced in 1987–88, when Arthur Scargill, who had opposed lifetime presidency of the NUM and wanted a new mandate after the divisive strike, put himself forward for re-election. Phil Bowen and Lyn Harper of Blaenant lodge held a meeting in Seven Sisters Rugby Club to back Scargill's opponent, John Walsh, while the rank and file of the Blaenant miners organised a meeting in Neath Rugby Club to support Scargill.[65] At Abernant, Martin James complained that they had a vote to mandate their delegates to vote for Scargill, but 'I think Blaenant they done the dirty on the boys, they wanted Arthur Scargill and the delegates voted for . . . I can't even remember the other one, you know, he's gone into the dustbin of history now, hasn't he?' Miners' wives such as Siân James and Ann Jones also campaigned for Scargill and acquired the name 'Scargill's angels'. She argued that John Walsh

deserved to be in the dustbin of history. With the sort of people who were supporting him. He would have been a puppet. He would have been. But the next thing we hear that John Walsh is speaking in Seven Sisters' Welfare Hall. So I said, 'Get off. He can't be,' and they said, 'Yes, he is.' So up we go to hear him speak up in Seven Sisters' Welfare Hall and they wouldn't let us in. So we stood outside windows and watched him through the windows. Heckling him through the windows and then they shut the curtains.[66]

'They weren't very democratic,' added Martin. That distinction between the dominant story of the 'feel-good' link with LGSM and the orderly return to work was challenged by the rank-and-file narrative which did not contest *Pride* – on the contrary – but which also wished to highlight the fact that the orderly return to work and the opposition to Scargill were the positions of the strike leaders in Blaenant, but not those of many ordinary miners.

The shared stories of the mining communities served to make sense of the struggle they had been through. These stories varied from one coalfield to another, highlighting repression and the fight for justice in Fife and

South Yorkshire; solidarity and redemption in County Durham and South Wales. Often there was a subordinate story, as well as a dominant one – that of Mother Jones behind Orgreave in Yorkshire and Scargill's angels behind *Pride* in the Dulais Valley. The Dirty Thirty have their own story of a happy few pitted against the odds. But in Nottinghamshire, there was no shared story, only competing ones of intimidation on the one hand and betrayal on the other.

16

CHILDREN OF THE STRIKE

The Miners' Strike will not die with those who took part in it. The mining families it impacted were composed not only of miners and miners' wives, but also their children. Some were children or teenagers during the strike itself and experienced the conflicts, hardships and pain for themselves. Others, the authentic 'strike babies', were born just before, during or just after the strike. They had no direct memory of the strike, but lived with its consequences and with the stories told by their parents. Also impacted were the grandchildren of miners and their wives, born well after the strike and learning about it much later, either from their grandparents or from their friends or from books, TV programmes and films. The experience of the strike and its legacy in material terms crossed generations. Memories of the strike were also intergenerational, handed down and thought about by children and grandchildren in very different ways. Some are able to recover the memories and others not; some are able to deal with the painful memories and others not. We will call these children variously casualties, survivors, heirs and redeemers of the strike.

Josie Potts, the miner's wife from Manton in Nottinghamshire, was very proud of her four daughters, born between 1969 and 1972:

They were happy kids. We used to walk miles, and you know, we used to walk to Clumber, which were lovely, and we used to walk by canal side past Manton pit. And they learnt swim in canal, when they were kids. We didn't have a lot, but we were better than what I had, if you know what I mean . . . My daughters used to be in the majorette band. All mining villages had one. We went down to Newcastle [-under-Lyme], competed there, and we stayed weekend they put us up. Yeah, and there were no drugs on the scene then.

Thirty years on, after the community had had its heart ripped out, everything had changed. One day, around the new millennium, her grandson Matthew came into her house with something he had found on some wasteland near the village:

He says, 'Look what I found,' and he thought it were a toy flask. Anyway, I opened it, and it were full of used needles, blood on them and the lot, and I were flabbergasted. And I'm getting really wound up about it, 'cause of his future. Now it's his kids' future.

This was the moment that started Josie on her campaign against the heroin epidemic in Manton, which was now fighting against joblessness, drugs and crime to feed the habit. The tragedy was that J., her youngest daughter, had also become an addict and Josie was bringing up Matthew, because her daughter could not cope. J. died, aged forty-nine, in 2021. During our interview with Josie, Matthew came in, now carrying his mother's casket. A moment of profound sadness descended. Rallying, Josie rejoiced in the Christmas celebrations she still hosted for the whole family, down to Matthew's daughter and son. Of the son, she said:

I can see me daughter in him. J. would have been the nan. And they are lovely. They call me nanny, and they call Billy granddad. And they lighten you up when they come, it's lovely. I love to see them. And more so him. Because I brought him up because of way my daughter were. She was a good daughter, but she had an addiction.[1]

379

One of Billy Potts's best mates was Andy Varley. They shared a common love of pigeon racing, the freedom and speed of which was perhaps as far from coalmining as they could get. But Andy's daughter Mandy and son S. had difficulties. Mandy became diabetic at four and was sacked as a hairdresser for her poor eyesight. She nevertheless had two strong sons and, said Andy, 'they're beautiful lads. I'm so proud of her.' His son S., born in 1981, was a talented young sportsman, but then 'went off the rails'. Andy and his wife Sue nevertheless stood by him:

> I suppose he got most attention, because he was a footballer. We'd been all over the country with him, Worksop Town level. Gainsborough, Frickley. He played for Worksop at seventeen. He were good. But he went off the rails. He'd got a partner, she were good-looking, they had our Jasmine . . . Then they split, then he started on drugs. Ended up going back to her, they had another lad, our Max. He's sixteen, he's another one who's quite bright. Then they split again, for good, she's remarried. So he had a hard time with them. He's got another lass, they got two kids. But he's done time. They gave him eighteen months. That was another hard job. The copper busted on him, got fed up with him. He said, 'Dad, they're going to send me down.' He did about three months. He were in Notts prison, locked up for twenty-three hours a day. I never missed one visit to him. They brought him out on tag. He said that's worse than going to jail. He's pulled himself round.[2]

Another miner's child who 'went off the rails' was the daughter of a member of the Dirty Thirty. She seemed to be particularly affected by her father's absences and infidelities, which broke up her parents' marriage. Her mother recalled, 'She went off the rails. She loved her dad. She went off the rails a bit, and she ended up, she started using drugs. And four years ago she went to a rehabilitation centre and, touch wood, for three years she's been off them.'[3]

A final example of a casualty was Lee Bonsall. Born in 1988 to Ken and Karen, who had got together after the strike, he grew up without the option of working in the mines like his father and grandfather. He chose the army, which had always been another option; but in 2006, within six months of joining up aged eighteen, he was sent out to Afghanistan as a private with the Royal Logistic Corps. One of his friends, another eighteen-year-old from Nottinghamshire, was killed in a Taliban ambush on the convoy they were both travelling in. By the time Lee returned to base three days later, said Karen,

> Andrew's stuff were just gone. His bed had been rolled up. Locker had been moved. The flag had gone. So, and I think, he just thought, 'Wow.' You know, 'We're here today, gone tomorrow. Nobody cares.'

Instead of being allowed to depressurise in Cyprus, Lee was sent straight back to Colchester barracks, from where he went absent without leave. When the army caught up with him, he was put in military prison; then he went AWOL again. Eventually he got out of the army, which registered that he was 'weak in both mind and body'. There was no recognition of the fact that he was suffering from post-traumatic stress disorder. Lee went to live with Serena, his girlfriend and then wife, in Tenby; but he had dark thoughts about the Taliban torturing prisoners and desecrating the graves of servicemen. Then, one evening, said Karen, 'in between her [Serena] going to work and her coming home, he'd hung himself. He were twenty-four. Just before his twenty-fifth birthday.'[4]

Ken and Karen were devastated, but soon discovered a pattern. Another young man in the neighbourhood who had been in Afghanistan committed suicide a week later. And there were others. They pressed the Ministry of Defence for more information, but were constantly frustrated. They formed a group of grieving families and wrote to Prime Minister David Cameron. They were approached by writer Toby Harnden, who was working on a BBC *Panorama* programme, *Broken by Battle*, aired in 2013, about the spike in the number of soldiers who took their own lives in 2012.[5] The greatest succour, however, came from Ken's band, Ferocious Dog, which Lee had named while still a toddler. Ken wrote songs such as 'Glass', in memory of the glass of water Lee left before he killed himself:

Had a fight in my head today and that's the state of my life now can't you see?
To walk away would be a bigger man
But there's bigger fights in my life now can't you see?

This world's not good enough for Lee
So I'll put the wine glass down. Leave it for eternity

I went to fight in a foreign land
And now I find that my depression fights with me
To fight a war at such an early age
They didn't prepare me for the things I had to see

This world's not good enough for Lee
So I'll put the wine glass down. Leave it for eternity[6]

The second group of children may be called survivors. They, too, belonged to families that were put under intense pressure by the strike and its aftermath, through redundancy or blacklisting, poverty and humiliation, early pregnancies or domestic abuse, mental health issues and addiction. Where they differed from the casualties is that they pulled themselves round by their own efforts and through the support of the family and wider community.

Claire Pinnegar, born in 1967, the younger daughter of Dirty Thirty leader Malcolm (Benny), remembers that 'we had the fun with my dad, and mum was the disciplinarian'. He was a generous father – and not only to them. When they went to Newquay for their summer holiday,

My dad would set a cricket field up for us and we'd be playing cricket and we'd always end up with all the other kids on the beach. Kids were drawn to him because he praised them so much.

Those happy days ended during the strike, when Malcolm was away so much and was then attacked by a strike-breaker in their own home. Claire lost her way, became pregnant and then fell victim to domestic violence:

I felt I lost my dad a bit to the strike, because he'd always been so hands-on and, you know, sort of properly involved in everything we did. I lost my dad through the strike really, but it sort of coincided with my first sort of serious relationship, which was very volatile. I was having a lot of trouble myself. I was pregnant at seventeen, I married the man. I took over the council house, didn't I? And I was in bother, really, I were in the shit really. I was in and out of women's refuges, had to go into refuges and stuff. I know it was massive thing as well for my mum and dad, because I know my dad wanted to kill this man, you know, not actually, properly, but mean, he did at one time.

Claire recovered in a new relationship, put together a career working for a bank and then running a pub, and her father 'became that man again, that hands-on, doting granddad, dad. The strike was done, so he reverted back to that strong family man.' When he died in 2012, her eldest son, Billy, asked if the grandchildren could carry the coffin, 'because Billy said he carried us all on his shoulders . . . he said he carried everybody all his life and they wanted to carry him. Well I just said, "Just don't effing drop him, please." ' Claire herself felt reconciled with her father, because 'I've always been – all my life, from very young to even now and he's been dead nine years – Benny's girl.'[7]

Some children of the strike were the victims of their parents breaking up after it. Kate Parker was born in 1973, the daughter of Harry Heaton, who worked at Welbeck colliery, and Anne, who came into her own during the strike through the Welbeck Women's Action Group. Kate had fond memories of her childhood; but these did not last. 'I remember play[ing] freely and catching butterflies and putting them in the jar and then letting them go,' she said. 'And I remember when Olympics used to be on because I used to want to be an Olympic runner.' She was thirteen in 1986 when Anne and Harry separated and Anne went with Kate back to her home-town of Wigan. But Kate really suffered there: 'I was just sort of panicking and I were lonely and I were sad, and I wanted to come home so I was crying and things, and I got bullied because of my accent.' To restore harmony, Anne decided to remarry Harry and move back to Warsop; but the marriage did not last more than a couple of years. Meanwhile, Kate was wrestling with what she wanted to do, began training for social care and then became a mother:

At one point, I think I wanted to go in the forces but I was a bit scared of everything, I wanted to go into the police forces but I was scared of the dark. I wanted to be a vet and I were a bit scared of dogs where the dog on the corner of the street used to try to bite me all the time. So I decided to go into social care and I did my first certificate and my first diploma and my Higher National Diploma in social care and psychology so that took me four years. But I was also, yes, so I did that. So, I qualified – well, I sat my exams when I was eight months pregnant and I found out I was pregnant . . . I finished my national diploma, eight months pregnant and then I've been a mum ever since, full-time mum to all three children.[8]

Twenty years younger than Kate, Yorkshire lad Adam Winter was also marked by the breakup of his parents during the strike. Born in 1992 on Barnsley's Kendray estate, his life was shattered by the closure of Grimethorpe colliery the following year, making his father, Paul, redundant. Paul took a job as a school caretaker in Wakefield and then formed a new relationship with a teacher. Adam, aged nine, found himself torn in two:

I were closer to me dad, I were like his shadow, but I had chosen to live with my mum because my dad had gone with the partner he's with now and my mum would have gone off rails completely without me being there.

Likewise, he was pulled between the Kendray estate, where his mother lived – its 'folk in drug-infested hovels with no carpets on the floors' – and his father's new middle-class environment:

I was just lost, I was taking ketamine to dumb myself down to the same level as me mates. I loved them dearly but they were as thick as shit. The rate of suicide in this culture and these places is much higher. I've got two close friends who have committed suicide that is drug-related and I know at least of another eight to ten. It's all to do with drugs and that alienation.

But Adam was rescued by his own pride and his father's determination. 'I knew that he'd got it in him,' said Paul. If there had still been pits, he said, Adam would have been 'a damn good pitman'. 'If there's one thing I've done in my life,' he asserted, 'my greatest achievement is pulling him back from the brink and saying to anyone who wants to listen, I didn't disown him, and there he is.' Adam spent two years at Ruskin College in Oxford, and then, aged twenty-seven, he took a degree in sociology and politics at the University of Huddersfield. He wrote an undergraduate dissertation on the 'Red Wall', started going out with a Polish student who was studying business and economics, and applied to take a master's degree course.[9]

Two hundred miles away, in the Dulais Valley, Jayne Headon, born in 1968, was also marked by family turbulence, but of a different kind. At the age of nine, she discovered that Jennifer – who she thought was her older sister – was in fact her mother, who had given birth to her out of wedlock. Jennifer had been sent away and Jayne brought up by her grandmother

Hefina Headon as her own daughter. She grew up shy and had few friends until, aged seventeen during the strike, she discovered the women's group and was taken under Mark Ashton's wing when LGSM visited Onllwyn.[10] When it was all over, she reflected, 'I didn't want to stay in the village but I didn't know how I could leave.' She decided to join the army, despite Hefina's warnings about becoming one of 'Maggie's boot boys'. On the day of her passing-out parade, devastating news came through that Jennifer had been killed in a motorbike crash in the United States.

Jayne was posted to Germany and tried to find another family in the army. 'To have a relationship with anybody really,' she explained, 'you're forced into becoming official. So there was a big group of us, about six or seven of us who all decided to get married at the same time.' Then another disaster struck. Her first child with Stuart was still-born, just as Hefina's had been. Hefina flew out to Belfast, where they were now based, but, said Jayne, 'She was an absolute mess. She just couldn't stop wallowing. She was upset. It was hard. It was hard for me and Stuart to grieve because we had to look after her.'[11]

Jayne and Stuart completed twenty years of marriage and had three sons; but then, it seems, Jayne was visited by the ghost of Mark Ashton. Through the fan club of Neath-born singer Katherine Jenkins, she met a student, Emily. They entered into a relationship and moved to Wrexham, where Emily continued her degree in psychology, while Jayne developed a new career as a National Vocational Qualifications assessor. Hefina died in 2013 and Jayne decided to write her story, returning periodically to the Valleys to interview people and to find Hefina's support group documentation in the archives.[12] A further tribute to Hefina was the repair café they opened in Wrexham, to recycle domestic appliances and reduce waste. 'I want to fight for my community. I want us to survive,' she said. 'You know, kind of like Hefina ethos.'[13]

At Glyncorrwg, twenty miles away from where Jayne Headon was brought up, Rachel Tudor Best, born in 1966, suffered her own family challenges. The daughter of communist doctor Julian Tudor Hart and his wife Mary, who were dedicated to research into miners' diseases and to making the world a better place, she felt agonisingly different from other children at school. After the summer holidays, 'I had to go school and everyone talked about Barry Butlins. "Where did you go, Rachel?" "Well I went to Czechoslovakia." '[14] She and her two brothers were expected to sell the *Morning Star* in the village every Saturday. At fourteen she had her 'first real head-on collision' with her parents, because she wanted to study arts subjects and they believed only in science. 'I had to do three sciences and history and French and I had to drop all the subjects I really enjoyed doing and was good at.' During the strike, in which her parents were heavily involved, she was at college in Neath, raised money, which she sent to the Neath, Dulais and Swansea Valleys Support Group, and was thanked by its secretary, Hefina Headon. But along with her boyfriend, who was in Militant Tendency, she took a more radical line and worked closely with Broad Left miners Ian Isaac and Phil White in Maesteg. Paying homage to her parents, she qualified in nursing in Cardiff, but then went to London to work at an AIDS Unit at St Mary's – 'probably the first thing I'd done that I really was personally drawn to'. Inspired by Third World revolution, she went to Honduras as a midwife and then came back to marry an Oxford-educated London lawyer, David Best.

Crisis then struck. Their first child, born in 1995, was delivered by forceps and had multiple fractures from birth. She was accused of child abuse and lost all faith in the medical profession:

> I had to take him every week to be checked over for bruising and really that's when I was reborn as a person, I would say. Because this NHS I had grown up in and lived with, it was our religion, it was our church. Of course it's not the experience I had.

She decided to abandon the NHS and throw herself into training as an artist. As far as her parents were concerned, 'I defected. It was like being a defector from Russia coming to England as a ballet dancer. The fact that

I'd committed this terrible crime of leaving the public services.' After the birth of their fourth child, Rachel persuaded her husband to move back to Wales and support her in developing her career as an illustrator. Her mother boasted that 'She's an illustrator but absolutely regards herself as a Valley girl.' Rachel was, in many ways, reconciled with Wales through her art, and when we met she was designing a large bowl 'filled with the names of every pit in South Wales coalfield'.[15]

In Ballingry, Fife, at the other end of the country, Anna Campbell and Margaret Todd were born in 1967 and 1969, respectively, the daughters of 'Red Ronnie' Campbell. Without resources during the strike Margaret went picking potatoes, while Anna, who left school in December 1984, found a job in a local shop and gave the £25 a week she earned straight to her mother Elizabeth. After the strike, Ronnie was blacklisted and jobless and sat at home for ten years. Margaret, aged seventeen, became pregnant, but subsequently built herself a career in retail. Anna then found her father a cleaning job in the Asda store where she was working. During our interview, his daughters sat protectively on either side of Ronnie; much slighter than they were, he would frequently have to cough and draw on his inhaler. Their mother Liz, exhausted by the strike and its aftermath, had died in 2006, and their brother Ronald died suddenly of a stomach ulcer, aged forty-two, in 2019. They held together as a family while they witnessed the devastation of the mining communities around them:

Ronnie: The amount of villages that we had in the Area was Ballingry, Lochore, Crosshill and Glencraig. Then you had Lochgelly, Lumphinnans and Cowdenbeath. Kelty. They were all mining communities, you know.

Q: And what's left of them?

Anna: Nothing.

Ronnie: Nothing.

Margaret: Nothing.

They felt angry about this dereliction which, in their eyes, had been visited on them by Mrs Thatcher. 'If I got my way, when she died, I would have put her down the Solsgirth pit,' said Anna. 'She was a horrible, horrible woman. She was out to destroy Scotland, she was out to destroy Britain, but she was gunning for Scotland.' What they were proud of, however, was the spirit of family and community that survived and was expressed not least at funerals. When Ronald died, one of their distant cousins came up from Didcot for the funeral. In the Ballingry pub, said Margaret, he was made to feel welcome and accepted:

These strangers were coming in, and they're like, 'Who's that boy, he's English, where's he from? What you doing here?' And he said, 'I'm up visiting my family.' And they said, 'Who's your family?' 'The Campbells.' 'Oh, you're alright then, mate.' Like that. And then, when our Ronald passed, they can't believe what it's like for people in this community to have the respect for people, to turn up, to pay their last respects. He just can't get his head round what it's like to be in a community, where everybody helps each other, looks out for each other. Your foodbanks, everybody is involved, you know what I mean. Your wee community groups and that, for children now, and it just, it's a community that's just growing, and growing, and growing.[16]

Raised in Lochore, adjoining Ballingry, James McShane and Janet Carson, the children of Doddy McShane, born respectively in 1962 and 1964, had to deal with the terrible impact of the strike on their family. Their father, said James, 'took the blame' for somebody else who threw a stone at a strike-breaker's house in Lochore and was sent to Saughton prison in Edinburgh while awaiting trial. 'I was just relieved that he'd been released,' said Janet, 'because again it made my mum ill'. Their mother especially continued to suffer after the strike and three years later, when Doddy was being feted in the Soviet Union. Janet, with toddler Kevin and heavily pregnant, accompanied her mother to a benefit office to get some money to pay for food. They were humiliated:

> We went in, we had to wait, pull a ticket, wait, and then we went back in for her appointment, and the lassie had said . . . she went away and she come back and she said, 'You do know that you'll not get much for this.' And she said, 'Aye, I understand, I'm on my own.' And they offered her £1.56. That's what she was offered to keep herself for a week. And she looked at my mum and she went, 'What are you going to do?' And to watch your mum break down in tears, and I did tell her to shove her money up her arse.

Doddy himself died of a heart attack in 2008 and their mother of cancer in 2018. James married in 1986 and had two children, but struggled with redundancy and stress:

> I was at Babygro for twelve years before being made redundant, then I moved onto Dunlop Textiles in Dunfermline, which was a tyre cord manufacturer. I was there for fifteen years, again made redundant. Now I'm now with an oil and gas company in Rosyth . . . I left for a couple of years and went back again . . . To be honest, I was a bit stressed at the time. I took another job which wasn't as well paid, and I started getting stressed financially, so eventually got the chance to go back, and seem to be a bit happier just now.

Janet worked at a woollen mill in Kinross, but then went into the care sector and the NHS, although this was interrupted by having to care for her sick mother:

> I started in care in 2000 with Scottish Autism, autistic adults, and then when my mum wasn't very well, I changed my job, went back to the wool mill for five years. Then when she passed away, I went back to

care . . . Just applied for NHS and this one came up . . . Healthcare support worker with forensic patients, it's a low secure unit.[17]

Like Anna and Margaret, James and Janet were also comforted by a sense of community that was manifested by the huge turnout at Doddy's funeral and by the continued existence of the Miners' Institute in Lochore, where they both celebrated their silver wedding anniversaries and where Janet's son Kevin was married.

A third group of children might be called heirs. Their approach to the strike and its consequences was to take inspiration from their parents – mothers as well as fathers, and even grandparents – who remained reliable models. They were able to draw strength for their own lives by remaining essentially faithful to their family, their community and their politics.

'I had a very happy childhood,' said Dafydd Francis, born in 1974, 'growing up in a very political family with my grandfather who was obviously a miner's leader.' Dai Francis, general secretary of the South Wales Miners' Federation until 1976, was also a Welsh nationalist. 'If he caught us speaking English he would say in Welsh, "What's this English you speak? What's this language you're speaking?"' Dafydd was also marked by his father Hywel's involvement in the strike. He remembered the convoys of strike-breaking lorries going along the M4 to Port Talbot and 'Literally everyone shouting at these lorries. Shouting "scab" and all other kinds of things and as a ten-year-old being quite scared.' When the strikers were picketing their own pit at Blaenant in the final weeks, he was allowed to join them and, he said, 'I remember going to school that day and being very, very proud saying, I've been on a picket line today.' After the strike, his father asked him to write to young Rhondda miner Russell Shankland, who had been convicted of killing the taxi driver taking a scab to work. 'I became good friends with Russell Shankland,' he said, 'I would send rugby programmes to Russell because [he] was a big rugby fan, a big Pontypool fan.' Dafydd studied sports science in Cardiff and worked for a period in

England, living in Aldershot and teaching in Farnborough. This did not last. Of his friend Cellan and himself, he said:

> We've both come back to raise our families in our respective communities, the Afan Valley and the Dulais Valley and maybe there's something about that. I can remember my mother always used to say, you know, the more you put in the more you get back and it's important to put something back into your community and I chose to come back. I don't work here. I could easily live in Cardiff but I chose to come back to live in my valley.[18]

Jude Bevan, born in 1972, was herself a child of Blaengwynfi in the Afan Valley. She was proud to be 'definitely working class. Absolute working-class family.' It was also a matriarchy, in which every Sunday night her mother, Donna Jones, put 'her cheque-book face on and now I realise she was balancing the books for the family'. During the strike, said Jude, 'I remember my mum shutting the kitchen door while she was taking these phone calls', because she was secretary of the support group. There was a rally 'on the rugby field of Maesteg Rugby Club and Arthur Scargill speaking and I remember there being lots of impassioned shouting, but when you're a child it felt like a day out that was quite fun'. Jude was close to her family and village and had a panic attack when she first arrived to study history at university, even though it was just down the road in Swansea. Perhaps there were echoes of her mother being forced to turn down an offer from Bristol University in order to support her family. Jude was encouraged to apply for a PhD at Cambridge, was accepted and secured funding – but then turned it down herself, because 'I just didn't think I was clever enough.'

Jude moved to London with her partner Tom, with whom she had done a master's at Swansea, and took up a post teaching in Maidstone, where his middle-class family came from. She differed from Dafydd Francis in that she did not choose to go back to the Valleys:

My mum still finds it quite strange that I will never go back and I'm not going back. [She] is used to having her mum and her sister all in the same street. I'd find that really claustrophobic. I couldn't handle that at all.

She was no longer sure what class she belonged to: 'I don't think I'm middle class. I don't think I'm working class. I don't know what I am actually. I'm just somebody who works.' But her experience of the strike taught her that 'the working class are the radicals. The middle class are not the radicals.' This is what brought her close to her mother. 'My mum and I were always the two that talk politics, always . . . You know, you must hate the police. You must hate Thatcher.' And this message she carried to her school in Maidstone, where she advised a colleague in the politics department who was making a film about the Miners' Strike and getting students to interview former mining families in the Kent coalfield.[19]

In County Durham, Samantha (Sam) Oldfield, the daughter of Dave and Dorothy Wray, born in 1969, remained faithful to her family and her community. 'I am the daughter of a miner and I couldn't be prouder of my dad,' she announced. She was taken every year to the Miners' Gala and 'I used to have the honour of holding the strings on the banners when I was little.' Aged fourteen during the strike, she was almost programmed to do her bit. She led a school strike against a practice of making the children of striking miners queue separately for their free school meals, and won. Her parents set up the soup kitchen in Leadgate. 'If my mum had asked us to peel a potato in the house, then I probably would have thrown a strop,' she laughed. 'But I loved being up there, I loved helping out, I loved all of that.' She experienced at first hand the politics of the strike and the divisions it inflicted on the village:

When people were at the house I would hear raised voices. Obviously as the strike went on there was the issue with people who went back to work, who were not particularly well liked. And my best friend's dad

393

actually went back to work. So we were best friends at school and we spent a lot of time together in the first half of the strike, we went to Beadnell with YMCA, they took us all for free, we went on a holiday there, surfing, kayaking, just a bit of caravan type holiday; it was much fun. We were really close . . . Then, as the strike wore on, near to the end, her dad actually went back to work and she then didn't speak to me.

'For as long as I can remember I've always wanted to be a nurse,' said Sam. 'Once I realised that I couldn't be a dolphin trainer.' She qualified in nursing in Durham and learned how to juggle professional and family life, with a first husband with whom she was 'more like brother and sister', and then with train driver Neville:

I was a staff nurse at the hospital I trained in and that was a general ward . . . Then, when I had my son, I left the hospital and I did a couple of nights in a nursing home just while he was a baby. And then I moved to the RVI, Royal Victoria Infirmary, that's in Newcastle. And I worked on the liver unit there. Then I had my daughter and after that I went on the nurse bank; child care obviously, when you have two children they are way more challenging than one.

After that, she worked for a GP unit, covering Newcastle, Northumberland and Tyneside. And all this time she remained faithful to the Miners' Gala. 'You kind of bump into people that you don't see any more,' she said. 'It reminds you of that time that it did feel like a community.'[20]

Peter Stratford, born in Great Lumley in 1982, did not have the same memories of the strike itself and, although he was heir to the mining tradition, did not have the chance of becoming a miner himself. He remembered visiting his grandfather and uncle in Easington, 'seeing the pigeons at the little colliery club. But now if you go to Easington, it's completely different. It's just a wasteland basically; just went downhill.' He remembered his father Paul no longer going out on shifts after the pit closed in 1993, but being at home all the time. This meant 'doing more stuff, like going out as a family' and his father also took them on camps with the Woodcraft Folk. However, Paul was not there as a model of a miner, as Paul's father had been for him. 'I had no idea when I was at school. I didn't even know what I wanted to do when I finished school,' he said. 'I went to this college at Durham and did catering, but apart from that I really had no idea.' Preparing frozen ready meals in a Chester-le-Street café was not quite what he dreamed of. He was true to his father, in that he found a job in the manufacturing industry, as an operative in a food-grade plastics factory. However, the power of the union was gone, because, said Peter, 'whoever was made union rep was basically sacked the year later'. The idea that someone who worked during a strike could be vilified and ostracised was also difficult for Peter to understand:

I've had conversation with me dad about scabs . . . stories of scabs like, there's still people now where certain working men's clubs, if some fellow is a scab, they still can't get in. And it's still like frowned upon. I wasn't there; I don't know what happened. I can see why you call a scab, but you also see why you went back to work. I don't know if I would. You've got to put yourself in that position, haven't you? I mean strikes aren't strikes anymore really . . . The strikes don't last very long, they do one-day strikes now.[21]

Lisa Potts, born a decade earlier – in 1971 – and brought up in the mining village of Warsop Vale, was arguably even truer to the legacy of her father Bill, a miner at Warsop Main. 'We were born here and I do mean literally here,' said Lisa. 'We were all born at home. My dad actually delivered me or so I was told later.' With three brothers she was a strong girl and inherited her father's fights. At school, she had a fight with John Proud, whose mining family came from County Durham:

John's father, who also happened to be called John, and my dad didn't get along. So, John and I didn't get along. And he was a bit of a bully.

I had always been taught to stand up to bullies, not that I needed teaching.

This was resolved during the strike, because John's father joined the strike; but on the other hand, her friend Zoe's did not – so they broke up. 'I remember her being nasty about the clothing vouchers and things like that. And I just, "At least my dad is not a scab."' Warsop Main was technically part of the Derbyshire coalfield and, she said, 'My dad still referred to Nottinghamshire until the day he died as "scabland".'

Lisa shared the sadness of her father when the pit closed in 1989 and the headstocks came down while they were away on holiday. It was as if something anchoring her father's life and her own had been taken away. 'The headstocks were always a landmark,' she explained. 'You always knew you're on your way home. And we couldn't see them when we came back. My dad probably knew they were scheduled to come down but he'd not said.' She completed her A-levels, got a BEd from the University of Derby, but failed to secure a job as a teacher. She found employment as a prison officer at Lowdham Grange, on the site of a former borstal and a 'brand-new 500-bed Category B prison for adult sentenced males'. Her father Bill, who died in 2020, would be proud of her.[22]

The last example of an heir is Lee Richardson, the second son of Pete and Sue Richardson of Askern. In many ways, he was like his father and was proud of him; but he also felt frustrated about the way in which the strike had affected his father and the family. The pride was evident in a story he told of being watched by a bouncer, aged eighteen, on one of his first trips into Doncaster with his mates:

And there was this bouncer, and he didn't take his eyes off me and I was shitting myself . . . I was thinking, 'This bouncer is going to do me, like.' Anyway, I got into the middle of the group and we left as a group and the bouncer put his hand out and dragged me in. He said, 'Are you a Richardson?' I said, 'Yeah.' 'Pete Richardson?' I said, 'Yeah.'

'Black-beard Richardson?' I said, 'Yeah, that's me dad.' He said, 'Get your sen back in.' He took us all back into the pub, bought us all drinks and started telling these stories about the stuff they used to get up to.[23]

Lee then told his own story about the Miners' Strike. When he was thirteen and fourteen:

We used to go on picket lines. It were cold, it were snowing, and back then snow was snow . . . We had a scab on our street, his son were a mate of mine, I wasn't allowed to talk to him. We used to come home from school, there were a brick for each of us, before we even get into house, throw a brick at the window. Best years of my life, it were ace.

But there was also the darker side, because his father was sacked on his older brother Wayne's birthday and twice sent to Durham gaol. Lee recalled the horror of visiting him:

I remember going up to the doors, and they were massive, like an old castle. They opened and you had to go and stand in a cage, and from one cage to another cage. Then we were walking to the visitors' room, but we had to walk past the prisoners. A bit intimidating, scary and stuff.

His own life unfolded very much like his father's, in terms of his fighting spirit: 'I finished school on the Friday and walked into Askern sawmills on the Monday. I got sacked on my twentieth birthday.' After that he went piling for Balfour Beatty, sinking the foundations of Wembley, the new Arsenal football ground and the Shard in London. At one point, he came back to the sawmill at Askern and set up a union, because, he emphasised, 'I'm a union man because of my dad.' He got 160 men to join the Transport and General Workers' Union and became shop steward, but a year later he was made redundant. What really united Lee and his father was taking him every year to the memorial for the two Yorkshire pickets who died during the strike – held every year at the statue of a grieving miner's family outside the Barnsley headquarters of the NUM.[24]

Frustration emerged at the end of the interview, when Lee complained that his father was still locked in the strike, and that the trips to Barnsley set him off – just as if the strike had been yesterday. Lee blamed it on the drugs his father was prescribed, but Pete's eyes gleamed as he insisted that if he was locked in the strike, it was because that desperate fight – in which he was engaged up to the hilt – had made him, for better or worse, the man he was:

Lee: Can I just say, right, he got the sack, yeah. He was so much involved with Miners' Strike before it finished and after it he was so involved. But he went to the doctors and the doctors screwed him over. They started him on these really bad anti-depressants, he got upped on them and he's never been the same since. He's locked in that era, he's locked in the '80s. He's still there, he still lives there. When I take him to this NUM every year it's still raw, as if it were yesterday. And that's the doctors. The tablets they give have screwed him up and made him into the man he is now.

Peter: I don't think they have.

Lee: Well they have.

Peter: They've made me able to sleep at night.

Sue: He can't move on.

Lee: It's crazy.[25]

The last group of children of the strike might be called redeemers. Like the others, they experienced the deprivation and pain of the strike and its defeat, and the devastation of its aftermath. But – exceptionally and consciously – they worked in later life to alleviate the ills suffered by the communities in which they had been brought up. Interestingly, this profile was found also among the few grandchildren of striking miners that we interviewed. The pain was felt intergenerationally by some who had not been alive at the time, and their commitment to redeeming their struggling communities was just as extraordinary.

In County Durham, Lynn Gibson, born in 1975 and brought up in Spennymoor, came from a long line of miners:

In the late 1800s, when the [Cornish] tin mines were all closing, my dad's family migrated up to the Durham coalfield, and so looking at my family tree, both of my grandfathers were hewers in the pits here in the Durham coalfield.

Her mother's father died of the miners' disease pneumoconiosis, aged sixty-three, at the beginning of the strike. Her father was a shift charge engineer at Easington colliery who passed on his hatred of Mrs Thatcher as one who had destroyed the miners and their communities:

During the strike, I do remember Thatcher being on the news loads, and my dad spitting every time he heard her name, which he still does to this day. And I can remember going onto free school dinners at school, which was something that I obviously wasn't used to before.

After her A-levels, she took a gap year – though it ended up as eleven years. She became an army nurse and was stationed in Saudi Arabia for two years; but after 9/11, she came back to Spennymoor and found a job at Durham University in the research office. Her Damascene moment came in 2015, when Jeremy Corbyn spoke at the Durham Miners' Gala:

I was just wide-mouthed and for the first time in my life I heard a Labour politician on that stage who wanted to be leader of the party speaking with my voice; and his ideas of socialism just matched mine.

She joined the Labour Party, voted for Corbyn to be leader and progressed to becoming Spennymoor branch secretary in 2017 and secretary of the Bishop Auckland Constituency Labour Party in 2019. She also became involved in the heritage side of Durham miners' history, helping to form a Women's Banner Group to commission a women's banner for the Gala to mark the centenary of women's voting rights in 2018. Another turning point came in December 2019, when Labour lost the Bishop Auckland seat it had held since 1935. This held out the possibility of redemption for Lynn, if she could be encouraged to stand for Parliament:

> I've been asked by a lot of people to stand [laughs]. For me a good candidate would be somebody that had solid socialist principles, that had roots in a working-class background and family; not somebody who has learned socialism from, you know, an academic textbook. Certainly not a Tony Blair. A female Jeremy Corbyn I think would be perfect for me.[26]

Less political, but no less committed, was the ambition of Helen Stratford, a genuine strike baby, born six months after the strike finished. The sister of Peter Stratford and the daughter and granddaughter of miners, she was above all inspired by her mother Mary. 'When I was a bit younger,' said Helen,

> I thought maybe she had helped out in the soup kitchens. Later people told me that she was involved in Women Against Pit Closures, in getting support for families who were struggling, making her voice heard, making sure that not the world but more people knew about the Miners' Strike.

It was not until her late teens that she learned 'quite what she did in the Miners' Strike and quite how empowered it made her'. Helen became aware that, for her mother, involvement in the strike was transformational. 'If the Miners' Strike hadn't happened,' she reflected, 'my mother wouldn't have gone to university and potentially I wouldn't have got to go to university.' She described how they studied side by side in Newcastle University Library, her mother doing coursework for her probation officer training, Helen doing a school project.

Helen was encouraged to go to university and was good at maths and sciences. But she also grew up to the sight and sounds of her grandfathers slowly dying of lung disease:

My father's dad had emphysema, my mum's dad had pneumoconiosis. My memories of him are of being on oxygen and coughing quite a lot, while my mother's dad got taken off the coal face when a doctor told him he had pneumoconiosis.

She applied to medical schools, but then asked herself, 'why go further than Newcastle, a world-class medical school on my doorstep?' Beginning her training in 2004, she soon decided that although she liked working in hospitals,

I didn't want to be a high-flying surgeon. I preferred the speciality where you got to follow the patient through. I quite liked respiratory. I was well aware of the impact of working down the mines on the lungs.

She was drawn to the idea of working with families and tracing illnesses – and attitudes to illness – from generation to generation. She worked on a series of GP placements in former mining communities – Herrington in 2014 and South Hetton in 2017 – before accepting a permanent position in Pelton Fell, where the pit had closed in 1965. She realised very quickly that she was picking up the terrible social and medical legacy less now of the pits than of the pit closures:

South Hetton's definitely got problems with drugs, alcohol, offending behaviour, crime, interlinked with the drugs to be honest, unemployment.

South Hetton was definitely the most deprived, had much higher levels of obesity, quite high levels of heart and lung disease linked to smoking . . . It was clear the impact that closing the mines had had. A lot of it was the younger males who have the drug-taking and the crime. Probably the ones who were less academic and would have followed generations of going down the mine but that choice wasn't there. Or their dad had become unemployed and struggled to find work elsewhere.[27]

Over the border in Fife, Lea McClelland from Dundonald, near Cardenden, inherited characteristics from both her parents. Her father, who travelled to the mine at Seafield, was a rebel outside the home, but very caring within it. Her mother was highly intelligent and might have gone to university if she had not fallen pregnant. At Auchterderran Junior High School, said Lea,

I wanted to be in the caring profession, but I just wasn't clever enough to be a nurse. And I was kind of more like my dad at the school. My sister was really clever and really well-behaved and got to help out at the school. And I never, because I was just a wee rocket, I was just so badly behaved.

During the strike, her father was sometimes on picket lines, but mainly dug his coal hole and entertained the miners in their welfares.[28] Lea left school to work in a café in Kirkcaldy, then had a burger van and an ice cream van which her father drove, because she could not. Later she found a job at the Sky call centre in Dunfermline, responding to customers in her Fife accent.

Tragedy struck in 2001, when her mother died of bowel cancer, and in 2014, when her older brother, John, committed suicide. In the community, a young mother survived a car accident which killed her partner and her boy at the primary school. The mother was pregnant and went on to have a baby, but, according to Lea, 'They had nothing, they had no insurance, they didn't have a bean.' Then a young local woman with brain cancer needed specialist treatment that was only offered in the United States. Lea and her friends – who drank together at the Red Goth pub in Lochore and danced at Pickwick's night club in Crosshill – set up the Benarty Fundraisers. Their motto was 'One for all and all for one'. Their fundraising started with getting sponsorship for them to jump in the lake in Lochore Meadows on New Year's Day 2015. Lea's desire to retie the threads of the local community then found political expression. She was motivated by the Scottish referendum because, with two Irish grandmothers, 'I believe in Irish freedom. I believe in any country that wants to govern itself, give them a chance.' Elected an SNP councillor in Willie Clarke's former stronghold of Lochgelly, Cardenden and Benarty in May 2017, she saw it as her mission to save the local communities that, in her eyes, had been destroyed by Mrs Thatcher, who left them to the scourge of drugs:

My hatred for Margaret Thatcher has definitely led me to where I am today. I absolutely hated the woman for what she'd done to the miners; and in death I still hate her. She pillaged communities. Every single thing that we're still going through yet, was thanks to her. Even the fact that we've not got mines, I attribute that to why we've got such a huge drug problem . . . I genuinely believe that the drug issues we have is definitely because of the pits not being here and the austerity caused everywhere is thanks to her. She believed, break the miners and she can break anybody . . . I will do everything in my power to undo what she did. And it starts around here in this village, or in this ward. I'll do everything to bring employment and to give people a purpose and try and make the next generation of young people not addicted to drugs like my generation is.[29]

Kevin Payne, brought up in Ballingry in a similar family of Irish origin, but four years older than Lea McClelland, was made acutely aware of the dangers of mining and the vanishing employment prospects by his father, a fireman whose job it was to check the gas levels before the men could go down. Kevin was the youngest of five sons, and his father refused to allow any of them to work in the mine, not only because of the insecurity, but also because of the danger. 'He had seen umpteen injuries and breathing conditions and he had broken his leg at least three times down the pit,' said Kevin. 'He had seen people round here been killed, aye, down in Glencraig pit.' Later, as the strike wore on, Kevin saw 'people who were really good friends that had turned against each other'; immediately after the strike, his father, aged fifty, was made redundant on £90 a week, 'the next step up from dole money', and not allowed to apply for other work.

Following his father's advice, Kevin avoided the mine and went into the construction industry. Employed by Miller Construction, Edinburgh, he helped build a new high school at Lochgelly and set up his own business in 1993. He was shocked by the growing unemployment and poverty in the area, with 'people going as far as, not quite Aberdeen, but it's about twenty mile, thirty mile short of Aberdeen, they were going as far as that picking vegetables'. He was asked to become involved in the children's gala, held every June; and from those beginnings, in 2014 he and Lea McClelland set up the Benarty Events Group, which sat along-side the Benarty Fundraisers. They revived a pipe band competition that used to be held in Lochore Meadows and attracted competitors, often with local roots, from Australia, Canada and the United States. In 2017, they launched a music festival, Rockore. 'We have had local bands, Paris Rebels, the Other Side,' said Kevin. 'We have had chart-hitting bands, we have had The South, which is former members of the Beautiful South, Bad Manners, Nazareth.' He added, 'Every penny that the Benarty Events Group raises goes back in the community.' It also rebuilt community solidarity by bringing back together people who had long left Benarty. As he reflected,

None of us had ever done a music festival before and we had a beer tent, and we had a queue there which was concerning me because it was stretched right across the middle of the field. I went over and I met a boy who came from here, this village, and he lives in Glenrothes now. He is going, 'What is wrong with you, Kevin?' I said, 'Look at this queue.' He said, 'Leave the queue, it's the best part of it.' He says, 'I'm meeting people here that I've no met for twenty and thirty year' . . . They were all coming back, aye, that's what everybody was saying, 'Such and such is over there, remember him he used to live in Craigie Street in the '70s.' So, everybody they have all said, that it is bringing back community spirit.[30]

Among the grandchildren of mining families, three stand out as young redeemers of their local community. Interviewed in Ballingry alongside Ronnie Campbell were his daughter Margaret's son Mark, born in 1987, and Anna's daughter Marissa, born in 1993. Confronted by the devastation wrought in their village, each had tried to leave to join the army. Mark was fascinated by the war in Iraq, but his grandmother forbade him from signing up, and he found work in a dairy. Anna likewise stopped Marissa from joining up and she began to study engineering; but, like her aunt, she had a teenage pregnancy, gave birth to Lewis, who turned out to have special needs, and subsequently became a mental health support worker.

Like their parents, Mark and Marissa came to understand the connection between the defeat of the strike and the destitution of the community. They also learned about the role their grandfather had played in the strike. Mark recalled that when he was about four, his granddad

took me a walk up to the loch which is just up there, and he sat me down by the water and he basically told me what it meant to be a Campbell. We spoke quite in-depth as I got older [about] how trade unions or charities or communities [were] pulling together, [and] Thatcher would do everything in her power to stop that, but also break the spirit of people.

When he was about eight or nine, someone he knew posted a picture of himself and Ronnie on Facebook, with the caption, '"The one and only Arthur Scargill", which my dey [Fife dialect for grandfather] got called, I believe.' He added, 'That's not the first time this person's put a photo up of my grandfather and seen him as a hero.'

The breakthrough for Marissa came later, when the commission of inquiry into the victimisation of Scottish miners during the strike, which organised hearings across the former Scottish coalfields, came to the Lochgelly Centre. She spent a long time persuading her grandfather – who insisted that 'The damage is already done. Why, why bring it up now? What's the point?' – to go. She took the view that

> my granddad has lost a lot of friends over the years that were miners and I sort of blackmailed him with that route. I was like, 'Look, they can't speak up and get justice with this, you have to do it for them. I'll come with you, I'll support you and you say your piece.' That meeting was the first time I'd seen my granddad cry.

She went on:

> It was really interesting to hear all these different stories but it all had the same theme. Everybody's personal experiences were horrible. Stuff they didn't want to talk about. Stuff they wanted to forget. Some people were more vocal than others. But it was just really endearing listening to these people, seeing how brave they were bringing this all up . . . Hearing about their community spirit, hearing about their wives that would run wee cafés and make meals for other families. Hearing these people fight for their work, fight for what they believed in, refused to be knocked down by anybody. Hearing about how they were convinced the army was on stand-by to just rally into these mines and hurt these miners. Do everything they can to destroy their livelihoods. It made me really glad I wasn't around then . . . Some even committed suicide.

There was a family that was at the meeting that me and my granddad were at and it was absolutely heartbreaking. It was a woman who was, I think, maybe late forties and she just absolutely broke down in tears. Her dad had committed suicide because he couldn't face the fact of going home every night with nothing, providing nothing for his family.

When the time came, Marissa herself stood up to address the inquiry. Aged twenty-six, she made the link that her mother, aunt and grandfather made between the defeat of the strike, the pit closures and the growth of unemployment, poverty and deprivation. She made the connection between her own work – which was 'helping people who have been in prison or been in hospital for three, four years come back and adjust to living in the community' – and the blight inflicted on those communities by the strike and its defeat:

One thing I do remember saying – this was just after my granddad had spoke – if you take a look in Fife alone, at all the mining communities, so Ballingry, Kirkcaldy, Leven, all of these wee villages are rife with poverty now. There's no jobs. There's nothing. There's nothing for kids. It's just poor communities absolutely rife with poverty. People relying on food banks. People relying on grants from the benefits to help them just get by till their next pay day. And all of these villages that are the worst hit in Fife all had mining communities. There were jobs when you walked out of school back then. You walked out of school and you went right into a job. You walk out of school nowadays and you walk to the Job Centre. There was one thing that really stuck with me from that meeting. Do you know what? I felt really supported because some of the guys started clapping. There was one man at the back who stood up and just said, 'I second her.'[31]

That man, according to her grandfather, was fellow blacklisted miner Sean Lee.

The last word will be left to Caitlin Oldfield, the daughter of Sam Oldfield and granddaughter of David and Dorothy Wray, a sixth-former when she was interviewed in 2020. She learned over time first about the Durham mining community that she grew up in and then about the strike. And her grandparents were central in both these processes:

> I have always been very close with my grandparents and like as a kid going to the Gala . . . I remember I was always very excited about it. Because I mean when I was a lot younger it was exciting because I got to march in the parade, and it was the big party and stuff. But then as I got older and I kind of realised what it was about it became a lot more meaningful. Because as I grew up I learned the stuff the granddad had to do with the Miners' Strike. It meant a lot more because I knew they fought for something that they really believed in.

As with Lynn Gibson, there was also a political awakening when she met Jeremy Corbyn, first at Redhills, when he stood aside because she had broken her leg and was on crutches, 'And then the second time it was in an outdoor garden and I saw him and my granddad told me, "It's Jeremy Corbyn over there." So I went and I got a picture with him.'

This political education from her grandparents was in tension with a sense of generational conflict. Caitlin was committed to equality and had protested with Black Lives Matter. She was also sharply aware of the climate crisis and environmental issues. She felt strongly that the older generations had 'messed up' on climate change and were liable to be more racist. She saw her own generation as much more activist than previous ones, willing to come onto the streets and use social media, and she argued that sixteen-year-olds should be given the vote and allowed to stand for election to positions of power:

> It makes me dead proud that as a generation we see all these issues and we don't just say, 'Oh, that's too much to handle. We are not even going

to bother.' And we say, like, 'It is a lot; but we might as well fight for it,' because who else is going to do it, you know? . . . So I think now it's all about getting our voices heard and letting the older generations know that like we are gonna get change, we are gonna fight for it and in like ten years' time I think we will really start to see that; sort of actually in the system.

In this fight, Caitlin came back to the Miners' Strike and to her grandfather as a model of action, courage and determination. This history and this memory inspired her own generation about how to redeem society and change the world:

I always think about the Miners' Strike and how they had the power to kind of dictate what happened. I always think about how strong they were and how like most people they went on strike and stayed on strike and they kept it that way. They didn't like falter. Like my granddad, he was always adamant he never kind of went back to work in the mines and stuff. So I always think that if they could do it and if they could stand the ground for what they believed in, why can't I?[32]

CONCLUSION

The story of the Miners' Strike and its aftermath is one of triumph and tragedy, resilience and retreat, reinvention and ruin. It was a defeat in the last great industrial battle of the twentieth century, but it transformed those who were involved and left a legacy that continues to resonate today.

The strike was a defeat for the miners, who held out to defend their jobs and their industry for a whole year. It started hesitantly, but then gained momentum, and the commitment around it strengthened. It was undermined because a majority of miners from Leicestershire and the much bigger coalfield of Nottinghamshire, given assurances that their pits would not close, were never on board. This meant that flying pickets were sent out from Yorkshire, South Wales and Kent to persuade the working miners to come out – an offensive that was felt locally as an invasion and a violation of a democratic right to ballot against the strike. Although the NUM rule book allowed its Executive to make strikes that broke out in individual coalfields official, it also provided for a national ballot. No such national ballot was ever held, for fear that it would be lost (only 19 per cent of Notts miners voted to strike in the March 1983 ballot). This meant that a deficit of legitimacy could always be used as a weapon against the strike leaders.

The miners had to fragment their forces by picketing not only scores of working pits, but docks, power stations and steelworks to which coal and

410

coke were being delivered. To counter this offensive, the government mobilised the full force of the police (to arrest miners) and the courts (to convict them). Footage of miners throwing stones at advancing police lines was routinely reversed to make it seem that the miners were acting first, and the media demonised 'the enemy within'. Miners who were arrested and appeared in court were very quickly dismissed by the Coal Board and were likely to be blacklisted, unable to find any job. From the late summer of 1984, police forces occupied mining villages to protect a small number of strike-breakers who were persuaded to return to work. As autumn turned into winter, and as hunger and cold bit harder, so the trickle of returning miners increased, provoking division and anger in the villages. This hostility was increased by the return to work in March 1985, when strike-breaking miners were protected by the Coal Board and those who abused them were liable to be dismissed. After the strike, the schism was consummated as the Nottinghamshire-based Union of Democratic Mineworkers broke away, undermining the effectiveness and authority of the NUM. The famous camaraderie of the miners was in tatters.

The defeat of the strike was followed very quickly by the closure of the pits it was launched to defend. By the time the coal industry was privatised in 1993, only 16 mines remained of the 219 operating in 1980.[1] Miners in Nottinghamshire, who had been promised that their pits would stay open, did not escape the cull. All this came as a profound shock. Mining was generally regarded as a job for life, since, in popular thinking, an industrial country would always need coal. Unlike in deindustrialising countries like France, the British government had no schemes to find work for miners without jobs: they were left to fend for themselves. Redundancy, as we have seen, was often felt as a loss or bereavement, and was related in miners' narratives to other losses, such as that of their father or spouse. Some redundant miners did not long survive the defeat. They were left with miners' diseases or grief, and were soon buried by their wives. The strike put marriages under pressure, as miners were often away picketing and campaigning and, treated as heroes, were not always faithful. Now they were defeated on the battlefield, no longer earning, languishing at home, while their wives went out to work.

Where they did find jobs, these did not require the same skills, pay the same wages or have the same status as minework. Now they were part of an increasingly globalised economy that was characterised by the casualisation of work, the outsourcing of production abroad and the in-migration of labour. Although as miners they had increasingly been forced to travel to pits, now they had to travel further to work on North Sea oil rigs or the Channel Tunnel, work as hauliers or move from contractor to contractor, factory to factory.

Closer to home, they might find work with the local council, but this would involve cleaning schools, mowing lawns or emptying bins. Periods of work would be combined with spells of unemployment, when they would go cap in hand to the job centre or benefit office. Some felt that they were competing for work or benefits with foreign workers. All this was a massive blow to the once proud miners' traditional sense of their masculinity, which was based on the three pillars of being a fighter, a breadwinner and a protector of their womenfolk (not to mention their patriotic sense of being English, Welsh or Scottish).

The slogan 'Close a Pit, Kill a Community' came to pass. Headstocks, which symbolised the presence of the mine, were demolished. Former bustling mining villages, even when they were places where miners lived rather than worked, were blighted. As the pits closed, so did other businesses, shops, post offices, cinemas and swimming pools. Local schools closed and children had to be bussed for their education to nearby towns. The Miners' Welfare and working men's clubs were frequented less and less. There was no love lost in the villages between those who had stayed out on strike and those who had gone back to work. As Dorothy Wray said of a strike-breaker in Leadgate, 'if you were on fire in the street I wouldn't spit to put it out'.

Generationally, the closure of the pits had a devastating impact on young people, particularly young men. Formerly, even with few or no qualifications, they would have begun work in the pit at fifteen and be given day-release training in the local college for several years. Now they had no prospects. Social problems developed – first alcoholism, then drugs – and there was an upsurge in the attendant crime. The children of miners were often the casualties of pit closures, unemployment and the increasing fragility of family life. Some struggled to keep afloat in their work and relationships; others succumbed along the way.

Politically, too, there was change. The traditional interlock of the Labour Party and the trade unions was broken, with Labour increasingly being regarded as middle class, distant, and no longer with the interests of working people at its heart. The austerity measures of Conservative governments after 2010, which undermined local services, were often blamed by voters on local Labour councils, rather than on central government. Brexit was seized upon by many in the former mining communities as an answer to their sense of disempowerment. An albeit small sample of ninety-six former miners and miners' wives voted 70 per cent to leave the EU in Leicestershire; 64 per cent in Nottinghamshire; 54 per cent in Yorkshire; 44 per cent in Fife; 33 per cent in South Wales; and 8 per cent in County Durham. 'I can't wait to get out of it, to be honest with you' was the terse comment of one ex-miner in the Dulais Valley. Nigel Jeffery, in Leicestershire, was concerned about immigration, sovereignty and what he perceived as a threat to Britishness:

> So, yeah, I voted to leave, Brexit, thinking, you just want this country to be more British and to stop growing. You know, we are only a small island. Do we need all these foreign people coming over? . . . Everywhere we go, it's all foreign, whether it be girls in the office, whether it be supervisors, whether it be foremen and what have you, they're all foreign. There's no English. And I think it's just got too much. It really has you know. We're just not British anymore, you know, it's just unreal . . . And personally, myself, I think Brussels is run by the Germans. The main people who have got the jobs up there are the Germans; now they're dictating all over Europe.[2]

And yet. The Miners' Strike and its aftermath was not all negative. The fact that 142,000 miners had held out against the Thatcher government, the Coal Board and the media for a whole year, accounting for the loss of 27 million working days, was a source of pride among miners and their supporters. They had been strongly supported by railway workers, who refused to move coal and forced the Coal Board to use fleets of lorries, which famously provoked picketing by men, women and children at Cartmore, outside Lochgelly, in June 1984. The strike was supported by a large number of other blue- and white-collar unions, including printers' unions, NALGO, NUPE and the NUT. Miners' children were invited on holiday by trade unions in Ireland and Europe; money and food flowed in from there, especially at Christmas time; and miners and miners' wives travelled there towards the end of the strike to raise money. After it was over, striking miners were treated as heroes in the United States and East Germany. Miners, their wives and supporters were steeled to support other strikes, such as the Wapping printers' strike of 1986. They were also politicised and moved to support other revolutionary movements globally, such as the anti-apartheid movement in South Africa and the Sandinistas in Nicaragua.

The closure of the pits forced miners and their wives to investigate other opportunities for work. Many of them went back to continue an education and training they had left at fifteen or sixteen for work or family, having been reminded how bright they were and having gained experience of the world outside their community during the strike. Adult education, especially for miners' wives, was developed at the DOVE workshop at Banwen, at the head of the Dulais Valley. The reforms of 1992, which elevated polytechnics to the status of universities, came at just the right time for this cohort. Dorothy Wray went to Newcastle Polytechnic before it became Northumbria University; Mary Stratford after. David Wray went to the University of Durham, Betty Cook to Sheffield, Siân James to Swansea. A few former miners went into research, reflecting on and writing about the mining industry and mining communities. Others, like David Hopkins and David Potts, taught at North Notts College in Worksop.

Here there was something of a gender revolution. Miners' wives had been transformed by the strike. They had been involved in setting up local support groups, which came together in Women Against Pit Closures. They learned to organise soup kitchens and the distribution of food parcels to striking families on a large scale. They stood on picket lines when their men had been arrested or were in danger of arrest. They became involved in fundraising, travelling to make speeches in support of the strike, meeting other trade unionists and left-wing groups that were hoping to promote it. They came into contact with middle-class feminists, learned a good deal from them, but developed a working-class feminism and broke with them when they felt patronised. The Welsh miners who met the London gays may not have been much affected, but their wives learned a great deal about sexuality and intimacy. It is often said that where the women wanted the men to stay out, they stayed out; where the women wanted them to go back to work, they went back. Women gained in experience and confidence and began to take a long, hard look at their marriages. Marriages had to evolve to take the strain, with the men happy to do child care if their wives had a public engagement. If the marriage could not bear it – and many did not – the women would move on and go back to education and better-qualified work without the men. The marriages that survived became more equal, and the men had to develop a new form of masculinity that was less macho and more caring. Very significant is the number of ex-miners who found work caring for old people, or children, or those with problems of mental health, alcoholism or drugs.

This brings us to the question of former mining communities. Given that there was so little government attempt at regeneration, and that what regeneration there was was so poor, communities had to be saved from the bottom up. It is significant that so many former miners and their wives went into professions that had a direct impact on their communities, weaving back together the social ties that had been pulled apart. In County Durham, for example, Mary Stratford became a probation officer, while Dorothy Wray, Peter Byrne and Kath Savory all became social workers. In Fife, meanwhile, a good batch of men – Sean Lee, Terry Ratcliffe, Peter McCutcheon – became carers of one sort or another. Expertise in welfare rights was developed by Pat Egan in Glenrothes, Anna Lawson in Consett and Darren Moore in Leicester, where his partner, Simone Dawes, worked with Rape Crisis.

Following a parallel line, many former miners and their families became involved in preserving the heritage of their communities. We have seen that there was a revival of banner making in the former pit villages of County Durham, which was part of what Dave Wray and Carol Stephenson called rebuilding them as 'emotional communities'. Organisations such as Education 4 Action in Durham and Mine 2 Minds in Nottingham were set up to pass on the mining heritage to children who may well never have encountered a lump of coal. Finally, a small but significant number of miners and miners' wives went into local politics – in Lochgelly, Cardenden and Benarty, Easington, Doncaster, Worksop and Neath – in order to deal with the challenge of redeeming their lost communities, while Siân James and Hywel Francis became MPs.

Generationally, we have seen that while some children in mining families were casualties or survivors of the strike and pit closures, others were their parents' heirs and redeemers. Some went into teaching and either – like Dafydd Francis – returned to work in the former mining community or – even if they did not return, like Jude Bevan – encouraged thinking about it. In County Durham, Helen Stratford, a strike baby, trained as a GP and worked in former mining communities, dealing with both old miners' lung diseases and the newer issues of alcoholism, drugs and obesity that haunted devastated former mining villages. In Benarty, Fife, a group of miners' children set up local fundraising and events organisations in order to help struggling local families; organise galas and concerts; and celebrate the history and culture of the local community.

Politically, former mining families, particularly in Fife, County Durham and South Wales, were by no means typical examples of a 'Red Wall' that crumbled into Brexit and voted for the Conservatives in the 2019 election. Kath Savory in County Durham voted Leave 'because it would be wonderful if we could have our country back again and have all those things'. She thought of voting in Boris Johnson 'because he seemed to offer more', but then she heard the voice of her dead miner father and 'at the last minute I changed my mind and voted Labour. Because I could hear my dad, "You better vote Labour. You cannot vote anything else." So I voted Labour.'[3] Meanwhile, Yorkshire miner Paul Winter, who had been at Orgreave, concluded that the British public had been taken in by the lies and illusion spun around Brexit:

> Brexit fetched all them people out who don't vote and were pillocked by a narrative, 'Let's get rid of all immigrants, let's put Britain first,' and then three words that Boris said, 'Get Brexit done,' and it won him an election. He hadn't a policy, he hadn't a manifesto, he hadn't got a fucking clue, hadn't Boris Johnson, but he said, 'Get Brexit done,' and he won an election and Corbyn lost. I can't believe that the public got pillocked like that, but they did.[4]

The Miners' Strike of 1984–85 still matters, forty years on. Admittedly, the coal industry does not have a good press in an era of climate crisis generated by fossil fuels. The authorisation of a new coal mine in Cumbria by the Conservative government in December 2022 met with widespread criticism on account of its effect on climate change targets. It may have been a challenge to the question of levelling up communities that were hollowed out by pit closures decades ago and that remain devastated; but a much more ambitious programme of levelling up post-industrial areas of the country is needed more urgently than ever. The question of the state's brutal suppression of the strike has been answered in part by Scotland, thanks to its devolved administration, and a pardon has been issued to miners who were unjustly convicted. In England and Wales, however, where an independent inquiry into what happened at Orgreave was refused by the Home Office in 2016, this question remains to be dealt with, and the Orgreave Truth and Justice Campaign is still live. Lastly, the breakdown of the neo-liberal project based on globalisation, privatisation, casualisation and immiseration has come up against the cost-of-living crisis and has provoked a series of strikes in 2022–23 not seen since the last century. The Miners' Strike and the voices of the men and women who sustained it for a year can offer guidance and hope.

LOCATIONS OF INTERVIEWEES

Location		Totals	Location		Totals
South Wales		**24**	**County Durham**		**27**
	Neath, Dulais & Swansea Valleys	16		Easington	1
	Afan, Llynfi & Cynon Valleys	7		Chester-le-Street & Lumley	12
	Cardiff	1		Durham City	4
Leicestershire		**14**		Stanley	2
	Coalville & Ibstock	5		Sacriston	1
	Barlestone & Desford	4		Leadgate & Blackhill	5
	Stoney Stanton & Stapleton	3		Spennymoor	2
	Loughborough	1	**Fife**		**27**
	Leicester	1		Lochore, Ballingry & Crosshill (Benarty)	19
Nottinghamshire		**23**		Lochgelly & Cardenden	2
	Annesley, Kirkby- & Sutton-in-Ashfield	6		Cowdenbeath	4
	Warsop	7		Glenrothes	1
	Worksop/Manton	10		West Wemyss	1
Yorkshire		**24**	**Outside activists**		**9**
	Askern	11		London	5
	Bentley & Dunscroft	3		Leicester	2
	Barnsley	7		United States	2
	Sheffield	2			
	Castleford	1	**TOTAL**		**148**

NOTES

INTRODUCTION

1. Interview with Thomas Watson, Ballingry, 16 June 2021.
2. Ferdynand Zweig, *The British Worker* (London: Penguin, 1952), 208.
3. Interview with Heather Wood, Easington, 25 June 2021.
4. See, for example, J.D. Chambers, *The Workshop of the World: British economic history from 1820 to 1880* (London: Oxford University Press, 1961); Peter Mathias, *The First Industrial Nation: An economic history of Britain, 1700–1914* (London: Methuen, 1969).
5. Roy Church, *The History of the British Coal Industry*, vol. III: *1830–1913: Victorian Pre-eminence* (Oxford: Clarendon Press, 1986), 2, 18–48, 86, 189–91.
6. Hywel Francis and David Smith, *The Fed: A history of the South Wales miners in the twentieth century* (London: Lawrence & Wishart, 1980), 11.
7. Hywel Francis, 'My community, my village: Onllwyn, Cwn Dulais', in Francis, *Stories of Solidarity* (Ceredigion: Y Lolfa, 2018), 87–90.
8. Gordon Smith, *Askern Spa* (1968), reprinted with further photographs added by Symeon Mark Waller (Sprotbrough: Doncaster History, 2013); Dave Fordham, *Askern Main Colliery and Instoneville: Early development* (Doncaster: Fedj-el-Adoum, 2010).
9. David Munro, *Lochore Meadows: The making of a Fife landscape* (Glenrothes: Fife Council, 2012), 24–5, 37–8.
10. Peter Bartrip and Susan Burman, *The Wounded Soldiers of Industry: Industrial compensations policy, 1833–97* (Oxford: Clarendon Press, 1983), 47.
11. Brian Elliott, *South Yorkshire Mining Disasters*, vol. I: *The Nineteenth Century* (Barnsley: Wharncliffe Books, 2006), 96–128.
12. John H. Brown, *The Valley of the Shadow: An account of Britain's worst mining disaster: The Senghenydd explosion* (Port Talbot: Alun Books, 1981); Jeremy Paxman, *Black Gold: The history of how coal made Britain* (London: William Collins, 2021), 144–55.
13. R. Page Arnot, *The Miners: A history of the Miners' Federation of Great Britain, 1889–1910* (London: George Allen & Unwin, 1949).
14. Richard Fynes, *The Miners of Northumberland and Durham: A history of their social and political progress* (Wakefield: S.R. Publishers, 1971), 17–40.
15. Ken Smith and Jean Smith, *Splendour of the Gala: The Durham Miners' Gala and the Northumberland miners' picnic* (Durham: Ergo Press, 2009), 2–6.
16. Huw Beynon and Terry Austrin, *Masters and Servants: Class and patronage in the making of a labour organisation: The Durham miners and the English political tradition* (London: Rivers Oram Press, 1994), 51–77.

17. Richard G. Neville, 'The Yorkshire miners and the 1893 lockout: The Featherstone "massacre"', *International Review of Social History* 21/3 (1976), 337–57.
18. Gwyn Evans and David Maddox, *The Tonypandy Riots 1910–11* (Plymouth: University of Plymouth Press, 2010).
19. R. Page Arnot, *The Miners: Years of struggle. A history of the Miners' Federation of Great Britain, from 1910 onwards* (London: George Allen & Unwin, 1953), 101–70; Beynon and Austrin, *Masters and Servants*, 19–21; Francis and Smith, *The Fed*, 14–27.
20. Arnot, *The Miners: Years of struggle*, 300–1.
21. ibid., 421–506; Huw Beynon and Ray Hudson, *The Shadow of the Mine: Coal and the end of industrial Britain* (London: Verso, 2021), 22–4; Paxman, *Black Gold*, 198–203.
22. Nina Fishman, *Arthur Horner: A political biography*, 2 vols (London: Lawrence & Wishart, 2010).
23. Arnot, *The Miners: Years of struggle*, 494–506; Alan R. Griffin, *The Miners of Nottinghamshire, 1914–44: A history of the Nottinghamshire miners' union* (London: George Allen & Unwin, 1962), 163–208; Robert J. Waller, *The Dukeries Transformed: The social and political development of a twentieth century coalfield* (Oxford: Clarendon Press, 1983), 108–29.
24. Barry Supple, *The History of the British Coal Industry*, vol. IV: *1913–46: The political economy of decline* (Oxford: Clarendon Press, 1987), 10.
25. Beynon and Hudson, *The Shadow of the Mine*, 34.
26. https://www.youtube.com/watch?v=708q7LjMGso
27. Interview with Peter Byrne, Blackhill, Consett, 9 Sept. 2020.
28. Arthur McIvor and Ronald Johnson, *Miners' Lung: A history of dust disease in British coalmining* (Aldershot & Burlington: Ashgate, 2007), 55–7.
29. Jim Phillips, 'The meanings of coal community in Britain since 1947', *Contemporary British History* 32/1 (2018), 43.
30. William Ashworth, *The History of the British Coal Industry*, vol. V: *1946–1982: The Nationalized Industry* (Oxford: Clarendon Press, 1986), 672–5.
31. Daryl Leeworthy, *Labour Country: Political radicalism and social democracy in South Wales, 1831–1985* (Cardigan: Parthian Books, 2018), 457.
32. Miles K. Oglethorpe, *Scottish Collieries: An inventory of the Scottish coal industry in the nationalised era* (Edinburgh and Newtongrange: Royal Commission on the Ancient and Historical Monuments of Scotland and the Scottish Mining Museum, 2006); Guthrie Hutton, *Fife: The mining kingdom* (Catrine: Stenlake Publishing, 1999).
33. Interview with Dave Douglass, South Shields, 15 Oct. 2020; interview with Maureen Douglass, Norwich, 3 May 2021.
34. Interview with David Amos, Eastwood, 21 May 2021.
35. Ashworth, *The History*, vol. V, 304.
36. Dave Douglass, *The Wheel's Still in Spin: A coalminer's Mahabharata* (Hastings: Read 'n' Noir, 2009), 70, 81–2, 102, 111; Interview with Dave Douglass, South Shields, 15 Oct. 2020; Douglass, *Pit Life in County Durham: Rank and file movements and workers' control* (Oxford: History Workshop, 1972); Douglass, *Pit Talk in County Durham: A glossary of miners' talk together with memories of Wardley colliery, pit songs and piliking* (Oxford: History Workshop, 1974).
37. Arthur Scargill, 'The new unionism', *New Left Review* I/92 (July/Aug. 1975).
38. Ashworth, *The History*, vol. V, 307–16.
39. ibid., 331–9.
40. Paxman, *Black Gold*, 43–5.
41. D.H. Lawrence, *Sons and Lovers* (Oxford: Oxford University Press, 1995), 6.
42. Beynon and Hudson, *The Shadow of the Mine*, 18.
43. David Hopkins, *Pit Talk: Memories of Manton colliery* (Nottingham: Nottinghamshire County Council, 2000), 61–3.
44. Fordham, *Askern Main Colliery*.

45. Alex Maxwell and Les Cooney (eds), *No More Bings in Benarty: An account of the rise and fall of coal mining in Scotland, and its influence on the lives of the people who lived there* (Benarty: Benarty Mining Heritage Group, 1992), 56–65.

46. Francis and Smith, *The Fed*, 55–8.

47. Interview with Kath Savory, Chester-le-Street, 13 Sept. 2020.

48. Interview with Josie Potts, Worksop, 17 May 2021.

49. Jayne D. Headon, *Mrs Hellfire 'You said it!': The life and endeavours of Hefina Headon with memoirs told by family and friends*, second edition (Wrexham: Headon Publishing, 2017), 29.

50. Interview with Ronnie and Anna Campbell, and Margaret Todd, Lochore, 17 June 2021.

51. Interview with Sean Lee, Lochore, 21 June 2021; interview with Carol and Robert (Rosco) Ross, Cowdenbeath, 15 June 2021.

52. Interview with Cliff Jeffery, Trearddur Bay, Anglesey, 20 July 2021.

53. Interview with David Potts, Everton, Notts, 19 May 2021.

54. Interview with Paul Stratford, Great Lumley, 11 Sept. 2020.

55. Interview with Steve Williamson, Clay Cross, 27 May 2021.

56. Interview with Betty Cook and Anne Scargill, Barnsley, 8 Oct. 2020.

57. Headon, *Mrs Hellfire*, 7–18.

58. Interview with Sue, Lee and Pete Richardson, Askern, 10 Oct. 2020.

59. Interview with Pete Richardson, Askern, 1 Sept. 2020.

60. Angela John, *By the Sweat of their Brows: Women workers at Victorian coal mines* (London: Croom Helm, 1980), 228–9.

61. Interview with Jean Crane, Askern, 5 Oct. 2020.

62. Interview with Dianne Hogg, Askern, 1 Sept. 2020.

63. Interview with Marilyn and Philip James, Seven Sisters, Dulais Valley, 9 Jan. 2020.

64. Interview with Christine Powell, Seven Sisters, Dulais Valley, 17 Sept. 2019.

65. Interview with Donna Jones, Blaengwynfi, 19 Sept. 2019.

66. Interview with Kath Savory, Chester-le-Street, 13 Sept. 2020.

67. Interview with Mary Stratford, Great Lumley, 11 Sept. 2020.

68. Lynn Abrams, 'Memory as both source and subject of study: The transformations of oral history', in Stefan Berger and Bill Niven (eds), *Writing the History of Memory* (London: Bloomsbury Academic, 2014), 89–109.

69. On the use of existing interviews, see Joanna Bornat, 'Secondary analysis in reflection: Some experiences of re-use from an oral history perspective', *Families, Relationships and Societies* 2/2 (2013), 309–17.

70. Hywel Francis, 'From the miners' library to the community university: A personal backstory (1959–94)', typescript, 2018, at https://collections.swansea.ac.uk/s/swansea-2020/page/miners-library

71. See https://www.bl.uk/national-life-stories

72. On the unreliability of memory see Lynn Abrams, *Oral History Theory* (Abingdon & New York: Routledge, 2010), 5–9.

73. Paxman, *Black Coal*; Beynon and Hudson, *The Shadow of the Mine*.

74. Raphael Samuel, Barbara Bloomfield and Guy Boanas (eds), *The Enemy Within: Pit villages and the miners' strike of 1984–5* (London and New York: Routledge & Kegan Paul, 1986); Seumas Milne, *The Enemy Within: The secret war against the miners*, fourth edition (London: Verso, 2014); Jim Coulter, Susan Miller and Martin Walker, *A State of Siege: Miners' Strike 1984 – Politics and policing in the coal fields* (London: Canary Press, 1984); Martin Walker and Susan Miller, *The Iron Fist: A state of siege*, vol. II: *A Report to the Yorkshire Area, NUM* (London: Yorkshire Area NUM & Greenwich NALGO, 1984); Chris Harman, *The Miners' Strike and the Struggle for Socialism* (London: Socialist Workers Party, 1985); Bob Fine and Robert Millar (eds), *Policing the Miners' Strike* (London: Lawrence & Wishart, 1985); David Reed and Olivia Adamson, *Miners' Strike, 1984–85: People versus state* (London: Larkin Publishers, 1985); and Peter Wilsher, Donald Macintyre and Michael Jones, *Strike: Thatcher, Scargill and the Miners* (London: Andre Deutsch, 1985).

75. David Waddington, Maggie Wykes and Chas Critcher, *Split at the Seams? Community, continuity and change after the 1984–5 coal dispute* (Milton Keynes: Open University Press, 1991); Andrew J. Richards, *Miners on Strike: Class solidarity and division in Britain* (London: Bloomsbury, 1996); Francis Beckett and David Henke, *Marching to the Fault Line: The 1984 miners' strike and the death of industrial Britain* (London: Constable, 2009); Beverley Trounce, *From a Rock to a Hard Place: Memories of the 1984/85 miners' strike* (Stroud: The History Press, 2015); and David Feickert, *Britain's Civil War over Coal: An insider's view*, ed. David Creedy and Duncan France (Newcastle upon Tyne: Cambridge Scholars Publishing, 2021).

76. Hywel Francis, *History on Our Side: Wales and the 1984–85 miners' strike*, second edition (London: Lawrence & Wishart, 2015); Ben Curtis, *The South Wales Miners, 1964–85* (Cardiff: University of Wales Press, 2013); Jim Phillips, *Collieries, Communities and the Miners' Strike in Scotland, 1984–85* (Manchester: Manchester University Press, 2014); Phillips, *Scottish Coal Miners in the Twentieth Century* (Edinburgh: Edinburgh University Press, 2019); Keith Pattison and David Peace, *No Redemption: The 1984–85 miners' strike in the Durham coalfield* (Newcastle: Flambard Press, 2010); Mary Patricia McIntyre, 'The response to the 1984–5 miners' strike in County Durham', PhD thesis, Durham University, 1992; Jonathan Winterton and Ruth Winterton, *Coal, Crisis and Conflict: The 1984–85 miners' strike in Yorkshire* (Manchester: Manchester University Press, 1989); Peter Gibbon and David Steyne, *Thurcroft: A village and the miners' strike* (Nottingham: Spokesman Books, 1986); Colin Griffin, 'Notts have a very particular theory', *Historical Studies in Industrial Relations*, 19 (Spring 2005), 63–99; Griffin, *The Miners of Nottinghamshire*; Harry Paterson, *Look Back in Anger: The miners' strike in Nottinghamshire thirty years on* (Nottingham: Five Leaves, 2014); David Amos, *The Miners of Nottinghamshire: A history of the Nottinghamshire miners' trade unions*, vol. IV: *1980–85* (Mansfield: Union of Democratic Mineworkers, 2013); Colin Griffin, *The Leicestershire Miners*, vol. III: *1945–88* (Coalville: National Union of Miners, Leicester Area, 1989); David Bell, *The Dirty Thirty: Heroes of the miners' strike* (Nottingham: Five Leaves, 2009); Diarmaid Kelliher, *Making Cultures of Solidarity: London and the 1984–85 miners' strike* (London: Routledge, 2021).

77. Vicky Seddon (ed.), *The Cutting Edge: Women and the pit strike* (London: Lawrence & Wishart, 1986); Joan Witham, *Hearts and Minds: The story of the women of Nottinghamshire in the miners' strike, 1984–85* (London: Canary Press, 1986); Jean Stead, *Never the Same Again: Women and the miners' strike, 1984–85* (London: Women's Press, 1987); Triona Holden, *Queen Coal: Women of the miners' strike* (Stroud: The History Press Ltd, 2005); Jean Spence and Carol Stephenson, 'Female involvement in the miners' strike 1984–1985: Trajectories of activism', *Sociological Research Online* 12/1 (2007), 1–11.

78. Holden, *Queen Coal*; Spence and Stephenson, 'Female involvement in the miners' strike'; Florence Sutcliffe-Braithwaite and Natalie Thomlinson, 'National Women Against Pit Closures: Gender, trade unionism and community activism in the miners' strike, 1984–5', *Contemporary British History* 32/1 (2018), 78–100; Florence Sutcliffe-Braithwaite and Natalie Thomlinson, *Women and the Miners' Strike, 1984-85* (Oxford: Oxford University Press, 2023).

79. Jackie Keating, *Counting the Cost: A family in the miners' strike* (Barnsley: Pen & Sword Books, 1991).

80. Linda McDowell, *Redundant Masculinities? Employment change and white working-class youth* (Oxford: Blackwell, 2003); Michael R.M. Ward, *From Labouring to Learning: Working-class masculinities, education and de-industrialization* (London: Palgrave Macmillan, 2015); Helen Smith, *Masculinity, Class and Same-Sex Desire in Industrial England, 1895–1957* (London: Palgrave Macmillan, 2015).

81. Ray Hudson and David Sadler, *A Tale of Two Industries: The contraction of coal and steel in the north east of England* (Milton Keynes: Open University Press, 1991); Christina Beatty and Stephen Fothergill, 'Labour market adjustment in areas of chronic industrial decline: The case of the UK coalfields', *Regional Studies* 30/7 (1996), 627–40; and Jim Phillips, 'Deindustrialization and the moral economy of the Scottish coalfields, 1947 to 1991', *International Labor and Working-Class History* 84/1 (2013), 95–115; Alice Mah, 'Memory,

uncertainty and industrial ruination: Walker Riverside, Newcastle-upon-Tyne', *International Journal of Urban and Regional Research* 34/2 (2010), 398–413; Jay Emery, 'Geographies of deindustrialization and the working class: Industrial ruination, legacies, and affect', *Geography Compass* 13/2 (2019), 1–14; Andy Clark, *Fighting Deindustrialisation: Scottish women's factory occupations, 1981–1982* (Liverpool: Liverpool University Press, 2022).

82. Eric Hobsbawm, 'The Forward March of Labour halted?', in Martin Jacques and Francis Mulhern (eds), *The Forward March of Labour Halted?* (London: Verso and NLB, 1981), 1–19; Ellen Meiksins Wood, *The Retreat from Class: A new 'true' socialism* (London: Verso, 1986); Ross McKibbin, *Ideologies of Class: Social relations in Britain* (Oxford: Oxford University Press, 1990); Selina Todd, *The People: The rise and fall of the working class, 1910–2010* (London: John Murray, 2014).

83. 'Boris Johnson faces backlash over Thatcher coal mines comment', 6 August 2021, https://www.bbc.co.uk/news/uk-politics-58107009

84. https://www.gov.scot/publications/independent-review-impact-communities-policing-miners-strike-1984-85

85. Deborah Mattinson, *Beyond the Red Wall: Why Labour lost, how the Conservatives won and what will happen next?* (London: Biteback, 2020).

86. https://leftfootforward.org/2023/02/mick-lynch-says-the-working-class-are-back-in-rousing-picket-line-speech/

CHAPTER 1 STOP–START

1. Telephone conversation with Siân James, Neath, 10 Mar. 2021.
2. The Ridley Report, July 1977. Margaret Thatcher Foundation, https://www.margaretthatcher.org/document/110795
3. Charles Moore, *Margaret Thatcher: The authorized biography*, vol. 1 (London: Penguin, 2013), 537; Paxman, *Black Coal*, 312.
4. Kenneth O. Morgan, *Labour People: Leaders and lieutenants, Hardie to Kinnock* (Oxford and New York: Oxford University Press, 1992), 291.
5. Phillips, *Scottish Coal Miners*, 281–2.
6. David Douglass, *Ghost Dancers: The miners' last generation* (Hastings: Read 'n' Noir, 2010), 3.
7. ibid., 13–19.
8. Interview with David Potts, Everton, Notts, 19 May 2021.
9. Ian Isaac, *When We Were Miners* (Carmarthen: Ken Smith Press, 2010), 14–18, 22.
10. Interview with Phil White, Maesteg, 9 Jan. 2020.
11. Hywel Francis and Siân Williams, *Do Miners Read Dickens? Origins and progress of the South Wales Miners' Library, 1973–2013* (Cardigan: Parthian, 2013); interview with Hywel Francis, Banwen, 16 Sept. 2019; tributes by Angela John, Dai Smith and Wayne David MP, at a celebration of Hywel's life, Onllwyn, 11 June 2022.
12. Interview with Phil White, Maesteg, 9 Jan. 2020.
13. Interview with Paul Stratford, Great Lumley, 11 Sept. 2020.
14. https://www.durhamminers.org/dave_hopper_1943_2016
15. Interview with Iain Chalmers, Cowdenbeath, 14 June 2021.
16. Interview with Sean Lee, Lochore, 21 June 2021.
17. Beynon and Hudson, *The Shadow of the Mine*, 88–9.
18. ibid., 89–91.
19. Moore, *Margaret Thatcher*, vol. I, 527, 608, 629–32.
20. ibid., 539.
21. ibid.
22. Morgan, *Labour People*, 293.
23. Michael Crick, *Scargill and the Miners* (London: Penguin, 1985), 90–3.
24. http://num.org.uk/wp-content/uploads/2015/11/1982-Presidents-Address-05-07-1982-Arthur-Scargill.pdf

25. http://www.margaretthatcher.org/document/104989. Cited in Robert Gildea, *Empires of the Mind: The colonial past and the politics of the present* (Cambridge: CUP, 2019), 138.
26. Phillips, *Scottish Coal Miners*, 234–5.
27. John McCormack, with Simon Pirani, *Polmaise: The fight for a pit* (London: Index Books, 1989), 14.
28. ibid., 14–16; Phillips, *Collieries, Communities and the Miners' Strike*, 61;
29. South Wales Coal Collection (SWCC) AUD 465, interview with Des Dutfield, conducted by Hywel Francis, 6 Mar. 1986.
30. Curtis, *The South Wales Miners*, 188–9.
31. SWCC AUD 466/2, interview with Peter Evans, conducted by Hywel Francis, 6 Mar. 1986.
32. SWCC AUD 574, interview with Emlyn Williams, conducted by Hywel Francis, 6 Jan. 1986.
33. Douglass, *Ghost Dancers*, 33
34. Interview with Dave Douglass, South Shields, 15 Oct. 2020.
35. Beynon and Hudson, *The Shadow of the Mine*, 102.
36. Phillips, *Scottish Coal Miners*, 236; Paxman, *Black Coal*, 313–14.
37. Phillips, *Scottish Coal Miners*, 238–9.
38. Interview with Tom Adams, West Wemyss, 17 June 2021.
39. McCormack, *Polmaise*, 17–28, 41–2; Phillips, *Collieries, Communities and the Miners' Strike*, 68–72; Phillips, *Scottish Coal Miners*, 236–9.
40. Interview with Iain Chalmers, Cowdenbeath, 14 June 2021.
41. Phillips, *Scottish Coal Miners*, 239.
42. Interview with Dave Douglass, South Shields, 15 Oct. 2020.
43. Douglass, *Ghost Dancers*, 35–6.
44. University of Sunderland, Murray Library NUM DA 1/3/54, NUM (Durham Area) Minutes of the Executive Committee, 1984.
45. Interview with David Wray, Shotley Bridge, 7 Sept. 2020.
46. Beynon and Hudson, *The Shadow of the Mine*, 112.
47. Curtis, *The South Wales Miners*, 199.
48. Isaac, *When We Were Miners*, 40.
49. SWCC AUD 514/1, interview with Lyn Harper, conducted by Hywel Francis, 21 Jan. 1986.
50. Interview with Phil and Kay Bowen, Resolven, 20 Sept. 2019.
51. Interview with Hywel Francis, Banwen, 16 Sept. 2019.
52. Interview with Ann and Dai John Jones, Hirwaun, 7 Jan. 2020.
53. Interview with Hywel Francis, Banwen, 16 Sept. 2019.
54. Interview with David Potts, Everton, Notts, 19 May 2021.
55. Nottinghamshire Archives DD NLHA/3/1/48, David Hopkins interview with himself, 13 Feb. 2000; interview with David Hopkins, Worksop, 20 May 2021.
56. Cited in David Amos, *The Miners of Nottinghamshire*, vol. IV, 50, 252.
57. Interview with Steve Williamson, Clay Cross, 27 May 2021.
58. Interview with David Amos, Eastwood, 21 May 2021.
59. *Leicester Mercury*, 23 Mar. 1984, cited in Griffin, *The Leicestershire Miners*, vol. III, 198.
60. Interview with Margaret and Claire Pinnegar, Hinckley, 15 Apr. 2021.
61. Interview with Mick Richmond and Marisa Cortes Richmond, Whitwick, Coalville, 14 Apr. 2021.
62. Interview with Kay Riley, online from Brittany, 20 Apr. 2021.
63. Interview with Nigel and Wendy Jeffery, Barlestone, 11 Apr. 2021.
64. Interview with Cliff Jeffery, Trearddur Bay, Anglesey, 20 July 2021.
65. Interview with Bobby and Sam Girvan, Ravenstone, 26 May 2021.
66. Interview with Mel Elcock, Loughborough, 13 Apr. 2021.
67. Interview with Darren Moore, Hinckley, 12 Apr. 2021.

CHAPTER 2 PICKETING OUT

1. Douglass, *Ghost Dancers*, 60.
2. Interview with Dave Douglass, South Shields, 15 Oct. 2020.
3. Barry Loveday, 'Central coordination, police authorities and the miners' strike', *Political Quarterly* 57/1 (1986), 60–73; Moore, *Margaret Thatcher*, vol. II, 147–9.
4. Sheffield City Archives (SCA), SY 691, interview with Mike Porter, 14 Jan. 1986.
5. SCA SY 691, interview with Peter Richardson, 13 Jan. 1986.
6. ibid.
7. SCA SY 692/1, Peter Richardson, 'Confessions of a Picket', vol. I.
8. Interview with Charlie Hogarth, Bentley, 6 Oct. 2020.
9. Interview with David Potts, Everton, Notts, 19 May 2021.
10. Interview with Paul and Adam Winter, Huddersfield, 23 Oct. 2021.
11. Alan Cowell, 'Thatcher debated using military in 1984 miners' strike', *New York Times*, 4 January 2014.
12. Interview with Dave Douglass, South Shields, 15 Oct. 2020.
13. Phillips, *Collieries, Communities and the Miners' Strike*, ch. 3.
14. Interview with Hywel Francis, Banwen, 16 Sept. 2019.
15. Interview with Phil and Kay Bowen, Resolven, 20 Sept. 2019.
16. Interview with Ali Thomas, Neath, 18 Sept. 2019.
17. Interview with Phil and Kay Bowen, Resolven, 20 Sept. 2019.
18. Interview with Darren Moore, Hinckley, 12 Apr. 2021.
19. Interview with Nigel and Wendy Jeffery, Barlestone, 11 Apr. 2021.
20. Interview with Bill and Elspeth Frostwick, Chester-le-Street, 16 Mar. 2020.
21. Interview with Mel Elcock, Loughborough, 13 Apr. 2021.
22. Interview with Nigel and Wendy Jeffery, Barlestone, 11 Apr. 2021.
23. Interview with Margaret and Claire Pinnegar, Hinckley, 15 Apr. 2021.
24. Interview with Paul Stratford, Great Lumley, 11 Sept. 2020.
25. Interview with Peter Byrne, Blackhill, Consett, 9 Sept. 2020.
26. Interview with David Wray, Shotley Bridge, 7 Sept. 2020.
27. Alex Maxwell, *Chicago Tumbles: Cowdenbeath and the miners' strike* (Glenrothes: the author, 1994), 38–40, 58; Phillips, *Collieries, Communities and the Miners' Strike*, 114–15.
28. Interview with Iain Chalmers, Cowdenbeath, 14 June 2021.
29. Interview with Tom Adams, West Wemyss, 17 June 2021.
30. Interview with Ronnie and Anna Campbell, and Margaret Todd, Lochore, 17 June 2021.
31. Interview with Sean Lee, Lochore, 21 June 2021.
32. Interview with Gary and Anne Fisher, Worksop, 20 May 2021.
33. Interview with Kevin Greaves, Worksop, 17 May 2021.
34. Interview with Frank Holmes, Askern, 7 Oct. 2020.
35. Jane Thornton, *All the Fun of the Fight* (Doncaster: Doncaster Library Service, 1987), 7.
36. SCA SY 689, interview with Jean Crane, 14 Jan. 1986.
37. SCA SY 689, interview with Dianne Hogg, 14 Jan. 1986.
38. Interview with Dianne Hogg, Askern, 1 Sept. 2020.
39. SCA SY 689, interview with Jean Crane, 14 Jan. 1986
40. Interview with Betty Cook and Anne Scargill, Barnsley, 8 Oct. 2020. See also Anne Scargill and Betty Cook, *Anne & Betty: United by the struggle* (Pontefract: Route, 2020), 136–8.
41. Interview with Anne Hubbell (formerly Heaton), Linda Randall and Katherine Parker, Warsop, 25 May 2021.
42. *Notts Women Strike Back*, directed by Simon Reynell, Steel Bank Film Co-op (1984).
43. Interview with Anne Hubbell (formerly Heaton), Linda Randall and Katherine Parker, Warsop, 25 May 2021.
44. Interview with Ann and Dai John Jones, Hirwaun, 7 Jan. 2020.
45. Interview with Ann Jones and Siân James, Kilgetty, 19 July 2021.

46. SWCC AUD 52/2, discussion group of 1984–85 strike; Curtis, *The South Wales Miners*, 223–4.
47. Interview with Ann Jones and Siân James, Kilgetty, 19 July 2021.
48. Interview with Dorothy Wray, Leadgate, 7 Sept. 2020.
49. Interview with Tom Adams, West Wemyss, 17 June 2021.
50. Interview with Sean Lee, Lochore, 21 June 2021.
51. Interview with Mary Coll, Lochore, 20 June 2021.
52. Interview with Ronnie and Anna Campbell, and Margaret Todd, Lochore, 17 June 2021.

CHAPTER 3 THE BATTLE FOR THE BALLOT

1. Interview with Steve Williamson, Clay Cross, 27 May 2021.
2. Winterton and Winterton, *Coal, Crisis and Conflict*, 44.
3. University of Sunderland, Murray Library NUM DA 1/3/54, minutes of the Durham Area Executive Committee, 14 Mar. and 9 Apr. 1984, 69–70, 77, 91–3, 103.
4. University of Sunderland, Murray Library NUM DA 1/3/54, minutes of the Durham Area Executive Committee, 24 Apr. 1984, 111–12.
5. Interview with Dave Douglass, South Shields, 15 Oct. 2020.
6. SCA SY 691, interview with Peter Richardson, 13 Jan. 1986.
7. David Hart, 'Impressions from the coalfield', 26 Apr. 1984, www.margaretthatcher.org/document/136217
8. Interview with David Amos, Eastwood, 21 May 2021.
9. Interview with Steve Williamson, Clay Cross, 27 May 2021.
10. Interview with David Amos, Eastwood, 21 May 2021.
11. Paterson, *Look Back in Anger*, 198–9.
12. Interview with Mick Marriott and Terry Stringfellow, Sutton-in-Ashfield, 26 May 2021.
13. Interview with Steve Williamson, Clay Cross, 27 May 2021.
14. Paul Foot, 'Hart in the right place', *Daily Mirror*, 18 October 1984. This was circulated the same day to the team close to Mrs Thatcher, including Robin Butler, Bernard Ingham and John Redwood. www.margaretthatcher.org/document/133637
15. SCA SY 691, interview with Peter Richardson, 13 Jan. 1986.
16. SCA SY 692 1–3, Peter Richardson, 'Confessions of a Picket'.
17. Interview with Steve Walker, Mapplewell, 9 Oct. 2020.
18. Interview with Dave Douglass, South Shields, 15 Oct. 2020.
19. Interview with Maureen Douglass, Norwich, 3 May 2021.
20. Interview with Pete Richardson, Askern, 1 Sept. 2020.
21. SCA SY 692 1–3, Peter Richardson, 'Confessions of a Picket'.
22. Peter Richardson papers, Askern, draft letter (unaddressed, n.d. but 1985).
23. Interview with Steve Walker, Mapplewell, 9 Oct. 2020.
24. Interview with Paul and Adam Winter, Huddersfield, 23 Oct. 2021.
25. Interview with Steve Williamson, Clay Cross, 27 May 2021.
26. Interview with David Amos, Eastwood, 21 May 2021.
27. Interview with Mick Marriott and Terry Stringfellow, Sutton-in-Ashfield, 26 May 2021.
28. Interview with Trevor and Susan Taylor, Sutton-in-Ashfield, 27 May 2021.

CHAPTER 4 ORGREAVE

1. See above, p. 29.
2. See above, p. 94.
3. Bernard Jackson, with Tony Wardle, *The Battle for Orgreave* (Brighton: Vanson Wardle Productions Ltd, 1986), 30–1.
4. See above, p. 87.
5. Interview with Kate Flannery, Sheffield, 12 Oct. 2020.

6. Interview with Sean Lee, Lochore, 21 June 2021.
7. Interview with Tom Adams, West Wemyss, 17 June 2021.
8. Interview with Pete Richardson, Askern, 1 Sept. 2020.
9. Interview with Kate Flannery, Sheffield, 12 Oct. 2020.
10. Interview with David Potts, Everton, Notts, 19 May 2021.
11. Douglass, *Ghost Dancers*, 79–80.
12. Interview with Dave Douglass, South Shields, 15 Oct. 2020.
13. Interview with Bill and Elspeth Frostwick, Chester-le-Street, 16 Mar. 2020.
14. Interview with Pat Egan, Glenrothes, 17 June 2021.
15. Interview with Carol and Robert (Rosco) Ross, Cowdenbeath, 15 June 2021.
16. Interview with Marilyn and Philip James, Seven Sisters, Dulais Valley, 9 Jan. 2020.
17. Interview with Pat Egan, Glenrothes, 17 June 2021.
18. Interview with Bill and Elspeth Frostwick, Chester-le-Street, 16 Mar. 2020.
19. Interview with Carol and Robert (Rosco) Ross, Cowdenbeath, 15 June 2021.
20. Interview with Dianne Hogg, Askern, 1 Sept. 2020.
21. Interview with Elsie and Lisa Potts, with Lisa's partner John Burton, Warsop Vale, 24 May 2021.
22. Interview with David Potts, Everton, Notts, 19 May 2021.
23. Jackson, *The Battle for Orgreave*, 122–5.
24. Interview with Marilyn and Philip James, Seven Sisters, Dulais Valley, 9 Jan. 2020.

CHAPTER 5 'CLOSE A PIT, KILL A COMMUNITY'

1. Interview with Jean Crane, Askern, 5 Oct. 2020.
2. SCA SY 689, interview with Jean Crane, 14 Jan. 1986.
3. See above, pp. 74–5.
4. Interview with Heather Wood, Easington, 25 June 2021.
5. Leaflet cited by McIntyre, 'The response to the 1984–5 miners' strike in County Durham', 188–9.
6. Interview with Heather Wood, Easington, 25 June 2021.
7. County Durham Record Office, North East Labour History Popular Politics Project, D/NELH/1/1/13, interview with Mary Stratford, 4 Apr. 2012.
8. Interview with Mary Stratford, Great Lumley, 11 Sept. 2020.
9. Interview with David Wray, Shotley Bridge, 7 Sept. 2020.
10. Interview with Dorothy Wray, Leadgate, 7 Sept. 2020.
11. County Durham Record Office, North East Labour History Popular Politics Project, D/NELH/1/1/13, interview with Mary Stratford, 4 Apr. 2012.
12. Interview with Mary Stratford, Great Lumley, 11 Sept. 2020.
13. Linda Erskine, 'Recollections of a Miner's Strike', notes to author, 18 June 2021.
14. Interview with Linda Erskine, Lochgelly, 19 June 2021.
15. Interview with Margaret and David Mitchell, Crosshill, 16 June 2021.
16. Interview with Mary Coll, Lochore, 20 June 2021.
17. Suzanne Corrigan, Cath Cunningham and Margo Thorburn, 'Fife women stand firm', in Seddon, *The Cutting Edge*, 43.
18. Interview with Carol and Robert (Rosco) Ross, Cowdenbeath, 15 June 2021.
19. Corrigan et al., 'Fife women stand firm', 34.
20. ibid., 44–5.
21. Interview with Hywel Francis, Banwen, 16 Sept. 2019.
22. Interview with Phil and Kay Bowen, Resolven, 20 Sept. 2019.
23. Interview with Hywel Francis, Banwen, 16 Sept. 2019.
24. Interview with Christine Powell, Seven Sisters, Dulais Valley, 17 Sept. 2019.
25. Interview with Phil White, Maesteg, 9 Jan. 2020.
26. See above, p. 21.
27. Interview with Jude Bevan, Maidstone, 21 Oct. 2019.

28. Interview with Donna Jones, Blaengwynfi, 19 Sept. 2019; interview with Mary Hart, Penmaen, Gower, 27 Sept. 2019.
29. Interview with Donna Jones, Blaengwynfi, 19 Sept. 2019.
30. Mave Calvert and Terry White, *The Hundred Year History of Warsop Vale and Warsop Main Colliery, 1889–1989* (Warsop: Warsop Vale Local History Society, 2000).
31. Interview with Elsie and Lisa Potts, with Lisa's partner John Burton, Warsop Vale, 24 May 2021.
32. *Notts Women Strike Back*, directed by Simon Reynell.
33. ibid.
34. ibid.

CHAPTER 6 'WE ARE WOMEN, WE ARE STRONG'

1. LSE Women's Library 7JMC B/01, Extracts from the diaries of Jean McCrindle, 12 May 1984.
2. LSE Women's Library 7JMC A19, The first WAPC book by Barnsley WAPC, 35–6.
3. British Library, Oral History Collection, BL C464/83, Interviews with Jean McCrindle, conducted by Louise Brodie, 5 Dec. 2011, 23 Feb. 2012, 13 Mar. 2012.
4. Sheila Rowbotham and Jean McCrindle, 'More than just a memory: Some political implications of women's involvement in the miners' strike, 1984–85', *Feminist Review* 23 (1986), 110.
5. British Library, Oral History Collection, BL C464/83, Interview with Jean McCrindle, conducted by Louise Brodie, 12 Mar. 2012.
6. British Library, Oral History Collection, BL C464/83, Interview with Jean McCrindle, conducted by Louise Brodie, 2 Mar. 2012.
7. LSE Women's Library 7JMC B/01, Extracts from the diaries of Jean McCrindle, 15 June 1984.
8. Rowbotham and McCrindle, 'More than just a memory', 117.
9. LSE Women's Library 7JMC A19, The first WAPC book by Barnsley WAPC, 9–10.
10. Scargill and Cook, *Anne & Betty*, 153.
11. LSE Women's Library 7JMC A20, comment by Anne Scargill.
12. LSE Women's Library 7JMC A/01, WAPC minutes 1984–85, meeting of 22 July 1984; Sutcliffe-Braithwaite and Thomlinson, 'National Women Against Pit Closures', 78–100.
13. LSE Women's Library 7JMC A/01, WAPC minutes 1984–85, meeting of 22 July 1984.
14. Interview with Barbara Jackson, Sheffield, 13 Oct. 2020.
15. Sheffield Women Against Pit Closures, *We are Women, We are Strong* (Sheffield: SWAPC, 1987).
16. Interview with Maureen Douglass, Norwich, 3 May 2021.
17. Interview with Betty Cook and Anne Scargill, Barnsley, 8 Oct. 2020.
18. LSE Women's Library 7JMC A/01, Barnsley Miners' Wives Action Group, minute book.
19. Interview with Elicia Billingham, Barnsley, 9 Oct. 2020.
20. Interview with Kath Connolly, Great Lumley, 14 Sept. 2020.
21. Interview with Bill and Elspeth Frostwick, Chester-le-Street, 16 Mar. 2020.
22. Interview with Kath Savory, Chester-le-Street, 13 Sept. 2020.
23. McIntyre, 'The response to the 1984–5 miners strike in County Durham', 60.
24. Interview with Anna Lawson, Langley Park, 13 Sept. 2020.
25. Interview with Mary Stratford, Great Lumley, 11 Sept. 2020.
26. Interview with Pat and Vin McIntyre, conducted by Pete Winstanley, 4 July 2012, https://nelh.net/resources-library/oral-history/oral-history-peace-movement/oral-history-peace-movement-vin-and-pat-mcintyre/; Remembering Pat McIntyre, 1935–2012, https://pat-mcintyre.muchloved.com/
27. Interview with Michaela Griffin, Durham, 16 Sept. 2010.
28. Interview with Lotte and Hugh Shankland, Durham, 17 Sept. 2020.
29. Interview with Jane Bruton and Paul Mason, Kennington, London, 8 Oct. 2021.

30. Interview with Kay Riley, online from Brittany, 20 Apr. 2021.
31. Bell, *The Dirty Thirty*, 50.
32. Interview with Kay Riley, online from Brittany, 20 Apr. 2021.
33. Interview with Helen Colley, Manchester, 18 Nov. 2021.
34. Interview with Carol and Robert (Rosco) Ross, Cowdenbeath, 15 June 2021.
35. Interview with Linda Erskine, Lochgelly, 19 June 2021.
36. SWCC AUD 510, interview with Hefina Headon, conducted by Hywel Francis, 19 Nov. 1985; *The Valleys' Star* (Voice of the Neath, Dulais and Swansea Valleys Support Group), no. 1 (May 1984); Francis, *History on Our Side*, 51.
37. Headon, *Mrs Hellfire*, 250–1.
38. Quoted in Tim Tate, with Lesbians and Gays Support the Miners, *Pride: The unlikely story of the unsung heroes of the miners' strike* (London: John Blake Publishing Ltd, 2018), 267.
39. Headon, *Mrs Hellfire*, 256.
40. Interview with Siân James, Neath, 24 Sept. 2019.
41. Interview with Ann and Dai John Jones, Hirwaun, 7 Jan. 2020.
42. Interview with Ann Jones and Siân James, Kilgetty, 19 July 2021.
43. Barnsley Miners' Wives Action Group, *We Struggled to Laugh* (Barnsley: BMWAG, 1987).

CHAPTER 7 CONNECTIONS

1. Interview with David Connolly, Great Lumley, 14 Sept. 2020.
2. Scargill and Cook, *Anne & Betty*, 146–7.
3. Interview with Jean Crane, Askern, 5 Oct. 2020.
4. SCA SY 689, Askern NUM Women's Support Group, letters from Butlin's, 27 July; Doncaster Metropolitan Borough Council, 1 Aug.; NUR, 8 Aug.; USDAW, 17 Aug; and Terry's, 17 Aug 1984.
5. Interview with Dianne Hogg, Askern, 1 Sept. 2020.
6. SCA SY 689, Askern NUM Women's Support Group, report of ACTSS 1/524 branch delegation to Askern, 12–14 Oct. 1984; programme of Askern visit to ACTSS, London, 3–7 Dec. 1984.
7. SCA SY 689, Askern NUM Women's Support Group, letters from Graham Dean, 6 Sept. and 9 Nov. 1984; interview with Jean Crane, Askern, 5 Oct. 2020.
8. Interview with Jean Crane, Askern, 5 Oct. 2020.
9. SCA SY 689, Askern NUM Women's Support Group, Liz Sullivan, Civil Service Union, letters of 1 Oct. and 17 Dec. 1984.
10. Mary Hart personal archive, Penmaen, Gower.
11. Interview with Mary Hart, Penmaen, Gower, 27 Sept. 2019.
12. Kelliher, *Making Cultures of Solidarity*.
13. SWCC AUD 515/1 interview with Ali Thomas, conducted by Hywel Francis, 1986.
14. Interview with Hywel Francis, Banwen, 16 Sept. 2019.
15. Interview with Phil and Kay Bowen, Resolven, 20 Sept. 2019.
16. Scargill and Cook, *Anne & Betty*, 148.
17. Barnsley Miners' Wives Action Group, *We Struggled to Laugh*, 55.
18. Interview with Elicia Billingham, Barnsley, 9 Oct. 2020.
19. McIntyre, 'The response to the 1984–5 miners' strike in County Durham', 199.
20. Interview with Mary Stratford, Great Lumley, 11 Sept. 2020.
21. Interview with Neil Griffin, Durham, 15 Sept 2020.
22. Interview with Sam Oldfield, Shotley Bridge, 8 Sept. 2020.
23. Maxwell, *Chicago Tumbles*, 52, 66–7.
24. Interview with Linda Erskine, Lochgelly, 19 June 2021; Cath Cunningham, 'Fife', in Vicky Seddon (ed.), *The Cutting Edge*, 224–5.
25. Interview with Carol and Robert (Rosco) Ross, Cowdenbeath, 15 June 2021.
26. Interview with Darren Moore, Hinckley, 12 Apr. 2021.
27. Interview with Simone Dawes, Hinckley, 12 Apr. 2021.

28. Bell, *The Dirty Thirty*, 76.
29. Interview with Bobby and Sam Girvan, Ravenstone, 26 May 2021.
30. Girvan papers, Bob Girvan to June Chenoweth, 20 Nov. 1984; Bob Girvan to Rosy Berry, 6 Dec. 1984 and 7 Jan. 1985; Marlborough and District Miners' Support Group, flyer, n.d. but November/December 1984.
31. Bell, *The Dirty Thirty*, 69–73.
32. Interview with Margaret and Claire Pinnegar, Hinckley, 15 Apr. 2021.
33. Quoted by Bell, *The Dirty Thirty*, 57–8.
34. Interview with Linda Burton, Coalville, 14 Apr. 2021.
35. SWCC AUD 552/2, interview with Terry Harrison (Kent), conducted by Hywel Francis, 5 July 1986.
36. SWCC AUD 515/2, interview with Ali Thomas, conducted by Hywel Francis, 1986.
37. ibid.
38. *The Valleys' Star*, no. 9, 19 Sept. 1984.
39. Interview with Phil and Kay Bowen, Resolven, 20 Sept. 2019.
40. Interview with Kay Jones, Ystradgynlais, 26 Sept. 2019.
41. County Durham Record Office, North East Labour History Popular Politics Project, D/NELH/1/1/13, interview with Mary Stratford, 4 Apr. 2012.
42. Interview with Mary Stratford, Great Lumley, 11 Sept. 2020.
43. Interview with Ernie Foster, Spennymoor, 10 Sept. 2020.
44. Interview with Bernard Regan, Enfield, London, 23 Sept. 2020.
45. Interview with Paul King, Polegate, Eastbourne, 28 Apr. 2021.
46. Jonathan Saunders, *Across Frontiers: International support for the miners' strike, 1984/85* (London: Canary Press, 1989).
47. Interview with Elsie and Lisa Potts, with Lisa's partner John Burton, Warsop Vale, 24 May 2021.
48. Interview with Tom Adams, West Wemyss, 17 June 2021.
49. See above, pp. 165–6.
50. British Library, Oral History Collection, BL C464/83, Interviews with Jean McCrindle, conducted by Louise Brodie, 13 Mar. 2012.
51. LSE Women's Library 7JMC A20, Marsha Marshall, 'How we survived the 84/85 strike'.
52. Interview with Phil White, Maesteg, 9 Jan. 2020.
53. Interview with Kipp Dawson, online from Pittsburgh, Pennsylvania, 24 Feb. 2021.
54. *The Militant: A socialist newsweekly published in the interests of working people*, 16 Nov. 1984.
55. Kipp Dawson papers, Pittsburgh, 'Chronology of visit to Britain', 18 Oct. – 6 Nov. 1984.
56. Interview with Ann Jones and Siân James, Kilgetty, 19 July 2021.
57. Kipp Dawson, 'Chronology of visit to Britain', 1 Nov. 1984.
58. Kipp Dawson papers, Pittsburgh, Richo Richmond to Kipp, 21 Nov. 1984.
59. Kipp Dawson papers, Pittsburgh, Richo Richmond to Kipp, 21 Nov. 1984; Kipp to Richo, 28 Nov. 1984.

CHAPTER 8 LESBIANS AND GAYS SUPPORT THE MINERS

1. Labour History Archive, Manchester, LGSM 1/1, minutes of meeting, 9 Sept. 1984.
2. SWCC AUD 547, interview with Dai Donovan, conducted by Hywel Francis, 10 Apr. 1986.
3. Interview with Mike Jackson, King's Cross, London, 9 Dec. 2019.
4. Interview with Mike Jackson, King's Cross, London, 9 Dec. 2019.
5. Labour History Archive, Manchester, LGSM 1/1, inaugural meeting of 15 July 1984; constitution.
6. Labour History Archive, Manchester, LGSM 3/2, interview with *Il Manifesto*, 21 Jan. 1985.
7. Interview with Mike Jackson, King's Cross, London, 9 Dec. 2019.

8. Quoted in Tate, with LGSM, *Pride*, 132.
9. Interview with Siân James, Neath, 24 Sept. 2019.
10. Interview with Jonathan Blake, Brixton, London, 24 Feb. 2020.
11. Interview with Siân James, Neath, 24 Sept. 2019.
12. Interview with Mike Jackson, King's Cross, London, 9 Dec. 2019.
13. Quoted in Tate, with LGSM, *Pride*, 187–8.
14. Interview with Siân James, Neath, 24 Sept. 2019.
15. Interview with Marilyn and Philip James, Seven Sisters, Dulais Valley, 9 Jan. 2020.
16. Interview with Jayne Francis Headon, Wrexham, 27 Sept. 2019.
17. Quoted in Tate, with LGSM, *Pride*, 188.
18. Quoted in ibid., 190.
19. Quoted in ibid., 194.
20. Interview with Mike Jackson, King's Cross, London, 9 Dec. 2019.
21. Interview with Jonathan Blake, Brixton, London, 24 Feb. 2020.
22. *The Valleys' Star*, no. 15, 31 Oct. 1984.
23. Labour History Archive, Manchester, LGSM 1/1, minutes of 4 Nov. 1984.
24. Labour History Archive, Manchester, LGSM 2/1, Mike Jackson to Hefina Headon, 15 Nov. 1984.
25. Interview with Mike Jackson, King's Cross, London, 9 Dec. 2019.
26. Quoted in Tate and LGSM, *Pride,* 213–14.
27. Interview with Siân James, Neath, 24 Sept. 2019.
28. Interview with Jayne Francis Headon, Wrexham, 27 Sept. 2019.
29. Quoted in Tate, with LGSM, *Pride*, 207–09.
30. Interview with Jayne Francis Headon, Wrexham, 27 Sept. 2019.
31. Quoted in Tate, with LGSM, *Pride*, 207.
32. Labour History Archive, Manchester, LGSM 3/2, Mike Jackson speech to LGSM conference, 30 Mar. 1985.
33. Tate, with LGSM, *Pride*, 190–1.

CHAPTER 9 A STATE OF SIEGE

1. Dave Douglass (ed.), *A Year of Our Lives: Hatfield Main – a colliery community in the Great Coal Strike of 1984–85* (London: Hooligan Press, 1986), no pagination.
2. Dave Douglass, *Come and Wet this Truncheon: The role of the police in the coal strike of 1984–85* (London: Aldgate Press, 1986), 2, 14, 29, 32.
3. Douglass, *A Year of Our Lives.*
4. Douglass, *Ghost Dancers*, 95–6.
5. Interview with Dave Douglass, South Shields, 15 Oct. 2020.
6. Interview with Heather Wood, Easington, 25 June 2021.
7. Interview with Paul Stratford, Great Lumley, 11 Sept. 2020.
8. Interview with Heather Wood, Easington, 25 June 2021.
9. Interview with Pete Richardson, Askern, 1 Sept. 2020.
10. SCA SY 692 1–3, Peter Richardson, 'Confessions of a Picket'.
11. Interview with Peter Robson, Askern, 12 Oct. 2020.
12. SCA SY 692 1–3, Peter Richardson, 'Confessions of a Picket'.
13. Interview with Ken and Karen Bonsall, Warsop, 19 May 2021.
14. Cited in Paterson, *Look Back in Anger*, 165.
15. www.margaretthatcher.org/document/147278
16. David Hart, 'Winning the war against Scargillism', 18 Sept. 1984, www.margaretthatcher.org/document/136219
17. Ian MacGregor, with Rodney Tyler, *The Enemies Within: The story of the miners' strike, 1984–5* (London: Collins, 1986), 220–7.
18. Interview with David Potts, Everton, Notts, 19 May 2021.
19. MacGregor, *The Enemies Within*, 228.

20. Interview with David Potts, Everton, Notts, 19 May 2021.
21. Interview with Ann and Dai John Jones, Hirwaun, 7 Jan. 2020.
22. Interview with Willie Clarke Jnr, Lochgelly, 24 June 2022.
23. Interview with Margaret and Claire Pinnegar, Hinckley, 15 Apr. 2021.
24. Phillips, *Collieries, Communities and the Miners' Strike*, 73.
25. MacGregor, *The Enemies Within*, 203–04.
26. Jim Phillips, 'Strategic injustice and the 1984–85 miners' strike in Scotland', *Industrial Law Journal* (2022), online advance publication at https://doi.org/10.1093/indlaw/dwac017
27. Interview with Pat Egan, Glenrothes, 17 June 2021.
28. Interview with Ronnie and Anna Campbell, and Margaret Todd, Lochore, 17 June 2021.
29. Interview with Tom Adams, West Wemyss, 17 June 2021.
30. Interview with Andrew (Watty) Watson, Ballingry, 15 June 2021.
31. Interview with James McShane and Janet Carson, Lochore, 22 June 2021.
32. Interview with David Williams, Coelbren, 25 Sept. 2019.
33. Interview with Kay Jones, Ystradgynlais, 26 Sept. 2019.
34. Interview with Martin and Siân James, Neath, 19 July 2021.
35. Interview with Martin and Siân James, Neath, 19 July 2021.
36. SWCC AUD 500/2, interview with Dane Hartwell, conducted by Hywel Francis, 17 Feb. 1986; AUD 513/1, interview with Tony Ciano, conducted by Hywel Francis, 27 Feb. 1986.
37. Gail Allen, dir., *Smiling and Splendid Women* (Swansea Women's History Group, 1986).
38. SWCC AUD 503/2, interview with Siân James and Margaret Donovan, conducted by Hywel Francis, 5 Nov. 1986.
39. Interview with Siân James, Neath, 24 Sept. 2019.
40. SWCC AUD 513/1, interview with Tony Ciano, conducted by Hywel Francis, 27 Feb. 1986.
41. Interview with Siân James, Neath, 24 Sept. 2019.
42. SWCC AUD 466/4, interview with Peter Evans, conducted by Hywel Francis, 6 Mar. 1986.
43. John I. Morgans, *Journey of a Lifetime: From the diaries of John Morgans* (Llanidloes: John & Norah Morgans, 2008), 370.
44. SWCC AUD 514, interview with Lyn Harper, conducted by Hywel Francis, 21 Jan. 1986.
45. Interview with Lyn Harper, Crynant, 17 Sept. 2019.
46. Interview with Phil White, Maesteg, 9 Jan. 2020.

CHAPTER 10 CHRISTMAS

1. Pattison and Peace, *No Redemption*, 11.
2. Interview with Anna Lawson, Langley Park, 13 Sept. 2020.
3. Interview with Linda Erskine, Lochgelly, 19 June 2021.
4. Interview with Marilyn and Philip James, Seven Sisters, Dulais Valley, 9 Jan. 2020.
5. Interview with Kath Savory, Chester-le-Street, 13 Sept. 2020.
6. Interview with Kay Riley, online from Brittany, 20 Apr. 2021.
7. See above, pp. 134–5.
8. Interview with Mary Stratford, Great Lumley, 11 Sept. 2020.
9. Interview with Allyson and Kenny McKitten, Great Lumley, 9 Sept. 2020.
10. Interview with Mary Stratford, Great Lumley, 11 Sept. 2020.
11. Interview with Nigel and Wendy Jeffery, Barlestone, 11 Apr. 2021.
12. Interview with Andy Varley, Worksop, 21 May 2021.
13. Interview with Elsie and Lisa Potts, with Lisa's partner John Burton, Warsop Vale, 24 May 2021.
14. Interview with Steve Walker, Mapplewell, 9 Oct. 2020.
15. Interview with Allyson and Kenny McKitten, Great Lumley, 9 Sept. 2020.

16. Interview with Mary Coll, Lochore, 20 June 2021.
17. Interview with Ronnie and Anna Campbell, and Margaret Todd, Lochore, 17 June 2021.
18. Interview with Willie Clarke Jnr, Lochgelly, 24 June 2022.
19. Interview with Mary Coll, Lochore, 20 June 2021.
20. Interview with Lea McClelland, Ballingry, 18 June 2021.
21. Interview with Terry Ratcliffe, Lochore, 16 June 2021.
22. Interview with Steve Walker, Mapplewell, 9 Oct. 2020.
23. Interview with Josie Potts, Worksop, 17 May 2021.
24. SCA SY 692 1–3, Peter Richardson, 'Confessions of a Picket'.
25. Interview with Donna Jones, Blaengwynfi, 19 Sept. 2019.
26. SCA SY 689, interview with Dianne Hogg, 14 Jan. 1986.
27. Interview with Dianne Hogg, Askern, 1 Sept. 2020.
28. Interview with Mary Stratford, Great Lumley, 11 Sept. 2020.
29. Interview with Allyson and Kenny McKitten, Great Lumley, 9 Sept. 2020.
30. Interview with Mary Stratford, Great Lumley, 11 Sept. 2020.
31. Interview with Ken and Karen Bonsall, Warsop, 19 May 2021.
32. Nottinghamshire Archives DD NLHA/3/1/48, David Hopkins interview with himself, 13 Feb. 2000.
33. Interview with David Hopkins, Worksop, 20 May 2021.
34. See above, p. 164.
35. See above, p. 182.
36. Interview with Betty Cook and Anne Scargill, Barnsley, 8 Oct. 2020.
37. Interview with David Connolly, Great Lumley, 14 Sept. 2020.
38. Connolly archives, Great Lumley, letter to Kamp-Lintfort, 21 Nov. 1984 and letter to churches, 23 Nov. 1984.
39. Interview with David Connolly, Great Lumley, 14 Sept. 2020; interview with Kath Connolly, Great Lumley, 14 Sept. 2020.
40. Interview with David Wray, Shotley Bridge, 7 Sept. 2020.
41. Hugh Shankland and Lotte Shankland, 'Johnny's book', unpublished manuscript, 2018, 80–1.
42. Interview with Bill and Elspeth Frostwick, Chester-le-Street, 16 Mar. 2020.
43. Interview with Paul King, Polegate, Eastbourne, 28 Apr. 2021.
44. Interview with Margaret and David Mitchell, Crosshill, 16 June 2021.
45. Interview with Tom Adams, West Wemyss, 17 June 2021.
46. Interview with Iain Chalmers, Cowdenbeath, 14 June 2021.
47. Interview with Christine Powell, Seven Sisters, Dulais Valley, 17 Sept. 2019.
48. Interview with Mary Hart, Penmaen, Gower, 27 Sept. 2019. See above, pp. 165–6.
49. Interview with Ann and Dai John Jones, Hirwaun, 7 Jan. 2020.
50. Interview with Dianne Hogg, Askern, 1 Sept. 2020.
51. Interview with Jean Crane, Askern, 5 Oct. 2020.
52. Interview with Lesley Merrifield, Askern, 7 Oct. 2020.
53. Interview with Dafydd Francis, Banwen, 19 Sept. 2019.
54. Interview with Jude Bevan, Maidstone, 21 Oct. 2019.
55. Interview with Sam Oldfield, Shotley Bridge, 8 Sept. 2020.
56. Interview with Lynn Gibson, Spennymoor, 15 Sept. 2020.
57. Interview with Ray Maslin, Worksop, 18 May 2021.
58. Interview with Gary and Anne Fisher, Worksop, 20 May 2021.
59. Interview with Josie Potts, Worksop, 17 May 2021.
60. Interview with Pete Richardson, Askern, 1 Sept. 2020.
61. Interview with Sue, Lee and Pete Richardson, Askern, 10 Oct. 2020.
62. Scargill and Cook, *Anne & Betty*, 159.
63. Interview with David Wray, Shotley Bridge, 7 Sept. 2020; telephone conversation with Martin Herron, Newcastle, 2 Nov. 2022.
64. Interview with David Connolly, Great Lumley, 14 Sept. 2020.

65. Scargill and Cook, *Anne & Betty*, 159–61; interview with Betty Cook and Anne Scargill, Barnsley, 8 Oct. 2020.
66. Interview with Elicia Billingham, Barnsley, 9 Oct. 2020.
67. Interview with Darren Moore, Hinckley, 12 Apr. 2021.
68. Interview with Ann and Dai John Jones, Hirwaun, 7 Jan. 2020.

CHAPTER 11 THE RETURN TO WORK

1. Francis, *History on Our Side*, 83.
2. Morgans, *Journey of a Lifetime*, 348, diary entry for 3 Mar. 1983.
3. Morgans, *Journey of a Lifetime*, 369, diary entry for 19 Nov. 1984.
4. Interview with Hywel Francis, Banwen, 16 Sept. 2019.
5. SWCC AUD 514/1, interview with Lyn Harper, conducted by Hywel Francis, 21 Jan. 1986.
6. SWCC AUD 515/3, interview with Ali Thomas, conducted by Hywel Francis, 1986.
7. John I. Morgans, 'Chapel and pit', unpublished manuscript, 1986, 69.
8. ibid., 75.
9. Morgans, *Journey of a Lifetime*, 377.
10. Douglass, *Ghost Dancers*, 111–14.
11. University of Sunderland, Murray Library NUM DA 1/3/55, minutes of the Durham Area Executive Committee, 4 Mar. 1985.
12. Interview with Paul Stratford, Great Lumley, 11 Sept. 2020.
13. County Durham Record Office, North East Labour History Popular Politics Project, D/NELH/1/1/13, interview with Mary Stratford, 4 Apr. 2012.
14. Interview with Mary Stratford, Great Lumley, 11 Sept. 2020.
15. Douglass, *Ghost Dancers*, 113.
16. Interview with Hywel Francis, Banwen, 16 Sept. 2019.
17. Darren Moore papers, Diary 1985.
18. Interview with Jane Bruton and Paul Mason, Kennington, London, 8 Oct. 2021.
19. Douglass, *Ghost Dancers*, 114.
20. Interview with Sean Lee, Lochore, 21 June 2021.
21. Morgans, *Journey of a Lifetime*, 378, diary entry for 5 Mar. 1985.
22. Interview with Ann and Dai John Jones, Hirwaun, 7 Jan. 2020.
23. SWCC AUD 509/1, interview with Christine Powell, conducted by Hywel Francis, 24 Nov. 1985.
24. Interview with Martin and Siân James, Neath, 19 July 2021.
25. Interview with David Williams, Coelbren, 25 Sept. 2019.
26. Interview with Ann Jones and Siân James, Kilgetty, 19 July 2021.
27. Interview with Phil White, Maesteg, 9 Jan. 2020.
28. SWCC AUD 551, interview with Philip Weekes, conducted by Hywel Francis, 2 Apr. 1986.
29. Phillips, *Scottish Coal Miners*, 250.
30. *The Strike* – a commemorative booklet published by the Fife Miners' Memorial Committee (1989).
31. Phillips, *Collieries, Communities and the Miners' Strike*, 155–6.
32. Interview with Tom Adams, West Wemyss, 17 June 2021.
33. Interview with Pat Egan, Glenrothes, 17 June 2021.
34. Interview with Andrew (Watty) Watson, Ballingry, 15 June 2021.
35. Interview with Carol and Robert (Rosco) Ross, Cowdenbeath, 15 June 2021.
36. Interview with Peter McCutcheon, Ballingry, 23 June 2021.
37. Interview with Kath Savory, Chester-le-Street, 13 Sept. 2020.
38. Interview with Peter Byrne, Blackhill, Consett, 9 Sept. 2020.
39. Interview with Paul Stratford, Great Lumley, 11 Sept. 2020.
40. Interview with Bill and Elspeth Frostwick, Chester-le-Street, 16 Mar. 2020.

41. Interview with Dorothy Wray, Leadgate, 7 Sept. 2020.
42. SCA SY691, interview with Mike Porter, 14 Jan. 1986.
43. SCA SY 689, interview with Dianne Hogg, 14 Jan. 1986
44. SCA SY 692 1–3, Peter Richardson, 'Confessions of a Picket'.
45. ibid.
46. Interview with Peter Robson, Askern, 12 Oct. 2020.
47. Interview with David Potts, Everton, Notts, 19 May 2021.
48. Interview with Andy Varley, Worksop, 21 May 2021.
49. *Worksop Guardian*, 5 Mar. 1985.
50. Interview with Andy Varley, Worksop, 21 May 2021.
51. Interview with David Hopkins, Worksop, 20 May 2021.
52. Interview with Steve Williamson, Clay Cross, 27 May 2021.
53. Interview with Ken and Karen Bonsall, Warsop, 19 May 2021.
54. Amos, *The Miners of Nottinghamshire*, vol. IV, 108–12
55. ibid., 117–18.
56. ibid., 32–41.
57. Interview with Ken and Karen Bonsall, Warsop, 19 May 2021.
58. Interview with Helen Colley, Manchester, 18 Nov. 2021.
59. SWCC AUD 546/2, interview with Malcolm Pinnegar, conducted by Hywel Francis, 30 Dec. 1986.
60. Interview with Nigel and Wendy Jeffery, Barlestone, 11 Apr. 2021.
61. Girvan papers, Bob Girvan to June Chenoweth, Marlborough, n.d. but March 1985.
62. Interview with Bobby and Sam Girvan, Ravenstone, 26 May 2021.
63. Interview with Nigel and Wendy Jeffery, Barlestone, 11 Apr. 2021.
64. Interview with Darren Moore, Hinckley, 12 Apr. 2021.
65. Mick Richmond papers, High Court Judgement, 13 Sept. 1985.
66. Griffin, *The Leicestershire Miners*, vol. III, 273–81.

CHAPTER 12 THE FIGHT GOES ON

1. Kipp Dawson papers, Pittsburgh, Mick Richmond to Kipp Dawson, 1 June 1985.
2. Interview with Kay Riley, online, 20 Apr. 2021.
3. Darren Moore papers, Scrapbook 2: After the Strike. *With the Sun on Our Backs*, programme.
4. Interview with Jane Bruton and Paul Mason, Kennington, London, 8 Oct. 2021.
5. Interview with Maureen Douglass, Norwich, 3 May 2021.
6. See above, pp. 170–1.
7. Interview with Neil Griffin, Durham, 15 Sept 2020.
8. I am grateful to Jim Phillips for this information.
9. LSE Women's Library 7JMC A/01, WAPC minutes, 21 Feb. 1985.
10. LSE Women's Library 7JMC A/01, WAPC minutes, 16 Mar. 1985.
11. Interview with Pat Egan, Glenrothes, 17 June 2021.
12. Bell, *The Dirty Thirty*, 107–08; interview with Nigel and Wendy Jeffery, Barlestone, 11 Apr. 2021.
13. Interview with Libby Lindsay, online from Chapmanville, West Virginia, 12 Mar. 2021.
14. Labour History Archive, Manchester, LGSM 3/5, programme of Welsh Women Make History, 25 May 1985.
15. Interview with Mair Francis, Banwen, 16 Sept. 2019; Mair Francis, *Up the DOVE! The history of the DOVE workshop in Banwen* (Ferryside: Iconau, 2008), 3–14.
16. Interview with Phil and Kay Bowen, Resolven, 20 Sept. 2019.
17. Labour History Archive, Manchester, LGSM 1/2, minutes of meeting 3 Mar. 1985; 5/2 programme of LGSM conference, 30 Mar. 1985; 3/2 transcript of speech by Mike Jackson, 30 Mar. 1985.
18. Interview with Mike Jackson, King's Cross, London, 9 Dec. 2019.

19. *Capital Gay*, 13 Sept. 1985; *Morning Star*, 5 Oct. 1985.
20. Interview with Mike Jackson, King's Cross, London, 9 Dec. 2019.
21. Interview with Hywel Francis, Banwen, 16 Sept. 2019.
22. Interview with Iain Chalmers, Cowdenbeath, 14 June 2021.
23. Interview with Darren Moore, Hinckley, 12 Apr. 2021.
24. Bell, *The Dirty Thirty*, 105.
25. Kipp Dawson papers, Pittsburgh, Richo Richmond to Kipp Dawson, 21 Sept. 1985.
26. Interview with Jane Bruton and Paul Mason, Kennington, London, 8 Oct. 2021.
27. Interview with Helen Colley, Manchester, 18 Nov. 2021.
28. John Lang and Graham Dodkins, *Bad News: The Wapping dispute* (Nottingham: Spokesman Books, 2011); Suellen M. Littleton, *The Wapping Dispute: An examination of the conflict and its impact on the national newspaper industry* (Aldershot: Avebury, 1992).
29. Interview with Paul King, Polegate, Eastbourne, 28 Apr. 2021.
30. Interview with Jane Bruton and Paul Mason, Kennington, London, 8 Oct. 2021.
31. Beynon and Hudson, *The Shadow of the Mine*, 148–9.
32. Douglass, *Ghost Dancers*, 269–70; Beynon and Hudson, *The Shadow of the Mine*, 150–1.
33. Douglass, *Ghost Dancers*, 279.
34. Scargill and Cook, *Anne & Betty*, 190–8.
35. Interview with Betty Cook and Anne Scargill, Barnsley, 8 Oct. 2020.
36. Interview with Trevor and Susan Taylor, Sutton-in-Ashfield, 27 May 2021.
37. Interview with Mick Marriott and Terry Stringfellow, Sutton-in-Ashfield, 26 May 2021.

CHAPTER 13 RUIN

1. Peter Richardson papers, letter to Jack Taylor, n.d. but probably Sept. 1987.
2. Interview with Pete Richardson, Askern, 1 Sept. 2020.
3. Peter Richardson papers, draft letter, n.d. but probably 1986.
4. Peter Richardson papers, letter from R.W. Gillies JP, Campsall, Councillor for Ward 15 (Askern), chairman of the Amenities and Leisure Services, Doncaster Metropolitan Borough Council, 8 Oct. 1986.
5. Interview with Pete Richardson, Askern, 1 Sept. 2020.
6. Peter Richardson papers, Open College prospectus, Sept. 1988.
7. Interview with Pete Richardson, Askern, 1 Sept. 2020.
8. Interview with David Potts, Everton, Notts, 19 May 2021.
9. Interview with Bobby and Sam Girvan, Ravenstone, 26 May 2021.
10. Kipp Dawson papers, Pittsburgh, Mick Richmond to Kipp Dawson, 24 June 1986.
11. Interview with Mick Richmond and Marisa Cortes Richmond, Whitwick, Coalville, 14 Apr. 2021.
12. Interview with Linda Burton, Coalville, 14 Apr. 2021.
13. Interview with Ronnie and Anna Campbell, and Margaret Todd, Lochore, 17 June 2021.
14. Interview with James McShane and Janet Carson, Lochore, 22 June 2021.
15. Interview with Sean Lee, Lochore, 21 June 2021.
16. Interview with Jean Crane, Askern, 5 Oct. 2020.
17. Interview with Dianne Hogg, Askern, 1 Sept. 2020; conversation with the author, 7 Oct. 2020.
18. Interview with Andy Varley, Worksop, 21 May 2021.
19. Interview with Dave Douglass, South Shields, 15 Oct. 2020.
20. Interview with Steve Walker, Mapplewell, 9 Oct. 2020.
21. Interview with Ken and Karen Bonsall, Warsop, 19 May 2021.
22. Interview with Trevor and Susan Taylor, Sutton-in-Ashfield, 27 May 2021.
23. Interview with Mick Marriott and Terry Stringfellow, Sutton-in-Ashfield, 26 May 2021.
24. Interview with Steve Williamson, Clay Cross, 27 May 2021.
25. Interview with Cliff Jeffery, Trearddur Bay, Anglesey, 20 July 2021.
26. Interview with Nigel and Wendy Jeffery, Barlestone, 11 Apr. 2021.

27. Interview with Martin and Siân James, Neath, 19 July 2021.
28. Interview with David Williams, Coelbren, 25 Sept. 2019.
29. Interview with Marilyn and Philip James, Seven Sisters, Dulais Valley, 9 Jan. 2020.
30. Interview with Bill and Elspeth Frostwick, Chester-le-Street, 16 Mar. 2020.
31. Interview with Allyson and Kenny McKitten, Great Lumley, 9 Sept. 2020.
32. Interview with Paul Stratford, Great Lumley, 11 Sept. 2020.
33. Interview with Carol and Robert (Rosco) Ross, Cowdenbeath, 15 June 2021.
34. Interview with Andrew (Watty) Watson, Ballingry, 15 June 2021.

CHAPTER 14 REDEMPTION

1. Interview with Hywel Francis, Banwen, 16 Sept. 2019.
2. See above, pp. 289–90.
3. Francis, *Up the DOVE!*, 9–21, 35–45; Tom Hansell, *After Coal: Stories of survival in Appalachia and Wales* (Morgantown: West Virginia University Press, 2018), 90–8; interview with Mair Francis, Banwen, 16 Sept. 2019.
4. Interview with Phil White, Maesteg, 9 Jan. 2020.
5. Tyrone O'Sullivan, *Tower of Strength: The story of Tyrone O'Sullivan and Tower colliery* (Edinburgh and London: Mainstream Publishing, 2001), 158.
6. Interview with Phil White, Maesteg, 9 Jan. 2020.
7. O'Sullivan, *Tower of Strength*, 171.
8. Interview with Ann and Dai John Jones, Hirwaun, 7 Jan. 2020.
9. O'Sullivan, *Tower of Strength*, 126.
10. Interview with Ann Jones and Siân James, Kilgetty, 19 July 2021.
11. Interview with Ann and Dai John Jones, Hirwaun, 7 Jan. 2020.
12. Interview with Siân James, Neath, 24 Sept. 2019.
13. Interview with David Wray, Shotley Bridge, 7 Sept. 2020.
14. Interview with Dorothy Wray, Leadgate, 7 Sept. 2020.
15. Interview with Peter Byrne, Blackhill, Consett, 9 Sept. 2020.
16. Interview with Mary Stratford, Great Lumley, 11 Sept. 2020.
17. Interview with Kath Savory, Chester-le-Street, 13 Sept. 2020.
18. Interview with Anna Lawson, Langley Park, 13 Sept. 2020.
19. Interview with Peter Robson, Askern, 12 Oct. 2020.
20. Interview with Frank Holmes, Askern, 7 Oct. 2020.
21. Scargill and Cook, *Anne & Betty*, 174–84, 222–4, 233–4.
22. ibid., 217.
23. Interview with Betty Cook and Anne Scargill, Barnsley, 8 Oct. 2020.
24. Interview with Paul and Adam Winter, Huddersfield, 23 Oct. 2021.
25. Nottinghamshire Archives DD NLHA/3/1/48, David Hopkins interview with himself, 13 Feb. 2000.
26. Interview with David Hopkins, Worksop, 20 May 2021.
27. Interview with David Amos, Eastwood, 21 May 2021.
28. Interview with Darren Moore, Hinckley, 12 Apr. 2021.
29. Interview with Simone Dawes, Hinckley, 12 Apr. 2021.
30. Interview with Linda Erskine, Lochgelly, 19 June 2021.
31. Interview with Terry Ratcliffe, Lochore, 16 June 2021.
32. Interview with Peter McCutcheon, Ballingry, 23 June 2021.
33. Interview with Linda Erskine, Lochgelly, 19 June 2021.
34. Interview with Carol and Robert (Rosco) Ross, Cowdenbeath, 15 June 2021.
35. Interview with Sean Lee, Lochore, 21 June 2021.
36. Interview with Pat Egan, Glenrothes, 17 June 2021.
37. Interview with Tom Adams, West Wemyss, 17 June 2021.
38. Interview with Heather Wood, Easington, 25 June 2021.
39. Interview with Kay Riley, online from Brittany, 20 Apr. 2021.

40. Interview with Ros Jones, Norton, 5 Oct. 2020.
41. Interview with Charlie Hogarth, Bentley, 6 Oct. 2020.
42. Interview with Josie Potts, Worksop, 17 May 2021.
43. Interview with Lyn Harper, Crynant, 17 Sept. 2019.
44. Interview with Ali Thomas, Neath, 18 Sept. 2019.
45. Interview with Hywel Francis, Banwen, 16 Sept. 2019.
46. Interview with Siân James, Neath, 24 Sept. 2019.
47. Morgans, *Journey of a Lifetime*, 399–400, diary entries for 31 Dec. 1986 and 15 Jan. 1987.
48. Interview with John Morgans, Cardiff, 25 Sept. 2019.
49. Interview with Donna Jones, Blaengwynfi, 19 Sept. 2019 (clipping shown at that time).

CHAPTER 15 SHARED STORIES

1. Interview with Kipp Dawson, online from Pittsburgh, Pennsylvania, 24 Feb. 2021.
2. Interview with Libby Lindsay, online from Chapmanville, West Virginia, 12 Mar. 2021.
3. Interview with Betty Cook and Anne Scargill, Barnsley, 8 Oct. 2020.
4. Scargill and Cook, *Anne & Betty*, 239–44; see also Marat Moore, *Women in the Mines: Stories of life and work* (New York: Twayne Publishers, 1996).
5. Jackson, *The Battle for Orgreave*.
6. Jeremy Deller, *The English Civil War Part II: Personal accounts of the 1984–85 miners' strike* (London: Artangel, 2003).
7. Granville Williams, 'Orgreave: The battle for truth and justice', in David Alsop, Carol Stephenson and David Wray (eds), *Justice Denied: Friends, foes and the miners' strike* (London: Merlin Press, 2017), 161–164.
8. Interview with Barbara Jackson, Sheffield, 13 Oct. 2020.
9. Interview with Barbara Jackson, Sheffield, 13 Oct. 2020.
10. Interview with Joe Rollin, Barnsley, 13 Oct. 2020.
11. With Banners Held High Facebook page (last viewed 6 September 2022).
12. Interview with Barbara Jackson, Sheffield, 13 Oct. 2020.
13. Interview with Joe Rollin, Barnsley, 13 Oct. 2020.
14. Interview with Kate Flannery, Sheffield, 12 Oct. 2020.
15. Munro, *Lochore Meadows*, 41; Maxwell and Cooney, *No More Bings in Benarty*.
16. Willie Clarke Jnr papers, Lochgelly, Willie Clarke, Speech at the Opening of the Willie Clarke Centre, 20 Apr. 2018.
17. Willie Clarke Jnr papers, Lochgelly, Willie Clarke Funeral Service, 13 Nov. 2019.
18. Interview with Andrew (Watty) Watson, Ballingry, 15 June 2021.
19. Phillips, 'Strategic injustice'.
20. Phillips, *Scottish Coal Miners*, 250–1.
21. https://www.gov.scot/groups/independent-review-policing-miners-strike/
22. https://www.parliament.scot/bills-and-laws/bills/miners-strike-pardons-scotland-bill/stage-3
23. I am grateful to Jim Phillips for this clarification.
24. Interview with Jim Coxon, Durham, 16 Mar. 2020.
25. Durham Record Office, Coalmining Oral History Project, interview with George Robson, 12 Sept. 2005.
26. Carol Stephenson and David Wray, 'The gala that would not die: Memory and heritage in the post-industrial mining communities', in Allsop et al., *Justice Denied*, 181–93.
27. Interview with David Wray, Shotley Bridge, 7 Sept. 2020.
28. Huw Beynon and Terry Austrin, 'The iconography of the Durham Miners' Gala', *Journal of Historical Sociology* 2/1 (1989), 66–81.
29. Carol Stephenson and David Wray, 'Emotional regeneration through community action in post-industrial mining communities: The new Herrington banner partnership', *Capital and Class* 29/3 (2005), 192.

30. ibid., 193.
31. Interview with Lotte and Hugh Shankland, Durham, 17 Sept. 2020.
32. Jim Coxon, 'Building a future on the ruins of the past: Identity, heritage and culture in a former mining area', PhD thesis, Durham University, 2020, 411–19.
33. Interview with Nigel and Wendy Jeffery, Barlestone, 11 Apr. 2021.
34. Interview with Bill and Elspeth Frostwick, Chester-le-Street, 16 Mar. 2020.
35. Interview with Margaret and Claire Pinnegar, Hinckley, 15 Apr. 2021.
36. Bell, *The Dirty Thirty*, 135–6.
37. Interview with Margaret and Claire Pinnegar, Hinckley, 15 Apr. 2021.
38. *Leicester Mercury*, 29 Sept. 2012.
39. *Leicester Mercury*, 12 Mar. 2012.
40. Jay Emery, 'Belonging, memory and history in the North Nottinghamshire coalfield', *Journal of Historical Geography* 59 (2018), 87.
41. https://www.nottsminingmuseum.org.uk/
42. https://www.nottsminingmuseum.org.uk/our-aims/
43. Nottinghamshire Ex- and Retired Miners Association, interview with Mary Joannou of the Cambridge Miners' Support Group and with Geoff Peace, Malcolm Howarth, John and Yvonne Woodhead, interviewed by Eric Eaton, 25 Aug. 2015. https://www.youtube.com/watch?v=JLxqxtQV4Js (accessed 1 February 2022).
44. Nottinghamshire Archives DD/NLHA/3/1/48.
45. Conversation with David Hopkins, Worksop, 7 June 2018.
46. Hopkins, *Pit Talk*.
47. Amos, *The Miners of Nottinghamshire*, vol. IV.
48. Mine2minds.com
49. Conversation with Natalie Braber and David Amos, Nottingham, 21 Sept. 2018.
50. David Amos and Paul Fillingham, *Banners and Beyond: People, parades and protest in the Nottinghamshire coalfield* (Blidworth: Thinkamigo Editions, 2020), 14–15.
51. Natalie Braber and David Amos (eds), *Coal in the Blood: An East Midlands coal mining anthology* (Nottingham: Trent Editions, 2021), 9, 141, 156.
52. Email to the author, 3 Dec. 2020.
53. Interview with David Amos, Eastwood, 21 May 2021.
54. https://www.bbc.co.uk/programmes/p0c725b1
55. Interview with John Morgans, Cardiff, 25 Sept. 2019.
56. Francis, *History on Our Side*.
57. Interview with Mike Jackson, King's Cross, London, 9 Dec. 2019.
58. Interview with Siân James, Neath, 24 Sept. 2019.
59. Interview with Jonathan Blake, Brixton, London, 24 Feb. 2020.
60. Interview with Mike Jackson, King's Cross, London, 9 Dec. 2019.
61. Interview with Jayne Francis Headon, Wrexham, 27 Sept. 2019.
62. Interview with Siân James, Neath, 24 Sept. 2019.
63. Interview with Mike Jackson, King's Cross, London, 9 Dec. 2019.
64. See above, p. 264.
65. Isaac, *When We Were Miners*, 135–40.
66. Interview with Martin and Siân James, Neath, 19 July 2021.

CHAPTER 16 CHILDREN OF THE STRIKE

1. Interview with Josie Potts, Worksop, 17 May 2021.
2. Interview with Andy Varley, Worksop, 21 May 2021.
3. Interview with mother, 2021.
4. Interview with Ken and Karen Bonsall, Warsop, 19 May 2021.
5. https://www.filmsforaction.org/watch/broken-by-battle-2013/
6. https://www.youtube.com/watch?v=VWg9f5Js49c

7. Interview with Margaret and Claire Pinnegar, Hinckley, 15 Apr. 2021.
8. Interview with Anne Hubbell (previously Heaton), Linda Randall and Katherine Parker, Warsop, 25 May 2021.
9. Interview with Paul and Adam Winter, Huddersfield, 23 Oct. 2021.
10. See above, p. 195.
11. Interview with Jayne Francis Headon, Wrexham, 27 Sept. 2019.
12. Headon, *Mrs Hellfire*.
13. Interview with Jayne Francis Headon, Wrexham, 27 Sept. 2019.
14. Interview with Rachel Tudor Best, Abergavenny, 8 Jan. 2020.
15. Interview with Rachel Tudor Best, Abergavenny, 8 Jan. 2020; interview with Mary Hart, Penmaen, Gower, 27 Sept. 2019.
16. Interview with Ronnie and Anna Campbell, and Margaret Todd, Lochore, 17 June 2021.
17. Interview with James McShane and Janet Carson, Lochore, 22 June 2021.
18. Interview with Dafydd Francis, Banwen, 19 Sept. 2019.
19. Interview with Jude Bevan, Maidstone, 21 Oct. 2019.
20. Interview with Sam Oldfield, Shotley Bridge, 8 Sept. 2020.
21. Interview with Peter Stratford, Great Lumley, 8 Sept. 2020.
22. Interview with Elsie and Lisa Potts, with Lisa's partner John Burton, Warsop Vale, 24 May 2021.
23. Interview with Sue, Lee and Pete Richardson, Askern, 10 Oct. 2020.
24. See above, pp. 351–2.
25. Interview with Sue, Lee and Pete Richardson, Askern, 10 Oct. 2020.
26. Interview with Lynn Gibson, Spennymoor, 15 Sept. 2020.
27. Interview with Helen Stratford, Great Lumley, 25 June 2021.
28. See above, p. 234.
29. Interview with Lea McClelland, Ballingry, 18 June 2021.
30. Interview with Kevin Payne, Lochore, 18 June 2021.
31. Interview with Mark Campbell, Marissa Carr and Ronnie Campbell, Ballingry, 21 June 2021.
32. Interview with Caitlin Oldfield, Shotley Bridge, 8 Sept. 2020.

CONCLUSION

1. Beynon and Hudson, *The Shadow of the Mine*, 155.
2. Interview with Nigel and Wendy Jeffery, Barlestone, 11 Apr. 2021.
3. Interview with Kath Savory, Chester-le-Street, 13 Sept. 2020.
4. Interview with Paul and Adam Winter, Huddersfield, 23 Oct. 2021.

SOURCES AND BIBLIOGRAPHY

INTERVIEWS BY THE AUTHOR

SOUTH WALES

Bevan, Jude, Maidstone, 21 Oct. 2019.
Bowen, Phil and Kay, Resolven, 20 Sept. 2019.
Francis, Dafydd, Banwen, 19 Sept. 2019.
Francis, Hywel, Banwen, 16 Sept. 2019.
Francis, Mair, Banwen, 16 Sept. 2019.
Francis Headon, Jayne, Wrexham, 27 Sept. 2019.
Harper, Lyn, Crynant, 17 Sept. 2019.
Hart, Mary, Penmaen, Gower, 27 Sept. 2019.
James, Marilyn and Philip, Seven Sisters, Dulais Valley, 9 Jan. 2020.
James, Martin and Siân, Neath, 19 July 2021.
James, Siân, Neath, 24 Sept. 2019.
Jones, Ann and Dai John, Hirwaun, 7 Jan. 2020.
Jones, Ann and Siân James, Kilgetty, 19 July 2021.
Jones, Donna, Blaengwynfi, 19 Sept. 2019.
Jones, Kay, Ystradgynlais, 26 Sept. 2019.
Morgans, John, Cardiff, 25 Sept. 2019.
Powell, Christine, Seven Sisters, Dulais Valley, 17 Sept. 2019.
Thomas, Ali, Neath, 18 Sept. 2019.
Tudor Best, Rachel, Abergavenny, 8 Jan. 2020.
Watkins, Betty Rae, Ystradgynlais, 23 Sept. 2019.
White, Phil, Maesteg, 9 Jan. 2020.
Williams, David, Coelbren, 25 Sept. 2019.

COUNTY DURHAM

Boyd, Lyn, Stanley, 12 Sept. 2020.
Byrne, Peter, Blackhill, Consett, 9 Sept. 2020.
Connolly, David, Great Lumley, 14 Sept. 2020.
Connolly, Kath, Great Lumley, 14 Sept. 2020.

Coxon, Jim, Durham, 16 Mar. 2020.
Foster, Ernie, Spennymoor, 10 Sept. 2020.
Frostwick, Billy and Elspeth, Chester-le-Street, 16 March 2020.
Gibson, Lynn, Spennymoor, 15 Sept. 2020.
Griffin, Michaela, Durham, 16 Sept. 2010.
Griffin, Neil, Durham, 15 Sept. 2020.
Lawson, Anna, Langley Park, 13 Sept. 2020.
McKitten, Allyson and Kenny, Great Lumley, 9 Sept. 2020.
Oldfield, Caitlin, Shotley Bridge, 8 Sept. 2020.
Oldfield, Sam, Shotley Bridge, 8 Sept. 2020.
Pallas, Jack, Stanley, 12 Sept. 2020.
Savory, Kath, Chester-le-Street, 13 Sept. 2020.
Shankland, Lotte and Hugh, Durham, 17 Sept. 2020.
Stratford, Helen, Great Lumley, 25 June 2021.
Stratford, Mary, Great Lumley, 11 Sept. 2020.
Stratford, Paul, Great Lumley, 11 Sept. 2020.
Wood, Heather, Easington, 25 June 2021.
Wray, David, Shotley Bridge, 7 Sept. 2020.
Wray, Dorothy, Leadgate, 7 Sept. 2020.

YORKSHIRE

Billingham, Elicia, Barnsley, 9 Oct. 2020.
Cook, Betty and Anne Scargill, Barnsley, 8 Oct. 2020.
Crane, Jean, Askern, 5 Oct. 2020.
Douglass, Dave, South Shields, 15 Oct. 2020.
Douglass, Maureen, Norwich, 3 May 2021.
Flannery, Kate, Sheffield, 12 Oct. 2020.
Hogarth, Charlie, Bentley, 6 Oct. 2020.
Hogg, Dianne, Askern, 1 Sept. 2020.
Holmes, David, Askern, 7 Oct. 2020.
Holmes, Frank, Askern, 7 Oct. 2020.
Jackson, Barbara, Sheffield, 13 Oct. 2020.
Jones, Ros, Norton, 5 Oct. 2020.
Merrifield, Lesley, Askern, 7 Oct. 2020.
Richardson, Pete, Askern, 1 Sept. 2020.
Richardson, Sue, Lee and Pete, Askern, 10 Oct. 2020.
Robson, Peter, Askern, 12 Oct. 2020.
Rollin, Joe, Barnsley, 13 Oct. 2020.
Scott, Dave, Castleford, 14 Oct. 2020.
Walker, Steve, Mapplewell, 9 Oct. 2020.
Wilkinson, Ken, Askern, 7 Oct. 2020.
Winter, Paul and Adam, Huddersfield, 23 Oct. 2021.

LEICESTERSHIRE (THE 'DIRTY THIRTY')

Burton, Linda, Coalville, 14 April 2021.
Dawes, Simone, Hinckley, 12 April 2021.
Elcock, Mel, Loughborough, 13 April 2021.
Girvan, Bobby and Sam, Ravenstone, 26 May 2021.
Jeffery, Cliff, Trearddur Bay, Anglesey, 20 July 2021.

Jeffery, Nigel and Wendy, Barlestone, 11 April 2021.
Moore, Darren, Hinckley, 12 April 2021.
Pinnegar, Margaret and Claire, Hinckley, 15 April 2021.
Richmond, Mick (known as Richo) and Marisa Cortes Richmond, Whitwick, Coalville, 14 April 2021.
Riley, Kay, online from Brittany, 20 and 29 April 2021.

NOTTINGHAMSHIRE

Amos, David, Eastwood, 21 May 2021.
Bonsall, Ken and Karen, Warsop, 19 May 2021.
Fisher, Gary and Anne, Worksop, 20 May 2021.
Greaves, Kevin, Worksop, 17 May 2021.
Hopkins, David, Worksop, 20 May 2021.
Hubbell (previously Heaton), Anne, Linda Randall and Katherine Parker, Warsop, 25 May 2021.
Marriott, Mick and Terry Stringfellow, Sutton-in-Ashfield, 26 May 2021.
Maslin, Ray, Worksop, 18 May 2021.
Potts, David, Everton, Notts, 19 May 2021.
Potts, Josie, Worksop, 17 May 2021.
Potts, Elsie and Lisa, and John Burton, Warsop Vale, 24 May 2021.
Taylor, Trevor and Susan, Sutton-in-Ashfield, 27 May 2021.
Varley, Andy, Worksop, 21 May 2021.
Williamson, Steve, Clay Cross, 27 May 2021.

FIFE

Adams, Tom (with Jim Phillips as co-interviewer), West Wemyss, 17 June 2021.
Campbell, Mark, Marissa Carr and Ronnie Campbell, Ballingry, 21 June 2021.
Campbell, Ronnie and Anna, and Margaret Todd, Lochore, 17 June 2021.
Chalmers, Iain, Cowdenbeath, 14 June 2021.
Clarke Jnr, Willie, Lochgelly, 24 June 2021.
Coll, Mary, Lochore, 20 June 2021.
Egan, Pat, Glenrothes, 17 June 2021.
Erskine, Linda, Lochgelly, 19 June 2021.
Lee, Sean (with Jim Phillips as co-interviewer), Lochore, 21 June 2021.
McClelland, Lea, Ballingry, 18 June 2021.
McCutcheon, Peter, Ballingry, 23 June 2021.
McShane, James and Janet Carson (with Jim Phillips as co-interviewer), Lochore, 22 June 2021.
Mitchell, Margaret and David, Crosshill, 16 June 2021.
Munro, William (known as Butch), Ballingry, 23 June 2021.
Nicoll, Kevin, Cowdenbeath, 22 June 2021.
Payne, Kevin, Lochore, 18 June 2021.
Ratcliffe, Terry, Lochore, 16 June 2021.
Ritchie, Senga, Lochore, 24 June 2021.
Ross, Carol and Robert (known as Rosco) (with Jim Phillips as co-interviewer), Cowdenbeath, 15 June 2021.
Watson, Andrew (Watty), Ballingry, 15 June 2021.
Watson, Thomas, Ballingry, 16 June 2021.

SOURCES AND BIBLIOGRAPHY

OUTSIDE ACTIVISTS

Blake, Jonathan, Brixton, London, 24 Feb. 2020.
Bruton, Jane and Paul Mason, Kennington, London, 8 Oct. 2021.
Colley, Helen, Manchester, 18 Nov. 2021.
Dawson, Kipp, online from Pittsburgh, Pennsylvania, 24 Feb. 2021 and 26 Oct. 2021.
Jackson, Mike, King's Cross, London, 9 Dec. 2019.
King, Paul, Polegate, Eastbourne, 28 April 2021.
Lindsay, Libby, online from Chapmanville, West Virginia, 12 Mar. 2021.
Regan, Bernard, Enfield, London, 23 Sept. 2020.

ARCHIVAL SOURCES

BRITISH LIBRARY

Oral History Collection C464/83, interviews with Jean McCrindle, conducted by Louise Brodie, Dec. 2011 – Mar. 2012.

COUNTY DURHAM RECORD OFFICE

Coalmining Oral History Project, interview with George Robson, 12 Sept. 2005.
North East Labour History Popular Politics Project, D/NELH/1/1/13, interview with Mary Stratford, 4 Apr. 2012.

LABOUR HISTORY ARCHIVE, MANCHESTER

Lesbians and Gays Support the Miners Collection 1/1, minutes of meetings and constitution, 1984;
1/2, minutes of meetings, 1985;
2/1, letter from Mike Jackson to Hefina Headon, 15 Nov. 1984;
3/2, interview with *Il Manifesto*, 21 Jan. 1985; transcript of Mike Jackson speech to LGSM conference, 30 Mar. 1985;
3/5, programme of Welsh Women Make History, 25 May 1985;
5/2 programme of LGSM conference, 30 Mar. 1985.

LONDON SCHOOL OF ECONOMICS, WOMEN'S LIBRARY

Jean McCrindle papers 7JMC A/01, Barnsley Miners' Wives Action Group, minute book;
7JMC A/01, Women Against Pit Closures (WAPC) minutes of meetings 1984–85;
7JMC A/19, The first WAPC book by Barnsley WAPC;
7JMC A/20, Marsha Marshall, 'How we survived the 84/85 strike';
7JMC A/20, WAPC contributions by Marsha Marshall and Anne Scargill, 1985;
7JMC B/01, extracts from the diaries of Jean McCrindle.

445

SOURCES AND BIBLIOGRAPHY

NOTTINGHAMSHIRE ARCHIVES

Nottinghamshire Living History Archive   DD NLHA/3/1/48, David Hopkins interview with himself, 13 Feb. 2000.

SHEFFIELD CITY ARCHIVES

South Yorkshire Collection   SY 689, interview with Jean Crane, 14 Jan. 1986;
SY 689, interview with Dianne Hogg, 14 Jan. 1986;
SY 689, Askern Women's Support Group, correspondence received, reports and programmes, 1984–86;
SY 691, interview with Mike Porter, 14 Jan. 1986;
SY 691, interview with Peter Richardson, 13 Jan. 1986;
SY 692 1–3, Peter Richardson, 'Confessions of a Picket' (1985).

SOUTH WALES MINERS' LIBRARY, SWANSEA

South Wales Coal Collection   AUD 52/2, discussion group about 1984–85 strike.
AUD 465–574, interviews conducted by Hywel Francis, 1985–86:
AUD 465 Des Dutfield (6 Mar. 1986);
AUD 466 Peter Evans (6 Mar. 1986);
AUD 500/2 Dane Hartwell (17 Feb. 1986);
AUD 503 Siân James and Margaret Donovan (5 Nov. 1986);
AUD 505 Donna Jones (5 Mar. 1986);
AUD 507 Hefina Headon and Christine Powell (24 Nov. 1985);
AUD 509 Christine Powell (24 Nov. 1985);
AUD 510 Hefina Headon (19 Nov. 1985);
AUD 513 Tony Ciano (27 Feb. 1986);
AUD 514 Lyn Harper (21 Jan. 1986);
AUD 515 Ali Thomas (unspecified, 1986);
AUD 546 Malcolm Pinnegar (30 Dec. 1986);
AUD 547 Dai Donovan (10 April 1986);
AUD 551 Philip Weekes (2 April 1986);
AUD 552/2 Terry Harrison (5 July 1986);
AUD 574 Emlyn Williams (6 Jan. 1986);
AUD 610 Philip James (9 Dec. 1985).

UNIVERSITY OF SUNDERLAND, MURRAY LIBRARY

NUM Durham Area   NUM DA 1/3/54, minutes of the Durham Area Executive Committee, Mar.–April 1984.

PRIVATE ARCHIVES

Willie Clarke Jnr papers, Lochgelly   Speech at the Opening of the Willie Clarke Centre, 20 April 2018;
Willie Clarke Funeral Service, 13 Nov. 2019.

Connolly archives, Great Lumley	Correspondence, 1984.
Kipp Dawson papers, Pittsburgh	'Chronology of Visit to Britain', 18 Oct.–6 Nov. 1984; 'Kipp's trips to Britain: an index to my journals', 1984–87; Letters to Mick (Richo) Richmond, 1984–88; Letters from Mick Richmond, 1984–87.
Linda Erskine, Lochgelly	'Recollections of a Miner's Strike', notes to author, 18 June 2021.
Girvan papers, Ravenstone	Correspondence, Nov. 1984–Mar. 1985; Marlborough and District Miners' Support Group, flyer (n.d.).
Mary Hart papers, Penmaen	Letter to potential donors from Mary Hart and Julian Tudor Hart, 5 Nov. 1984.
Darren Moore papers, Hinckley	Diary, 1985; Scrapbook 1: The Strike; Scrapbook 2: After the Strike.
Peter Richardson papers, Askern	Correspondence, 1985–91.
Mick Richmond papers, Whitwick	Address Book, 1984–85; High Court Judgement, 13 Sept. 1985.

NEWSPAPERS AND PERIODICALS

Capital Gay
Leicester Mercury
The Militant
Morning Star
The Valleys' Star
Worksop Guardian

PRINTED SOURCES

Abrams, Lynn, *Oral History Theory* (Abingdon & New York: Routledge, 2010).

Abrams, Lynn, 'Memory as both source and subject of study: The transformations of oral history', in Stefan Berger and Bill Niven (eds), *Writing the History of Memory* (London: Bloomsbury Academic, 2014), 89–109.

Allsop, David, Carol Stephenson and David Wray (eds), *Justice Denied: Friends, foes and the miners' strike* (London: Merlin Press, 2017).

Amos, David, *The Miners of Nottinghamshire: A history of the Nottinghamshire miners' trade unions*, vol. IV: *1980–85* (Mansfield: Union of Democratic Mineworkers, 2013).

Amos, David and Paul Fillingham, *Banners and Beyond: People, parades and protest in the Nottinghamshire coalfield* (Blidworth: Thinkamigo Editions, 2020).

Arnold, John H. and Sean Brady (eds), *What is Masculinity? Historical dynamics from antiquity to the contemporary world* (Basingstoke: Palgrave Macmillan, 2011).

Arnot, R. Page, *The Miners: A history of the Miners' Federation of Great Britain, 1889–1910* (London: George Allen & Unwin, 1949).

Arnot, R. Page, *The Miners: Years of struggle: A history of the Miners' Federation of Great Britain, from 1910 onwards* (London: George Allen & Unwin, 1953).

Ashworth, William, *The History of the British Coal Industry*, vol. V: *1946–1982: The Nationalized Industry* (Oxford: Clarendon Press, 1986).

Barnsley Miners' Wives Action Group, *We Struggled to Laugh* (Barnsley: BMWAG, 1987).

Bartrip, Peter and Susan Burman, *The Wounded Soldiers of Industry: Industrial compensations policy, 1833–97* (Oxford: Clarendon Press, 1983).

Beatty, Christina and Stephen Fothergill, 'Labour market adjustment in areas of chronic industrial decline: The case of the UK coalfields', *Regional Studies* 30/7 (1996), 627–40.

Beckett, Francis and David Henke, *Marching to the Fault Line: The 1984 miners' strike and the death of industrial Britain* (London: Constable, 2009).

Bell, David, *The Dirty Thirty: Heroes of the miners' strike* (Nottingham: Five Leaves, 2009).

Beynon, Huw and Terry Austrin, 'The iconography of the Durham Miners' Gala', *Journal of Historical Sociology* 2/1 (1989), 66–81.

Beynon, Huw and Terry Austrin, *Masters and Servants: Class and patronage in the making of a labour organisation: The Durham miners and the English political tradition* (London: Rivers Oram Press, 1994).

Beynon, Huw and Ray Hudson, *The Shadow of the Mine: Coal and the end of industrial Britain* (London: Verso, 2021).

Bornat, Joanna, 'Secondary analysis in reflection: Some experiences of re-use from an oral history perspective', *Families, Relationships and Societies* 2/2 (2013), 309–17.

Braber, Natalie and David Amos (eds), *Coal in the Blood: An East Midlands coal mining anthology* (Nottingham: Trent Editions, 2021).

Brown, John H., *The Valley of the Shadow: An account of Britain's worst mining disaster: The Senghenydd explosion* (Port Talbot: Alun Books, 1981).

Calvert, Mave and Terry White, *The Hundred Year History of Warsop Vale and Warsop Main Colliery, 1889–1989* (Warsop: Warsop Vale Local History Society, 2000).

Chalmers, Iain, *Beneath the Kingdom: Memoirs of a miner* (Dysart: the author, 2023).

Chambers, J.D., *The Workshop of the World: British economic history from 1820 to 1880* (London: Oxford University Press, 1961).

Church, Roy, *The History of the British Coal Industry*, vol. III: *1830–1913: Victorian Pre-eminence* (Oxford: Clarendon Press, 1986).

Clark, Andy, *Fighting Deindustrialisation: Scottish women's factory occupations, 1981–1982* (Liverpool: Liverpool University Press, 2022).

Coulter, Jim, Susan Miller and Martin Walker, *A State of Siege: Miners' Strike 1984 – Politics and policing in the coal fields* (London: Canary Press, 1984).

Coxon, Jim, 'Building a future on the ruins of the past: Identity, heritage and culture in a former mining area', PhD thesis, Durham University, 2020.

Crick, Michael, *Scargill and the Miners* (London: Penguin, 1985).

Curtis, Ben, *The South Wales Miners, 1964–85* (Cardiff: University of Wales Press, 2013).

Deller, Jeremy, *The English Civil War Part II: Personal accounts of the 1984–85 miners' strike* (London: Artangel, 2003).

Douglass, Dave, *Pit Life in County Durham: Rank and file movements and workers' control* (Oxford: History Workshop, 1972).

Douglass, Dave, *Pit Talk in County Durham: A glossary of miners' talk together with memories of Wardley colliery, pit songs and piliking* (Oxford: History Workshop, 1974).

Douglass, Dave, *Come and Wet this Truncheon: The role of the police in the coal strike of 1984–85* (London: Aldgate Press, 1986).

Douglass, Dave (ed.), *A Year of Our Lives: Hatfield Main – a colliery community in the Great Coal Strike of 1984–85* (London: Hooligan Press, 1986).

Douglass, Dave, *The Wheel's Still in Spin: A coalminer's Mahabharata* (Hastings: Read 'n' Noir, 2009).

Douglass, Dave, *Ghost Dancers: The miners' last generation* (Hastings: Read 'n' Noir, 2010).

Elliott, Brian, *South Yorkshire Mining Disasters*, vol I: *The Nineteenth Century* (Barnsley: Wharncliffe Books, 2006).

Emery, Jay, 'Belonging, memory and history in the North Nottinghamshire coalfield', *Journal of Historical Geography* 59 (2018), 77–89.

Emery, Jay, 'Geographies of deindustrialization and the working class: Industrial ruination, legacies, and affect', *Geography Compass* 13/2 (2019), 1–14.

Evans, Gwyn and David Maddox, *The Tonypandy Riots 1910–11* (Plymouth: University of Plymouth Press, 2010).

Feickert, David, *Britain's Civil War over Coal: An insider's view*, ed. David Creedy and Duncan France (Newcastle upon Tyne: Cambridge Scholars Publishing, 2021).

Fine, Bob and Robert Millar (eds), *Policing the Miners' Strike* (London: Lawrence & Wishart, 1985).

Fishman, Nina, *Arthur Horner: A political biography*, 2 vols (London: Lawrence & Wishart, 2010).

Fordham, Dave, *Askern Main Colliery and Instoneville: Early development* (Doncaster: Fedj-el-Adoum, 2010).

Francis, Hywel, 'NUM united: A team in disarray', *Marxism Today* (April 1985), 28–34.

Francis, Hywel, *History on Our Side: Wales and the 1984–85 miners' strike*, second edition (London: Lawrence & Wishart, 2015).

Francis, Hywel, *Stories of Solidarity* (Ceredigion: Y Lolfa, 2018).

Francis, Hywel and David Smith, *The Fed: A history of the South Wales miners in the twentieth century* (London: Lawrence & Wishart, 1980).

Francis, Hywel and Siân Williams, *Do Miners Read Dickens? Origins and progress of the South Wales Miners' Library, 1973–2013* (Cardigan: Parthian, 2013).

Francis, Mair, *Up the DOVE! The history of the DOVE workshop in Banwen* (Ferryside: Iconau, 2008).

Fynes, Richard, *The Miners of Northumberland and Durham: A history of their social and political progress* (Wakefield: S.R. Publishers, 1971).

Gibbon, Peter and David Steyne, *Thurcroft: A village and the miners' strike* (Nottingham: Spokesman Books, 1986).

Griffin, Alan R., *The Miners of Nottinghamshire, 1914–44: A history of the Nottinghamshire miners' union* (London: George Allen & Unwin, 1962).

Griffin, Colin, *The Leicestershire Miners*, vol. III: *1945–88* (Coalville: National Union of Miners, Leicester Area, 1989).

Hansell, Tom, *After Coal: Stories of survival in Appalachia and Wales* (Morgantown: West Virginia University Press, 2018).

Harman, Chris, *The Miners' Strike and the Struggle for Socialism* (London: Socialist Workers Party, 1985).

Headon, Jayne D., *Mrs Hellfire 'You said it!': The life and endeavours of Hefina Headon with memoirs told by family and friends*, second edition (Wrexham: Headon Publishing, 2017).

Hobsbawm, Eric, 'The forward march of labour halted?', *Marxism Today* (Sept. 1987), 279–86.

Holden, Triona, *Queen Coal: Women of the miners' strike* (Stroud: The History Press Ltd, 2005).

Hopkins, David, *Pit Talk: Memories of Manton colliery* (Nottingham: Nottinghamshire County Council, 2000).

Hudson, Ray and David Sadler, *A Tale of Two Industries: The contraction of coal and steel in the north east of England* (Milton Keynes: Open University Press, 1991).

Hutton, Guthrie, *Fife: The mining kingdom* (Catrine: Stenlake Publishing, 1999).

Isaac, Ian, *When We Were Miners* (Carmarthen: Ken Smith Press, 2010).

Jackson, Bernard, with Tony Wardle, *The Battle for Orgreave* (Brighton: Vanson Wardle Productions Ltd, 1986).

John, Angela, *By the Sweat of their Brows: Women workers at Victorian coal mines* (London: Croom Helm, 1980).

Kanagasooriam, James and Elizabeth Smith, 'Red Wall: The definitive description', *Political Insight* 12/3 (2021), 8–11.

Keating, Jackie, *Counting the Cost: A family in the miners' strike* (Barnsley: Pen & Sword Books, 1991).

Kelliher, Diarmaid, *Making Cultures of Solidarity: London and the 1984–85 miners' strike* (London: Routledge, 2021).

Lang, John and Graham Dodkins, *Bad News: The Wapping dispute* (Nottingham: Spokesman Books, 2011).

Lawrence, D.H., *Sons and Lovers* (Oxford: Oxford University Press, 1995).

Leeworthy, Daryl, *Labour Country: Political radicalism and social democracy in South Wales, 1831–1985* (Cardigan: Parthian Books, 2018).

Littleton, Suellen M., *The Wapping Dispute: An examination of the conflict and its impact on the national newspaper industry* (Aldershot: Avebury, 1992).

Loveday, Barry, 'Central coordination, police authorities and the miners' strike', *Political Quarterly* 57/1 (1986), 60–73.

McCormack, John, with Simon Pirani, *Polmaise: The fight for a pit* (London: Index Books, 1989).

McDowell, Linda, *Redundant Masculinities? Employment change and white working-class youth* (Oxford: Blackwell, 2003).

MacGregor, Ian, with Rodney Tyler, *The Enemies Within: The story of the miners' strike, 1984–5* (London: Collins, 1986).

McIntyre, Mary Patricia, 'The response to the 1984–5 miners' strike in County Durham', PhD thesis, Durham University, 1992.

McIvor, Arthur and Ronald Johnson, *Miners' Lung: A history of dust disease in British coalmining* (Aldershot & Burlington: Ashgate, 2007).

McKibbin, Ross, *Ideologies of Class: Social relations in Britain* (Oxford: Oxford University Press, 1990).

Mah, Alice, 'Memory, uncertainty and industrial ruination: Walker Riverside, Newcastle-upon-Tyne', *International Journal of Urban and Regional Research* 34/2 (2010), 398–413.

Mathias, Peter, *The First Industrial Nation: An economic history of Britain, 1700–1914* (London: Methuen, 1969).

Mattinson, Deborah, *Beyond the Red Wall: Why Labour lost, how the Conservatives won and what will happen next?* (London: Biteback, 2020).

Maxwell, Alex, *Chicago Tumbles: Cowdenbeath and the miners' strike* (Glenrothes: the author, 1994).

Maxwell, Alex and Les Cooney (eds), *No More Bings in Benarty: An account of the rise and fall of coal mining in Scotland, and its influence on the lives of the people who lived there* (Benarty: Benarty Mining Heritage Group, 1992).

Meiksins Wood, Ellen, *The Retreat from Class: A new 'true' socialism* (London: Verso, 1986).

Milne, Seumas, *The Enemy Within: The secret war against the miners*, fourth edition (London: Verso, 2014).

Moore, Charles, *Margaret Thatcher: The authorized biography*, 3 vols (London: Penguin, 2013–19).

Moore, Marat, *Women in the Mines: Stories of life and work* (New York: Twayne Publishers, 1996).

Morgan, Kenneth O., *Labour People: Leaders and lieutenants, Hardie to Kinnock* (Oxford and New York: Oxford University Press, 1992).

Morgans, John I., 'Chapel and pit', unpublished manuscript, 1986.

Morgans, John I., *Journey of a Lifetime: From the diaries of John Morgans* (Llanidloes: John & Norah Morgans, 2008).

Munro, David, *Lochore Meadows: The making of a Fife landscape* (Glenrothes: Fife Council, 2012).

Neville, Richard G., 'The Yorkshire miners and the 1893 lockout: The Featherstone "massacre"', *International Review of Social History* 21/3 (1976), 337–57.

O'Sullivan, Tyrone, *Tower of Strength: The story of Tyrone O'Sullivan and Tower colliery* (Edinburgh and London: Mainstream Publishing, 2001).

Oglethorpe, Miles K., *Scottish Collieries: An inventory of the Scottish coal industry in the nationalised era* (Edinburgh and Newtongrange: Royal Commission on the Ancient and Historical Monuments of Scotland and the Scottish Mining Museum, 2006).

Paterson, Harry, *Look Back in Anger: The miners' strike in Nottinghamshire thirty years on* (Nottingham: Five Leaves, 2014).

Pattison, Keith and David Peace, *No Redemption: The 1984–85 miners' strike in the Durham coalfield* (Newcastle: Flambard Press, 2010).

Paxman, Jeremy, *Black Gold: The history of how coal made Britain* (London: William Collins, 2021).

Phillips, Jim, 'Deindustrialization and the moral economy of the Scottish coalfields, 1947 to 1991', *International Labor and Working-Class History* 84/1 (2013), 95–115.

Phillips, Jim, *Collieries, Communities and the Miners' Strike in Scotland, 1984–85* (Manchester: Manchester University Press, 2014).

Phillips, Jim, 'The meanings of coal community in Britain since 1947', *Contemporary British History* 32/1 (2018).

Phillips, Jim, *Scottish Coal Miners in the Twentieth Century* (Edinburgh: Edinburgh University Press, 2019).

Phillips, Jim, 'Strategic injustice and the 1984–85 miners' strike in Scotland', *Industrial Law Journal* (2022), online advance publication at https://doi.org/10.1093/indlaw/dwac017 (last accessed 18 November 2022).

Reed, David and Olivia Adamson, *Miners' Strike, 1984–85: People versus state* (London: Larkin Publishers, 1985).

Richards, Andrew J., *Miners on Strike: Class solidarity and division in Britain* (London: Bloomsbury, 1996).

Rowbotham, Sheila and Jean McCrindle, 'More than just a memory: Some political implications of women's involvement in the miners' strike, 1984–85', *Feminist Review* 23 (1986), 109–24.

Samuel, Raphael, Barbara Bloomfield and Guy Boanas (eds), *The Enemy Within: Pit villages and the miners' strike of 1984–5* (London and New York: Routledge & Kegan Paul, 1986).

Saunders, Jonathan, *Across Frontiers: International support for the miners' strike, 1984/85* (London: Canary Press, 1989).

Scargill, Anne and Betty Cook, *Anne & Betty: United by the struggle* (Pontefract: Route, 2020).

Scargill, Arthur, 'The new unionism', *New Left Review* 1/92 (July/Aug. 1975).

Seddon, Vicky (ed.), *The Cutting Edge: Women and the pit strike* (London: Lawrence & Wishart, 1986).

Shankland, Hugh and Lotte Shankland, 'Johnny's book', unpublished manuscript, 2018.

Sheffield Women Against Pit Closures, *We are Women, We are Strong* (Sheffield: SWAPC, 1987).

Smith, Gordon, *Askern Spa* (1968), reprinted with further photographs added by Symeon Mark Waller (Sprotbrough: Doncaster History, 2013).

Smith, Helen, *Masculinity, Class and Same-Sex Desire in Industrial England, 1895–1957* (London: Palgrave Macmillan, 2015).

Smith, Ken and Jean Smith, *Splendour of the Gala: The Durham Miners' Gala and the Northumberland miners' picnic* (Durham: Ergo Press, 2009).

Spence, Jean and Carol Stephenson, 'Female involvement in the miners' strike 1984–1985: Trajectories of activism', *Sociological Research Online* 12/1 (2007), 1–11.

Stead, Jean, *Never the Same Again: Women and the miners' strike, 1984–85* (London: Women's Press, 1987).

Stephenson, Carol and David Wray, 'Emotional regeneration through community action in post-industrial mining communities: The new Herrington banner partnership', *Capital and Class* 29/3 (2005), 175–99.

Supple, Barry, *The History of the British Coal Industry*, vol. IV: *1913–46: The political economy of decline* (Oxford: Clarendon Press, 1987).

Sutcliffe-Braithwaite, Florence and Natalie Thomlinson, 'National Women Against Pit Closures: Gender, trade unionism and community activism in the miners' strike, 1984–5', *Contemporary British History* 32/1 (2018), 78–100.

Sutcliffe-Braithwaite, Florence and Natalie Thomlinson, *Women and the Miners' Strike, 1984-85* (Oxford: Oxford University Press, 2023).

Tate, Tim, with Lesbians and Gays Support the Miners, *Pride: The unlikely story of the unsung heroes of the miners' strike* (London: John Blake Publishing Ltd, 2018).

Thornton, Jane, *All the Fun of the Fight* (Doncaster: Doncaster Library Service, 1987).

Todd, Selina, *The People: The rise and fall of the working class, 1910–2010* (London: John Murray, 2014).

Trounce, Beverley, *From a Rock to a Hard Place: Memories of the 1984/85 miners' strike* (Stroud: The History Press, 2015).

Waddington, David, Maggie Wykes and Chas Critcher, *Split at the Seams? Community, continuity and change after the 1984–5 coal dispute* (Milton Keynes: Open University Press, 1991).

Walker, Martin and Susan Miller, *The Iron Fist: A state of siege*, vol. II: *A Report to the Yorkshire Area, NUM* (London: Yorkshire Area NUM & Greenwich NALGO, 1984).

Waller, Robert J., *The Dukeries Transformed: The social and political development of a twentieth century coalfield* (Oxford: Clarendon Press, 1983).

Ward, Michael R.M., *From Labouring to Learning: Working-class masculinities, education and de-industrialization* (London: Palgrave Macmillan, 2015).

Wilsher, Peter, et al., *Strike: Thatcher, Scargill and the Miners* (London: Andre Deutsch, 1985).

Winterton, Jonathan and Ruth Winterton, *Coal, Crisis and Conflict: The 1984–85 miners' strike in Yorkshire* (Manchester: Manchester University Press, 1989).

Witham, Joan, *Hearts and Minds: The story of the women of Nottinghamshire in the miners' strike, 1984–85* (London: Canary Press, 1986).

Zweig, Ferdynand, *The British Worker* (London: Penguin, 1952).

ONLINE SOURCES

Burton, Richard, appearance on *The Dick Cavett Show* (4 April 1980) at https://www.youtube.com/watch?v=708q7LjMGso (last accessed 30 May 2022).

Cowell, Alan, 'Thatcher debated using military in 1984 miners' strike', *New York Times*, 4 January 2014, at https://www.nytimes.com/2014/01/04/world/europe/margaret-thatcher-miners-strike.html (last accessed 10 June 2022).

Ferocious Dog (Ken Bonsall), 'The Glass', *Ferocious Dog*, track 1 (2013), at https://www.youtube.com/watch?v=VWg9f5Js49c (last accessed 17 Aug. 2022).

Francis, Hywel, 'From the miners' library to the community university: A personal backstory (1959–94)', typescript, 2018, at https://collections.swansea.ac.uk/s/swansea-2020/page/miners-library (last accessed 18 November 2022).

Joannou, Mary (Cambridge Miners' Support Group), Geoff Peace, Malcolm Howarth, John and Yvonne Woodhead, interviewed by Eric Eaton (25 August 2015), at https://www.youtube.com/watch?v=JLxqxtQV4Js (last accessed 1 February 2022).

Jones, Danny, 'Mick Lynch makes rapturous speech as Enough is Enough campaign gathers momentum' (18 August 2022), at https://www.joe.co.uk/news/mick-lynch-speech-enough-is-enough-campaign-london-rmt-354531 (last accessed 29 August 2022).

McIntyre, Pat and Vin, interview conducted by Pete Winstanley (4 July 2012), at https://nelh.net/resources-library/oral-history/oral-history-peace-movement/oral-history-peace-movement-vin-and-pat-mcintyre/ (last accessed 27 June 2022).

Mine 2 Minds, Community Outreach initiative, at http://www.mine2minds.com (last accessed 2 February 2022).

Miners' Strike Pardons (Scotland) Bill, at https://www.parliament.scot/bills-and-laws/bills/miners-strike-pardons-scotland-bill/stage-3 (last accessed 15 August 2022).

Nottinghamshire Mining Museum, information at https://www.nottsminingmuseum.org.uk/ (last accessed 16 August 2022).

'Remembering Pat McIntyre, 1935–2016', at https://pat-mcintyre.muchloved.com/ (last accessed 27 June 2022).

Scargill, Arthur, Presidential address to National Union of Miners (July 1982), at http://num.org.uk/wp-content/uploads/2015/11/1982-Presidents-Address-05-07-1982-Arthur-Scargill.pdf (last accessed 9 June 2022).

Scott, John, 'Policing during miners' strike: Independent review' (2021), at https://www.gov.scot/groups/independent-review-policing-miners-strike/ (last accessed 31 January 2022).

Temple, Dave, 'Dave Hopper 1943–2016' (8 August 2016), at https://www.durhamminers.org/dave_hopper_1943_2016 (last accessed 8 June 2022).

SOURCES AND BIBLIOGRAPHY

Thatcher, Margaret, Reports, documents, diaries, speeches and press reports, at https://www.margaretthatcher.org (last accessed June 2022).
'With Banners Held High' Facebook page, at https://www.facebook.com/withbanners.held-high.50 (last accessed 6 September 2022).

AUDIO-VISUAL SOURCES

Daldry, Stephen, dir., *Billy Elliot* (Universal Pictures, 2000).
Graham, James, creator and writer, *Sherwood* (BBC, 2022), 6 episodes. Online at https://www.bbc.co.uk/iplayer/episodes/p0c724lz/sherwood (last accessed 16 August 2022).
Harnden, Tony, reporter, *Broken by Battle* (BBC, 2013). Online at https://www.filmsforaction.org/watch/broken-by-battle-2013/ (last accessed 6 September 2022).
Herman, Mark, dir., *Brassed Off* (Film Four, 1996).
Reynell, Simon, *Notts Women Strike Back* (Steel Bank Film Co-op, 1984).
Sutherland, Janice, dir., *Strike: When Britain Went to War* (Channel 4, 2003).
Warchus, Matthew, dir., *Pride* (20th Century Fox, 2014).

INDEX